RETURN to TAHITI

Portrait of Bligh, charcoal drawing by John Smart, 1803

RETURN to TAHITI

*Bligh's
Second Breadfruit
Voyage*

Douglas Oliver

UNIVERSITY OF HAWAII PRESS
Honolulu, Hawaii

Published in North America by
University of Hawaii Press
2840 Kolowalu Street
Honolulu, Hawaii 96822

First published in Australia by
Melbourne University Press
Carlton, Victoria 3053

Printed in Australia

Library of Congress Cataloguing-in-Publication Data

Bligh, William, 1754–1817.
    [Log of H.M.S. Providence, 1791–1793]
    Return to Tahiti: Bligh's second breadfruit voyage/ [edited by]
Douglas Oliver.
      p. cm.
    Previously published: The Log of H.M.S. Providence,
    1791–1793. Surrey, Eng.: Genesis Publications, 1976. With
    new introd. and annotations.
    Bibliography: p.
    Includes index.
    ISBN 0-8248-1184-4
    1. Oceania—Discovery and exploration. 2. Providence (Ship)
I. Oliver, Douglas L. II. Title.
DU20.B53 1988
919'.04—dc19   88-14298
                                          CIP

To my wife
Margaret McArthur

Contents

Illustrations

Plates

Unless specified, all are watercolors by George Tobin. They, and Bligh's sketches, are reproduced by courtesy of the Mitchell Library, Sydney.

ILLUSTRATIONS

Figures

Acknowledgments

It is a gratifying duty to acknowledge the assistance provided by several institutions and individuals that made this book possible.

First, is the Mitchell Library of the State Library of New South Wales, the Mecca of any scholar undertaking historical research on early European voyaging in the South Pacific. I am indebted to 'The Mitchell', as her denizens fondly call her, not only for access to Bligh's and Tobin's own holographic journals of the *Providence* voyage, but for permission to reproduce exerpts from them, along with many of their pictorial and cartographic illustrations. Equally heavy is my debt to London's Public Record Office, which supplied me with copies of all the official, Admiralty-deposited journals of the *Providence* (and *Assistant*) voyage, and gave permission to publish exerpts from certain of them. I am also indebted to the National Maritime Museum (Greenwich), the British Museum, the University of London, and the Australian National University—all for allowing me access to their library collections, and to the John Simon Guggenheim Memorial Foundation for generously assisting me financially in my research visits to Australia and England. Also, I wish to thank London's National Portrait Gallery for supplying me with, and permitting me to reproduce, the portrait of Bligh used herein.

Several individuals provided me with indispensable assistance at one or another stage in this project's long course. For moral support in undertaking it, I am grateful to Jean Guiart (Paris), Harry Maude (Canberra) and Alexander Spoehr (Honolulu). In London, Madge Darby and Harold Carter (of Bristol) added new perspectives to my research. And at Harvard University, Joy Spalding and some Argus-eyed students (including J. W. Love) saved me from purblindness by deciphering hundreds of pages of faded and in some places amorphous eighteenth century script contained in the logs. Joy Spalding, especially, has through the years pressed me to keep working at this book, which was begun so many years ago and interrupted by so many other projects *en route*. I wish also to thank Mary Hutchinson (Melbourne) for compiling the map of the Torres Strait.

The Bibliography lists the many writings from which I have extracted information and ideas, but I wish to mention one in particular that has been of paramount help. I refer to Gavin Kennedy's *Bligh*, the best balanced, most comprehensive and detailed account of the life of that complex man.

Finally, I tender my thanks to three individuals who helped me to transform my own illegible handwriting into editor-ready manuscript, by means of—what else?—a word-processor. Peter Pirie served to introduce me to that baffling machine and William Russell to find and restore recordings ineptly lost by me in its depths. And my wife, Margaret McArthur, stood by me throughout the whole painful process, patiently extricating me from numerous pitfalls and softening—but only partially!—my geriatric resistance to the new-fangled thing.

Preface

The core of this book is a verbatim reproduction, with annotations, of the Journal entries written by William Bligh during a brief but most crucial phase of his second and this time successful expedition to obtain breadfruit plantings for West Indian plantations. It focuses on sixteen weeks of a voyage that lasted two years. Bligh being who he was, his complete Log of the entire voyage merits a kind of treatment it has not yet received. Bligh himself was unsuccessful in his efforts to have it published.* A facsimile of its official, clerk-transcribed, Admiralty-deposited, version was published in 1976, but without annotations and in a limited and costly edition.† Also, excerpts of the entire Journal, many of them abridged or reworded, were published in 1920,‡ but the annotations that accompanied them do not do justice to the richness of the text. In fact, what the Journal as a whole requires is a thorough, 'Beagleholean', treatment;§ alas, I am no John Beaglehole, and do not even attempt to emulate him. What I do is concentrate on the expedition's stay in Tahiti, and devote only a quarter of the book's pages to its origin and its passage there and back. Moreover, in keeping within the limits of my own specialized knowledge I am concerned, not with Bligh's seamanship or leadership, etc., but with his perceptions of the persons he encountered and the events he witnessed in Tahiti.

---

* 'In March, 1795, Bligh himself wrote to [George] Tobin's father: "I cannot possibly say when my voyage will be printed.—This some time past my drawings have been done, but I do not know if I shall be able to get the Admiralty to assist me . . . At present books of voyages sell so slow that they do not defray the expence of publishing, and unless the Admiralty will indulge me in paying for the engravings it will be out of my power to introduce anything but what is absolutely necessary."' (Mackaness 1953: 81)

† Captain W. Bligh, *The Log of H.M.S. Providence.* London, 1976.

‡ Ida Lee (Mrs C. B. Marriott), *Captain Bligh's Second Voyage to the South Sea.* London: Longmans, Green and Co., 1920.

§ Reference here is to the late J. C. Beaglehole, whose three-volume work, *The Journals of Captain James Cook,* represents the acme of the genre.

I began this project with a more ambitious objective in mind. I had hoped to present Bligh's journal entries about Tahiti as an example of how that worldly-wise and in many respects typical Englishman perceived the behavior of persons of another, exotic culture, and to try to explain *why* he perceived as he did: in other words, an essay on one aspect of the intellectual history of an era characterized (it is asserted) by radical changes in Englishmen's ideas about 'primitive' mankind. Regrettably, that proved beyond my reach. In the first place, I am unable to establish the typicality of Bligh's recorded ideas and ways of perceiving. And secondly, I cannot discover how he came to view Tahitian behavior the way he did, there being virtually nothing discoverable about his education in such matters, formal or otherwise. Volumes have been written about what philosophers and other Europe-bound intellectuals of his nation thought about 'primitives', but little has been published in the form of generalizations concerning what Bligh and his like thought about them.* Consequently, my annotations are designed mainly to provide an ethnographic context for what Bligh wrote, it being left to more widely informed scholars to decide how Bligh's Journal entries relate to the history of other Englishmen's ideas.

While the protagonist of this study is Bligh, excerpts from the journals of some of his companions will also be presented, especially when they record matters other than or perceptions different from his. Also, while the focus will be on the *ethnographic* observations of Bligh and his companions, some of the annotations will draw attention to the conditions under which those observations were made, including shipboard routine, food, and health, especially the health of Bligh himself.

Finally, the reader is reminded that, although the focus of this book is on Bligh's ethnographic observations, such most certainly was not what he himself viewed his mission to be. To him it was first and foremost to obtain a large collection of breadfruit for West Indian plantation workers—thereby exonerating his earlier failure to do so and, he doubtless hoped, advancing his naval career. For those purposes he seems to have recognized the necessity of having a working knowledge of some aspects of Tahitian culture. However, he chose also to observe and record common practices and specific events that had little or no direct bearing on his primary mission. Some of that choice may have been influenced by a desire to court the favor of Britain's Royal Society, and particularly its President, Sir Joseph Banks (who was Bligh's patron throughout much of his career). But in addition it is possible to detect in his Journal a personal, non-calculative, curiosity about Tahitian culture, along with a measure of affection for those Tahitians he held to be allies.

* A noteworthy exception is the article by Glyndwr Williams listed in the Bibliography.

In short, my revised purpose in resurrecting these long-buried records of a forgotten voyage is to reveal a little-known, highly admirable, side of a man whom I came to respect in the course of my own work,* and one who deserves a better memorial than Hollywood and other fiction-vendors have made for him.

* Douglas Oliver, *Ancient Tahitian Society*, 3 volumes. Honolulu: University Press of Hawaii, 1974.

Conversions

1 inch	2.54 centimetres
1 foot	0.30 metre
1 mile	1.61 kilometres
1 nautical mile	1.85 kilometres
1 ounce	28.35 grams
1 pound	0.45 kilograms
1 ton	1.02 tonnes
1 pint	0.57 litre
1 gallon	4.55 litres

Editorial Note

Two versions of Bligh's Journal of the *Providence* voyage are known to exist. The original is deposited in the unrivalled Mitchell Library collection of Sydney's Library of New South Wales. It was written by Bligh himself on a daily, sometimes hourly, basis, even during his lengthy periods of illness on the passage from England to Table Bay. This version, which henceforth will be identified as ML (for Mitchell Library) contains many corrections and deletions (by crossing-out, not erasing) apparently made by Bligh himself— for reasons that were either literary (e.g., to correct misspellings or polish composition) or political (e.g., to retract words and statements that on second thought appeared impolitic). Some of these corrections and deletions appear to have been made before, others after, the Journal was copied into the version that Bligh delivered to the Admiralty upon completion of the voyage. This second, official, version of the Journal was made by Edward Hatfull, clerk aboard the *Providence*, and is now deposited in the Admiralty Division of the Public Record Office in London (and henceforth will be identified as the PRO version). It is written in the clerk's copperplate script and contains many of the latter's corrections of ML version misspellings, word use, and sentence structure. It also contains several additional words in a different script; most of these appear to have been added by Bligh himself.

Differences between the scripts of the two versions may be seen in Figures 1 and 2, which record Bligh's 'Remarks' accompanying his entry of February 9th 1791 concerning arrival in Tasmania's Adventure Bay.

Both versions of the Journal consist of two kinds of entries. The first kind, the 'log account', is a one-page record for each day at sea. (See Figure 3) It contains noontime observations regarding the vessel's location (weather permitting); an hourly account of winds and temperature, the vessel's course and distance travelled; along with terse statements about matters on and off ship, such as 'set fore Top Sail', 'Saw many porpoises', 'Strong Gale and Cloudy weather', 'Worked and cleaned below', 'Armourer at the Forge',

'Served thick Portable Soup Gruel for breakfast', and on most Sundays, 'Mustered and saw every person clean dressed' and 'Performed Divine Service'.

The second kind of entry, written on separate pages, consists of more extensive 'Remarks'. A few of these were recorded while under way (e.g., while skirting a coast) and they were the standard form of record kept while in port.

The version of Bligh's Journal reproduced in this book is the PRO one, to which I have added its differences from Bligh's original, the ML version. The editorial signs employed to reveal those differences are:

« » enclose words found in PRO but not in ML, or words in PRO that are wholly different from those in ML. (Not indicated, however, are the clerk's corrections, in PRO, of Bligh's misspellings, etc.)

< > enclose words found in ML but not in PRO. In instances where PRO words were subsequently changed in PRO (presumably by Bligh), one letter of each PRO word so corrected is underlined.

/ /enclose words added to PRO (presumably by Bligh).

As for the spelling of English words, I have not attempted to modernize Bligh's or his clerk's eighteenth century spellings except when comprehension seems to require. (Nor have I tried to standardize the many inconsistencies in such spellings, some of which occur on the same Journal page.) I have however spelled out many abbreviations, such as *weather* for *wthr*, and I have made an effort to standardize the various and often bizarre attempts by Bligh and his companions to deal with Tahitian words, by adding more phonemically accurate spellings: e.g., Bligh's rendition of Oreepyah becomes Ari'ipaia and his Teppahoo becomes Te Pau, which like all of my textual emendations will be enclosed in square brackets when inserted into the texts of the journals. In this connection the (') in Ari'ipaia (and in many other Tahitian words that I have rendered phonemically) is the glottal-stop consonant, which was—still is—an essential sound of the Tahitian language.

Punctuation is not so simply dealt with; the journals abound with inconsistencies and omissions, and with myriads of dashes, but I have standardized or added marks only when sense requires. As for capitalization, which by modern standards of English is, to say the least, profuse, I have left it as I found it, despite many inconsistencies between and within separate journals.

And now for the Voyage itself . . .

Stone adze on wooden handle

INTRODUCTION

H.M.S. *Providence* and her tender, H.M.S. *Assistant*, departed from England on August 3rd 1791 bound for the South Pacific—some 271 years after the first European vessels, under command of the Portuguese Magellan, had crossed that vast island-strewn ocean. During the next two-and-a-half centuries many other European vessels—Spanish, Dutch, and English—had ventured into the South Pacific, but it was not until 1767 that one of them 'discovered' Tahiti, that having been the English armed frigate, H.M.S. *Dolphin*, Samuel Wallis commanding. In short order several other European vessels touched at Tahiti: the French *La Boudeuse* and *L'Etoile*, under command of Louis Bougainville; the *Endeavour*, under James Cook; three visits by the Peru-based Spanish ship, *Aguila*; *Resolution* and *Adventure*, under Cook; and *Resolution* and *Discovery*, also under Cook. After that there was a pause of eleven years until H.M.S. *Bounty* arrived there in October 1788. For its commander, Lieutenant William Bligh, that visit marked his second encounter with Tahitians; he had served as Master on the *Resolution* during its 1777 visit of seven weeks (plus another ten weeks elsewhere in the Society Archipelago).

At the time of his appointment as Master of the *Resolution* Bligh was only twenty-one years old—a remarkable achievement, given even a minimal conception of the responsibilities attending that post on that particular voyage. In the Royal Navy of that period a master was a warrant, not a commissioned, officer, but a most important official in the navigation and management of a ship.

Lacking evidence to the contrary, it appears that Cook selected Bligh on the basis of having seen some of the latter's chart work, and in line with Cook's wish to have on board some young officers who, 'under my direction could be usefully employed in constructing charts, in taking views of the coasts and headlands near which we should pass, and in drawing plans of the bays and harbours in which we should anchor.' (Cook, quoted in Mackaness 1931: I 12)

1

Bligh did indeed produce many charts during the voyage (Spate 1984), but there is no record of what if any contact he had with the Tahitians during the ships' sojourn at Tahiti. (Whether Bligh himself kept a journal is not known, none having come to light.)

In any case, the mapping that Bligh did on the voyage was good enough to arouse, or perhaps increase, the interest and approbation of Sir Joseph Banks, who seven years later was instrumental in having him appointed to command the *Bounty* on that famous and ill-starred first expedition to obtain Tahitian breadfruit. (And Bligh's connection with the *Bounty* voyage led directly to his command of *Providence*.) But let us look astern even farther, in search of other connections and events prior to his voyage on the *Resolution* that could have influenced what Bligh wrote about Tahitians in his *Providence* Journal.

William Bligh was born in Plymouth on September 9th 1754. His father, Francis, a customs officer, was descended from an ancient Cornish line that had produced town mayors, a general, an admiral, and a collateral branch promoted to an English peerage. Little is known about William's mother, Jane, a widow before her marriage to Francis, except that she was related to a family named Bond, one of whose members served as Bligh's First Lieutenant aboard the *Providence*.

The earliest certain information we have concerning the life of the young William is dated July 27th 1770, when, shortly after the remarriage of his widowed father, he entered active service aboard H.M.S. *Hunter*, a 10-gun sloop. Before that, in 1762, his name was for six months on the muster roll of H.M.S. *Monmouth*, as 'Captain's Servant'; this however does not certify that the seven-year-old lad went to sea. In that period it was common practice for Navy-destined boys of well-connected families to be given such positions. If such a boy went to sea he usually received special tutoring in naval-related matters and a privileged introduction to life in the Royal Navy. And even if he did not leave shore he received official credit for sea-service towards a lieutenancy, which required that a candidate have six years at sea. (Also, the ship's captain, whose 'servant' he was, drew a ration in his name. It was of course a fraud but a common and relatively harmless one; even the upright James Cook took part in it, having entered the names of his young sons on his muster when out of port.) It is not known whether the seven-year-old William actually went to sea; if he had it would have been a most appropriate nursery for him. And even if he had not, Plymouth itself would have provided an ideal setting for a boy headed, as William evidently was, for a naval career. Presumably he had some formal schooling; whether it was in the Plymouth Free Grammar School or under a tutor on a Navy ship is not known, but it almost surely included effective training in mathematics, as indicated later on by his outstanding achievements in navigation and cartography.—But back to the documented certainties of his career, which, as noted above, began with his entry on the pay-sheets of H.M.S. *Hunter* at the age of fifteen.

The fact that he was listed on the *Hunter* as an A.B. (able-bodied seaman) was subsequently used by some of Bligh's post-Mutiny detractors to support their charge that he had begun his naval career as a common, forecastle, seaman, and not as a midshipman (i.e., a 'young gentleman' of quarter-deck status and destined for Admiralty-commissioned officer rank). In the Navy of that period seamen did occasionally become commissioned officers, but it was held in some circles that persons of that social background were not and could never become 'gentlemen', and therefore were unsuited to govern 'gentlemen'. What his detractors failed or chose not to see was that Bligh's posting as an A.B. was a temporary expedient and a very commonly practised one. Depending on its size and mission each Navy vessel was allowed a numerically limited and specifically graded complement, including midshipmen. But if for some reason (including return of a favor) a ship's captain wished to take along an additional 'Young Gentleman' he had him signed on as an A.B. and eventually promoted to midshipman when a vacancy occurred. Meanwhile the temporary A.B.s messed with the officially designated midshipmen and usually had their kinds of duties as well. James Cook, even Horatio Nelson, had entered the Navy hierarchy in this way, and so did Bligh, whose promotion to midshipman took place after six months as a nominal A.B.

Up to this point Bligh's naval progress had been propelled mainly by the backing of his relatives and their friends and associates—a kind of mechanism, explicitly labelled 'interest', which was, and was unabashedly acknowledged to be, a powerful and pervasive social force. In the words of one writer: 'Careers in public service [including the Navy] required sponsorship ashore, and the wider and more influential the interest a person could set to work in his behalf, the more assured he was of advancement. Family ties could be crucial, if these were lacking, patrons were sought among the high-ranking families.' (Kennedy 1978: 3n) In Bligh's case, while the 'interest' of his own family had been instrumental in his becoming a midshipman aboard the *Hunter*, it was not powerful enough to push him farther up the naval ladder, so for the next few years his advancement depended entirely upon his own performance. After *Hunter* he served three years on the 36-gun *Crescent*, and after that on the *Ranger*. His performance must have been noteworthily good, for within three days of his discharge from the *Ranger* he was selected by James Cook to be Master aboard the *Resolution*. Meanwhile, Bligh stood and passed his examination for a lieutenancy, although his promotion to that rank did not take place until 1781, five months after the *Resolution's* return from the Pacific.

During the next seven years Bligh led a varied and eventful life. On February 4th 1781 he married Elizabeth Betham, member of an affluent and influential family of the Isle of Man. Ten days later he was appointed Master of a frigate then engaged in the war with France, and for the next two years—now a commissioned lieutenant—he served aboard warships engaged in the war. At war's end he, along with hundreds of other officers, was placed on reserve, at half pay. His two shillings a day having been insufficient to support his growing family he obtained clearance from the Navy and entered the mercantile service of Duncan Campbell. The latter, an uncle of Bligh's wife, was a wealthy shipowner and was pleased to engage such an experienced young officer to captain one of his ships carrying goods between England and the West Indies. Bligh was employed in that commerce for the next four years, thereby gaining valuable experience in commanding ships and in managing commercial transactions—along with the life-long friendship of Campbell, whose 'interest' reached into high levels of the Navy.

The most fateful event in Bligh's life occurred in 1787, shortly after his return from one of his voyages to Jamaica. That of course was his selection to lead the Government's expedition to Tahiti to collect breadfruit and transport it to the West Indies, for what was expected would be an acceptable food for plantation slave laborers. Quoting from a recent study:

Up until the 1770's, there was no breadfruit crop in the West Indies, no mango crop, not even a sizable banana crop, but mainly plantains, maize and ground provisions; since this was insufficient, a large portion of the food consumed in the islands came from continental North America. This was an expensive method of feeding the large slave population. Because of the American War of Independence, none but British ships were allowed to trade with the British West Indies, and so the American food supply was cut off. (Powell 1973: 8)

In addition, the study continues, a number of droughts and hurricanes during the period 1780–1787 destroyed so many of the local crops that about 15 000 slaves died from starvation and attendant causes:

Something had to be done to arrest this horrible loss of life and the planters saw a very timely ray of hope. Between 1768 and 1780 Captain Cook made three voyages of discovery to the South Seas, and enthusiastically told about the tree which supplied the islanders in that part of the world with bread for 12 months of the year— nine months with fresh fruit and 3 months with a paste preserved in leaf-lined holes in the ground. This was envisaged as the plant to solve the food problem in the sugar islands. (ibid: 9–11)

The West Indian planters and merchants began by offering money and a gold medal to anyone supplying them with breadfruit plants, but when this offer was not taken up they sent an emissary to England in 1786 to persuade the Government to obtain plantings of it from Tahiti. The emissary found a powerful ally in Sir Joseph Banks—who had learned about bread-fruit first hand in 1769, when he accompanied the *Endeavour* to Tahiti; who was now President of the Royal Society (Britain's premier scientific organization); and who was himself an eminent botanist and very active in promoting the transplanting and development of useful plants. He was also rich and very influential. Having won King George III's support for the Tahiti expedition Banks himself was placed in charge of organizing it, and soon thereafter named Bligh to lead it. The steps by which he had fixed on Bligh are not exactly known but can be plausibly inferred. Banks knew that Bligh had been to Tahiti and he knew about his skills in navigation and car-tography. He also knew about Bligh's familiarity with the West Indies—a qualification that may well have been endorsed by (or perhaps proposed by?) Duncan Campbell, who also supported the enterprise and who doubtless fre-quented the same circles as Banks. The rest of this chapter of Bligh's life is one so well known—though so often distorted and fictionalized—that it need not be repeated here.* Some of the ethnographic fruits of Bligh's *Bounty* visit will be reproduced later on in the present book, as annotations to entries in his *Providence* Journal. But about the rest of Bligh's life before the *Provi-dence* voyage, the question that is most relevant to the present book is: What had he experienced (in addition to his *Bounty* visit) and what had he read, that could have shaped the way he viewed the Tahitians during *Providence's* fourteen-week visit there?

During his several voyages to the West Indies Bligh may have encountered some American Indians there, but by the time of those visits the few of them that remained had long since lost most of their indigenous identity. Earlier, during his visit to Tahiti aboard the *Resolution*, he cannot have failed to have formed impressions about the local people and their way of life but, as noted earlier, he left no known record of those impressions. As for his visit there in the *Bounty*, the records he kept of Tahitian personalities and practices are in general fresher and more detailed than those recorded in his *Providence* Journal, and many of them will be reproduced below. From those it will be seen that many of his perceptions about Tahitian culture had been shaped prior to the *Providence* visit, and in part by his own experiences there and in other parts of the Pacific during his voyage on the *Resolution*. There remains to consider, then, what other sources of information and attitude may have influenced the way he viewed Tahitians and their culture during his *Provi-dence* visit. In other words: What had he read from the accounts of other writers about 'primitives' in general, and Tahitians in particular?

* The most recent summary of the whole expedition and its aftermath, and the most credible analysis of 'What *really* happened on the *Bounty*', is presented in Gavin Kennedy, *Bligh*, London: G. Duckworth & Co. Ltd, 1978.

That Bligh had engaged in some reading about other 'primitive' peoples is certified: in his *Providence* Log entry of 27th May 1791 he compared a Tahitian practice with one that he had read about in a travel book on Siberia. And while that is only one instance, in view of his known interest in geographic exploration it is reasonable to assume from it that he had read quite widely in books of this kind. It is also recorded, in his *Providence* Journal entry of July 11th 1791, that he had had several books with him aboard the *Bounty*—which upon the return of the ship to Tahiti after the Mutiny had found their way into Tahitians' hands; and it is certain that they included descriptions about Tahitians and other South Pacific peoples. The question becomes: Which of such writings would have been readily available to him before his *Providence* voyage?

Bligh had had ready access to, and had certainly read, Hawkesworth's *Voyages*, published in 1773; this three-volume compilation dealt (often erroneously) with Cook's first voyage and also with the voyages of Byron, Wallis, and Carteret. Bligh also would have read the compilations of the Admiralty Hydrographer, Alexander Dalrymple, whom he once described as his 'friend'. (*Providence* Journal of August 2nd 1792) Perhaps he also read John Callander's *Terra Australis Cognita*, which was published in 1766–68 and which, in addition to Byron's Journal of his voyage in the *Dolphin*, was based largely (actually translated from) Charles de Brosses's *Histoire des Navigations aux Terres Australis* (1756).

Concerning Tahiti in particular Bligh unquestionably would have read the (then unpublished but readily accessible) *Dolphin* journals of Wallis and Robertson (see under Carrington in Bibliography), the *Endeavour* journals of Cook and Banks, and the posthumously edited *Endeavour* journal of Parkinson. Several writings about Cook's second voyage would have been accessible to him, including Cook's own journals, along with those (to list the more ethnographic ones) of Clerke, Mitchel, and Wales; Cook's *A Voyage towards the South Pole . . .* etc. (1777); George Forster's *A Voyage Round the World . . .* (1777); Wale's *Remarks . . .* (1777); and Marra's *Journal* (1775). (Sparrman's Swedish original of *A Voyage round the World with Captain James Cook in H.M.S. Resolution*, was first published in 1802 and 1813, and the English translation of it in 1944.) As for writings about Cook's third voyage, which Bligh had accompanied, he would most certainly have read all of the more substantial of the officially deposited ones; moreover, he himself contributed plans and charts to the official publication about the voyage, for which he received a part of the royalties.

In April 1768 the French frigate *La Boudeuse* and its storeship *L'Etoile*, commanded by Louis-Antoine de Bougainville, anchored for nine days off Tahiti's eastern coast and engaged in active relations with the local natives, aboard ship and ashore. Bougainville—soldier, diplomat, aristocrat, and sophisticate—was charmed by the Tahitians and by their island, which he named *Nouvelle Cythere* (after Kithira, the Aegean island where Aphrodite first rose out of the sea!). The first edition of his journal, published in 1771, expressed his initial impressions: of an Eden-like isle inhabited by a healthy, happy, peaceful, sexually uninhibited people. Conversations with 'Aoutourou' (Ahutoru?), the Tahitian who accompanied the expedition back to France, led Bougainville to describe some of the darker and seamier sides of Tahitian life as well. That, and a second, augmented edition published in 1772, were read widely but had less influence upon European literary and philosophical circles than did two other accounts of the voyage.

One of the latter, an anonymous *Newsletter* published in two parts dated July 20th and August 1st 1769, four months after the expedition's return, was—except for its account of human sacrifice—a rapturous panegyric of the Tahitians and their way of life. (Hammond 1970) The other account was an equally rapturous letter written by Philibert Commerson to a colleague and published in the *Mercure de France* in November 1769. Commerson, a renowned naturalist, had accompanied the Bougainville expedition and was a devotee of the 'Noble Savage' philosophy expounded most recently and influentially by Jean Jacques Rousseau. (Commerson was also either a poor observer or a wily actor: it was not until the expedition's arrival in Tahiti that it was discovered—and by Tahitians—that his young 'male' servant was actually a female.) Both Commerson's letter and the earlier *Newsletter* represented Tahitians to be the very embodiment of Noble Savages: tall, handsome, and white-skinned!; gentle and affable; sexually hospitable; law-abiding; owning all things in common; etc., etc.

(Although not directly relevant to this book's main concern, it may be of interest to note that the effusions of Commerson were more influential among French intellectuals than were the harder facts presented by Bougainville. See Jacquier 1944)

Bligh very probably had read at least one edition of the Bougainville account, which was translated into English by J. R. Forster and published in London in 1772. (In fact, a copy of one—unidentified—account of Bougainville's voyage was taken on the *Providence*.) He would not however have read the *Newsletter* or Commerson's letter unless he could read French—an uncertainty I cannot dispel. But even had he done so it is unlikely that, after two visits to Tahiti, he would have been anything but irritated and perhaps amused by them.

We turn next to the Spanish vessels that had visited Tahiti before the *Providence* (i.e., between 1772 and 1775). It is improbable that Bligh had had access to, or been able to translate, their several logs and journals, which remained unpublished for decades and did not appear in English translation until 1913–1919. (Corney 1913, 1915, 1919) The only sample of their contents that was published before *Providence*'s departure was a German translation, by Georg Forster, of a brief abridgment of one journal.(G. Forster 1780) Even assuming that Bligh read German it is therefore doubtful that his ideas about Tahiti had been extensively informed, much less shaped, by those of his Spanish predecessors there.

In conclusion, it would be impractical, and probably not very useful, to try to summarize the large numbers of facts and fictions about Tahiti read by Bligh before 1791. Nor can I discover what he knew about, or felt about, the contemporary philosophical—and ethnological, and ultimately political —issues centered in the Noble Savage concept.* So, instead of pursuing these laborious and unpromising objectives, I shall reproduce here a few examples from the accounts he had surely read, in order to indicate that even those did not provide him with *unequivocal* perceptions and interpretations about the matters reported. The topics selected for this demonstration are *property* and *adultery*—but any number of other topics would serve as well, to reveal how differently some of Bligh's predecessors in Tahiti viewed and interpreted what they 'saw' and 'heard'.

Property

Every one gathers fruits from the first tree he meets with, or takes some in any house into which he enters. It should seem as if, in regard to things absolutely necessary for the maintenance of life, there was no personal property amongst them, and that they all had an equal right to those articles. (Bougainville 1772: 252; translation of J. R. Forster)

After walking a few miles the boat rowing along shore, we came up to a number of double Canoes and [were] surprized to find in them a great number of our friends an[d] acquaintance. Here we made sure of geting some [provisions] but were here again disappointed, for altho Cocoa-nut trees were full of fruit, our friends had no property in them or in any thing we wanted . . . (James Cook, in Beaglehole 1955: 109)

. . . if any one be caught stealing . . . the proprietor of the goods may put the thief instantly to death; and if any one should inquire of [the proprietor] after the deceased, it is sufficient to acquit him, if he only inform them of the provocation he had to kill him. (Anderson, in Cook III, 1784: 172)

Adultery

Chastity indeed is but little valued especialy among the midling people; if a wife is found guilty of a breach of it her only punishment is a beating from her husband. (Banks, in Beaglehole 1962: 340)

* For a broad resumé of those issues see H. N. Fairchild, *The Noble Savage: A Study in Romantic Naturalism*, New York: Columbia University Press, 1928. And for a learned and succinct essay about them in the context of eighteenth century South Sea voyaging, see the article by Glyndwr Williams listed in the Bibliography.

. . . the favours of Maried women and also the unmarried of the better sort, are as difficult to obtain here as in any other Country whatever. (Cook, in Beaglehole 1961: 238-9)

So very solicitous & zealously desirous are our good friends here for the attaining of these red feathers and so thoroughly convinc'd of their efficacy with their Sovereign Deities that they will very chearfully oblige us in good natur'd but rather unhallow'd rites for the possession of them to render back religious Ceremonies by way of Propituation to their Jolly Gods. (Clerke, in Beaglehole 1961: 383, n)

And from one and the same observer writing on different days:

Besides [another] instance of the immorality and selfishness of the great, I can add another; *Wainee-ou* and *Potatou* her husband, were so greedy after the possession of red parrots feathers, that having sold all the hogs, which they possibly could spare, together with a fine helmet, several breast-plates, and a mourning dress, they agreed to prostitute *Wainee-ou*, and she in consequence offered herself to Captain Cook, and appeared a ready victim. (J. R. Forster 1778: 391-2; Cook declined!)

Their women are modest enough, when married, & I believe there was not one instance of a woman's yielding that was married though the offerred bribe were ever so great. (J. R. Forster, in Hoare 1982: 401)

PREPARATIONS

The failure of the Voyage under my command in his Majesty's Armed Vessel
Bounty when it was in a fair way of succeeding, led His Most Gracious Majesty to
direct it to be put into execution a second time, and with the Ship I was to
command, a small Vessel was likewise to be procured about 100 Tons burthen to go
in company with me.

Thus begins William Bligh's Log of a voyage that lasted two years and that
fulfilled beyond expectations its primary mission: 'to carry the Breadfruit
Plant from the Society Islands to the West Indies'. The expedition also discovered several unmapped islands in the Fiji Archipelago, located and
charted a new and safer passage through the labyrinthine Torres Strait, and
accomplished all the above with little sickness (save for the Captain's), with
only (!) four fatalities, and no disabling internal discord.

Bligh had returned to England from the *Bounty* expedition on
March 14th 1790, having travelled to Europe from Batavia, via the Cape of
Good Hope, aboard a Dutch vessel. He retained his commission as commander of the *Bounty* until October 22nd, on which day he was brought to
court martial, and speedily exonerated, for loss of the *Bounty*. In the interim
he was busy, in serving as relief commander of H.M.S. *Cumberland* and in
writing his account of the *Bounty* mutiny and the open-boat voyage to Timor.
Meanwhile, news about those events spread throughout the nation, and,
wrote one of his biographers: 'Bligh's name was on the nation's tongue, and
he was almost universally praised for his courage, skill, and daring in having
accomplished the longest and most arduous boat journey in naval history.'
(Mackaness 1931: I 247) In official recognition of his personal, if not
substantively successful, accomplishment he was presented to the King, promoted to the rank of commander (and placed in command of the 14-gun sloop
Falcon). Then, on December 15th he was raised to the rank of post-captain—
the customary three-year service in the rank of commander having been
waived. Clearly, a powerful 'interest' was also being wielded on his behalf.

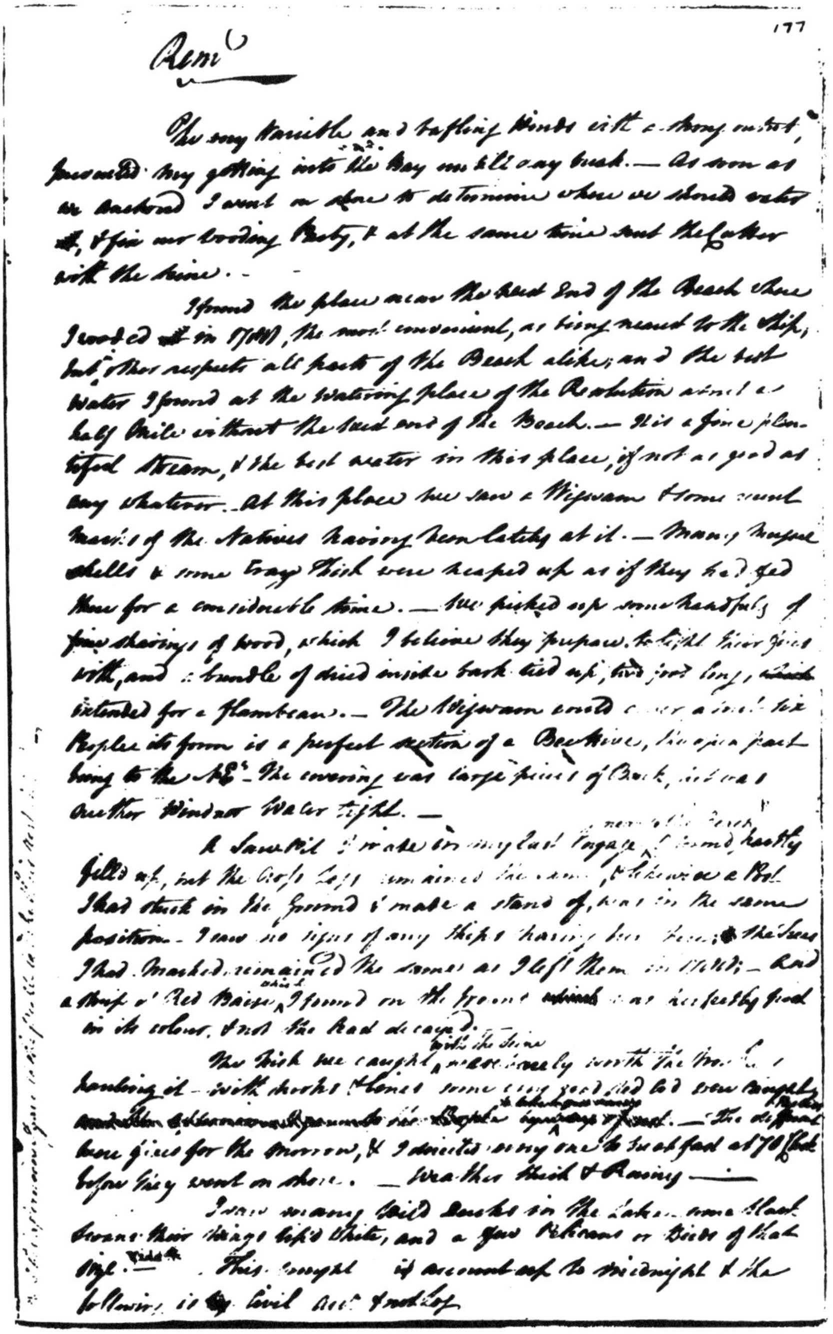
177

Remks

The very variable and baffling Winds with a strong outset, prevented my getting into the Bay until 2 o'clock. — As soon as we anchored I went on shore to determine where we should water &c, & fix our Wooding Party, & at the same time sent the Cutter with the Seine. —

I found the place near the West End of the Beach where I wooded in 1788, the most convenient, as being nearest to the Ship, but in other respects all parts of the Beach alike; and the best Water I found at the watering place of the Resolution about a half Mile without the West end of the Beach. — It is a fine plentiful Stream, & the best water in this place, if not as good as any whatever. — At this place we saw a Wigwam & some recent marks of the Natives having been lately at it. — Many Muscle shells & some Cray Fish were heaped up as if they had fed there for a considerable time. — We picked up some handfuls of fine shavings of wood, which I believe they prepare to light their fires with, and a bundle of dried inside bark tied up, two feet long, [illegible] intended for a flambeau. — The Wigwam could cover about six People its form is a perfect section of a Beehive, the open part being to the NE. — The covering was large pieces of Bark, but was neither Wind nor Water tight. —

A Sawpit I made in my last Voyage near the Beach I found partly filled up, but the Cross Logs remained the same, & likewise a Bolt I had stuck in the Ground to make a stand of, was in the same position. — I saw no signs of any Ships having been here; & the Trees I had marked remained the same as I left them in 1788. — And a strip of Red Baize, which I found on the ground was perfectly good in its colour, & not the least decayed. —

The Fish we caught with the Seine [illegible] hauling it — with sticks & stones [illegible] — The [illegible] were given for the Morrow, & I directed every one to breakfast at 7 o'Clock before they went on shore. — Weather thick & Rainy. —

I saw many Wild Ducks in the Lakes, some Black Swans their wings tip'd White, and a few Pelicans or Birds of that Kind. — Vide * This brought up account up to midnight & the following is Civil Acct. [illegible]

Figure 1 Facsimile of page from Bligh's *Providence* Journal written by himself (the Mitchell Library version)

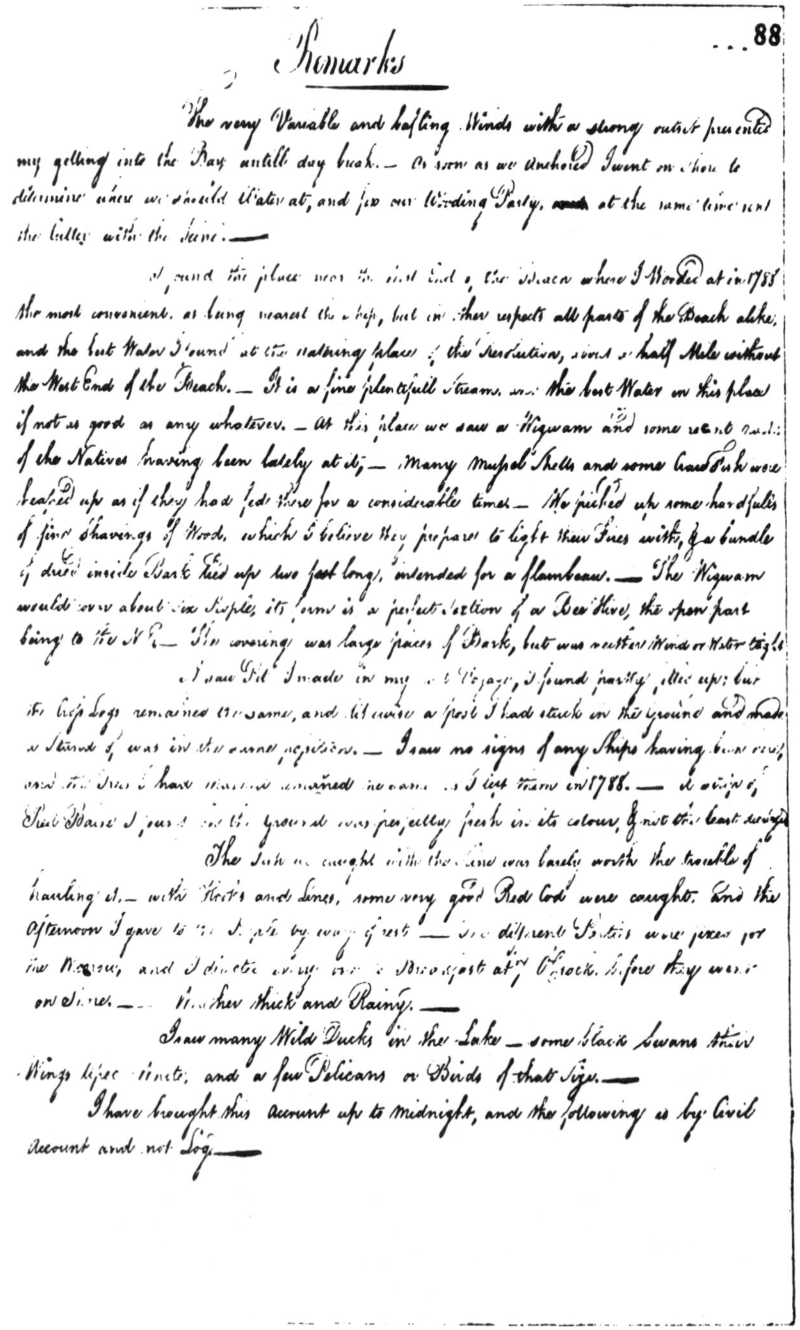

Remarks ... 88

The very Variable and baffling Winds with a strong outset prevented my getting into the Bay untill day break.— As soon as we Anchored I went on shore to determine where we should Water at, and fix our Wooding Party, and at the same time sent the Cutter with the Seine.—

I found the place near the East End of the Beach where I Wooded at in 1788 the most convenient, as being nearest the Ship, but in other respects all parts of the Beach alike, and the best Water I found at the Watering place of the Resolution, about a half Mile without the West End of the Beach.— It is a fine plentifull Stream, and the best Water in this place if not as good as any whatever.— At this place we saw a Wigwam and some recent marks of the Natives having been lately at it;— Many Mussel Shells and some Craw Fish were heaped up as if they had fed there for a considerable time.— We picked up some handfulls of fine Shavings of Wood, which I believe they prepare to light their Fires with, & a bundle of dried inside Bark tied up two feet long, intended for a flambeau.— The Wigwam would cover about six People, its form is a perfect section of a Bee Hive, the open part being to the N.E.— The covering was large pieces of Bark, but was neither Wind or Water tight.

I saw the Pit I made in my last Voyage, I found partly filled up; but the Cross Logs remained the same, and likewise a post I had stuck in the ground and made a Stand of, was in the same position.— I saw no signs of any Ships having been here, and the Trees I have marked remained the same as I left them in 1788.— A piece of Salt Beef I found in the ground was perfectly fresh in its colour, & not the least decayed.

The Fish we caught with the Seine was barely worth the trouble of hauling it.— with Hooks and Lines, some very good Red Cod were caught. In the Afternoon I gave to the People by way of rest — The different Parties were fixed for the Morrow, and I directed every one to Breakfast at 7 OClock before they were on Shore.— Weather thick and Rainy.—

I saw many Wild Ducks in the Lake — some black Swans their Wings tipt white; and a few Pelicans or Birds of that Size.—

I have brought this Account up to Midnight, and the following is by Civil Account and not Log.—

Figure 2 Facsimile of clerk's copy of Figure 1 (the Public Record Office version)

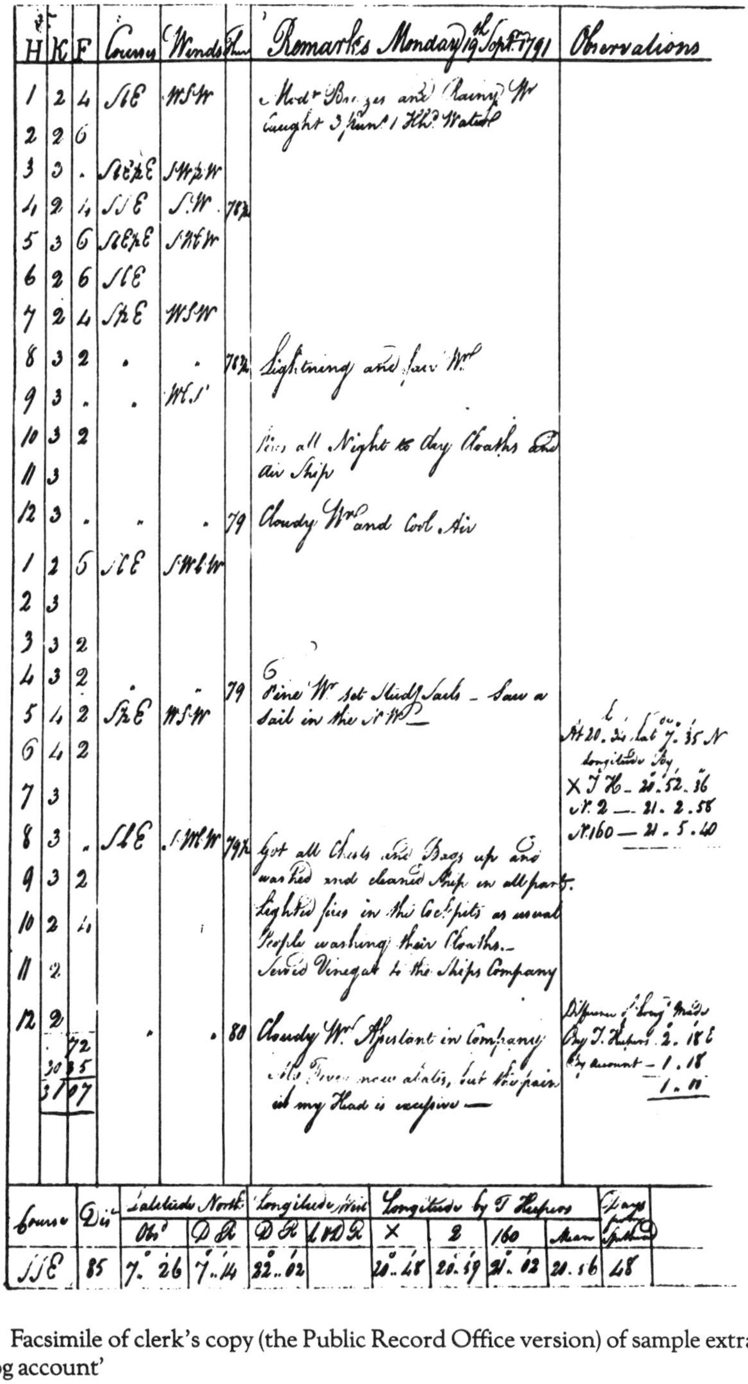

H	K	F	Courses	Winds	Ther	Remarks Monday 19th Sept. 1791	Observations
1	2	4	SE	WSW		Modt. Breezes and Rainy Wr Caught 3 Puncheons 1 Hhd. Water	
2	2	6					
3	3	.	SEbE	SWbW			
4	2	4	SSE	SW	78½		
5	3	6	SEbE	SWbW			
6	2	6	SE				
7	2	4	SbE	WSW			
8	3	2	.	.	78½	Lightning and fair Wr	
9	3	.	.	WbS			
10	3	2				Fires all Night to dry Cloaths and air Ship	
11	3						
12	3	.	.	.	79	Cloudy Wr and Cool Air	
1	2	5	SE	SWbW			
2	3						
3	3	2					
4	3	2	.	.	79	Fine Wr Set Studg Sails – Saw a Sail in the NW	
5	4	2	SbE	WSW			At 20. 20 lat 7. 35 N Longitude by
6	4	2					× T K – 20. 52. 36
7	3						N. 2 – 21. 2. 58
8	3	.	SSE	SWbW	79½	Got all Chests and Bags up and washed and cleaned Ship in all parts.	N. 160 – 21. 5. 40
9	3	2					
10	2	4				Lighted fires in the Cockpits as usual People washing their Cloaths. – Served Vinegar to the Ships Company	
11	2						
12	2	.	.	.	80	Cloudy Wr Assistant in Company. My Fever now abates, but the pain in my Head is excessive —	Difference of Longd Made By T. Keepers 2. 18 By account – 1. 18 / 1. 00
	.	72					
	30	35					
	31	07					

Course	Dist	Latitude North Obs.	Latitude North D.R.	Longitude West D.R.	Longitude West L by D.R.	Longitude by T. Keepers ×	2	160	Mean	[illegible]
SSE	85	7°. 26	7.. 14	22.. 02		20.. 48	20. 59	21. 02	20. 56	48

Figure 3 Facsimile of clerk's copy (the Public Record Office version) of sample extract from Bligh's 'log account'

The wielder was Sir Joseph Banks, who was at the time pressing for another breadfruit expedition—urged, again, by the West Indian planters (who had awarded Bligh five hundred guineas for his valiant even though unsuccessful first try). Final approval for the second expedition came from the Admiralty in March 1791—but let Bligh himself narrate the chain of events through his Journal's introductory 'Remarks', written at Spithead on July 16th 1791. (This passage is a verbatim copy of his clerk's transcription of Bligh's original draft, and differs only slightly and insignificantly from the latter. An explanation of my editorial treatment of subsequent Journal entries is set forth in the Editorial Note.

On the 10th of March 1791 I received orders to search after such Vessels as I thought would answer. The only elligible Ship that I could find was on Mr Perry's Slip at Blackwell, and she was purchased on the 23rd, upon conditions of being ready to be launched in one Month.

In the course of this time I got a small Vessel of the Tonnage prescribed, and that the utmost dispatch might be used, she was taken into a Merchants Yard to undergo a repair, and to have every thing done that was necessary.

On the 16th April I had the honor to receive my Commission to command the Providence, and she was launched with that Name on the 23rd as Mr Perry had engaged. On the same day she was taken to Woolwich to be coppered, and on the 30th was brought up to Deptford.

The small Vessel was greatly forward, and named the Assistant. The Command of her was given to Lieutenant Nathaniel Portlock. Her burthen was 110 Tons, length of Keel for Tonnage 51ft 4in, Extreme breadth 20ft 1in, and depth of Hold 9ft 10in.

The Providence was a superior Ship of her Class, with three Decks and 420 Tons burthen. Her length of Keel for Tonnage was 98ft 11in, the breadth 29ft, depth in the Hold 12ft 10in.

Her Compliment was 100 Men including 20 Marines, and that of the Assistant 27 including 4 Marines.

On the 7th of March we began to fit out, but owing to a strict Press, and a large Armament, we got so few Men, that untill the 19th June we were not ready to go down the River. Ship's draught of Water forward 14ft 10½in, Aft 15ft 2in.

On the 22 June we dropt down to Galleons, and having taken on board 12 Carriage Guns and 14 Swivels, and the Assistant 4 four pounders and 8 Swivels, with all Gunners Stores, we sailed on the 6th July.

On the 7th July anchored at the little Nore. We were joined by Lieut. Pearce, one Sergeant, 2 Corporals, 1 drummer and 15 private Marines from Chatham Division.

I found the Ship to require more ballast. I had permition of

Admiral Dalrymple to go into Sheerness, and on the 8th after mooring along side the Hulk we began to clear the Hold, where we took in 20 Tons of Iron ballast and 15 Tons of Shingles.

On the 12th July in the morning we sailed from Sheerness. Ships draught of water 15ft 9in aft 10ft forward.

On the 13th passed through the Downs, and on the 16th anchored at Spithead and Moored in 8 fms Water. South Sea Castle E b N ½ N 3 Miles Monkton [?] NW ½ W, and St. Helens point S b W. Lord Hood Commanded here with 36 Sail of the Line, and Admiral Roddam in the Harbour.

'The Providence was a superior Ship of her class.' That 'Class' was the West Indiaman, a type of vessel designed for the West Indies trade—i.e., for its economy, and not for its speed, in transporting large amounts of goods. Those of this period had three lofty masts with the normal complement of sails. Most of them had two decks; *Providence* (a 'superior' ship of the class) had three. Bligh was evidently pleased with the ship, which was larger, broader, and deeper than the *Bounty*, and almost double the latter's burthen.

Providence's companion, *Assistant*, was a small brig, a two-master, square-rigged merchantman, intended (among other duties) to assist *Providence* in finding and charting passage through the hazardously intricate Torres Strait. (Plate 2)

The Admiralty's 'Instructions' for the expedition were straightforward and detailed, and contained none, 'secret' or otherwise, tangential to that of obtaining breadfruit and other 'useful Productions' for the West Indies and, supplementarily, for England's Kew Gardens. Incidental to them, they assigned to the expedition two men, James Wiles and Christopher Smith—'Gardeners by Profession'. Also specified in the 'Instructions' were the routes to be followed, namely, around the Cape of Good Hope to Tahiti, and via the Torres Strait, Timor, and the same Cape *en route* to the West Indies and home. (The entire 'Instructions', along with other official correspondence relating to the expedition, are preserved in London's Public Records Office, documents ADM 55/152–3.)

It took over three months to obtain the required complements of seamen— 'owing to a strict Press' and a 'large Armament'. Bligh's reference to a 'strict Press' and a 'large Armament' are, to this editor, not entirely clear. 'Armament' was synonymous with 'mobilization'; the one referred to here, I suppose, was occasioned by Britain's tension with Russia over sovereignty of the Black Sea port of Oczakov, and it anticipated a mainly naval war. 'Press' referred to *impressment*, the forceful recruitment of men to man the larger fleets just then required; but what Bligh meant by 'strict' I cannot say. Perhaps he was referring to the acceleration in impressment of the current armament—what was usually called a 'hot press'—and the competition that

15

it presented to his own recruitment efforts. Or, he may have been referring to the 'strict' criteria that had to be applied in selecting from already impressed men those who qualified for the very special, very demanding, very lengthy voyage he was preparing for (criteria regarding seafaring experience, special skills, health, etc.). In partial support of this latter interpretation is Bligh's entry for July 31st 1791, where he recorded having received orders to desist pressing. (This order, however, may have been issued to the Navy in general, and not to Bligh in particular.) In any case, at least some of the new crew were volunteers, as indicated in his entry for July 20th 1791, which records the payment of bounty money to some (or all?) of them, a perquisite limited to volunteers. (Lloyd 1968; Lewis 1960) Who and what those seamen were I cannot discover—not even the proportion of experienced seamen to landsmen. Few of them were named or otherwise identified in the expedition's records, and those mainly for misfortunes of some kind—illnesses, accidents, and misconduct.

A similar anonymity obtained for the accompanying Marine privates. The journals record that they regularly held drills and practised target shooting, and occasionally fired diplomatically useful salutes to Bligh's Tahitian supporters, but their main purpose, it appears, was to provide him with the kind of sanction that was so fatefully lacking aboard the *Bounty*.

The officers were more conspicuous in the annals of the expedition. Some of them deserve to be remembered largely for their satisfactory—or in some instances, unsatisfactory—performance of prescribed duties, but others among them warrant singling out for additional acts.

Francis Godolphin Bond, First Mate of the *Providence*, was born in 1765, a son of Bligh's half-sister, Catherine. (Mackaness 1949; 1953) Like Bligh, he had 'entered' the Navy at a tender age, in his case nine. At age fourteen he became a midshipman and at seventeen a commissioned lieutenant. By age twenty-six when he was appointed to the *Providence*, he had seen service on a dozen ships, including first lieutenancies on two. Thus, although his kin tie undoubtedly led to his selection for the *Providence* posting, he was also professionally well qualified for the job, and that kin tie seems not to have afforded him any specially privileged treatment from his uncle. On the contrary, his treatment by Bligh, only eleven years older, was generally overweening and on occasion gratuitously abusive.(In sharp contrast were the generous and solicitous efforts that Bligh made *after* the voyage, to advance Bond's naval career. See Mackaness 1949; 1953.) Like all of the principal officers on the expedition, Bond kept a journal, but his goes beyond brief daily entries (concerning position, ship routine, etc.) only during the sojourns in Tasmania and Tahiti, and during passage through the Torres Strait. Even his account concerning Tahiti totals only about three thousand words.

Lieutenant James Guthrie, *Providence*'s Second Mate, had been promoted to a lieutenancy in November 1790. Beyond that nothing is recorded about him in any of the official naval biographies of the period, nor in the *Dictionary of National Biography.* (Personal communication of February 1987, from C. J. Ware, National Maritime Museum, Greenwich, London) Like all other officially required journals of the voyage, his was handed over to the Admiralty upon the return to England, and is now in the Public Record Office (Adm 51 4551). It is written in a neat, copperplate script; what can be read from its few unfaded pages is limited to matters like the following, written while at Matavai Bay:

Mod[erate] breezes & fair wea[ther]. sent 96 Garden Pots ashore the Cutter. PM Dark cloudy wea[ther]. At 4 mod[erate] breezes & fair wea[ther]. Got the Spare Anchor out of the Main Hold. Caulking the Sides & marking Rafters for a Greenhouse. Served fresh Pork & Breadfruit etc. Rec[eived] a moderate supply of Pigs. At Noon Mod[erate] breezes & fair.

Evidently a 'mod[erate]' young man, with even less than a moderate impulse to record what he however cannot have failed to have seen, in that magnificent setting and among those exotic people!

(Another *Providence* journal attributed to Guthrie is in the National Library of Australia, Canberra (MS 4235/NK 718). It is written in a markedly different hand and covers only that part of the voyage from England to the arrival in Tahiti.)

Turning next to *Providence's* Third Mate, Lieutenant George Tobin, a sharper contrast to Guthrie in literary impulse is difficult to imagine.

Tobin was born in 1768 in the West Indies, the son of a wealthy merchant and of a mother who was related to the wife of Horatio Nelson. In 1780 he entered the Navy as midshipman, and was promoted to lieutenant in 1790. From 1780 until his appointment to the *Providence* he served in a number of ships, saw a large quota of naval actions, and voyaged extensively—to the West Indies, North America, India and China. The impression of him given through his personal journal is that of a well-educated (where, I cannot discover), modest, amiable, witty, benevolent, and tolerant young man. (Horatio Nelson, writing in 1796 to his wife, described Tobin as a 'fine young man' with whom he was 'exceedingly pleased'.) Tobin also had a talent, apparently untutored, for sketching and watercoloring, as reproductions of some of his pictures in this book will reveal. In addition to the cut-and-dried log that he kept on the *Providence*, he made personal notes from which he subsequently compiled the lengthy Journal just referred to in the form of letters to his brother, James. It is from this yet unpublished holograph Journal, now in the Mitchell Library of Sydney, that excerpts have been used in the present book to complement and supplement the basic text, Bligh's Journal.

The fourth person on board the *Providence* meriting mention was Matthew Flinders, aged seventeen at the beginning of the voyage. Born in

Lincolnshire, the son of a surgeon, Matthew was educated in local schools until he was fifteen. Then, having developed a longing to go to sea (partly through reading *Robinson Crusoe*) he entered the Navy in 1790 as a midshipman on board H.M.S. *Bellerophan*, whose Captain, evidently impressed by his promise, arranged for his transfer to the *Providence*, as an anticipated means of forwarding his career. Flinder's *Providence* Journal, now in the Public Record Office (Adm 55 97) is written in a neat and easily legible hand and, considering the writer's tender age and inexperience, contains some crisp (though rather two-dimensional) descriptions of events witnessed and places seen, some of them also sketched by himself—a forerunner of his subsequent accomplishments in charting the coasts of Australia's eastern half. His *Providence* Journal entries concerning Tahiti, which total about two thousand words, provide an interesting portent of the man he was to become, but they add little to the descriptions of Bligh and Tobin.

      The next member of the expedition we have to consider is Lieutenant Nathaniel Portlock, hand-picked by Bligh to command the *Assistant*. Born in America in about 1748 (and thus about six years older than Bligh), he eventually joined the British Navy, and in 1776 became a member of James Cook's third voyage to the Pacific. He entered on board the *Discovery* as an A.B., but eighteen days later was promoted to master's mate—evidently on account of his considerable experience aboard merchant ships. After Cook's death in Hawaii, in 1779, Portlock was transferred to the *Resolution* to serve as master's mate to Bligh, a relationship that seems to have been so mutually satisfactory as to lead the latter to select him to captain the *Assistant*. Between his discharge from the *Resolution* and his posting aboard the *Assistant*, Portlock served first in the British Channel Fleet, and then in command of one of two merchant vessels charged, with Government backing, with opening up the fur trade on North America's north-west coast. (Dixon 1789)

      Bligh's choice of Portlock was a fortunate one. Throughout the voyage the two vessels worked in tandem, always in mutual sight. When passing through hazardous waters it was usually the smaller *Assistant*'s job to go ahead to feel out safe channels. Especially in the Torres Strait, Portlock's seamanship contributed greatly to locating and charting the way. A large portion of his official Journal (that dealing with the post-Tahiti part of the voyage) is reproduced, in somewhat condensed form, in the book by Ida Lee; some (non-condensed) extracts from the Tahiti portion of it will be reproduced in the present book.

ENGLAND to TASMANIA

Shortly after noon ('civil', i.e., shore time) on August 2nd 1791 *Providence* and *Assistant* weighed anchor and sailed amid 'Moderate Breezes and fair Weather' for the Cape of Good Hope, the first leg of their outward voyage. (In 'log' time, in which log entries were recorded at sea—i.e., from one noon-time locational observation to the next—the date was August 3rd.) On August 28th (log time) the vessels anchored in the St. Cruz Road of Teneriffe, the main island of the (Spanish) Canary Islands. During the voyage hither the activities aboard them had settled into a routine, which merits our notice mainly as background to what the voyagers experienced and recorded at Tahiti.*

The log-time dated day began at noon, when observations were made, weather permitting, to fix the vessel's longitude and latitude. For this recording aboard the *Providence* the average of the readings of her three sextants was timed by the average shown on her three chronometers.

The solar day, on the other hand, began for those aboard ship at about four or five a.m.; breakfast was at about eight, dinner about midday, and supper about five. Between rising (which for the forecastle men meant rolling smartly out of hammocks—or else!) and supper, weekdays and Saturdays were spent working at some job or another, depending upon one's specialty, or upon established routine or weather or situational need. Among the specialists, the armourer (for example) worked at the forge, the carpenter repaired boats, the Marines exercised their guns, and so on, while the rest of the crew cleaned ship—an almost daily chore, or worked the pumps, or serviced the rigging, or worked up punk, or manufactured pointers and

* None of the journals of this expedition provides a detailed description of the daily routines aboard ship, or of the organization and division of labor of the crew. For that, one must refer to such books as those by Michael Lewis and Christopher Lloyd (see Bibliography)—with the understanding, however, that while *Providence* and *Assistant* were armed navy vessels they were not meant nor manned to engage in naval warfare.

gaskets—or performed one or more of the other 'necessary duties of the ship'. In addition, much of each (solar) Saturday was spent by the crew in mending and cleaning their garments. And at 10 a.m. on most Sundays the whole ship's company assembled on deck, where the crew were inspected for cleanliness of body and clothes, and where the Captain conducted Divine Service. Weather, of course, had a powerful influence on work routine and physical comfort; for example, during exceptionally wet spells fires were kept burning to help dry clothes, which were otherwise continually wet.

Concerning clothing, officers in the Navy had been provided uniforms since 1748, but it was not until 1857 that uniforms were issued to seamen. Until then the latter were *usually* expected to provide their own clothing, of whatever kind, and for those afloat the usual means of replacing worn-out garments was to purchase them aboard. Such replacements were called 'slops'; they were periodically placed on sale by a ship's purser, who received a shilling per pound sterling for all those sold, payments having been debited against the purchasers' wages. I wrote 'usually' because I am not sure whether the slops that were periodically distributed aboard the *Providence* were in fact sold, or were issued *gratis*. For example, in his entry for October 2nd 1781, two months out of England, Bligh recorded having 'served slops to the Ships Company'—i.e., 'served' not 'sold'. Another entry by another commander on another voyage suggests that the slops aboard the Providence were issued free, because of the similarity between that other voyage and Bligh's. Reference is to a journal entry by James Cook for November 24th 1772 on board the Resolution and headed towards the Antarctic: 'Judging that we should soon come into cold weather, I order'd Slops to be served to such as were in want, and gave to each man', to which he added, 'which were allowed by the Admiralty'. (Beaglehole 1961: 52)

And now to the food provided aboard ship—a topic no less exotic than unappetizing to most twentieth century palates.

The ships were victualled with twelve months of standard navy food, which for two hundred years preceding the voyage of *Providence* and *Assistant* had remained the same for ships at sea: for each man one pound of salt pork or two pounds of salt beef, on alternate days; one pound of biscuit and one gallon of beer every day; and a weekly issue of two pints of pease, three pints of oatmeal, eight ounces of butter, and one pound of cheese. One pint of wine or one-half pint of brandy was usually substituted for beer on longer, and especially southern, voyages, because beer did not keep well at sea. Altogether, a diet that was large in quantity (larger than persons of seamen's means would have eaten ashore) but deplorably, even dangerously, deficient in nutritional balance. The consequences of that deficiency were all too evident in the high incidence of dysentry and scurvy, especially scurvy, about which one naval historian wrote:

The most serious disease which began to afflict the European mariner as soon as long voyages became common was scurvy. It was only in the [twentieth] century that it was found that this is a dietary deficiency disease due to lack of vitamin C. All that was certain in the days of sail was that after five or six weeks at sea on salt provisions pimples appeared on the gums, teeth began to fall out, large dark blotches began to appear on the skin, old sores re-opened, an intolerable lethargy overcame the sufferer and any sudden movement, such as that resulting from a stroke with a rope's end wielded by a boatswain, killed a man outright. Half the shipwrecks in history have been due to crews enfeebled by scurvy, and the navy's manning problem was always exacerbated by the number of seamen rendered unfit for duty because they were suffering from this curse of the sea. (Lloyd 1960: 45)

The most effective preventative for scurvy, the juice of citrus fruits, was experimentally established in 1747, and widely publicized in 1753, but another forty years passed before the Admiralty decreed that lemon juice be issued, and then only after six weeks on salt provisions. Meanwhile, steps had been taken by some naval surgeons and some ship commanders (notably James Cook) to vary and supposedly improve the nutritional quality of shipboard fare. Thus by the time of the *Providence*'s departure, such foods as vinegar, bore cole (sauerkraut), and 'portable soup' had become fairly common—the latter a dried concentrate of veal broth. And it had become recommended procedure to substitute, whenever possible, fresh provisions for shipboard fare.

Another established procedure of the period was to withhold meat one day each week; I do not know whether this practice—called 'Banyan Day', after Hindu vegetarianism—was introduced to improve nutrition or to save money, but suppose the latter to have been the case.

As noted, wine or brandy were usually substituted for (cereal-mash) beer on voyages lasting more than about one month. That evidently occurred on the *Providence* voyage, as indicated in Bligh's entry of August 29th 1791, at Teneriffe, where the vessels anchored to take in more supplies: 'Sent Empty Water Casks on Shore & directed the Contractors Messrs Collagan [sp?] to supply us with 930 Gallons of Wine.' Further to that he wrote in his accompanying Remarks:

The Changes since my last visiting this place in 1788 were,—the Contractors had lowered their contract price of Wine from £10 per Pipe [a large cask] to 9£ 10S, a pernicious alteration to the Seamen as it lessens the quality of the Wine more than the difference of Price should effect it, & which is ever the case, however it may be asserted the quality is the same, it is a very miserable saving to Government.

Two months out of England Bligh ordered the brewing of a batch of 'spruce beer', which was issued thereafter every four to seven days until November 5th, when the batch ran out. Spruce beer was a fermented beverage made from an extract from leaves and branches of spruce fir. The *Oxford*

English Dictionary characterizes it as a 'powerful diuretic and anti-scorbutic'; that being so it is likely that it was issued aboard the *Providence* as a dietary prophylactic rather than as a substitute for the standard issue of wine or cereal-mash beer.*

The one item of Navy food and drink that resisted most innovative or substitutive efforts was 'grog', a mixture of rum and water that was by regulation issued daily to all hands (in some cases twice a day). Several ships commanders took steps to increase the water component of grog in order to reduce drunkeness, but a mix of more than three parts water usually led to grumbling, while arbitrary and wilful deprivation of it could lead to outright disaffection. There are few references in the journals of *Providence* and *Assistant* to the serving of grog, but when at sea it was evidently issued every day, as indicated by a sentence in Bligh's Log entry for April 5th 1792, shortly after arrival in Tahiti: 'I thought it proper to put the People to short allowance of liquor, only to serve it three days a week while we have such abundance of fine Cocoa nutts.' (This curtailment seems to have been acceptable to the crew—at least there is no record of any vocal opposition to it.)

As pointed out above it was the Navy's recommended procedure at that time to substitute fresh provisions for standard ship-board fare whenever possible. One reason for this practice on long voyages was the need to augment supplies. Another was the concern of some ship commanders to make their men's meals more appetizing—although, as James Cook recorded in a well-known dictum, the average seaman was notoriously conservative in his food preferences.† A third basis for substituting fresh provisions for shipboard fare was for known or supposed reasons of health—reasons that weighed especially heavily with Bligh.

All the foregoing on food and drink concerns especially the lower deck, but the nature of the food and of much of the drink was the same for officers as well, although the food was doubtless more appetizingly prepared and served for the latter, some of whom also were served better wine and spirits, and a few of whom brought along wines and spirits of their own.

The matters of the ships' command structures and social levels having already been touched upon, it is pertinent to add a word about other aspects of shipboard organization aboard the *Providence*.

There were of course small groups of specialists who worked

---

* Such at least was the practice of James Cook (Bligh's mentor in this and many other matters) who, upon learning of the presence of scurvy in the *Adventure* (*Resolution*'s companion vessel on the Third Voyage), advised its captain to 'brew Beer of the Inspissated [condensed] juce of Wort, Essence of Spruce and Tea plants (all of which he had aboard) for all hands, if he could spare Water, if not for the Sick . . .' (Beaglehole 1961: 187)

† 'To interduce any New article of food among Seamen, let it be ever so much for their good, requires both example and Authority of a Commander, without both of which, it will be droped before the People are Sencible of the benefits resulting from it.' (Beaglehole 1961: 187)

together whenever required: for example, the master and his assistants (i.e., 'mates'), the armorer and his, and so on. Also, everyone except the captain—who often ate alone—ate in one of several separate messes: the commissioned officers, lieutenant of Marines, and surgeon in the ward room mess; the midshipmen in one of their own; and all others in separate messes of about eight members each. For the regular jobs of working and maintaining a naval ship, its company was divided into alternating shifts, or watches; most commonly there were two watches, starboard and larboard, but in some ships a less unremitting three. Thus, thirteen days out of England Bligh recorded:

As an encouragement to the People to be alert in the execution of their duty, as well as considering it conducive to their health, I ordered them in future at three Watches—the Master to keep no regular Watch but to be ready at all calls. (August 16th 1791)

In addition, a Navy ship's company was usually divided into divisions, each under a lieutenant, who 'was responsible for seeing that the men in his division were clean, healthy, and fit for duty, and who could order summary punishments ranging from extra scrubbing duty to a dozen lashes.' (Lloyd 1968: 234) On large warships there were usually four such divisions; *Providence*, having had only three naval lieutenants presumably had as many divisions as well. In any case, the only mention of divisions in Bligh's Journal occurs in Sunday entries, where the ship's company is sometimes referred to as assembling 'in Divisions'. Finally, it is likely that the Marines aboard the *Providence* were separate from all others aboard in some respects—certainly in some of their activities and possibly in messing and assembling as well.

After a stay of four days at Teneriffe the two vessels resumed the voyage to the Cape. They anchored at Porto Praya in the Cape Verde Islands but remained there only overnight because of the Port's insalubrity and the unavailability of fresh fruit and vegetables. After that the only untoward events to take place before reaching Table Bay were a bout of disobedience and violence on the part of the Quartermaster (for which he received thirty lashes) and the illness of the Captain, which lasted acutely for over a month and was so severe and disabling that he withdrew temporarily from active command:

I was extremely doubtfull how long I might survive, and therefore while I had power to think, I sent for Lieutenant Portlock to remain on board here, that I might give every necessary information and advice to render the Voyage successful, and Lieutenant Bond I sent to command the Assistant. (Entry of August 31st 1791)

Bligh first described his illness as 'severe Fever, of a very putrid tendency', and attributed it to the ('remarkable and uncommon') burning heat then gripping St Cruz. In those times 'fever' referred to a range of diseases, from yellow fever and malaria to typhus, while 'putrid fever' was applied to both typhus and diptheria and bore the implication of gangrene. As Bligh's illness continued, his 'putrid tendency'—whatever that was— was replaced by what he described as a 'nervous' fever: 'I was constantly afflicted with a dreadful head Ach and burning heat in my Skin, with a distracted brain on the least noise'. (Entry of September 12th 1791)

Whatever the malady was—heatstroke? migraine?—its symptoms diminished when the ship sailed farther south into a cooler climate, and disappeared during the stay at the Cape—but the 'nervous Fever' was to return.

The vessels anchored in Table Bay on November 11th and remained there for eight weeks. During that lengthy stopover the ships' companies were fed fresh provisions, the invalids were stationed ashore and returned to seemingly good health, those staying aboard were refreshed by shore leave, and the expedition's commander enjoyed a 'vacation' in the countryside around Cape Town. While thus engaged he (characteristically) recorded many observations regarding the region's geography and people, but those records are not directly relevant to the narrower focus of this book.* In any event, the vessels left Table Bay on December 23rd and headed for Tasmania, which was to be the last lengthy stopover before reaching Tahiti.

The passage to Tasmania, then called Van Dieman's Land, required forty-eight days. During it the vessels passed within sight of the Island of St Paul but because of foggy weather did not risk a landing there. Later, after rounding Tasmania's southeast cape they anchored in Adventure Bay, which Bligh had visited in the *Bounty* and before that in Cook's *Resolution*. For the following fortnight the ships' supplies of water and wood were replenished and many excursions were made ashore: collecting new species of plants, encountering a few native Tasmanians, investigating and charting details of the region's geography, and so on. In the course of this visit Bligh and his officers made and recorded many new discoveries—geographical, botanical and ethnographic; some of these are listed in the book by Ida Lee, which also contains excerpts from the journals of Bligh and Bond. They merit a much fuller scholarly treatment than they have hitherto received—but not in the present book, which is concerned mainly with Tahiti, towards which the vessels next sailed.

* For the high points of Bligh's record of his visit to the Cape, see Ida Lee 1920.

TOWARDS TAHITI

Providence and *Assistant* left Tasmania's Adventure Bay in the early evening of February 24th 1792. During the first few days in the Tasman Sea the course was east-southeast. Then, upon approaching New Zealand a more southward one was followed, ('to give [New Zealand] a wider berth') to a latitude just south of 48 degrees, which it was intended to keep to until reaching the approximate longitude of Tahiti. At first the temperatures were low and the ships had to battle gale-force winds. After a fortnight the winds moderated and the ships, always keeping together, remained on that track until April 21st, when they turned north at about longitude 140 degrees west and began working towards Tahiti. During the eastward passage from Tasmania many sea birds and porpoises were seen, and on two occasions the ships passed through huge colonies of phosphorescent seaworms (Pyrosoma). In Bligh's words: 'the water had the appearance as if thousands of small lamps were lighted thereon, and it looked beautiful beyond description.' (Entry of March 16th) It is to be wished that this sight provided some respite from the pain that had resumed: 'I am never free from headaches all day long.' (Entry of March 14th)

While on their northward course (Figure 4) the ships passed within about five hundred miles of Pitcairn Island, where, unknown to Bligh and the rest of the world, Fletcher Christian and eight other *Bounty* mutineers, along with their Tahitian companions, were attempting to survive. (What lively material for Hollywood had Bligh himself only known!) As it was, the first land seen by Bligh and his shipmates on the Tasmania–Tahiti passage was Tematangi, a small and hitherto uncharted atoll in the Tuamotu Archipelago; for the next century it was known by Europeans as Bligh's Lagoon Island. With this landfall we take up our voyagers' daily journal entries, beginning with Bligh's own hourly Log.

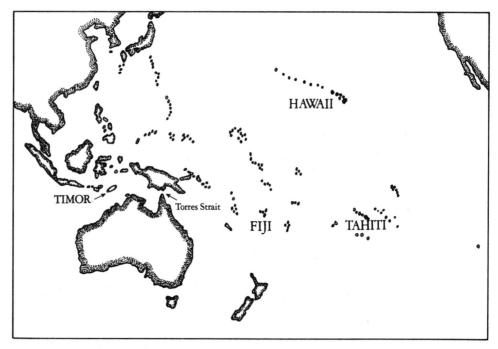

Figure 4   Map of the Pacific Basin

April 5th 1792

      10 AM.   Saw a low lagoon Island from SW to W ½ N, by the W distant four or five miles. Made the signal [to Assistant] and hauled up for it.

      12 AM.   Squally Weather. The Island E by N ½ N 3 or 4 miles to S by E ¾ E about 5 miles. Tremendous surf on the shore. Saw dark brown Noddys with a white spot on the Head [Anous stolidus pileatus ?], Men of War Birds [Fregata minor ?] and Tropic [Family Phaethontidae]. A few cocoa Nutt trees on SW part. No inhabitants.

Remarks

The weather was so very hazy, and the land so low, that it was a mere chance we had not passed it without knowing of being <that we were> near any land whatever. We saw the break of the Surf as soon as the Island was discovered. Its extent of coast is about 22 Miles. From the East to the West point is 8 Miles, and nearly 9 Miles from SW to NE across a Lagoon which takes up most of the Isle. In some parts it is covered with Bushes and some Trees common to these Islands in this*

---

  * This notation, it will be recalled from the Editorial Note, indicates that the italicized words, 'of being', which appear in the PRO version of Bligh's Journal (and in the first draft of the ML version) were subsequently changed to 'that we were' in the ML version.

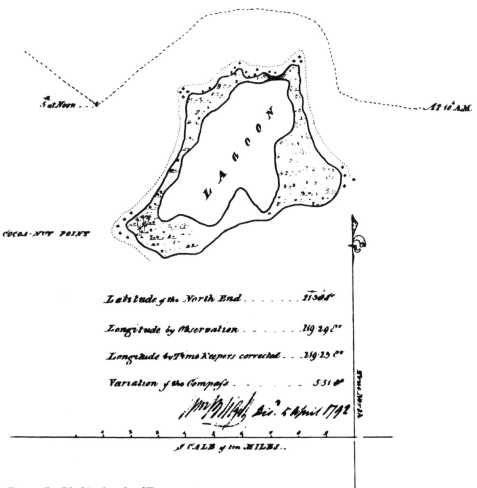

Figure 5   Bligh's sketch of Tematangi

Sea, in others a bare sandy Beach, over which in some places the Sea broke in a most tremendous manner. On the North side are several very large Rocks, but in every other place it is a White Sandy Beach Shore. On the W part I saw a few Cocoa Nutt Trees, and near the point was a cluster of seven very tall ones, remarkable from their situation. [See Figure 5]

I do not believe the Island to be Inhabited. Its nearest situation to any known Land is N by 8 degrees E distance 59 Miles from Osnaburgh Island [Mururoa] discovered by Captain Carteret [in 1767], which is in Latitude 22 00 S and Longitude 218 degrees 20 minutes E.

I am doubtfull if it w<u>as</u> <is> possible for a Boat to land, so *high was the Surf on the lee side of the Island; it was however of too little consequence to me to delay any time in search of it, although I dare say there are many Turtle and abundance of Fish. I did not see any opening into the Lagoon.*

First Mate Bond labelled the atoll Margin Island in his Journal:

This island we discovered in fine weather at the distance of about 6 miles; it is exceedingly low and composed of sand. A little under-wood grows on the margin, with a few fragments of coral rock in some parts on the beach. At the west point are six or seven cocoa-nut trees, the production perhaps of some nuts driven by the trade wind from neighboring islands. The border is so narrow in one place, that a communication must inevitably exist between the lagoon and the sea, which indeed is the most rational way of accounting for its existence, tho we had no opportunity of trying whether it was fresh or salt-water. I imagine the length to be 7 miles—the lagoon 5 or 6. On the N [?] side the surf breaks with great fury, and even to leeward we had no reason to suppose there was anchorage. A convulsion of nature must have given birth to the spot, which appears to be too barren and too unhospitable for the human race.

And from the Journal of Nathaniel Portlock:

At 10 a.m. the Commodore [i.e., Bligh] made the signal for seeing the land; answered it and saw very low land bearing from SSW to WNW, distant 6 or 7 Miles. Hauled in the Studing sails and stood the Course to W by N ½. Bent the small Bower anchor and Buoy Ropes and got the Best Bower anchor all clear the Remainder of the Forenoon steering down along the north side of the Island at the distance of about 2 or 3 miles and shows [?] it to be a Lagoon Isle wooded tolerably well with trees of a very moderate height whose [?] kind we could not well distinguish. Cocoanutt trees we saw on the West Point of the Island a few, I think not more than half a dozen. In rounding the North Point of the Isle I saw from the Mast head a Bay just around the land's Point turning in to the SE, perfectly sheltered from the SE Trade and the water in the head of the Bay appeard quite smooth for landing in the launch and no appearance of foul ground in the Bay. If there is anchorage in this bay ships that [?] make little draft might get an abundant supply of Turtle from the Lagoon, its true we saw none off its coasts and some people may infer from that the Isle may not abound with them but that reasoning will not hold good for in the Voyage of the Resolution and Discovery [i.e., James Cook's third voyage, 1776–1780, on which Portlock served as Master's Mate to Bligh] near Christmas Isle, that was discovered in that Voyage we saw no Turtle at the Distance of three miles from the shore, a very few close to the shore or Reef, but an abundance in the Lagoon and just within the Reefs, but we found them not abundant just within the Points that formed the breaks in the Reefs leading into the Lagoon. I conclude there are no Inhabitants in this Isle as we saw none make their appearance. Birds we saw a few such as the Man of War bird and Noddy.

Bligh's chartered location of Tematangi was off by only a few miles. Also, his description and sketch map of the island were remarkably accurate, considering that he viewed it from a distance of one to three miles off its northern shore. (But of course, he had practised his cartographic skills under the demanding eye of James Cook.) However, his conclusion that the island was uninhabited at the time may have been incorrect.

When Tematangi was visited by H.M.S. *Blossom* thirty-four years later it was very visibly 'inhabited'; to quote from one account of that visit:

After steering W by S 41 miles, we made Bligh's Lagoon Island, bearing SW . . . [which] is inhabited. The Natives made fires on several parts of the beach, when we approached, and on our sending a boat to look for a good landing place, & for the purpose of gaining information, and establishing traffic with them, they made unequivocal signs of hostility, motioning to our people to depart, and menacing them with stones. They picked up some bits of iron that were thrown to them with great eagerness, but nothing would induce them to venture off to the boat, & our party were as unwilling to trust themselves on shore, and quickly returned to the ship. These Natives had long lances. There were no cocoanut trees, and the Island was like the others, composed of patches with trees on them & reefs. (Gough 1973: 109)

Thirty years later the inhabitants of the island figured in an incident that may help to explain Bligh's inference about their inexistence—and to confirm the above judgment about their hostility.

In April 1856 the schooner *Sarah-Ann* took on a cargo of pearl shell at Mangareva and sailed for Tahiti with seventeen persons aboard, including the captain's wife and child. When after several months it had not arrived it was assumed ship-wrecked—a common enough occurrence for boats passing through the 'Dangerous Archipelago', i.e., the Tuamotus. In June 1857 another schooner passed close enough to Tematangi for its captain to see what he believed to be remains of a wrecked vessel, along with colored bits of European clothing bedecking the natives seen on shore. Thinking that he was seeing remnants of the *Sarah-Ann* and her passengers, but dissuaded by hostile gestures from landing, he returned to Tahiti and reported his suspicions. Acting quickly, the French authorities dispatched a rescue ship with a company of marines. The latter scoured Tematangi and found signs of hasty departure but no natives or Europeans, so after burning a few canoes and huts they returned to Tahiti.

Undaunted by the failure of the official expedition, the mother of two of *Sarah-Ann*'s passengers charted another schooner to press the search. *En route* she stopped off at nearby Anaa and recruited twenty-five of its men, including their chief, Teina. Once again the search party saw no humans on the beach at Tematangi, so they fanned out through the pandanus thickets, leaving Teina to bring up the rear. After the noisy party had left him in the quiet their chief saw a human hand emerge from a pile of coral and begin to clear an opening into the cavern where its owner and several other Tematangans were hiding. Teina called back his men, who opened the cavern and captured all sixteen of its inmates. Elsewhere on the Island were found many human remains, including a head with long blond hair—clear proof (to the searchers) that these presumed passengers of the *Sarah-Ann* had been eaten (an inference strengthened by earlier reports of the existence of cannibalism in some other islands of the Tuamotus). The prisoners were taken to Tahiti, three having died *en route*. I do not know what eventually happened to them, but their sometime habit of hiding from strangers in their cave may explain Bligh's conclusion about the island's uninhabited state.

A footnote to this island's grisly, yet poignant, history: when it was visited, and finally 'pacified', by a certain Lieutenant de Kertanguy in 1880 the sixty or so natives living there were 'very suspicious, and frequently reduced to great straits through hunger, they having only the fruit of the pandanus to live on'. (*Revue Maritime et Coloniale* 1881: 138–43) And most recently, the Island was reported to be 'usually uninhabited . . . as the only livlihood afforded [there] is pearl fishing'. (*Pacific Islands Pilot* 1957: 93–4)

At noon on Thursday April 6th (log time; still April 5th civil time) the ships resumed course towards Tahiti, and for the next forty-eight hours Bligh's Journal recorded only the usual occurrences of everyday routine, for example:

April 6: 6PM.   Let fresh Water into the Ship and Ventilated with the pumps. [Hauled] in 1st Reefs and furled the Main Sail.
11:00 PM.   Squally. In 2nd Reefs.
12:00 PM.   Fair Weather and Haze.
4:00 AM.   Out Reefs and Set Steering Sails.
7:00 AM.   Served thick Portable Soup Gruel for breakfast Krout-Sweet Wort at 10 o'clock—Portable Soup and Bore Cole in the Pease for Dinner.
8:00 AM.   Exercised Boats Crews and fired [i.e., target practice by Marines]. Armourer [working] at the Forge. Carpenters finishing the Boats. People washing.

April 7: 12:00 AM.   Fair Weather but exceedingly Hazy. Broached a Puncheon of Spruce Beer for the People. Saw a peice of Wood like a rough stave. Assistant in Company.
1:00 PM.   Fresh Trade and Hazy Weather. Saw flying fish and Mother Careys Chicken [storm petrel; it may however have been not a true storm petrel but à variety of sawbilled petrel. See Beaglehole 1955: 39 note 2].
3:00 PM.   Exercised the Marines at firing at a Target. They put in ⅓ of the number of shot fired.
4:00 PM.   People Employed mending [their] Cloaths.
6:00 PM.   Let fresh Water into the Ship and worked the Pumps as usual. In Steering Sails and 1st Reefs.
8:00 PM.   Fine bright Moon light Night but the Clouds passing so thick cannot get Observations.
4:00 AM.   Out Reefs and set Steering Sails.
7:00 AM.   Served thick Portable Soup Gruel for Breakfast Sweet Wort at 11 oclock. Krout.

9:00 AM.   Exercised Marines and Boats Crews at small Arms and fired. Armourer at the Forge.

10:00 AM.   Saw a forked Tail Gull like what are called Ganneps in the North Sea [Family Sulidae] they are never far from Land.

April 8: 12:00 AM.   Fair Weather and Hazey. Saw two Tropic Birds Mother Careys Chicken and a Sheerwater [Family Procellariidae]. Assistant in Company.

During this Saturday afternoon the regular routine was augmented with two proceedings designed specifically to prepare for the arrival in Tahiti:

2:00 PM.   The Surgeon examined the Ships Company to discover those that were tainted with the Veneral disease.

5:00 PM.   Took an Account of every Man's Cloaths to prevent them <their> trafficking them away.

The action of 'taking account of every Man's Cloaths' was not further discussed in the Remarks accompanying the Log entry; it was however nothing more than an inventory of the 'People's'—every man on board? all except officers?—garments to discourage them from bartering them away for native food or 'curiosities' or sexual favors. Bligh knew from experience the inveteracy of such trafficking. (How effective the measure proved to be is not known, there having been no mention of a check-up at the end of the visit in Tahiti.) Curious to relate, Portlock's Log does not mention having carried out a similar inventory on the *Assistant*.

As for the 'Veneral' examination: that did incite further remarks from Bligh and others, and it appears to have been applied to *Providence*'s entire company—excepting the Captain himself and, probably, the examining surgeon. (Again, there is no mention in Portlock's Journal of an examination on the *Assistant*.) Bligh's expanded Remarks about this examination read:

Agreeable to an Order I gave the Surgeon dated the 7th he examined the Ships Company to discover if any disease was among them, particularly the Venereal. His report to me by letter was, he had examined them individually, and found Mr. Gillespie, George Harford, John Currey, and William Morgan to have such remains of it, as might convey the infection, and therefore their intercourse with Women should be prevented if possible. With respect to any other complaint there was not any, on the contrary the Ship's Company was in perfect Health.

In Bligh's own handwritten original—the Mitchell Library version—the list read: 'Lieut Tobin, Mr Gillespie, Geo Harford, Jno Curry and Wm Morgan to have such remains of it . . .' but someone, presumably Bligh himself, had crossed out the individual names and written 'five of them' in the interline space above them, possibly to spare those individuals, and particularly the commissioned officer, Tobin, the censure of posterity.

31

The examination was merely mentioned in the Journal of Lt. Bond, and it was referred to with approval in that of Flinders:

The Examination . . . might possibly be not very agreeable to the Parties concerned, yet it was certainly done with a good Intention and will free us from any Share of the Guilt attending the Communication of the Venereal Disease to this modern Cypress.

Most comment on it was supplied by Tobin in his Journal written five years later:

In the afternoon, with but little distinction, the whole body corporate, passed through the hands of our worthy associate Ned Harwood; and never did the Doctor take a pinch—of snuff, with more solemnity, or handle—a subject, with less risible countenance. It was ever his nature to be gentle, and memory tells me there were moments, and but moments, when I paid him in a different coin—Yet never, but that it recoiled on me with double force. It was his duty now to examine—the affairs of men—with a scrutinizing eye; in his report, to 'nothing extenuate or set down aught in malice'. The Report was favorable, and such as to acquit the crew of the Providence of a fresh importation of misery to this still cheerful Island. If two subjects could not strictly 'pass muster', we will not doubt, from their situation in the ship that a sense of benevolence restrained them from error.

Four?, five? two?: we shall never know the actual count in this well-intentioned muster!

The following morning began as usual on *Providence* with a breakfast of portable soup gruel and a cleaning of the ship.

Thereafter, as was the usual Sunday morning routine, the Captain assembled the entire company, inspected their clothing ('saw every person clean dressed') and performed Divine Service. Regarding the inspection he wrote:

No men were ever in better health; not a complaint in the Ship except the Venereals, and on their account only has there been a Sick List necessary [during] the Voyage.

In addition to these routine procedures Bligh made further preparations for the arrival in Tahiti by giving out 'Orders for establishing an amicable intercourse with the Natives of any Island we might be at, and promised disgrace and punishment to those who disobeyed them'.

In promulgating those 'Orders' Bligh was repeating a line of practice that went back at least as far as 1768, to the 'Hints' offered to Captain Cook and other members of the *Endeavour*, on Cook's first South Sea voyage. The formulator of those 'Hints' was James Douglas, 14th Earl of Morton, who was at the time President of the Royal Society, the organization that sponsored *Endeavour*'s mission to observe the transit of Venus. Douglas's 'Hints' ranged from the very general (for example):

To have it still in view that sheding the blood of these people [i.e., the natives] is a crime of the highest nature: They are human creatures, the work of the same omnipotent Author, equally under his care with the most polished Europeans; perhaps being less offensive, more entitled to his favor.

to the very particular (for example):

Opening the mouth wide, putting the fingers towards it, and then making the motion of chewing, would sufficiently demonstrate a want for food. (Beaglehole 1955: 514–15)

Cook reformulated and abbreviated the 'Hints' into a set of five, characteristically direct and practical, 'Rules':

Rules to be observ'd by every person in or belonging to His Majesty's Bark the Endeavour, for the better establishing a regular and uniform Trade for Provisions etc. with the Inhabitants of Georges Island [i.e., Tahiti].
1st   To endeavour by every fair means to cultivate a friendship with the Natives and to treat them with all imaginable humanity.
2d   A proper person or persons will be appointed to trade with the Natives for all manner of Provisions, Fruit, and other productions of the earth; and no officer or Seaman, or other person belonging to the Ship, excepting such as are so appointed, shall Trade or offer to Trade for any sort of Provisions, Fruit, or other productions of the earth unless they have my leave to do so.
3d   Every person employ'd a Shore on any duty what soever is strictly to attend to the same, and if by neglect he looseth any of his Arms or working tools, or suffers them to be stole, the full Value thereof will be charge'd against his pay according to the Custom of the Navy in such cases, and he shall recive such farther punishment as the nature of the offence may deserve.
4th   The same penalty will be inflicted on every person who is found to imbezzle, trade or offer to trade with any part of the Ships Stores of what nature soever.
5th   No Sort of Iron, or any thing that is made of Iron, or any sort of Cloth or other usefull or necessary articles are to be given in exchange for any thing but provisions. (Beaglehole 1955: 75–6)

On his second South Sea voyage Cook's 'Rules' were even more specific, and directly relevant to the situation in Tahiti. (Beaglehole 1961: 201 fn 1) As far as I can discover Cook did not publicly promulgate any official rules of this kind relating specifically to Tahiti during his third voyage, but prior to his arrival there he did so at Tonga:

Knowing from experience, that if every body was allowed to traffick with the natives according to thier own caprice, perpetual quarrels would essue, to prevent this I ordered that particular person(s) should manage the traffick both on board and ashore, and prohibited the trade to all others. I also ordered that no curiosities should be purchased till the Ships were supplied with Provisions and leave give[n] for that purpose. (Beaglehole 1967: I 97)

Bligh, who was aboard the *Resolution* during Cook's third-voyage

33

visits to these islands, was well aware of the risks attending barter and other interaction with the Tahitians. Accordingly, he promulgated a similar set of rules on the *Bounty* and on the *Providence*. The *Providence* 'Orders' are recorded not in Bligh's own Journal but in Flinders's, where they read as follows:

Rules to be observed by every Person on board or belonging to H.M.Ship Providence for the better establishing a Trade for Provisions and good Intercourse with the Natives of the South Sea Islands, wherever the Ship may be at.

    1st.   At the Society or Friendly Islands [i.e., Tonga] no seaman or officer is ever to speak of the Loss of the Bounty, or that Capt. Cook was killd by Indians.

    2nd.   No man or officer is ever to speak or give the least hint that we have come on Purpose for the bread-fruit plant.

    3rd.   Every Person is to study to gain the good will and esteem of the Natives, to treat them with all kindness and not to recover by violent means any thing that may have been stolen from them, but to acquaint me with it.

    4th.   Every Person employd on any Service whatever, is to take care that no Arms or Implements of any kind under his Charge are stolen, the Value of any such being lost shall be charged against his Wages, besides a severe punishment for his Neglect.

    5th.   No man is to embezzle or offer to sale directly or indirectly any Part of the Kings Stores, of any kind whatever.

    6th.   A proper Person or Persons will be appointed to regulate Trade with the Natives & no Officer or Seaman or other Person belonging to the Ship shall trade or offer to trade for any kind of Provisions or Curiosities without my leave.

    7th.   The Mate of the Watch will be answerable for all Neglects of the Centinals and he is to see that they do not lounge or sit down.

    8th.   No Canoe is to come on board after eight at Night and on no Pretence what ever is a Canoe to be under the Bows, or any thing to be handed in or out, but [rest of line cut off]

    9th.   All boats when moored, to have every thing handed out of them at Sun down.

    10th.   The Awnings to be always set at Sun-rise, & furled at Sun-sett wet or dry except the After one—But they are occasionally to be spread or furled in variable Weather in the daytime as Circumstances will allow, the object in this being to keep them from rotting and tearing to pieces.

    11th.   Every Night the Tarpaulins are to be ready for the Hatchways and Care taken that no Wet gets below.

    12th.   The Officers of the Watch on any Pretence whatever, are not to get into Conversation with the Indians, but to be cautiously up on the look-out, lest the Indians draw their attention from their Duty and commit some violence or Theft.

    13th.   All Boats are to be moord alongside & to have stern fasts and a Boat-keeper in each. If it is found necessary to veer a Boat astern, two Men must be kept in her.

    14th.   Any Person having the Venereal Disease on him & is found to have connection with the Women shall receive a very exemplary Punishment.

15th.   No Curiosities are to be kept between Decks.

16th.   No Person whatever is to take fire Arms with him on shore at Otaheite until he has my Permission.

Lastly, Any transgression to the foregoing orders, will be punished with the utmost severity—a total Loss of my good wishes towards the Offender the remainder of the Voyage & be publickly noted as such.

With all these preparations in hand, *Providence* (and presumably *Assistant*) were ready for Tahiti, but *en route* they paid a brief visit to Me'etia, the easternmost island of the Society Archipelago, and closely linked with Tahiti in social ties. At 9 a.m. on April 8th the position of this island was computed by Bligh to bear N 77 degrees W and to be 44 miles ahead. By noon the Island was in sight, bearing W ¼°S and about 7 leagues ahead, and received the following entry in Bligh's Journal:

I steered to the North of the Island and hauled round under the Lee of it, where I brought too about 2 Miles distant from the Shore. Four small Cannoes came off to us with whom I traded for a few Cocoa Nutts, two baked Breadfruit, and a small bunch of Plaitains. The Men were all but one, of the lowest class, or Toutous [teueu, servant]. Some of them recognized <recollected> me. The superior Man said he was the Erree ra high [ari'i rahi, paramount chief; see below] of the Island, but I soon found that he was deceiving me, a circumstance not at all uncommon among these People; he had on an European Shirt <an European Shirt on> which he said was given to him by one Pahteenee, but I could not make out who this Pahteenee was. [A footnote added to PRO states: 'Pateene. A seaman called Martin belonging to the Bounty'] He [the 'superior Man'] was desirous to go to Otaheite in the Ship, and on my refusing him, he told me he would follow to Morrow. He said two Ships had passed about 3 Months ago, but he knew not from what country they came. The lee side of this Island has no plantations on it, it being so remarkably steep to the summit of the Mountain that scarce any Soil will lie on it. The Weather side appeared cloathed with Cocoa Nutt Trees.

On the face of it Bligh's refusal to transport the 'superior Man' to Tahiti seems churlish; in fact it was wise. He knew that his mission would be dependant upon the good will of the leaders residing at his proposed anchorage, Matavai Bay, and could not risk identification with someone who was quite possibly an enemy of theirs—or rather, quite *probably*, since Me'etia's closest ties on Tahiti were with the chiefly dynasty of Taiarapu, who were rivals of the leaders then in authority at Matavai.

Tobin's retrospective account of this brief visit is less laconic:

By four in the afternoon, while passing the north side [of Me'etia; Plate 3] at about the distance of a mile, three canoes were observed paddling with great exertion to overtake us; the vessels were in consequence brought to the wind. With the hearty confidence of an unoffending people they soon jumped on board, and bartered some bread fruit and Cocoa nuts for nails and other articles. One among our visitors, who called himself an Eree or Chief, and who, from having taken copiously of an intoxicating beverage called Yava was quite riotous, entertained us in no small degree. He was dressed in a European shirt of which he was not a little vain, and gave us to understand it was procured from a ship (pahee) [pahi] that had recently visited the island. We afterwards were informed that it was from the Matilda Whaler he had got his finery. The vessels drifted East from the land which about sun set occasioned the departure of our visitors who did not wait the canoes coming along side, but jumping over board with their English goods in one hand, with the other they swam to them. This little Island, not above a League in circuit, is one of the most beautiful spots that can be conceived, being in most parts well-clothed with a variety of trees; the bread fruit, plantain, and cocoa nut, being among the number. The very summit is nearly destitute of verdure for a small space where there is a chasm apparently by some convulsion of nature, probably it is the seat of a volcano. There were several courses from this part of the Island to the sea, similar to what are to be seen in most mountainous countries from the effects of heavy rain. The habitations of the natives, like those of O'tahytey are near the sea.

The first recorded European ship to sight Me'etia (Maitea, Mehetia, etc.) was H.M.S. *Dolphin*, on June 17th 1767, during a voyage in search of new lands (including a fabled 'Southern Continent', which many Europeans believed to exist in the Pacific between New Zealand and Cape Horn—a belief based partly on the theory that a large land mass in the southern Hemisphere was essential for the stability of the global Earth). Wallis, *Dolphin*'s Commander, named Me'etia 'Osnaburg' Island, for the second son of George III, Frederick Augustus, who had been elected Bishop of Osnabrug (also, Osnaburg) at the age of six months. Philip Carteret, whose sloop, *Swallow*, was to have accompanied *Dolphin* throughout the expedition but which went on alone after being separated from her in Magellan Straits, applied the name 'Osnaburg' to another island discovered by him. That was the Tuamotuan island, Mururoa, of present-day nuclear-testing notoriety. In John Beaglehole's words: 'Cook's English predecessors were more notable for loyalty to the House of Hanover than for romance in their choice of names'. (1955: 72n)

At Me'etia *Dolphin*'s barge and cutter rowed close in to shore and engaged in some barter with natives in their canoes: 'toys' in exchange for a pig and some fowl and fruit. They did not land, because of the presence on the beach of a hundred or so men armed with 'picks and sticks'. (Carrington 1948: 132–3) From Me'etia the *Dolphin* sailed northwest and 'discovered' Tahiti on June 19th.

Following the *Dolphin*, Me'etia was sighted from Bougainville's ships in April 1968 (and named by Bougainville 'Le Boudoir') and again from the *Endeavour* a year later, but the first Europeans known to have landed there were from the Spanish frigate *Santa Maria Magdalene* (alias *El Aguila*), Don

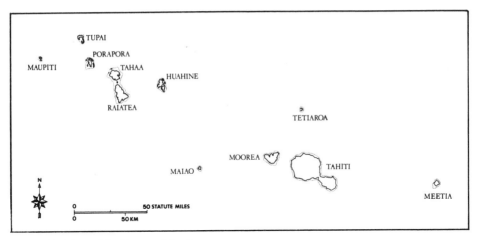

Figure 6   Map of the Society Islands

Domingo Boenechea commanding, in November 1772. The island, renamed by him 'San Cristobal', was explored by a shore party, which estimated its population to be about two hundred and which recorded a brief but informative account of its observations. (Corney 1913: 292–7) After that, Me'etia was sighted again by Cook in 1773 and 1777, by Bligh (in the *Bounty*) in 1788, and by Vancouver in 1791—but visited by none of them. By that time it had come to serve European voyagers as a familiar and welcome prelude to the grander drama of Tahiti.

Me'etia, the easternmost and geologically youngest island in the Society Archipelago (Figure 6), is less than 1 square mile in area, with a highest elevation of 1500 feet. In Bligh's time canoes plied regularly, two or three times a year, between Me'etia and Tahiti—mainly Tahiti's peninsula, Taiarapu, whose chief was described by one writer of that era as having exercised a kind of suzerainty over the Me'etians. (Rutter 1935: 201) The Spaniard, Andia y Varela, wrote that Me'etia served the Taiarapu chief as a place of banishment of subjects in disfavor. (Corney 1915: 264) Whatever their political relationships may have been, the Me'etians and Tahitians shared the same culture, including language, and regularly exchanged goods. After European goods became common on Tahiti some of them, especially iron, were sent to Me'etia in exchange for stools (and other carved wooden objects), bark cloth, mats, pigs, etc.—along with pearls and pearlshell (the latter from the nearer Tuamotuan atolls, Me'etia having been an *entrepot* between them and Tahiti). (Rutter 1935: 201) It is not reported what items went from Tahiti to Me'etia before the advent of European goods—perhaps red feathers?—but something evidently did. For, although the Me'etians' goods may have been regarded as 'tribute' (an expression of their reported 'subjection' to the Taiarapu chief), in the culture shared by both parties 'tribute' was usually reciprocated by 'gifts' of *noblesse oblige*. Also, the natives of these islands would not likely have travelled empty-handed on such a long voyage to a known and friendly destination.

Leaving Me'etia, *Providence* and *Assistant* set their sails for the northern coast of Tahiti, only sixty-five nautical miles ahead.

ARRIVAL at MATAVAI

Bligh's Log 'Remarks' upon approaching Tahiti—his third arrival there—were factual and succinct:

The Night [after leaving Me'etia] came on boisterous, and the morning so much that I was obliged to lye by for some time, for I was not able to see the land [Tahiti] distinctly. Towards Noon the Weather came <became> fair, and we anchored in Matavia <Matavai> Bay without accident.

In the greater detail supplied by his hourly Log:

Hauled round the Dolphin Bank [the sandbank where Wallis's ship Dolphin went aground] and worked up into Matavai Bay, where I anchored in 9 fathoms and Moored with an open Hawse to the Sea. Point Venus N 30 E ⅔ of a Mile; West head of Tarra S 25 [degrees] W; East Head S 3 [degrees] W, 1 Mile; End of Reef N 10 [degrees] W; Morai [Marae] Point at Oparre S 40 [degrees] W; Extremes of Morea [Mo'orea] S 11 [degrees] W to S 88 [degrees] W, its High Mountain S 76 [degrees] W. The Best Bower [anchor] lay in 15 fathoms. [See Figures 7, 8a, 8b]

The Journal entries of Bond and Portlock were just as matter-of-fact. Not so that of George Tobin, whose retrospective Journal expresses vividly his reaction to one of nature's most romantic landscapes—Tahiti in the morning sunlight when approached by sea:

At day light we were gratified with a sight of the long wished for Island, but at too remote a distance to distinguish, even with our glasses, more than its blue mountains. When about eight miles from point Venus, the most northern part of the Island, our expectations were more than realised in the many delightful views opening in succession as the vessels passed a short league from the shore. The heavy showers of the preceding night, had given additional verdure to the lower grounds, while they served to form numberless white cataracts, serpentining amid the foliage on the distant mountains. The beach was tumultuously crouded with natives from their huts, scattered under the umbrage of the luxuriant bread fruit or towering cocoa nut whose leafy plumes waved towards the opposite horizon, on every projecting point of the Isle, from the cease-

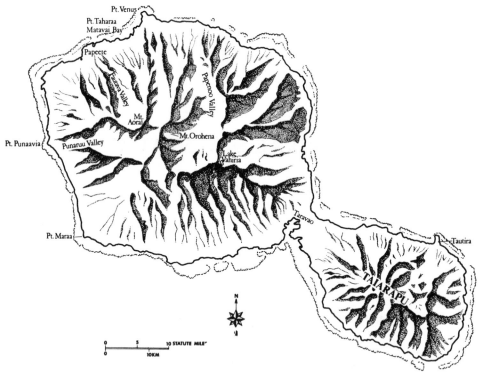

Figure 7   Topographic map of Tahiti

less pressure of the eastern breeze. Numberless canoes were in motion within an angry reef that seemed to gird the Island, yielding security to these pigmy vessels, and on the reef itself, where in a few spots the sea did not force a passage, the natives of both sexes were industriously employed, in procuring shell and other fish; yet not without indulging a respite from their daily avocation, in viewing the Providence and Assistant as they passed.

By Noon we were safely anchored in Matavai bay [Plates 4, 5, 6], after a passage from Spithead of thirty six weeks.

Returning to Bligh's Log 'Remarks':

[After anchoring] I was immediately visited by my old acquaintances, and to my surprise by a Whale Boat of a Ship that was lost, called the Matilda, Matthew Weatherhead Master. I found that Captain Vancouver had been there <and> Captain Edwards in the Pandora, and <heard> many <and> various accounts respecting them. Every person I saw gave me joy of my safe return to Otaheite.

I had not many Cannoes off to the Ships, for the People of Oparre and M̲atavia <Matavai> were at War, on account of the M̲atavia <Matavai> People refusing to share the things <of which> they had robbed the

40

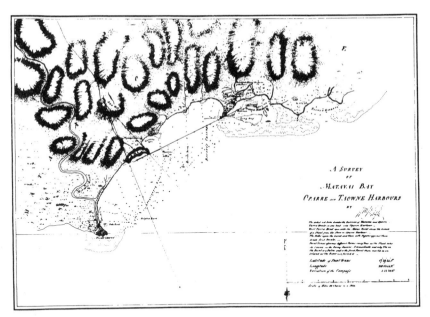

Figure 8a   Bligh's chart of Matavai Bay and environs

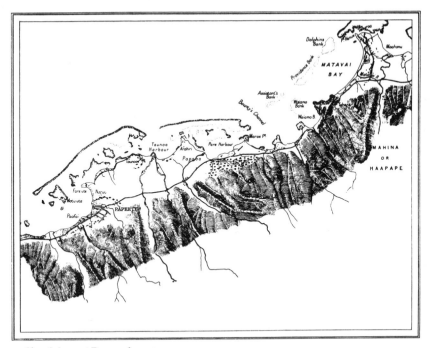

Figure 8b   Matavai Bay and environs

41

Seamen of the Matilda. I heard this News with some concern, as it militated against my plans of immediately beginning to get the Bread Fruit. The People who came off to me were Iddeah the Queen (her husband was from home), Tootaha an old Preist <Priest>, and Oreepyah and Whydooah, the Brothers of Tynah.

> *Here Log Account Ends and Civil [time reckoning—i.e., from midnight to midnight rather than noon to noon] begins, this page taking in 36 Hours.*

Before adding other journal accounts of these events some editorial comments are called for. First, regarding the survivors of the *Matilda*, the story of that affair will unfold in subsequent entries by Bligh and others. The mention of Vancouver refers to the visit to Tahiti of H.M. Ships *Discovery* and *Chatham*, from the end of December 1791 to January 24th 1792. That visit, which had for its principal mission the exploration of the North Pacific (Lamb 1984), will figure again in later entries by Bligh. H.M.S. *Pandora* was the ship, commanded by Captain Edward Edwards, which was sent to these waters to search for and capture the *Bounty* mutineers. She reached Tahiti on March 23rd 1791, and proceeded to arrest all twenty-two of the *Bounty* people still on the island—two members of the original crew having been killed earlier on Tahiti, and the others having left aboard the *Bounty* for what turned out to be Pitcairn Island, 1130 nautical miles to the southeast. After leaving Tahiti the *Pandora* carried out a widespread but vain search for the latter and was eventually wrecked on Australia's Barrier Reef, with the loss of thirty crew members and four prisoners. (Thomson 1915)

Bligh's references to Oparre and Matavai, to the 'old acquaintances' who greeted him aboard the *Providence*, and to the offices of 'Queen' and 'Priest' stand in need of some introductory explanations, which subsequent Journal entries and annotations will serve to amplify.

Oparre [Pare] and Matavai were geographic areas on Tahiti's northwest coast. They were also territorial-political units, though of different orders of complexity. But before describing that kind of unit let us take a more comprehensive look at some aspects of the culture shared by the natives of Tahiti and of the other islands in this chain, from Me'etia in the southeast to Maupiti in the northwest.

The basic social-residential unit of these islands was the household (*'utuafare*), a group of from about five to twenty persons, interrelated mainly by familial ties, who dwelt together in a single compound of huts (sleeping, cooking, working) and who cooperated in producing their own food and clothing. Each household also had its own *marae*, a temple where its members petitioned their own tutelar spirits, including one or more ancestral ghosts.

With few exceptions households were located near the coasts and were clustered into separate neighborhoods—but straggling ones, not com-

The Bread Fruit of Otahytey. GT 1792 Page 193
about the size of a Shaddock

Section of the Fruit

Artocarpus incisa
of Linn

Plate 1   Breadfruit
Watercolor by George Tobin

Plate 2   *Providence* and *Assistant*
Watercolor by George Tobin

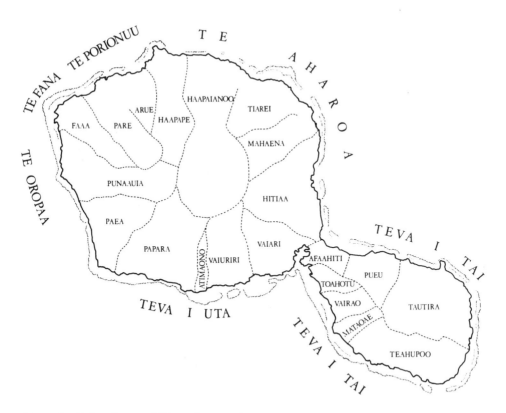

Figure 9   Political map of Tahiti, showing districts

pact villages. Ties of kinship also obtained among most of the residents of any neighborhood. In many of them such ties were reinforced by economic cooperation (e.g., by joint land clearing or fishing) but even where that did not take place all the permanent residents of each neighborhood formed a separate religious congregation, with its own temple (*marae*) and set of tutelar spirits, which in perhaps most instances were those of the household of the neighborhood's headman. In addition, the neighborhood was this society's most common type of (corporate) land-owning unit. Individual households held uncontested use-rights in their own house sites and gardens and groves, but when they ceased to use them ownership reverted to their neighborhood as a whole, for re-allocation by its headman.

Centuries earlier, when these islands were less populous, most neighborhoods were politically autonomous, hence their headmen were what may be called chiefs—a leader subject to the authority of no one else. By the middle of the eighteenth century, however, all of Tahiti's neighborhoods had become parts of larger polities, which may be called (autonomous) districts. (Figure 9). In most cases the boundaries between districts were topographic—e.g., mountain ridges or swampy embankments—but there were cases where a single district extended over two or more valleys, or occupied only part of one. Like neighborhoods, each district had its own temple, or *marae*, and its own tutelar spirits, which in many instances were those of its chief's own neighborhood, or even his own household. Cooperation among members of a district consisted mainly of doing things for their chief, for example, building his houses, supporting his ceremonies, fighting what were mainly his wars. Also, a chief was, *ex officio*, head priest of his district, just as he was a paterfamilias of his household and a headman of his neighborhood; in practice, however, that office in a district was often delegated to some other individual, or to some other family line.

A district's chief also had some control over the lands in his district of neighborhoods other than his own. That control was not as direct or as priestly or as supernaturally sanctioned as the kind he exercised over his own household and neighborhood lands, but at the very least he received tribute in the form of food and other objects produced on those lands, and he had the power to impose restrictions on what their owners harvested—say, in order to build up supplies for a district-wide feast. And in instances of extreme *lèse-majesté* he sometimes exiled all members of a family or neighborhood and confiscated their land, temporarily or in perpetuity, for the exclusive use of himself and his heirs.

Relations *between* districts varied widely, from continual 'hot' or 'cold' warfare, to shifting alliance, or long-standing confederation (a state of affairs that Bligh understood well, as his Journal will relate). Most influential of the factors that shaped such relations were the kind of (or lack of) kin ties between chiefly dynasties, plus the ambitions and abilities of individual chiefs.

The foregoing is an oversimplification but it is sufficient for the present; the extraordinarily complex nature of Tahiti's 'governments' will emerge little by little, as did Bligh's comprehension of it.

In comparison with what the British visitors would have found in, say, Fiji or New Caledonia, the Tahitians' ideas about consanguineal relationships were quite similar to those held by Bligh and his shipmates. Children were deemed to be the corporeal and spiritual offspring of *both* their parents, and learned to make little or no distinction between relatives of the two. And while the Tahitians' acceptance of polygyny was alien to the legal code of the visiting Englishmen, most were conjugally monogamous in practice.

Another facet of Tahitian society comfortably familiar to the visitors was its social stratification: an upper class (*ari'i*), a lower class (*manahune*), and a 'middle' class of *ra'atira* in between. Pedigree, rather than occupation or disposable property, was the decisive criterion in this stratification, especially at the top—a consideration that rendered the aristocratic *ari'i* even more

44

caste-like than their English counterparts (e.g., in Tahiti the issue of *mésalliances* were usually killed at birth). Another not unfamiliar discriminating principle in Tahitian consanguinity was birth order: a first-born inherited the largest portion of each parent's spiritual component (i.e., his and her 'godliness', since all descent lines began with gods), a last-born the smallest. Thus, in this pervasively hierarchic society the *ari'i* were the offspring of lines of first-borns, while *manahune* were those of lines of later-borns—or were so low-born as to have no pedigrees worth recall.

Such, at least, was the dogma. In the course of actual (versus mythical) history this arithmetically flowing scheme had been diverted many times: for example, by reproductive vagaries or by individual disparities or by family feuds. Nevertheless, the dogma was influential enough to support a society-wide hierarchy of social rank that in several localities differed from hierarchies of secular authority. Bligh appears to have understood enough of this dualism to be able to maneuver within it (there were, after all, English parallels) but evidently he never did uncover its Tahitian rationale, which I shall now summarize.

The belief that an individual inherited some of each parent's godliness, or sanctity—the amount having diminished with order of birth—led to a graded hierarchy of sanctity within families, and also between families sharing historical or legendary lines of descent. Moreover, consciousness of this form of hierarchy was so universal that high-ranking families, or dynasties, were graded one with another even if their members had no known or supposed ancestors in common (although such families did not always agree on their standing *vis à vis* each other!). And, it should be added, it was this spiritual criterion for hierarchy that was the basis of, or provided the rationale for, the society's class stratification.—However, a *caveat* is here called for. Although individuals and whole families were judged, by themselves and others, to be members of this or that social class—or, within the upper class, of this or that dynasty—the actual building blocks of the sanctity hierarchy were not specific individuals or families (which had only transitory lives and careers) but named kin-Titles, which, ideally, existed forever.

The Tahitian language contained generic names for many kinds of roles and offices: for example, 'father', 'first-born', 'brother-in-law', 'bond-friend', 'warrior', 'priest', 'district-chief', and so on. It also contained proper names—'Titles'—for important offices associated with the official temples of the more powerful political units: for example, Deep Thinker of Such-and-Such Temple. (Actually, such Titles were the property of the leading family lines associated with such temples, hence my label *kin*-Title.) Historically, political units waxed and waned in power and influence; the same was doubtless true of the prestige and privileges of kin-Titles associated with them, although with some lag in time.

Kin-Titles passed from parent to child, preferably to eldest son

45

hence from father to son. But not invariably: females could and often did hold kin-Titles, therefore some individuals, male and female, held kin-Titles from both parents, and either from the same temple (and political unit) or from different temples and political units, with privileges and duties in each. (The latter had mainly to do with religious matters, but provided opportunities for exercising secular authority as well.)

None of the above would have seemed markedly alien to the English visitors, except that the important kin-Titles of England were associated more directly with territorial estates (although some of the English Titles carried religious privileges and duties as well). There was however one feature of Tahitian kin-Titles that was not only unfamiliar to the English visitors, but was so alien—so 'unnatural'—to them that it provoked perennial comment. That feature had to do with the timing of the devolution of kin-Titles, the more important of them having been transferred at the time of a successor's *birth*. Thus, among the *ari'i*, when the socially acknowledged spouse of the holder of an important dynastic office—a kin-Title—bore her first male child, the more important kin-Titles of her and her husband passed immediately to that child. Thereafter, the child's father continued to perform the secular jobs associated with his released kin-Titles during his heir's minority, but the religious rights and duties associated with those kin-Titles were transferred to the heir. (Since females did not perform religious duties, and seldom if ever any secular administrative ones, the duties associated with their kin-Titles usually passed *through* rather than *to* or *from* them.)

And now back to Bligh. His 'Opare' ('it-is-Pare') was a territorial section of the autonomous political district of Pare-Arue (Figure 9), but by Bligh and his English predecessors 'Opare' was applied to the district as a whole. Pare-Arue was in fact more populous than most other Tahitian districts, but the circumstance that made it outstandingly prominent in European annals, and eventually in Tahitian politics, was its proximity to Matavai harbor, which since their first visit, in the *Dolphin*, had been the main anchorage for English ships. The residents of bordering Matavai constituted only a neighborhood, which traditionally had been part of the sparsely populated and loosely united district of Ha'apape, but which during Bligh's visits was intermittently, and usually reluctantly, subordinate to the chief of Pare-Arue.

We turn now to the 'old acquaintances' named by Bligh in his *Remarks*: first to the absent 'Tynah', the husband of 'Iddeah' and brother of 'Oreepyah' and 'Whydooh'.

'Tynah' (i.e., Tina) seems to have been the principal natal personal name of this man, but in time, like most other Tahitians, he received or chose additional ones, such as (in his case) 'Mate' and 'Vaira'atoa'. Soon after his birth (as a first-born son) he also received his most important kin-Title, which, insofar as I can judge, was 'Tu Nui ae i te Atua' (Great Tu, begotten of a god). At some age that I cannot discover he assumed still another name, 'Pomare', which came to be applied (by the English, at least) not only to himself but to his successors—and in fact to his whole family dynasty. (One account of the origin of this name is given in Bligh's entry of April 19th.) In any case, the man Tina (or Vaira'atoa, etc., or Pomare I) was about forty years old at the time of *Providence*'s visit. Until the birth of his son and successor (the new Tu Nui ae i te Atua, or simply Tu, or in English records Pomare II), *circa* 1780, Tina had been the titular chief (*Te Ari'i*: *The* Chief) of Pare-Arue district both in kin-Title rank and in actual secular authority. In 1792 he was no longer *Te Ari'i* in religious matters (and as will be seen was required to respect the superior sanctity of his successor), but he continued to exercise most of his former secular authority.

In this non-literate society pedigrees, having been orally transmitted, were subject to occasional revision, either to enhancement or disparagement, according to competing social and political ambitions. This was especially so in the case of Tina and his family, who were the center of controversy in consequence of their inordinate political ambitions and of the advantages they enjoyed—and attempted to monopolize—as the result of their direct access to visiting English ships. The versions of their pedigree promulgated by their rivals imputed a Tuamotuan (hence a *manahune*, lower class) origin to their paternal line; the version proclaimed by the Pomares themselves made no mention of Tuamotuan forebears and traced its lines back some forty generations through holders of kin-Titles of several of the most venerated temples on Tahiti and on neighboring Mo'orea. Whatever may have been the 'true' version of the ancient pedigree of this dynasty, its entry into documentable history (according to a genealogy recorded by Georg Forster on Cook's second voyage and revised by Bligh in his *Bounty* Journal) took place about 1705 with the birth of Tina's paternal grandfather, Ta'aroa Manahune. The latter, as a first-born son, succeeded to most of the kin-Titles (all of high-ranking, *ari'i* grade) of his immediate forebears, and was officially *Ari'i Rahi* of Pare-Arue. He died before 1767. His first-born son and successor, known to the English as Hapai, and Teu, was born *circa* 1728; and although he lived until 1803, by the time of *Dolphin*'s visit his principal kin-Titles had already passed to *his* son, our man Tina (who was at the time about sixteen).

Hapai appears briefly in Bligh's *Providence* Journal, as will be seen, but his most noteworthy role in the dynasty's history resulted from his marriage to 'Oberroah' (Peroa?), also called Tetupaia, who was eldest child of Tamatoa III. The latter was the highest-ranking kin-Titleholder of Ra'iatea Island, and much of his sanctity, *sans pareil*, was passed on to Tina through Peroa-Tetupaia. The quality or intensity of the sanctity entailed in those

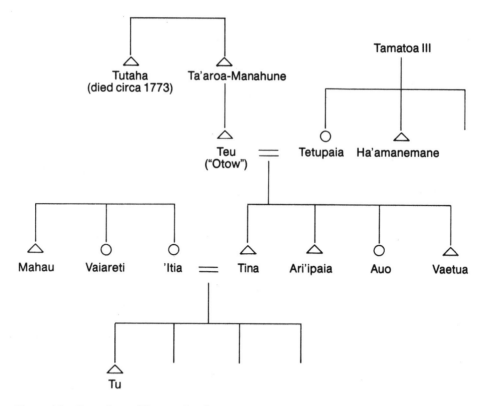

Figure 10 Genealogy of Pomare family

Ra'iatean kin-Titles figures so prominently in some of the events recorded by Bligh that an account of them will be given here. (Figure 10)

Earlier in this commentary was the statement that consciousness of the hierarchy of sanctity was so pervasive in Tahitian society that the kin-Titles of certain family dynasties were inter-graded even if they had no known or supposed ancestors in common. Also, it was noted that such families did not always agree on their standings relative to each other; nevertheless, there was one widely dispersed family-grouping of kin-Titles that was acknowledged throughout the archipelago as being the very *highest* in rank. The source of those kin-Titles was the district of Opoa on the Island of Ra'iatea, whose premier temple, *Taputapuatea*, was dedicated mainly to the worship of the high-god 'Oro, especially to his avatar as God of War. Several spirits were venerated by the Tahitians as high-gods—as being more powerful than all their myriad fellow spirits. Over the centuries the objects of such veneration had doubtless changed from time to time and from place to place; during the second half of the eighteenth century the one most widely courted was 'Oro-God-of-War. Explanation of that focus is not reconstructable; perhaps it was the islands' increasing population, hence increasing competition for resources, hence warfare. Whatever the reason, the assistance of 'Oro-God-of-War was sought by the leaders of nearly every district engaged, or about to be engaged, in war. And that is where the Opua kin-Titleholders entered the picture: to obtain the support of 'Oro it was necessary to offer him a *human* sacrifice, and the only persons qualified to preside over such a sacrifice were holders of certain Opoa kin-Titles, probably no more than about four or five in all the archipelago. Such persons were universally known as *Ari'i Rahi* (Great Ari'i) and as *Ari'i Maro 'Ura* (Red-girdled Ari'i), so named for the loin-cloths covered with red (and sometimes also yellow) feathers that they donned on certain ceremonial occcasions, especially when presiding over rites of human sacrifice. In addition, such rites could be performed only at temples labelled *Taputapuatea*, i.e., those dedicated to 'Oro-God-of-War, and in the presence of images serving as occasional receptacles of that god.

As result of all those circumstances, if a Tahitian Believer—and all Tahitians were such in Bligh's time—desired the assistance of 'Oro in the waging of war it was necessary to secure the services of a Red-girdled *Ari'i* to preside over the human sacrifice required by 'Oro, however unfriendly one's relations with that *Ari'i* might have been. Such was the powerful position occupied by Tina—until, that is, his Red-girdled kin-Title had passed to his successor (about whom we shall later on read).

Returning now to Tina the individual (Plates 7a, 7b): he was described by one English observer as being the tallest man in Tahiti. He may have been physically strong as well but some English visitors characterized him as being timid in battle, better suited to political maneuver than to martial combat. Like several other Tahitian grandees of that era he was ambitious to extend the influence and authority of himself and his family; and he was quick to seize the opportunity for doing so provided by the periodic visits of English ships to the bay bordering his own district. Through such visits he acquired a near monopoly of the European goods that entered Tahiti, and he used some of these to buy support, however fleeting, from other chiefs and sub-chiefs. Also, through his frequent and direct and ever-helpful contacts with the English he came to be regarded by them as their principal ally, a man deserving, and quite often needing, their recognition and support. In fact, so firm was James Cook in this conviction that he vowed publicly to avenge any attack upon Tina. To the English visitors, for whom monarchy was the usual, indeed the most appropriate form of government, it was only natural that Tahiti should also have a king; and who else but Tina, who readily declared himself to be so. Bligh himself came to know better (as his Journal will reveal) but continued to label Tina 'King', and in order to accomplish his own mission also treated him as such.

Of the several women who shared Tina's sleeping mat from time to time there were three whose relations with him had some institutionalized permanence. The first and most 'official' was 'Itia (Bligh's 'Iddeah'), who was mother of Tina's four known offspring, including his successor, Tu (i.e., Pomare II). (The second of Tina's consorts will appear later in Bligh's Journal; the third came onto the scene after Bligh's departure.) 'Itia (Tetuanui Rei i te Ra'iatea) was distinguished indeed, including connections with some of the highest-ranking kin-Titleholders of Tahiti and Mo'orea. She was also a woman of strong and independent character and of amiable disposition—but not (according to George Vancouver) of physical beauty:

The queen-mother, although destitute of any pretensions to beauty, and having in her person a very masculine appearance, has yet, in her general deportment, something excessively pleasing and engaging; free from any austerity or pride, she is endued with a comparative elegance of manners, which plainly bespeaks her descent, and the high situation in which she is placed. Although her figure exhibited no external charms of feminine softness, yet great complacency and gentleness were always conspicuous; indicating, in the most unequivocal manner, a mind possessing, and alone actuated by those amiable qualities which most adorn the human race. All her actions seemed directed to those around her with an unalterable eveness of temper, and to be guided by a pure disinterested benevolence. Self, which on most occasions is the governing principle in the conduct of these islanders, with her was totally disregarded; and indeed, such was her very amiable disposition, that it counterbalanced any disadvantages she might labour under in a deficiency of personal attractions. (Lamb 1984: 430)

Of the two brothers of Tina who greeted Bligh on his arrival at Matavai, Ari'ipaea ('Oreepyah'), born *circa* 1758, was the more agreeable and responsible by far. Vaetua ('Whydooh'), somewhat younger, was a bold warrior, but a 'very impudent, dissolute young man', much addicted to *'ava* (i.e., kava, an intoxicating infusion made from the root of the pepper shrub, *Piper methysticum*).

The fourth of the 'old acquaintances' was 'Tootaha an old Priest'. Several individuals named Tutaha appear in the annals of this era, including one, nicknamed 'Hercules' by Joseph Banks, who was *de facto* leader of Pare-Arue during Tina's (secular) minority, and who died in battle in 1773. The Tutaha referred to here, also named Ha'amanemane, and Mauri, was a brother to Tina's mother. He had left Ra'iatea in 1788, having been forced to flee before a conquering force of Boraborans. He was characterized by Bligh in the latter's *Bounty* Journal as a 'Cheif of much consequence . . . a Priest [with] great Knowledge.' (Bligh 1937: I 385; II 45) Tutaha, now Ha'amanemane, remained closely attached to the Pomare family and came to exercise a weighty influence in Tahiti's political affairs.

According to George Tobin, Bligh's old acquaintances brought him 'a present of cloth [bark cloth], hogs and fruit, the former being wrapped round him by her Majesty.' (See his description on April 10th of this customary form of greeting.) And as a postscript to the accounts of this eventful day, Tobin added:

As the sun declined, the Canoes returned on shore, leaving by far the most desirable part of their freight among our crew, which after the trying self-denial of a long voyage, shut out from the dearest solace life affords, could not but be truly acceptable. Edeea ['Itia] was among the number, attended by her favorite Towtow *[teuteu, servant] Mideedee . . . The natives in the course of the day had been dexterous enough to make my pocket lighter by the handkerchief. With our other visitors came an incredible number of flies.*

Providence and *Assistant* remained anchored in Matavai Bay until July 19th. In keeping with Bligh's own record of that visit, his account of it, along with my annotations, will be presented on a daily basis.

MATAVAI BAY

Tuesday, April 10th

Bligh's Journal entry for this, his first full day at Matavai, is lengthy and detailed:

Very fine Weather. Wind ENE but I believe more Easterly at Sea. Thermometer 80 to 80 ½ Degrees. Ships Draught of Water forward 14 feet 3 inches abaft, 16 feet 3 inches astern. People Employd drying and unbending Small Sails and cleaning Ship of everything that could be stolen by the Natives. Got on board a Launch Load of Water. <My> Thermometer is kept in the coolest part of the Ship.

> *I had only a few Oparre Cannoes off to me but a sufficiency of Hogs, Breadfruit and Cocoa Nutts to feed every Person sumptiously. My Visitors were the same as Yesterday, and Iddeah ['Itia] assured me a Cannoe was sent away to Moreah [Mo'orea] for Tynah [Tina] her Husband and his Father and Mother. These People are necessary to my well doing, notwithstanding Ideeah and Oreepyah [Ari'ipaea] seem sufficient to effect my plans, assisted by Otoo (Ereerahigh) [Tu, Ari'i Rahi, Tina's eldest son and successor], who yet a Boy continues to be instructed by them. Tomorrow I intend to pay him a Visit, and my endeavours will be to establish a Peace, which I have some hopes will be lasting <a lasting one>. Nothing could exceed the joy of these People at seeing me.*

> *I received a letter to day, directed to any of His Majesty's Ships that might touch here, from Matthew Weatherhead Commander of a Ship called the Matilda. It relates, that in the Latitude of 22 degrees S, and Longitude 139 degrees 45 minutes W from London, the Ship was lost on a Shoal, He begs my [sic] assistance as follows*

> > *'I beg your assistance in rectifying the Wrongs I have received on this Island by one Tabyroo. After the misfortune of losing the Matilda, We were 6 days in the Boat, landed at Matavia <Matavai> and put ourselves under the protection of the above mentioned Man. I had with me one Box containing <the> most of my*

papers—407 Dollars, 17 Guineas and one half, between 3 & 4 lbs. of English silver. A Bag containing <with> a few Necessary Cloaths. After being in <the> House 6 Days I was turned out without any thing to shift myself with only one Shirt.

> Parry Otaheite   Your Most Hble Servant,
> March 29th 1792   Matthew Weatherhead

PS—Sir the Chief Mate and Carpenter will explain the matter more clearly if required.'

On enquiry I found that the Matilda, Captain Weatherhead, and [the] Mary Ann, Captain Munro, were two ships that had been at Port Jackson [Sydney, New South Wales] with Convicts. They left England the 27th March 1791. Arrived at Port Jackson 1st August 1791 and Sailed the 28th December 1791 bound to the Coast of Peru. On the 14th February 1792 both Ships anchored in Oaitepeha Bay [Vaitepiha Bay, southeastern Tahiti], where having got a plentiful supply of Hogs and Fruit, they sailed on the 17th after a stay of two Days. A few days after they Sailed the Masters of the Ships agreed to part company, and to meet again in the Latitude of 10 degrees South, when they should arrive on the Coast [of South America] to Fish for Whales.

On the 25th February the Matilda in a dark Night run <ran> aground upon a Shoal which was of some extent, perhaps about 8 or 10 Miles. They cut away their Masts, lowered their Boats down, and having put a few necessaries into them (7 Muskets, 3 Pistols, ammunition, 2 or 3 Cutlasses) they left the Ship about 10 OClock in the Morning.

The Ship's Company consisted of 28 Men and Boys; but a Convict having secreted himself at Port Jackson, the number at this time were 29. They divided themselves into four Boats, and without examining minutely into their situation, they left the Shoal without knowing if any Island or Land was near it. <I cannot discover that any Person saw anything that was green.>

They proceeded fortunately to Maitea [Me'etia], and after a Nights rest and kind treatment, they Sailed for Otaheite on the 5 March. On the next Night, by bad Weather, the Boats were separated, two arrived at Matavai, one at Oaitepeah, and the other round by Attahooroo [Atehuru]. The People at Oaitepeeah were too hostile to induce the Boat to remain with them, she therefore preceeded to Matavai and joined the Party that had got there before them. Afterwards, in the course of eight Days, the Men who had landed at Attahooroo also came to join their Companions. It however appeared so much the opinion of the Captain that they should not all remain in one place, that some resided at Matavai, some at Oparre, and some at Attahooroo. They were all dispossesed of their Cloaths & Articles they had with them; but the greatest <great> prize fell in <into> the hands of the Matavai People, under the command of Poeeno the Chief, and Tabyroo, a Person of some power. The circumstances no sooner became known than

Otoo demanded the Articles taken at Matavai, consisting of Money & Arms, in behalf (he asserts) of his Friends the English; but no restitution was made. Some deliberation immediately took place, <the> result of which was, that on the 19th March War was proclaimed, and the Oparre People came to Matavai destroying Houses and all the provision kind they could lay their Hands on. The Matavians made very considerable resistence; still retain their Booty, and at this instant the Parties are violently at War with other.

Notwithstanding our Countrymen were robbed of their Cloaths, they were treated afterwards with much kindness and attention, it would however have been better if the whole had gone to Oparre under the protection of Otoo, and as there were three at this time absent with the Matavians; the first step I took was to order them to join their Ship Mates.

The War was interrupted by the Arrival of a Schooner called the Jenny (a) from Bristol burthen 90 Tons. [(a) refers to the following marginal note: 'Arrived 25th March Sailed 5 Weeks after me from England and came by the Cape Horn.'] This Vessel remained here until the 31st March, when she Sailed for the NW Coast of America and by this opportunity Capt. Weatherhead with Two Boys and One Man, had the means of returning home. He [Jenny's Captain] had one passenger more than expected, a Seaman <having> secreted himself on board sailed with them as it is supposed, for he has not been heard of since.

While the Jenny remained here the Second Mate, Campbell [of the Matilda] undertook to go away in one of the Whale boats for Port Jackson. It was fitted up in a miserable manner with Mat Sails, and himself with two Men, Phillip Cristall & John Basster sailed <on> the same Day.

The Number of Men now remaining on the Island are 21, including the Convict who has absented himself. Among them is [are] the Chief Mate, Surgeon, Boatswain & Carpenter. The whole of them I directed to stay at Oparre where they are well taken care of.

I find that about 2 Months after I left Otaheite in the Bounty [marginal note in ML version: 'some say 5 months'], Christian returned with her to the very great astonishment of the Natives, whose enquiries were numerous and affectionate, doubting even to the last that things had gone well with me, and those who were absent. [In ML, 'even to the last that' is crossed out and replaced with a few illegible words.] The first questions were

Where is Bry?
He is gone to England
In what Ship?
In Tootes [Cook's] Ship
How came you to meet Toote and where is he?
We met at Whytootacke <Whytootackee> [Aitutaki] where he is going to live, and has sent me for all those who will come and live with him. The Bull

and Cow and as many Hogs as you will send him [animals left at Tahiti by Cook]

What is become of the Breadfruit?

He has sent it home to England with Bligh.

Every thing was now given to him [Christian] that he asked, and in Eight or Ten Days he left Matavai with several Men and Women (a) & every thing they had. [(a) refers to marginal note: '10 Men 2 Boys 9 Women 1 Girl See 2 May']

In (b) one Month after Captain Cox left this place [(b) refers to marginal note: 'October 1789'. John Cox was Captain of the Swedish brig, Mercury, which anchored at Matavai August 13 to September 2, 1789.] Christian arrived again, and having landed 16 of his Villains [in ML 'Villains' is crossed out and replaced with 'Associates'], he sailed in the Course of a Day [[but]] I cannot find that any person was acquainted with the route he intended to take.

It may readily be believed that I found <felt> great satisfaction and pleasure to hear of these Wretches all being taken by Captain Edwards [on H.M.S. Pandora] except two who were killed by the Indians. [marginal note: 'See 28th April'. In ML Bligh crossed out 'by the Indians'; he also crossed out 'to hear of these Wretches all being' and substituted 'in hearing that all these Mutineers were'.]

From the best accounts those taken in the Pandora were as follows—

George Stewart [Midshipman]—acting Masters Mate

Peter Hayward—Midshipman

James Morrison—Boatswains Mate

Thomas Burkit[t]—AB

John Millward—AB

Henry Hil[l]brant—Cooper

William Musprat—Taylor [rated Commander's Steward]

Thomas Ellison—AB

Richard Skinner—Barber [rated AB]

Michael Byrne— AB

Joseph Coleman—Armourer

Charles Norman—Carpenter's Mate

Thomas McIntosh—ditto crew

Charles Churchill—Master at Arms (a)

Matthew Thompson—AB

[John] Sumner—AB

[(a) refers to footnote: 'Thompson killed Churchill who was made Eree of Tiaraboo & the Tiaraboo people killed Thompson'.]

George Stewart, Thomas McIntosh, and Richard Skinner each had a Daughter by the Women they lived with, and Thomas Burkit and John Millward [each] had a Son—I have seen none of them—and some are said to be dead. The Man who Captain Cox left here called Brown, had a <one> Son. He

sailed with Captain Edwards about 4 Months before <Captain> Vancouver arrived
<here>.

> *Captain Vancouver and Lieutenant Broughton arrived here after*
the Pandora and stayed about five weeks. After he sailed [marginal note: '12th
January 1792. See 6th April'] a disease afflicted the Natives that killed many of
them, so that they speak of the Ships with a degree of horror and declare it was
caught on board.

> *The Anchor which Christian left the Natives got and delivered*
it to Captain Edwards.

Focusing first on the affair of the ill-fated *Matilda*, there is little that can be
added to Bligh's account of its course up to this date. The nearest name to
Poeno (Bligh's 'Poeeno') I can find on the most relevant recorded genealogy
(i.e., that of the principal persons associated with the Farẽroi temple of
Ha'apape District) is Paino. (Oliver 1974: 1178) Clearly however this Poeno
was headman of Matavai during both of Bligh's Breadfruit visits. In fact, during the *Bounty* visit Bligh and Poeno became bond-friends (*taio*). Moreover,
according to Bligh (1937 II: 6) Poeno had been headman of Matavai, and
Cook's official 'Protector' during his last visit there, in 1777. (Cook himself
did not mention Poeno by name in his Journal; the Matavai headman was so
far out-ranked by Tina and some other principal persons who visited Matavai
that he seems to have escaped the interest of the Great Navigator.) As already
reported, Matavai had earlier been a part of the District—the chiefdom—of
Ha'apape; and while it seems to have been allied with Pare-Arue during parts
of the last third of the eighteenth century, it was very much of an off-and-on
relationship, as witness the *Matilda* affair now under discussion. As for
Bligh's Tabyroo (Tapiru), the 'Person of some power' associated with Poeno,
a statement by Lt. Bond, in his Journal's general essay, provides a clue to his
identity and motives:

A native of the district . . . whose name is Tupira, and who had accompanied Christian on
his expedition to the island of Tooboai [Tubuai], finding his influence increased by a knowledge
of firearms, joined the chief of the same part [i.e., Poeno], to shake off the yoke of subjection
to the reigning king [i.e., Tu]. Accordingly when the Matilda's people landed . . . they got from
them five muskets and some ammunition. A formal demand was made by Otoo [Tu] the sover-
eign at Oparre, for the arms alluded to, which on the part of Poeenow and Tupira, was peremp-
torily refused. In consequence of which, on our arrival at Matavy Bay, we found both armies
in the field, that is to say, in a state of hostility.

Bligh's concern to recover the articles taken by the Matavians from
the *Matilda* people seems to have been based mainly on legal and moral
scruples against robbery, but like the Pare-Arue chief he doubtless was aware
of the political consequences of so many firearms in the hands of Poeno and
his people. As will be seen, the five muskets now held by the Matavians were

only three less than all those in the hands of the leaders of Pare-Arue, and the latter knew from experience the overwhelming strategic and tactical superiority of firearms over slingstones, clubs and spears. As for Tu's assertion that he wished to recover the firearms 'in behalf of his Friends the English', Bligh's skepticism of that noble sentiment is revealed by his parenthesis.

Bligh's remarks concerning the departure of the *Matilda*'s whaleboat for Port Jackson—some 3300 nautical miles distant—is the last known mention of that ill-considered attempt. Judging by his own even longer launch voyage to Timor in 1789, Bligh himself could probably have made it, but not many other men.

Turning now to Bligh's account of the members of the *Bounty* crew who had remained at Tahiti after Christian and his associates had departed for the last time, the reference to Thompson and Churchill requires some emendation. At first all sixteen of the Tahiti-beached crew had resided at Matavai, where they had been hospitably received—the Tahitians knew nothing at that time about the mutiny and the treatment of Bligh. Soon however one of the crew moved to the District of Papara and two others, Thompson and Churchill, moved to Taiarapu at the invitation of that District's chief, Vehiatua. Tahiti's leaders placed high value on what they knew or believed to be the special skills possessed by the Englishmen, especially the latters' knowledge of firearms. In the case of Churchill, the *Bounty*'s Master-at-Arms, he became so highly regarded by Vehiatua that the latter made him his bond-friend and principal aide. Moreover, when a few months later Vehiatua died, and without issue, his leading supporters elected Churchill to succeed him. However, the ill-tempered Churchill did not enjoy his position for long. Within a month he had quarrelled so violently with Thompson that the latter killed him—and was himself killed by Vehiatua's supporters to avenge the death of their English chief.

The parts played in Tahiti's affairs by the fourteen other *Bounty* crew during their eighteen months on the island will be touched on later, when commenting on more relevant entries in Bligh's Journal.

Regarding the reference to Vancouver's visit, it is not possible to identify the disease believed by the Tahitians to have been introduced by his ships, but it was clearly deadly, and epidemic.

The Journal entry written by Lt. Bond adds little to Bligh's account of this day's events:

Throughout the night light winds and fine weather. At noon calms. Edeea the Queen with some chiefs visited the ship and were assiduous in making tyos (friends). Launch made [?] in [?] turn of Water. Served Breadfruit, Cocoa Nuts and fresh Pork to the ship's company. Aird and unbent the small sails and steering sails. Broached a puncheon of spruce Beer. At noon moderate breezes and fine weather.

57

Moderate breezes and fine weather. Saw the Natives on shore march armed towards another district; and by enquiring that they were at war with their neighbors. Down Topgallent yards.

Moderate breezes and fair weather.

Bond's reports of the visits by 'Itia and some 'chiefs', and on the natives marching off to war, are more fully covered in other journals. In fact, from this day on during the stay at Tahiti Bond's daily Journal contains few remarks concerning anything but details of ship management, including the daily food rations of the crew. Instead, after leaving the island this officer wrote a 3000-word general essay of the Tahitians' 'manners and customs' with the following prefatory disclaimer:

So much has already been said of the island of Otaheite by Captain Cook, that very little remains for the cursory Voyager, indeed that celebrated navigator displayed the greatest sagacity in all the observations he made on this wonderful country; for every acute observer must allow his account of the manners and customs of the natives of the South Seas to be unequald for truth and precision.

In examining minutely into the ceremony of their religious sacrifices and publick festivals, we found the strictest veracity in every thing he had advanced; and it was with admiration we reflected on that wonderful penetration which so conspicuously marked this great man. For my own part, when I consider it necessary to strengthen my future memory by a few remarks, however desultory they may be, I readily embrace the opportunity sur le champ, and attempt to arrange my ideas, collected during a stay of near four months, in the following lines.

However, rather than reproduce Bond's essay separately and in full, only those excerpts from it will be presented that emend matters mentioned by Bligh.

Assistant's Commander, Lt. Portlock, was almost as economical in recording his daily activities and observations during the Tahiti visit. And here again, his Journal entries will be reproduced only on those rare occasions when they throw additional or different light upon matters discussed by Bligh.

Not so with George Tobin, whose entries either complement or supplement Bligh's on many occasions, and with a perception refined by his artist's eye and by his vantage point of a younger, unmarried, and less officially responsible man. Here are his remarks about this days events:

The natives in their canoes were about us by early dawn and the stock of hogs and fruit encreased rapidly. For a Toey [to'e] (a flat piece of iron made for the purpose in England, and which the natives fasten to a handle and use as an adze) a moderate sized hog was procured.

Many Chiefs (Erees) visited the ship, and we all began to establish our individual friends. Edeea ['Itia] examined all the cabins, seemingly quite `at home' and well acquainted with a ship . . . I exhibited my Stock in Trade, and everything I conceived would gratify her; when on presenting her with a few ornaments she offered to become my Tayo [taio], or friend, which distinguished honour I most readily accepted. As the dinner hour arrived, she sat down

Plate 3   Me'etia Island
Watercolor by George Tobin

Plate 4   *Providence* and *Assistant* in Matavai Bay
Watercolor by George Tobin

Plate 5   Scene in Pare Harbour
Watercolor by George Tobin

Plate 6   Near the Watering Place, Matavai Bay
Watercolor by George Tobin

at Table with us, used her knife and fork not awkwardly, and drank many bumpers of Teneriffe
[rum] with great good will . . . In the evening she presented me with a large hog and two pieces
of the Island cloth [bark cloth, tapa], when we underwent the ceremony of O'tahyteean Friend-
ship. The smaller piece, which was of a thick texture about a yard wide and three in length, in
the center of which there was a hole, I was instructed to put my head through, the ends falling
before and behind and leaving the arms at freedom. This done, the other piece, above a dozen
yards in length, was wrapped round my waist until I became so swaddled as to be nearly immo-
bile. We then kissed, joined noses, and exchanged names. Her Majesty in return received a pre-
sent from my Store of every thing she desired, seemingly quite rejoiced with the Treaty . . .
Most of the Mess [officers' Mess?], soon established their Tayos, going through a similar
ceremony.

Individual Europeans came to know well some aspects of the
Tahitian institution of *taio*, bond-friendship, but it comprised a wider range
of behavior than any one of them was able to observe. It warrants our attention not merely as another exotic custom, but because it served as the principal kind of bridging relationship between Tahitians and their European
visitors—much more important, politically and economically, than that
based on sexual intercourse.

Among the Tahitians of that era most of an individual's day-to-day
interactions took place with persons identified as kinsmen, or with those
who had more, or less, authority than oneself. Interaction did however take
place between individuals whose ties of kinship, or of more or less authority,
were tenuous enough to ignore or override in favor of a relationship of
untrammeled friendship. Like humans everywhere Tahitians formed many
such friendships, brief or long-lasting, with other Tahitians: males with
males, females with females, and males with females (the latter not always
accompanied by sexual intercourse). Most such friendships received no public sanction or reinforcement beyond the sentiments of the principals themselves, but some of them became institutionalized by means of a formal
contract, called *taio*.

There is good reason to hold that *taio* relationships were formerly
contracted only between males (although there may have been cases of such
between females and homosexual males). Another criterion for *taio*-ship was
social class: as far as I can discover the partners in most *taio* pacts were members of the same. Within these bonds, the prototype of the male–male
relationship was a mutuality so close as to approximate social identity. The
partners exchanged names, gave objects to each other without (implied)
expectation of return, succored one another in time of war even if on rival
sides, etc. Also, to simulate the unity-making nature of the contract the partners were permitted sexual access to each other's wife—but not sisters or
daughters, which would have been regarded as incestuous.

Ideally, the contract contained all the above terms and was permanently binding. Indeed, in some cases the ritual that initiated a *taio*-ship

resembled that performed for marriages and child adoptions, and served to implicate the principals' near kin as well. In practice however many *taio*-ships were piecemeal and short-lived, as for example when a travelling dignitary exchanged names and presents with a dignitary met *en route*.

The ideal behind *taio* pacts seems to have been benevolent, altruistic friendship, but as more and more Europeans appeared on the scene the custom became even more perverted to self-interest. And at the same time it was adopted by Tahitian females as a means of obtaining cloth, etc. from the visiting Europeans (sometimes in exchange for sexual favors).

Returning to Tobin's remarks, there is no evidence that his *taio* pact with 'Itia involved anything more than a periodic two-way exchange of objects and an entirely platonic friendship. (The young and presumably comely officer doubtless had a choice of much younger and prettier women.) Speculation aside, whatever may have been the relationship between Tobin and 'Itia, his description of the ceremony that initiated the pact merits interest on two counts. It underlines the importance of native bark cloth as an item in Tahitian exchanges, especially in ceremonial exchanges. And it exemplifies very nicely one way in which the bark cloth was ceremonially presented—i.e., by swaddling the donee in long strips of it. (The length in this instance was only 'above a dozen yards'; on some occasions they were many times longer.) Another way—more interesting perhaps to most visiting Europeans—was to swaddle a young female in the cloth; the recipient then held the loose end of it while she unwound herself of all of it, and of anything else she wore.

Wednesday, April 11th

Very fine Weather with a regular Trade at ESE without, but at E by N here. Thermometer 76 to 82 Degrees. Employd Caulking the larboard Side, getting fresh Water off and trading with the Natives for Hogs, Breadfruit, Tarro, Plantains, Cocoa Nutts and some Fowls, so that every person had much more than they could use. Began to kill some very large Hogs for Salting.

Early in the Morning I went to Oparre to see Otoo. He was overjoyed to see me. When I was here in the Bounty he was rather an ill looking Boy, but he is now grown a fine Youth. None of the ceremony took place between us that did then, he was very familiar and always kept hold of my hand, altho carried on a Mans Shoulder where he rode as on a horse, and carried a Switch with which he beat back the Croud <Crowd>.

He received a very handsome Present of Cloaths and Iron Tools with great thankfullness, and pressed me hard to bring the Ships down to Oparre. He had only a few Body Guards with him, the whole district being employed against Matavai. After a short stay, for I was seized with a very Violent Nervous head ach, (which is always more or less upon me,) I took my leave. Three fine Hogs were put in <into> the Boat, & I might have had her loaded with Fruit.

Among my old Friends who used to be with me here, I saw Terrano the Wife of Teppahoo a great Chief of Tettahahi <Tettahah>. This Old Woman with her Sister clung about me and literally thanked God for saving me after I had lost the Bounty, for they were informed of the whole transaction. Teppahoo she told me was Dead from the Cancer that was in the Roof of his Mouth when I was here before. (See page 210 of last Voyage) I found also that Mowworoah the Uncle of Tynah, was dead and lying in State on a Toopapow in Oparre [ML contains following marginal note: This man died 1 Month after C. Vancouver sailed, Feb. 7 1792], and that Terreenahroah, Eldest Daughter of Tynah & Iddeah, had died of a decline soon after I left them.

Odidee they told me was gone with Captain Edwards in the Pandora to Ulietea [Ra'iatea] and the rest of the Society Islands.

In our return to the Ship I saw a multitude of Men on the low land of Matavai all armed, preparing for an Attack on the Matavians who <whom> they had already driven from the Spot, and burnt all their Houses <whose Houses they had burnt>. The Afternoon produced the result of their determination. The Oparre people drove the others to the Mountains, killed one Man, & returned victorious. I have been sollicited very much to join Otoo's Army, but I only promised to interfere should the Matavians attempt to go near Oparre, in which case I assured them I would land a Party of Men & drive them back, which gave great pleasure to our Oparre Friends. I also sent the Surgeon of the Matilda to Poeeno and Tabyroo, to order them to return the Captains effects, if they ever ['ever' crossed out in ML] wished to be on good terms with us, & he brought me back Word from them, that everything would be returned. The Surgeon informed me that he was conducted through an immense number of Men armed with Spears, Clubs & Slings, who appeared extremely anxious to know the Message he had brought, & if I intended to act against them. They behaved with much decorum and some attention to the Chief who went with him; for the front of each army was so near to each other as to use their Slings, hostilities ceased during the parley. These Men when heaped together in such numbers armed with Spears 12 or 14 feet long or more, have a tremendous appearance, they nevertheless do little mischief to each other, for I believe they seldom come to a serious charge, but content themselves with the execution they are able to effect by Slinging Stones, by which means some Men are Maimed and sometimes killed.

It is of the utmost concern to me, but I dare not yet send any party on shore. I have not yet seen any Chief of consequence, but Oreepyah and his Brother, and Tynah still remains at Morea.

When the Matilda C[aptain] Weatherhead passed Matavai,

some of the Natives swam off to him with Notes that some of the Discovery's
People had given them to recommend them as Tyo's, these Notes were dated the
12th January 1792, which I suspect was the time they Sailed. [marginal note: 'See
16th April']

The Villains that <People whom> Christain landed were
permitted to have Sails and various implements, <so that> they built a Vessel
about 25 or 30 Feet long with two Masts, and the Natives tell me that Captain
Edwards took this Vessel with him, which gave me much pleasure, as I think he
may derive a great advantage from her in going through between New Holland and
New Guinea. [ML originally read 'through Endeavour' but 'Endeavour' has been
crossed out and replaced with 'the Straights'.]

Our Friends here have benefited very little from the intercourse
they have had with Europeans since I left them. Our Countrymen must have taken
great pains to have taught them such vile & blackguard expressions as are in the
Mouth of every Otaheitean. I declare I would rather forfeit any thing than to have
been in the list of Ships that have touched here since April 1789. [In ML this whole
sentence has been crossed out—still another post-PRO afterthought? Bligh doubtless
felt that Vancouver's ships were among the guilty ones but that it would be
impolitic to imply as much.]

Bligh's visit to the young Tu (Pomare II), a feather-girdled *Ari'i* and
the sovereign Chief of Pare-Arue, was a diplomatic necessity. The boy, now
about twelve years old, resided in his own household compound which was
located inland from Pare Harbour, where in fact he had dwelt, separately
from his parents, since shortly after his birth. In families associated with very
highly-ranked kin-Titles it was customary for the children to be moved into
a household separate from their parents' within a year or so after birth.
Thereafter the parents, and especially the father, had little to do with them
until, many years later, the restrictions on interaction had been lifted by
means of desacralization (*amo'a*) rites—a practice that will be discussed later
(April 17th), in connection with Bligh's own remarks about it. Meanwhile,
it is sufficient to the present passage to note that while in 1792 the young Tu
was still 'sacred' enough to require some ceremonious respect and to be carried about (so that the ground would not be rendered too sanctified, hence
dangerous, for common use), he had evidently been ritually freed of some of
the taboos that had formerly surrounded him, as described in Bligh's *Bounty*
Log of November 1st 1788:

After a walk of five minutes Otoo [who was then Tina] stopt me, and telling me
no person could see his son that was covered above the shoulders, he made Signs
for me to stop. He was obliged to do it himself and also his Wife & therefore
requested I would. I was about it when it occured to me I risked my health in
being exposed in such a Manner to a burning heat, and I therefore told him that

if I could not see his Son upon any other Conditions, I would leave my present with my best wishes to him. I said I had no objection to go as I would to my own King, who was the greatest in all the World, and this had such an Effect, that on my pulling off my Hat he threw a piece of Cloth round my shoulders and we went on.

About a quarter of a Mile farther towards the Hills through the delightful Breadfruit flats of Oparre, we again stopped at the side of a Serpentine River where they said our Ducks and Geese swarmed in. Here a lane was made by the Natives, and I was in view of a House on the other side about 50 Yards distant. It had a beautiful and picturesque appearance, as had all the country about it, to which, no description could do justice.

The Young King was now brought out on a Man's shoulder cloathed with a piece of fine white Cloth, and I was now to salute him by the name of Too Eree-rahigh [Tu, Ari'i Rahi]. Otoo [i.e., Tina] standing by me told me what I was to say. The present was now divided into three parts, and two other Children brought out in the same Manner. The first present I was ordered to give to a Messenger, who attended for that purpose, and Otoo told me to say, that was for the King, that I was his Friend, hated thieves and that I came from Britannia. The second part of the present was sent in the same manner with a similar message and likewise a third. As I could not see the King distinctly I desired I might now go over to him, but Otoo said no, that cannot be, we must go back, I did not therefore persist but returned as readily as he wished me.

I can say nothing more of these Children than that the King appeared about 6 years Old, and that besides these three another is at Matavai so that Otoo has four children.

Reverting to Bligh's *Providence* Journal, the 'old Friend' who greeted him this day was Terano, relict of Tu Mataroa, who during the *Bounty* visit held the kin-Title of Te Pau, the highest-ranking one of Fa'a. This small district, which was situated between the larger and more populous districts of Pare-Arue and Puna'auia, was from time to time allied with one or both of them, nevertheless retained its autonomy throughout most of this era.

Maua Roa ('Mowworoah'), another of Bligh's former acquaintances, had died about six weeks previously. 'Toopapow' (i.e., *fare tupapa'u*, ghost house) were biers on which corpses of notable persons were kept for several weeks or months before final disposal. (More will be said about their con- struction, and on the subject of mortuary practices in general, in the entry for May 29th.) Bligh had good reason to regret Maua Roa's death; the deceased had been a brother of Tina's father, a leading member of the Arioi sect (see comment accompanying entries for April 23rd, below) and hence a learned sage, and as such one of Bligh's most useful informants.

The Hitihiti ('Odidee', also Mahine) mentioned by Bligh in this entry was a familiar name in the annals of this era. He was born on Borabora circa 1757 and claimed kinship with that island's great and warlike Chief, Poni. At Ra'iatea in August 1773 Captain Cook added him to the ship's complement as a replacement for a Marine who had recently died. For the next few months Hitihiti—reportedly a personable, quick-witted, eager youth—made himself very useful to the expedition, especially in its dealing with natives in other Polynesian islands visited by the ship, with most of whom he was able to communicate. Back in Tahiti, where Tina—the then titleholding Tu—appointed him to serve as his aide (mainly because of Hitihiti's fluency in English and his knowledge of firearms and other English ways) and married him to a kinswoman of his. Alas, the fame was more than the youth could bear. Three years later, when Cook next visited Tahiti, his surgeon's mate, David Samwell, wrote of Hitihiti:

We had been told by those who had been in the Resolution last Voyage that he was a fine sensible young fellow . . . which made it some disappointment to us to find him one of the most stupid Fellows on the Island, with a clumsy awkward Person and a remarkable heavy look . . . he frequently came on board to see us . . . and was almost constantly drunk with Kava. (Beaglehole 1967: 1058-9)

Nevertheless, Hitihiti retained his skill with firearms, and hence his privileged position with Tina. In 1790 he led a force to Mo'orea and skilfully put down a 'rebellion' against a Tina ally, and shortly thereafter played a leading role in Tina's successful—*Bounty*-crew assisted—war against Atehuru.

Bligh's remarks about the war between the supporters of Poeno and those of Tu—evidently a mismatched one in view of the latters' numerical superiority—are succinct, to say the least. Portlock's account is slightly more expansive:

During this afternoon the warring parties met on the Plains of Matavai and Continued Skirmishing for some time, at length about 4 Oclock they had rather a Serious set too with Spears Stones thrown from a Sling (at which they are very Expert) and Musketry (for each party have several musketts) and Continued pretty warmly at it for about half an hour or more. The Matavians began then to give way and soon after on one of their party being shot through the head with a Muskett Ball by one of the Oparre people, gave way on all Sides and took to their Mountains next the Border of low land, the Oparre people pursued them for some time and we heard the report of Musketts frequently and Indeed from the Ship I saw some of the Matavia party amongst whom was Tubira as they were passing over the hills make short stands and fire their musketts at the opposite party that were pursuing them. In the Evening when the Chiefs returnd from the pursuits they informed us that Tubira who appears to be their principal Warrior, with most of the Party have retreated to Ope'ana [Ha'apaino'o] a district about 8 Miles to the Eastward of Matavia.

Tobin also adds an interesting detail not elsewhere recorded:

Old Hamaneminhay [Ha'amanemane], a Priest, the Tayo of Pearce [the Lieutenant of Marines], now came on board in a state of great agitation expressing much dissatisfaction that the Royal party [i.e., Tu and his family] was not assisted by King Georges people, who they considered as their allies, urging that hostilities were undertaken solely on this account. The old man raged violently, but was pacified in some measure by Captain Bligh assuring him that the Matavaians should not pass the heads of Taira (one tree Hill) a clift of some extent dividing the two districts.

And Bond, in his general essay, summarized this war as follows:

Several rencountres had taken place before we made our appearance, but every skirmish ended without much damage to either party. These effeminate sons of luxury, like the quarrels of school boys, seldom did more than sling stones at each other; by which, few disabled warriors returnd from the field; and it was but seldom they dared charge their enemies with the Oomooree ['omore], which is an unwieldy club of about 9 or 10 feet long. The presence of Captain Bligh soon put a period to the rebellion, tho a jealousy continued to reign in the bosoms of each party; and during the whole campaine only one man lost his life, and that by a musket ball.

None however of this expedition's chroniclers provides a comprehensive account of Tahitians' war-making. In a summary statement near the end of his Journal, Tobin wrote:

The soft voluptious disposition of these people but ill qualifies them for hostile operations, nor do they indeed at all boast of being warlike; on the contrary acknowledge their inferiority as Tata Toas [ta'ata toa, warrior] to the inhabitants of many of the Islands near them; particularly of Bola Bola.

'Voluptious' and/or 'effeminate' some Tahitians may have been, but armed conflict was one of the most habitual of their activities, and was practised in a distinctively Tahitian way—until the injection of European firearms and advisors transformed it into a more European and deadly kind of game.

In pre-European times economic factors were far less conducive to warfare than political ones, and among the latter the principal cause was desire of this or that leader to extend his own authority or to curb such ambitions in others. Weapons consisted of spears (both throwing and jabbing), clubs (both battering and cleaving), rasps (edged with sharks teeth or stingray vertebrae), and slingstones. Bows and arrows were also present but, inexplicably, were used only for sport. Early European observers disagreed about the effectiveness (but not the ferocity) of hand-to-hand fighting; most of them agreed however about the large and deadly role played by slingsmen. Shields were not in use; instead, there were various kinds of armor, including torso wraps of coconut fiber or bark cloth, wicker-work breast plates, and thick bark cloth turbans. Many leaders also wore high and elaborately decorated helmets, which served both to signify their status—and to target enemy attack!

Every able-bodied male was expected to fight in his chief's wars; on some occasions a few women also joined in the fray. Specialists included slingsmen (who usually held together); *aito* (champions in the use of hand weapons); *tarai-aro* ('battle shapers', the chiefs and other leaders who marshalled the troops and sometimes led the assaults—but who had little influ-

65

ence over events once the general fighting had begun); and *rauti* ('exhorters,' whose job it was to animate the fighters before and during battles by their stirring chants and commanding persons). In addition, there were specialists in the religious side of war—in keeping with the belief that spirits played a major, perhaps the decisive, role in victory and defeat. These included diviners (to foretell the outcome and thereby encourage or discourage the undertaking of a war) and various types of priests (to empower and guide one's own weapons or ward-off those of the enemy, and to secure the aid of specific spirits, through petition backed by sacrifice). In earlier eras each district probably had its own tutelar deity to be invoked in times of war, but during the second half of the eighteenth century the paramount war god of most Tahitians was 'Oro, whose patronage was sought by every leader embarking on war—a circumstance that served to augment immeasurably the influence of incumbents of a feather-girdled kin-Title, who alone were entitled to preside over the kind of sacrifice, namely that of a human, most acceptable to that deity. (In the case of the Matavai 'rebels', Poeno and Tapiru, it is not known how much weight they attached to the religious advantage possessed by their 'Oro-backed opponent, Tu, in this conflict, but they evidently were pragmatic enough to retain their faith also in their firearms.)

Another facet of Tahitian warfare, graphically reported by Bligh, was the havoc almost invariably wreaked by victors upon their opponents' possessions: burning their houses and canoes, killing their animals, destroying their gardens and groves, and not infrequently slaying those of their enemies unable to flee. So thorough was the devastation in many cases that the communities affected were considered by their residents to be 'ill' (*mai*), and hence requiring religious rites to render them healthy again.

A final note on Tahitian warfare: prior to and in the early years of European contact, some wars were fought wholly or in part at sea, sometimes with the engagement of huge flotillas (such as that reviewed by Cook in 1773). By 1792, however, nearly all of the war canoes had rotted or been destroyed, and warfare took place only on land.

Thursday, April 12th

Fair Weather and regular Trade Wind E b N in the Bay and ESE out. Thermometer 80 to 83 Degrees. Carpenters Employed Caulking the larboard side. Loosed Sails and unreeved the running Ropes. A few Cannoes trading with Hogs and sufficient supplies.

This Morning, word was brought me that the Matavians were drove <driven> to the Mountains, and that War would cease as soon as Tynah came from Morea, and they assured me he was sent for. Oreepyah appears very desirous for me <that I should> remain on board untill Tynah comes, and it appears to me that his presence is absolutely necessary, to regulate some busyness which they dare not do without him.

In the Afternoon an Indian was caught thieving on board the Assistant; he was sent on board «of» me and confined untill Oreepyah returned on board, when I released him, for Oreepyah told me he was insane. At 8 in the Evening the same person was again found swimming about the Cable. The Night was dark, it was therefore with some difficulty that he was taken. I put him in Irons.

Several inferior Chiefs were on board today, they were remarkably glad to see me, and thanked their God for his protecting me from the hands of Christian. Their manner of expressing themselves was literally to that effect.

Portlock's entry for this day adds a detail about the continuing war not mentioned by Bligh:

The Oparre people seem to consider the Matavians as completely beaten off and Several of them begin to take advantage of their absence for they are taken down loading their Canoes and carrying down to Oparre the small remains of Houses that have Escapd the Ravage of war and Conflagration.

In explanation: the building elements of most Tahitian houses—tree trunks, limbs, coconut-leaf thatch plates, and plant-fiber cordage—were so standardized in composition and shape, and so easy to assemble, that they were often taken apart and then put together again in another location.

The Tahitians perceived behavioral abnormalities—what Bligh here calls 'insanity'—to be of two kinds: temporary and permanent. Concerning the former, James Morrison (one of the *Bounty* crew) wrote as follows:

The Insanity is only temporary, and perhaps may proceed from too great a flow of Blood & spirits and a Want of Exercise, as it generally Commences when the Bread-[fruit] begins to be ripe—at which Season others are troubled with Boils on their legs and thighs, this being the Wet Season and the Sun over head when they are More Confined to their houses by the rain; this generally leaves them when the Sun returns to the Northward, and it is Not Common for a Man or Woman to have it return, tho during its stay with them they are very Mischevious and go quite Naked. With some it stays longer than others & they have it in different degrees from a heavy dull Melancholy to Raving Mad. They never bind them but let them run and some travel all round the Island Naked in the time of their Madness and none interrupts them unless they do some Mischief as they suppose them posessd with some evil spirit. This is Common to Weomen as well as Men, who are not restrained but sufferd to take their own Course till the spirit leaves them when they return home and wear their Cloaths as usual. (Rutter 1935: 228-9)

'Permanent' insanity was described by the London Missionary Society missionary, William Ellis, writing in the 1820s:

Insanity prevailed in a slight degree, but individuals under its influence met with a very different kind of treatment. They were supposed to be inspired or possessed by some god, whom the natives imagined had entered every one suffering under mental aberrations. On this account no control was exercised, but the highest respect was shewn them. They were, however, generally avoided, and their actions were considered as the deeds of the god, rather than the man. Under these circumstances, when the poor wretch became his own destroyer, it was not regarded as an event to be deplored. (Ellis 1829: II 274)

In Tahitian eyes the thief confined aboard the *Providence* seems to have been of the 'permanent' kind of madman; in fact, he was so persistent in his madness that we shall meet him again.

Friday, April 13th

On this, his fourth full day at Tahiti, Bligh's impatience to get on with the job of collecting breadfruit plants moved him to take matters into his own hands. Although he acknowledged that he needed the cooperation of the Pomare family in doing so, and although he was on most occasions tolerant of the characteristically dilatory natures of most of them, he knew also how dependant they were on the approbation and recognition of himself and other visiting English ship captains:

Fine Weather. Wind at ENE and much Swell in the Bay. Thermometer 82 to 84 Degrees. The heat oppressive.

Carpenters Employed <in> Caulking the larboard side. Not many Cannoes, we have nevertheless as much as we possibly make use of: Hogs, Breadfruit, Plantains [mei'a; Musa paradisiaca], Tarro [Colocasia esculenta], Cocoa Nutts and Vees [vi; Spondias dulcis, the native 'mango']. Through the whole day I have some of the Natives welcomeing me here, and it is great fatigue to me to show proper attention and in assorting the Presents I give to them.

In the Morning I ordered the Small Bower Anchor to be shifted nearer the Shore in 12 fathoms. When Moored again Point Venus bore N 22 [degrees] E, Distance, ⅔ of a Mile, Point of the Reef N 13 [degrees] W, and the West head of Tarrah S 29 [degrees] W. Aired Sails.

In the Afternoon Ideeah and her friends teased me to send my Boat for Tynah, and said if I did not send for him he would not come. I saw this was a plan of her own, and insisted on her sending for him herself if she meant to be on a friendly footing with me. The way I did it gave her some alarm; she ordered a Boat to be ready, and Sailed, promising me to be back in two Days if the Weather would permit.

A great inveteracy is still held against the Matavians, particularly Poeeno the Chief. As it was necessary for me to do it away as soon as possible, I told Oreepyah I would wait no longer for Tynah's arrival from Morea; and in the Morning I should go on Shore to prepare a Place for my Plants, in which it was his interest to assist me, but that he might do as he liked; for I would have no more fighting. This brought him about, and he engaged to assist me to morrow, as soon as I had determined on the part <where> I intended to have <fix> my Post.

Beginning with this exemplar, someone—Bligh?—went through the ML (but not the PRO) version of the Journal and 'corrected' some mispellings, including crossing out the second 'n' in some spellings of 'canoe'. I have not transferred those alterations to the PRO version of the text, the one reproduced in this book.

Saturday, April 14th

Moderate Breezes and fine Weather. Wind at NE b E. Thermometer 83 to 85 degrees. Carpenters Employed Caulking the larboard side. Washed & Cleaned Ship Below.

We have plentifull supplies of Hogs and fruit, and every man has more than he can consume.

At day dawn I sent away Mr. Norris Surgeon of the Matilda with a Message from me to Poeeno & Tabyroo for Mr. Weather heads Money, & some other Articles that were in their possession, particularly the Musquets. After a troublesome Walk of Six Miles he found Poeeno & Tabyroo at Wapyhanoo [Ha'apaiano'o; marginal note: 'a district next to Matavai']. They received him in a very friendly manner and promised that the Money should be returned as soon as it could be got from Teturoah [Tetiaroa; marginal note: 'A small Isl north of Point Venus'] where they had sent it for security. They refused to give up the Musquets, unless by mutual <general> consent all those that were on the Island were to be given to me; in that case they had no objection to comply, but in their present situation they could not think of it, as it was necessary for them to preserve some Means to regain their property, or to establish themselves in another situation. They would do anything to serve me, and hoped I would not be angry with them; it was the Mob, they said, had taken away the [Matilda] peoples Cloaths, and hauled the Boats on Shore. They endeavoured to restrain them, but could not. If I came after them, they said, all that could be done, was for them to fly farther. They called Matavai my Country, and described <lamented> that the People of Oparre had destroyed their Houses, Barked their Trees, destroyed what I had left among them, and done the Country irreparable injury. I am sorry to say I found it too much the Case; it will not however affect my plan, as the Plants are numerous.

According to my promise I landed with Oreepyah & Toota'ah and fixed on a rising ground for my Post, about a ¼ of a Mile from Point Venus along the Beach. Matavai River runs close to the back of it, which makes the Situation vastly desirable and advantageous for the Plants. By Orrepyah's assistance I got the lines marked out, and by Night I got a fence and Shade two thirds completed, (about 30 Yards long and 6 Wide,) to receive my Plants. I also got necessary posts for Houses, & everything ready for erecting them on to morrow, which is vastly preferable to erecting my own Tents.

Thus happily we were going on well, and I got ready a Party of 27 Men & Officers under the command of Lieut. Guthrie & Lieut. Pearce <two Lieutenants>, all capable of bearing Arms, twenty of them being Marines.

Tobin's account of Norris's mission to recover the *Matilda* articles contains some information not included in Bligh's:

By the return of Mr Norris it was learnt that Poenow had quitted the Matavaian district for Whappiano a few miles to the East of it, whose inhabitants had given him protection. He received Mr Norris with real kindness, but refused in the most determined manner, parting with the arms, at the same time promising solemnly that the money should be speedily returned, urging as an excuse for not sending it before that it had been conveyed to a distant part of the Island. If his enemies, he said, would deliver to Captain Bligh all the arms in their possession, he would readily do the same, without which, nothing should induce him to leave himself in a defenceless state, as in such an event after the departure of the ships his district would become a prey to the Oparreans, which he had no dread of while he had no firearms to oppose.

In case of an attack from the English, it was his intention to fall back to a narrow pass in the mountains where we should never take him alive. Tupira, the colleague of this enterprising Chief, had received a wound in the late battle and was importunate with the Surgeon [i.e., Mr Norris] to bring him to a speedy cure. The whole of their ammunition did not exceed forty balled cartridges.

Tobin on this day was sent by Bligh to Pare to bring back a member of the *Matilda*'s crew still residing there. Ever mindful of protocol—especially in the furtherance of his own objectives—the Captain sent along a present for Tu, who was of course sovereign of Pare. Tobin's description of the encounter throws some additional light on the restrictions surrounding the youthful Ari'i:

[Tu] made his appearance carried on one of his Towtows shoulders, they [sic] style in which he ever travelled. He seemed about twelve years of age, his countenance free and open, yet with much curiosity painted in it. The ornaments of dress did not much incommode the young Monarch, having nothing but a wrapper of fine white cloth round his loins. In signifying that these were presents from Captain Bligh I was instructed to give them to his attendants, and afterwards learnt that, the custom is strictly observed, it being considered derogatory to his dignity to soil his fingers with any thing until reaching his own house. During the whole of this intercourse, Otoo [Tu] examined with searching looks our different dresses, and was particularly pleased with the sleeve buttons of the petty officer. I had scarcely any thing about me to offer him but a knife, (Tepey) [tipi] which was received by one of his suite while the man on whose shoulders the King rested withdrew several paces. On returning, he begged my acceptance of a hog (Boa) [pua'a] but as the mate had now joined which was the chief object of my mission, and being anxious to lose no time in reaching the ship, I took leave, promising to return to Oparrey er'e long. There was a vast crowd about the boat who waited no solicitation to assist in launching her from shore.

The observant Tobin also recorded brief descriptions of Tahitians' canoes and canoeing (Plate 8), and of the ever-popular subjects of sharks and tattooing:

A number of sailing canoes arrived in the afternoon at Oparrey from Moreea. These canoes

70

carry a very loft narrow sail of matting and in smooth water, are able to beat to windward, yet the natives never attempt to lose sight of the Island but with a fair wind, so that from Orieteea [Rai'atea], Huhahayney [Huahine], and the other Society Islands, a voyage to O'tahtey is never undertaken with the usual trade wind, which is also as adverse to a canoe reaching Maiteea [Me'etia] from O'tahytey. Accidents frequently happen, and Canoes have been driven to sea nor more heard of. Orepaia stated that a short time previously to the arrival of the Providence, his Canoe overturned coming from Tetheroa [Tetiaroa], a low Island in sight to the northward, and after remaining several hours in the water with his Wife and Towtows, they were saved by another canoe. Like the common canoes, they are fitted with an outrigger on one side, the double ones indeed, do not require this security being fastened to each other from the Gun whales, about their own breadth assunder. The natives have a singular, yet very simple way of clearing them of water when leaky or from other causes. It is common to see them leap overboard, and by the motion of quickly moving the Canoe backward and forward, force the water over at each end. It surprised us on these occasions to observe the little apprehension entertained of sharks. Yet are the natives sensible it is a fish of prey. It had the desirable effect of giving the crew [of Providence and Assistant] such confidence that the major part bathed along side every evening, which in many tropical countries would have filled them with fears. Only one shark was taken along side during our stay, but from the vast number of their teeth used by the natives in their different ornaments, it would seem that they are not a scarce fish. The shark is called Mow [ma'o]; another kind named by seamen Shovelnosed Shark, Mow-Tamowtow) [ma'o tamoutou], the latter part signifying the bonnet worn by the women.

Continuing Tobin's Journal entry:

The operation of Tatowing [tatau] was this day performed by a native on one of the seamen. The marking instruments are of various breadths, from a quarter of an inch to two formed of fish bone with teeth like a comb. This is fastened to an handle, forming an adze. After being dipped in a black composition it is applied to the part intended to be marked, and struck sharply with a small wooden spatula. The blows produce blood, as well as considerable pain, and infrequent inflamation, but this ceases er'e long, when the ornaments, which are various, remain indelible. It is frequently necessary to repeat the operation from the accute pain endured when applied to the more susceptible parts of the body. There are many marks adopted by particular classes, The Eareoyes [Arioi] have generally a large spot under the left breast. About the time of entering their teens, the young girls become fit subjects for the tatowing instruments, the swell of the hip and its environs, being chosen for the field of operation. This is sometimes done in curved lines, and at others in a broad one two or three inches, which on a clear nankeen coloured skin has a lively effect, giving great relief to the eye. Some prefer the Vandyke fashion diverging o'er the smooth surface of their more fleshy part, forming a star of nearly half a foot in diameter.

No girl at any of our fashionable finishing seminaries in the neighborhood of Queen, or Bloomsbury Squares, when she takes leave of her tucker [a frill of lace worn round the neck] feels warmer hopes than do these damsels when they submit to this short lived pain. The deeper the wounds, the greater the triumph, the more their boast, nor is perswasion at all required to gain an exhibition of these proud stains.

The sight was interesting and novel. Their contempt of pain at so early an age, we *could not but admire, yet not more than their complacency in anticipating our most critical researches. The operation is sometimes performed with such severity as to raise the skin considerably, nor were subjects wanting, on whom the rays of light were not necessary, to prove their being tatowed, a Basso-relievo being very evident to another of the senses.*

As whim and notoriety, seem my dear James, to be the 'order of the day' among you, it has surprised me much, that some of our dashing demi-reps have not come forward— backward might have been said—compleatly tatowed. If on the embossed skin of the Otahytean fair one it proves so interesting, how heavenly would it appear in contrast with the snowy whiteness of the ignoble part of our own country women! And then, the luxury,—with what trembling timidity, would the gazing operator, lost in admiration, apply the instruments.

The facts behind Tobin's coy circumlocution are simply stated: that the most common body area for tattooing was the buttocks; that women took pride in revealing their buttock tattoos; and that the tattoo marks were in some cases raised enough, in the form of scar tissue—'*basso relievo*'—for exploring hands to discover even in the dark.

In their Journal entries for this day both Tobin and Portlock wrote about commerce. First, Portlock's:

. . . we get a Good supply of hogs and Every other Article of food and much more reasonable than might be Expected when we consider the Quantity that must have been taken off, by the different Ships, we get a fine hog weighing 150 Pounds, for a hapenny or an Eightpenny hatchet—we get 10 or 12 heads of bread fruit for a Sheathing nail and as many Cocoanutts, for a Sheathing nail also—this I think cheaper than we found it when here in the Resolution and Discovery.

The different kind of commerce that Tobin wrote about was apparently very common aboard both ships and ashore, but was either unnoticed or ignored by Bligh (and probably never engaged in by him):

In the evening a scene presented itself the most repugnant possible to human nature, a father and mother bargaining for the untasted charms of their child, and it was difficult to discover, which expected the greatest delight, the parents or their daughter at her being engaged to yield her virgin treasures for a few foreign ornaments, for such were considered a couple of shirts, and three or four strings of beads. Miti t' Parawhay [maita'i te pareo] (good shirt) was often heard from the lips of these damsels when particularly interested in pleasing their english visitors. The teenless [?] fair one, if the expression may be used to a lovely face, partaking more of the olive than either the Lily or Carnation, recieved the tempting bait, which the mother took from her with eager joy, leaving her on board 'nothing loth' without that remorse—it is yet to be hoped—which would attend the most depraved European in a transaction of such a nature.

This was not the only instance of the kind that had occurred since our arrival, and it is an indisputable truth that the O'tahytean considers it as but a mark of confidence and attention, the offer of a moiety of his wife, and the entire of his sister or daughter to him, with whom he has entered on the terms of Tayoship. Of the turpitude of such an action among ourselves there can be but one opinion. Of its effects on these less rigid people, there is no reason to believe them inimical to order on the most cordial harmony. Never does it take place but with the most hearty and unreserved concurrence of all parties. You may call it indifference if you please, and doubtless to the jealous monopolizing european it cannot but appear so. For your friend 'He'd rather be a toad and live upon the vapour of a dungeon than keep a corner in the thing he loves for other uses'.

The pliant O'tahytean argues differently. Yet even there, where the fond swain seldom breathes his warm wishes unheeded, the chilling repulsive denial is sometimes heard. Happily for them, such instances are rare.

The instructed daughters of chastity of our colder regions, no doubt, in their own strength, look with pity and contempt on the infirmity of these poor Islanders. True, from their infancy they are taught that this alone will pave their way to heaven. This jewel inviolate, every discordant passion may riot without impeachment or controul; The children of these Southern Isles know no such doctrine, nor, are they the less happy for it; If frail, yet do they largely teem with charity and benevolence. Then condemn them not too harshly, for, with all the frothy aid of systematic instruction, yet do our own fair fall, and deep indeed, for such is the prejudice of an unfeeling world—that the once fond mother who sedulously watched their infant years, and sisters who shared the warm confidence of their bosoms—must know them no more. T'is a heartrending truth—Better then, perhaps do the thoughtless South Sea Islanders act in looking with a benevolent eye on what mankind has from the 'beginning,' and will to the 'end,' err in, even should civilized institutions—which is hardly possible—become more severe—and a still greater restraint be imposed on the laws of all powerful nature.

The practice of offering one's sister to one's *taio* was likely a new one and confined to European 'pseudo' *taio*; among Tahitians coitus with a *taio*'s sister was considered to be incestuous.

Sunday, April 15th

A steady breeze all day from the Westward, and Cloudy Weather. Thermometer 82 to 84 [degrees].

Washed and Cleaned Ship. Mustered the People, and saw every Person Clean dressed. Performed Divine Service. Plentifull supplies of every thing. I thought proper to put the People to short allowance of liquor, only to serve it three days a Week while we have such abundance of fine Cocoa Nutts. This enables me to assist <the> Weatherhead's People [i.e., the beached members of the Matilda crew], and Acts against necessity from <to provide against the consequences of> any delay I may meet with in my Passage to Timor.

In the course of this Day I got my Post so forwardly <nearly> fitted up, that I determined to land the People in the Morning. I have at present given up all thoughts of going [i.e., of moving the ships] to Oparre, as there is a risk in getting the Ship in and out, and I have a chance or rather certainty of fine Weather at this Season of the Year which will render my situation here more elligable.

<I have now got my Gardeners tolerably acquainted with the manner of proceeding, and some intelligent men [i.e. Tahitians] to go with them

73

*who assisted me last Voyage. A number of Natives I have employed in making
Mats of Cocoa Nut leaves for coverings to the Plants which can be taken off and
put on occasionally, and the Chiefs are highly pleased that King George has again
sent for the Breadfruit.>*

The ever-agreeable Portlock had this to say about Bligh's decision to
reduce the ration of grog:

*. . . the Commodore in order to make our Liquor [run?] out and to guard also against any
[Accident?] has come to the determination of Serving Grog only three times a week, that is on
Sundays, Tuesdays, and Fridays. Grog is an Article that can be well done without here where
every man gets as many fine Cocoanutts as he chuses to make use of, and the Milk of the
Cocoanutt before the kernel becomes hard and firm is exceedingly pleasant to drink.*

Bligh's decision to establish his shore nursery at Matavai rather than
at some spot adjacent to the somewhat better protected Pare Harbour was
probably reinforced by a survey carried out by Portlock, who wrote:

*I have been orderd by the Commodore to hold the Assistant in readiness to proceed down to
Oparre as he has some Intention of procuring the Plants there and my remaining to protect them
and the people who will have the care of procuring them; he does not think it safe to risk the
Providence in. Indeed there is little difuculty in geting in but a good deal with such a ship as
she in geting out, as the Entrance is not above 65 fathoms and laying in the winds Eye of the
prevailing trade and without it the Navigation renderd dangerous and uncertain by a number
of shoal water Coral Banks whose situations at present are not well known.*

Monday, April 16th

*Moderate and Cloudy Weather which towards the middle of the Day became
Squally and at Night smart Rain. Wind about E b S and the Thermometer 82 to
83½ Degrees.*

*In the Morning I sent the Second Lieutenant of the Ship Mr.
Guthrie [and] Lieutenant Pearce of the Marines with his party and those of the
Assistant, amounting to 20 Men, and three non Commissioned Officers, a Mate and
two Midshipmen, to guard our Breadfruit Walk. I ordered also the Surgeon of the
Matilda to be of the Party, who with the two Botanists <Gardeners> made 27
Men capable of using Arms. (Plates 9 and 10)*

*Not many Cannoes about the Ship, but very sufficient supplies.
Carpenters employed caulking the Larboard side. Finished Salting 4 Hogsheads of Pork.*

*The favorable Wind yesterday brought me over [from Mo'orea]
my friend Tynah. He came on board about two OClock in a covered Cannoe with his
two Wives, Iddeeah & Whyareddee. His Father Old Otoo came in another Cannoe.
There appeared a natural degree of affection in Tynah & his Father that gave me
much pleasure. We all thank God (he said) [to me] that you are safe. we were told
you were put into a little Boat & sent a drift without anything to eat or drink,*

Plate 7a   Tina, in 1773
Crayon drawing by
W. Hodges

Plate 7b   Tina, in 1802
Pencil drawing by J. W. Lewin

Plate 8   Tahitian canoes
Watercolor by George Tobin

and that you must perish. You have a fine Ship now. Have you good Men? Have you a bad Man among them? Have you seen King George? What did he say to you? and many various <other> questions he put to me respecting every person he knew. I asked him how he came to be so friendly to Christian, for that proved to me he was not sincere in what he said. He replied—'I really thought you was living and gone to England untill Christian came back the second time. I was then from home, but all my Friends, as soon as they heard from the Men who came on Shore, on their questioning them, that you was lost, from that time we did not profess any friendship to him, and Christian knew it so well that he only remained a few hours, and went away in such a hurry, that he left a second Anchor behind him. One of the Anchors we got I gave it to the Pandora.' Thus he freed himself from any suspicion on my side, & with his usual good nature and cheerfulness regained my esteem & regard.

Poeeno & the Matavai People seem to be objects of great dislike to Tynah and his Father, they requested I would undertake the War with them to destroy those people as well as the Inhabitants of Paparrah & Oaitepeeah, who had a number of Musquets. They knew it was an object worth their most strenuous <earnest> endeavours to persuade me to <engage with them> but they had the good sense not to be seriously offended at my refusal when I told them it would interfere with the busyness I was sent on <upon>. I however still threatened the adverse Party unless they brought in the Arms & Money.

Tynah brought me a large Hog and some Cloth, Breadfruit, Plantains and Cocoa Nutts. His Wife Whyareddee also put a few peices of Cloth about me, but there was very little of the ancient Custom of the Otaheitean; all that, was laid aside; it is rather a difficulty to get them to speak their own language without mixing a jargon of English, and they are so generally altered, that I believe no European in future will ever know what their ancient Customs of receiving Strangers were.

It surprised me to find Tynah to have <had> another Wife, while Iddeeah was living, it is however the Case. She is a Woman of Iddeeah's Stature <. . . a younger sister>, but has a much handsomer Countenance. She was the Wife of Whaeeahtuah, the Chief of Tierraboo who is dead. They all slept on board together, & the Women were on the best of terms with each other.

Tynah brought with him Captain Cook's Picture, and on the back of it, underneath my Memorandum is as follows—

His Britannick Majesty's Ship Pandora Sailed from Matavai Bay Otaheite 9th May 1791.

His Britannick Majesty's Ship Discovery and armed Tender Chatham Sailed from Matavai Bay 24th January 1792.

I should have been happy to have received a letter from Capt. Edwards to have known how he had proceeded, it would have been delivered to me as safe as the Picture, and I might have assisted in finishing the object of his Voyage.

> *Tynah observing the Man in Irons wҺo \<whom\> I had confined for being about the Assistant's Cable in the Night, laughed at me exceedingly for confining a Mad Man—Nainaivah [neneva], as he called him, which also implies foolish. At his request he was liberated & told not to come any more near the Ships.*
>
> *The presents I made to Tynah and his Friends gave them much pleasure, particularly a Suit of Crimson coloured Cloth with Gold Lace about the Cape and Sleeves, and printed Callico Night Gowns to the Women. To these I added every thing they wished for in Iron and Trinkets.*
>
> *I had forgot to mention that I saluted Tynah on his Arrival with 10 Guns.*

Before commenting on Bligh's entry for this day, it may be noted that Tobin's contains his personal opinion about the character of the shore party, and a lively water color of the shore establishment in its natural setting:

> *A party under command of Guthrie landed this day and took possession of our Post near Point Venus. Pearce, with his marines served to give it quite a military appearance [Plates 9 and 10]. I am not writing for the world it is true, but I cannot resist bearing, even to you [i.e., his brother, James], my humble testimony to the unremitting attention and good conduct of Pearce and his small party from Chatham [Division of Marines]. Indeed, in essential points of service this truly valuable Corps have rarely been found remiss.*

The arrival of the Pomare family from Mo'orea added a new and not altogether beneficial element to the conduct of Bligh's mission. Although the presence of Tina—the 'Regent'—probably lent some weight to the local support needed for collecting the breadfruit plantings, Tina's younger brother, Ari'ipaea, had already proved himself willing and able to facilitate the work of the expedition. And while Bligh's pleasure in seeing his former friends was doubtless sincere, their constant presence during the following weeks clearly became burdensome to him, especially in view of his nagging preoccupation with the welfare of the growing plant nursery and his delicate state of health.

We can sympathize with Bligh's 'surprise' on finding Tina to have a second wife: even today our understanding of Tahitian 'marriage' in that era is, to say the least, vague.

Alongside their own notions about, say, 'kingship' and 'sexual decency', the Europeans who visited Tahiti during that era brought with them some conventional and highly specific ideas about 'marriage'. Those held by Bligh may have differed in some respects from those of, say, the urbane Joseph Banks or of the English missionaries (who arrived there in 1797), but common to all of those Europeans was a core of ideas—rules, memories, expectations—that shaped their perceptions about relationships between Tahitian men and women. The circumstance that some of those relationships did in several respects *resemble* European ideas about marriage led the observers (who were in general better at observing, say, canoe-making

76

and tattooing, than social institutions) to assume that English and Tahitian institutions of 'marriage' were much more alike than they actually were.

A search through all known published reports originating in that era leads me to characterize (for what in lack of a better word can be called) Tahitian 'marriage' as, a male–female relationship that involved the following: (1) coitus, with open—in contrast to clandestine—corresidence for a period of at least several weeks; (2) tacit agreement to exchange certain services and objects (i.e., a conjugal division of labor and other goods); (3) tacit agreement by themselves to regard as 'legitimate' (i.e., for purposes of inheritance) any surviving offspring thought by them to be their own; and (4) some degree of public recognition of and kinfolk sanction for their relationship—sometimes but not necessarily marked by a 'wedding' ceremony. (For a fuller treatment of this subject, see Oliver 1974: 445–65, 799–828.) In addition to 'marriage', as here defined, there were among Tahitians other kinds of heterosexual unions that were more or less regularized.

Unvalidated unions in Tahiti were those characterized by all the above features of 'marriage' except for the circumstance that one or both of the families of the partners had deliberately witheld recognition of the union, as manifested by their refusal to recognize the 'legitimacy' of the couple's progeny. Unions of this kind occurred most usually between persons of different social class—i.e., when an 'inheritance' of one of the partners was important enough to warrant protection from social debasement. Some 'unvalidated' couples were driven into exile, or remained childless as a result of the slaying of their newborns by objecting relatives, but some others lived fairly normal lives, complicated only by the ambiguous status of their living offspring.

A third kind of union, that between a man and his 'secondary' wife, was quite common, especially between members of the upper class. In fact, many men with high-ranking kin-Titles usually had one 'primary' wife, through whom heirs were appropriately assured, along with a secondary wife or two—in addition to long-lasting concubine relationships and any number of casual, unregularized, sexual affairs. The young woman who appears in this day's Journal entry of Bligh's—Tina's 'another Wife'—was clearly a 'secondary' one in the sense defined above. Years later Tina acquired yet another secondary wife; and while these secondaries appear to have replaced 'Itia, the primary wife, on Tina's sleeping mat, 'Itia remained throughout his life a loyal supporter and valuable counsellor to him—as well as the respected mother of all of his 'legitimate' offspring, including his successor, Tu.

Some upper-class and duly 'married' women (including 'Itia) came to have unions with other men that were open and durable and domestic enough to warrant calling the latter 'secondary husbands'—to distinguish them from other, exclusively sexual, partners, both casual and longer-lasting.

As will be seen below, in his Journal entry of 26 May, Bligh confessed to his inability to discover the existence of any wedding ceremony *per se*. In this opinion he was partly correct; for, while the kind of ceremony that initiated some primary 'marriages' was part of a whole series of rites that had other objectives as well (see April 17th, May 27th), it nevertheless contained some features that had to do directly with the marriage it served to validate.

Getting back to Tina's new secondary wife introduced in this Journal entry, she was, as stated, a younger sister of 'Itia, and the widow of Vehiatua, *The Chief—Te Ari'i*—of the Seaward Teva, the large and politically united population of Tahiti's Taiarapu Peninsula. This Vehiatua (the third at least in the succession bearing that name), who had died in March 1790, at the age of about twenty-two, was the man who was for a short time succeeded by the *Bounty* mutineer, Churchill (see entry of April 10th).

Tobin's Journal entry for this day provides some details about the Pomares' visit aboard *Providence* not mentioned by his more circumspect Captain:

Pomaurey paid us his first visit to day, but without any form or ceremony. He was accompanied by his father Otow a venerable old man apparently about seventy, very grey and infirm, and whose skin was much affected from drinking of Yava.

In the dress of Otow and his son there was no difference from the other Chiefs, but the canoe in which they came was covered with an awning of canes and network. Edeea was of the party, and her sister Whyhereddy, a younger and more handsome wife. My Tayo [i.e., 'Itia] brought me a hog, some fruit, and a quantity of cloth, the latter being wrapped round me as when we became friends.

In honor of the Regents visit some guns were fired which rather alarmed him, nor did he quit the side of Whyhereddy, the whole cannonade. Edeea now complained of hunger, nor was she many minutes in devouring full two pounds of pork, with as much brandy and water as would have staggered any seaman in the ship. Pomaurey and his two wives slept on board. Poor Edeea seemed neglected for those charms still in bloom of her younger sister, and was seldom allowed to share her Lords bed.

Still more details about the Pomares' visit are supplied by Lt. Portlock, who was in position to compare this visit with ones made fifteen years earlier, aboard the *Resolution*, on whose sister-ship *Discovery* he had served as master's mate:

The King who formerly bore the name of Otoo and is now called Tynaa (his Eldest son taking the name of Otoo) passed us in a double Canoe with a shed over her fore part, and went onboard the Providence he had just arrivd from Morea and this was his first Visit to the ships, on which Occasion Captain Bligh saluted him with a few guns, which pleasd exceedingly, he made his visit with very little state and was very thinly attended on the Occasion, it usd to be quite different formerly, for on his coming to the Resolution he was generally attended by a Number of Canoes and many of the chiefs, and the Canoes that were about the ship trading were always thrown into a bustle to get out of the way; he must now be advancing in Years and his son Otoo

78

is growing a fine lively lad its most probably that the respect that used to be shewn to the father now devolves on the son. At 6 PM) I went onboard the Providence, were I found the King [i.e., the ex-'King', Tina] his father whose name is Oteu, Edea, and another wife of the Kings whose name is Whyride this lady is younger sister to Edea and appears to have supplanted her Intirely in the Kings Affections, it was a very happy meeting of old friends and their Joy was so great that it was perfectly visable in all countenances, few of them in speaking of the fate that they Expected Captain Bligh and his companions had met with could refrain from tears, the King in particular who is one of the most friendly and best disposd men in the world could not enough Express his happiness at this unexpected visit from Captain Bligh, he still looks remarkable well, is much belovd by his subjects; but from his Imoderate use of Wine or Spirits (or when he cannot get them, the Gava) he too often renders himself Incapable of doing them or his country much Service. Urepia his next brother (between who and the King there appears to be much Friendship and Affection) is the ruling man, and pickd from the remarks I have been able to make of him I think there cannot be a better, he appears to be a Sensible Vigilant and all his countrymen allow him to be one of their best warriors. He is about five feet ten Inches high, an Excellent figure of a man remarkably strong and Active and of a commanding Aspect.

Both Tobin and Portlock wrote of the Pomare party having arrived in an awning-covered canoe. The natives of the Society Islands built three types of boats (*va'a*). A *pu ho'e* consisted of a single hollowed-out log sometimes capped with thin gunwale strips of wood. Such boats had rounded bottoms, convex cutwaters and slightly raised bows, and slightly raised and pointed sterns. Few of them were longer than about fifteen feet; they were used mainly for inshore fishing. Larger dug-outs (called specifically *va'a*) consisted of rounded hulls of two or more dug-out bottoms fitted together, and built-up wooden sides. They had long flat bow-pieces and high upward-curving sterns. The largest one actually measured (by Joseph Banks) was 72 feet long. A third kind of boat, a *pahi*, consisted of a definite keel, made of one or more hollowed-out logs, and rounded sides made of tiers of wide planks; both bow and stern were curved upward. Such boats measured in length from 30 to 100 or more feet.

Pu ho'e were always stabilized by a single outrigger float, *pahi* by joining two hulls together (i.e., a double canoe), and *va'a* by either outrigger or double hulls. All three types were propelled by pole, paddle, or sail—or by two sails, one stepped in each hull of a double canoe. Steering was by paddle or larger paddle-shaped rudder. When sailing an outrigger canoe a balancing board was often lashed across the gunwales so as to extend several feet beyond the hull opposite the outrigger; by moving along this board crewmen were able to keep the boat on an even keel. Washboards were added when travelling in rough water, and wooden bailing scoops were usually carried because of invariable leakage and of water taken over the sides.

The *va'a* and *pahi* were often fitted with additional features for special uses, such as platforms (for long-distance travelling) and awnings (for protection against the elements), such as the one mentioned by Tobin and

Portlock. (See Oliver 1974: 194-219, for additional information on boat construction, management, navigation, and ritual.)

These islands could only have been settled by means of oceangoing boats, and there were doubtless times in their history when the Society Islanders voyaged many hundreds of miles beyond the archipelago's bounds. But during the era now under examination voyaging took place only within the archipelago itself (including Me'etia), and possibly to the nearer Tuamotuan atolls (as was described by Tobin in his Journal entry for April 14th).

Tuesday, April 17th

On this long-awaited day was begun the actual collection of breadfruit plants—the principal, indeed the only major objective of the expedition:

All the Morning Light Variable Winds Easterly. In the Evening the Wind varied to the NW and West, and kept steady all Night with Cloudy Weather inclinable to Rain. Thermometer 81 to 83½ degrees.

Employed Caulking, Drying Sails and Salting Pork, the Natives supplying us with more Hogs than we can keep alive.

This was the first day of my beginning to collect my Plants. We had 32 in the Pots at Sun Set.

I had a Visit today from the Young King. He was brought to the Post on a Man's Shoulders in his usual way; but would not come off to the Ship. After receiving a few presents he returned to Oparre.

Tynah, his Wives, Oreepyah and Tootaha, after they had all eaten voraciously, went to Oparre in the Cutter, nothing pleases them more than this mark of attention I always show to them, and my saluting on his arrival delights him. He says it will show all his enemies that we are good Friends. He has none but Friends about him just now, for the Matavai People are fled, and their habitations all destroyed, the whole Plain seems desolated, which I have seen replete with Cheerfulness and Wealth <Plenty>. By the Matavai People being away, I have lost an intercourse with full thousand People <Persons>, so that I have not half the bustle I had in my last Voyage, which is <in some respects> «so far» a fortunate circumstance, <as> my Nervous Head Ach being <is> at times scarce <scarcely> bearable.

<Before I was aware of it the Botanists had potted some of the Plants without putting any pieces of Shells or anything at the bottom of the Pot to prevent the water laying and souring. I therefore ordered them to be turned out and potted anew.>

Regarding the last paragraph (which appears only in Bligh's original version, i.e., the Mitchell Library Journal), it is interesting to note that he, this *sailor* par excellence, found it necessary to instruct his 'Botanists' in so elementary a botanical matter as the correct method of potting plants. It is also note-worthy that he did not have this episode recorded in the official version of the Journal. As in the case of the earlier venereal inspection carried out before reaching Tahiti, he appears to have wished to shield members of his crew from the criticism that may have resulted, in this case, had the Botanists' ignorance of botanical matters become 'officially' known.

Lieutenant Portlock's account of this day's events augments the more laconic one of Bligh:

The Botanists reported to Captain Bligh that they have found a very good place for procuring bread fruit plants at [?], in the Valley leading to the Southward from Matavia and about 1½ mile off. (AM) the sun being very hot and Captain Bligh Indisposd he did not Venture on shore I visited the post where I found all perfectly in order and work finishd [on building] the houses and [on] bounding the post by a ditch of four feet broad and 4 feet deep going on very well, the ditch made by our own people, whilst I was at the Post the Young King Otoo came carried as usual on a mans shoulders I made him a present from Captain Bligh and one for myself which he directed his attendants to receive, for it appears he never in public takes anything of the kind himself and was highly pleasd with them, he had lernt my Name and spoke it and several English words very plain his behavior was truly friendly and he gave me a pressing Invitation to see him at Opare, this prince I think is about 13 or 14 Years of age well grown and with a countenance that commands respects already from the Inhabitants, I think he possesses a very different disposition to that of his father, having an Active and lively turn of mind.

The Indian that was in confinement onboard the Providence was by request of the King set into liberty on conditions that he was not to return to the ships again, the poor wretch who had laid his account down to be killd, receivd his liberty with every demonstration of Joy and gratitude that he could show, lept into the water and swam on shore. At Noon light Westerly breeses with hot Sultry weather. I returnd onboard the Providence and reported to Captain Bligh the proceedings on shore.

PM) a gentle breese from the westward with hot sultry weather, ships Company Employd in the Necessary duty of the ship, our supply to day from the Natives (and which we buy very cheap) are an abundance of Cocoanutts and bread fruit, but few hogs we get for a nail about 1½ Inch long 6 or 10 large heads of bread fruit one head sufficient for a man per day and for Cocoanutts we give the same kind of nail for 8 or 10. in general a nutt containing very near a Quart of most Excellent and healthy drink which we in general call Milk in the Evening I accompanied Captain Bligh on shore we visited the Post and found the botanists had lodged in the Plant House 32 Potts each containing on average two fine bread fruit Plants the weather was showery and much in favour of the Plants, thus we had the satisfaction of seeing the first of this business the object of our voyage happily begun.

The excellent Portlock—Bligh evidently judged him to be so—having been continually absorbed in administering the 'Necessary duty of the ship,' had not the time, and perhaps not the inclination, to delve more deeply into Tahitian customs, but here as elsewhere in his Journal he provides valuable information concerning rates of barter-exchange—valuable because of the light it casts on the value-setting processes at work in this frontier market. Rather than comment on those exchange rates piecemeal, however, they will be discussed all together in the editorial commentary later on (entries of May 23rd).

Tobin, who was less duty-bound than Portlock for supervising everyday ship-keeping, had the time and the opportunity—along with, it seems, the inclination—to observe and ponder native ways. Also, it should be remembered, his Journal was written primarily for the amusement of himself and his brother, and not for bleak-eyed Admiralty types. And unlike Bligh's and Portlock's Journals, Tobin's was written wholly *after* the Tahiti visit, hence each day's entry was informed by knowledge acquired throughout the whole visit:

Facts are all, I deal in; you, who have more leisure and research, may reason on them as 'seems wise'. It was my destiny this morning, to stumble on Orepaia, brother of the King Regent in an unequivocal situation with Whyhereddy. It was by accident be assured, as it has ever been my maxim—and ever shall—not to interfere with the private avocations of any one—nor, should I have entered the six foot cabin of my friend Guthrie—at least without knocking—had I in the slightest degree suspected it had been converted into a rendezvous for gallantry. The discovery however served to convince me that, the Royal family were as incontinent as those in a more subordinate sphere. An enjoinment of secrecy took place, not only from the parties, but stranger to tell, from Edeea, the neglected and almost repudiated Edeea. But I am disposed to suspect that she had her weak moments, and that Pomaurey was dupe of both. The very high bred hacknied dames of quality of our own Island might here take a lesson in courtly indifference.

Dining with Captain Bligh I found Pomaurey of the party who never contaminates his hands with the touch of food, but is crammed like a Turkey by one of his attendants, nor is it possible to consider anything more ludicrous than this operation. He received several glasses of wine from me, which I was instructed to pour down his eager throat as he sat with his hands totally unemployed. Pomaurey appeared about five and Forty, as well as his brothers his skin was darker than that of most of the natives, nor was it much tatowed. In height he was above six feet, and of a strong muscular frame, but an awkward stoop, with a vacant unmeaning countenance, in which indolence and good nature were leading features. Certainly it must be confessed that Whyreddy evinced taste, although at the extreme of constancy, in preferring Orepaia, who was a most interesting figure, and bore the character of a great warrior, while that of the Regent was quite the reverse.

Pomaurey had but little external distinctions paid him, nor was it uncommon for the towtows to converse peculiarly with him and sit in his presence. The Women it is true, were not allowed to eat in his company, indeed the sexes among all classes at O'tahytey, separate when at their meals. It was however dispensed with on board the Providence, Edeea, and Whyreddy constantly joining at our dinner table with the Chiefs.

Many of the Matavaians having with drawn from the district, their antagonists availed themselves of it to plunder the houses of the few articles left in them.

Tobin's surprise concerning the 'infidelity' of Vaiareti ('Whyhereddy') seems to have been occasioned mainly by the connivance in it of 'Itia, the cuckold's 'repudiated' primary wife. What Tobin did not weigh in the matter was 'Itia's apparent affection for Vaiareti, her younger sister. And what he may not have known was the prevalence of 'infidelity' between Tahitian men and their brothers' wives—a practice which Bligh had described in his *Bounty* Journal:

Were the Women moderately Chaste and to Marry I really believe the Island would swarm with Inhabitants, and it would be absolutely necessary that every inch of Ground should be Cultivated, but at present I am convinced there is not that fear or that necessity. The Women have too great an intercourse with different Men. An Elder Brother has connection with another Brothers Wife, and the Younger Brothers with their different Brothers Wives whenever Opportunities offer without giving Offence, it is considered no infidelity, for I have known a Man to have done the Act in the presence of his own Wife, and it is a common thing for the Wife to assist the Husband in these Amours. But what is remarkable, it is not so among those who are not related to one another; it is then a violation if a married Couple err on either side, for if a Man finds another with his Wife he'll kill him if he can, and if the Woman discovers infedelity of the Husband she will certainly take revenge on the Woman. (Bligh 1937: II 78)

And what was suspected by Tobin about 'Itia's own 'infidelity' had been well known to Bligh during his *Bounty* visit:

He [Tina] left the Table soon after dinner, when Oreepyah (his Brother) and Odiddee [Hitihiti] told me of a peice of Scandal I had never heard of with certainty before. This was that Iddeah, Tynahs Wife, kept a Gallant called Taerree, and that he was a towtow and the very person who had fed Tynah at dinner. They said also that Tynah knew it, and it was so far agreeable to both parties that both men cohabited with the Wife in the same hour, and in the presence of one another. As I appeared to doubt of the fact, they took several Opportunities to convince me in the course of the day by mentioning it to some others who all declared it was true, and I have no longer any doubt of it, not but I beleive it is more or less the case as far as I can find throughout the whole Island. The Virtue and chastity of the cheif Women is by no means equal to what it has been represented, and it certainly is not a fact that they will not grant certain favors if opportunity and convenience offers. (Bligh 1937 I: 399)

The restriction against self-feeding here reported by Tobin piqued the interest of many Europeans, including Bligh, as reported in the latter's *Bounty* Journal:

Tynah as usual dined with me, and this is always a convenient Opportunity to make enquiries; it was particularly apropos to the subject I was on, and have long been endeavoring to get a certain knowledge of, the reason of his not feeding himself.
    This circumstance is not confined to the Erree rahigh, but is common among all Cheifs who are married and have Children. When the Mother is

83

delivered, the Father, who is always present, has the New born infant given to
him before any other person but the Midwife touches it. As soon as he is
satisfied with viewing the Child he returns it to the Mother, and from that
moment untill the Child is grown up and considered a Man, he never tastes any
food or nourishment but what is put into his Mouth by another person.

It is the same with Idddeeah, Tynahs Wife, for about ten Months,
when she performs a ceremony Aammo-Aammo, which is presenting some
Cocoa Nutt, Sugar Cane and a Small bough of a Shrub called Errow-woah in
each hand held to her forehead to the Child; this being done she is at liberty to
feed herself.

It is the same with the Cheifs of Districts, but the Aammo is performed
in a shorter space of time; some people tell me that both the Father and Mother
are at liberty to feed themselves in ten Months after the Child is born.

This never happens with the Mana-hownes or Towtows [*manahune* or
teuteu, commoners or servants]. (Bligh 1937: II 43)

The clue to the self-feeding restriction is to be found in the name
given to the rite that lifted it, namely, what Bligh called 'Aammo' (*amo'a*, literally, sanctity-neutralizing, or as some early observers called it, 'head-freeing').
To comprehend this rite one must recall the concept of an individual's god-
derived sanctity, which was described earlier in the commentary on social
hierarchy accompanying the journal entries of April 9th. In the belief of the
Tahitians of that era, every newborn contained some of the sanctity of each
parent, the amount (or intensity, or whatever) diminishing with order of
birth and hence with collateral distance from each line of first-born descendants of the primagenital ancestral god. As we have seen, the possession of
sanctity entailed the right to communicate effectively with spirits—the more
sanctity the greater the effectiveness; and coupled with those religious rights
were some (but not necessarily matching) political rights as well. However, as
with a current of electricity (the analogy is suggestive if not carried too far),
a high concentration of sanctity in one person was believed to be dangerous
to those having less of it, hence rites had to be performed to insulate that
danger, as a protection to other persons and as a means of enabling the high-
sanctity possessor to lead a more unrestricted everyday life.

One such restriction already met with in the journals was the
necessity for the young Tu to be carried when away from home; any other
ground touched by his feet would have been rendered unusable for their
occupants. (The same thing held for others' houses, including European
ships.) The logic is somewhat less transparent when applied to the eating
restriction, but appears to derive from the extreme vulnerability attributed
to the stomach and bowels (which in Tahitian belief were the site of a person's
soul). Thus, the reasoning seems to have been, food touched by the hand of
someone associated, 'contagiously', with 'super-sanctity'—as was Tina with
his super-sanctified son, Tu—would have endangered that someone's
stomach, and hence soul. (A similar line of reasoning was manifest in the

event of a death, when a person who had touched the corpse had to be fed by someone else until ritually freed of that restriction; in this case, however, the danger seems to have stemmed less from the sanctity of the deceased than from the pollutive effects of decay, i.e., from spirits associated with that death and decay.)

As Bligh stated in the *Bounty* Journal entry quoted above, sanctity-neutralizing rites were not performed on behalf of servants ('Towtows', *teuteu*) or members of the lower class ('Mana-hownes', *manahune*)—indeed, such persons possessed too little sanctity to require neutralizing. Beginning with the middle class (i.e., the *ra'atira*), however, the restrictions upon a new-born and its close consanguines increased in kind and in duration corresponding to its amount of sanctity.

In the case of some individuals the neutralizing was accomplished gradually, through a series of rites, which in the case of a person such as Tu were spun out over two decades or more. (One observer recorded that some socially pretentious parents spun out the rites for periods beyond what the associated sanctity warranted.) In some instances the rites were performed separately and devoted only to sanctity-neutralizing; in other instances, such as nuptial and bond-friendship ceremonies, the sanctity-neutralizing ritual was performed as one part of the event (e.g., to permit the groom and his male in-laws to share food).

Now to consider another small but pregnant passage of Tobin's, namely, 'the sexes among all classes at O'tahyety, separate when at their meals', a custom that had some elements in common with the eating restriction just described.

In the smaller households of lower-class Tahitians, both males and females usually ate under the same roof, although spatially separate. But in larger households, and especially those of the upper class, males and females ate (and usually slept) in separate houses. Moreover, it was generally held that females ought not to eat any food that had been touched by males—the prohibition not having applied in reverse. It is improbable that this rule was strictly observed within the smaller families of lower-class persons; little was reported about this segment of society (European observers were generally more interested in persons of 'the Better Class') but lower-class Tahitians, who were in most matters quite pragmatic, are unlikely to have submitted, day in and day out, to measures as onerous as those would have been. However, within upper- and middle-class families, and especially the larger ones, the sex-segregation food rule does appear to have prevailed—even to the extent of using different earth ovens, different sets of cooking utensils, and separate food plants.

In the absence of recorded native explanations on this point we cannot know for certain the ideological basis for this prohibition, but one possible rationale was the distinction between *ra'a* and *noa*. It was a basic premise of Tahitian ideology that males were or could become *ra'a*, while females always remained *noa*. (A familiar albeit inadequate gloss for this contrasting pair of terms would be 'sacred' versus 'secular'.) *Ra'a* applied to spirits and everything associated with spirits, including temples, images, and persons formally engaged in worship; *noa* applied to entities lacking *ra'a*. *Ra'a* was dangerous to persons in a state of *noa*; conversely, persons in a state of *noa* impaired *ra'a*. In everyday life all persons were normally *noa*, but most males could through ritual become *ra'a*, temporarily, in order to associate with spirits effectively and safely. Females, on the other hand, along with specially designated male domestic servants (i.e., of some upper-class females) were always *noa*, never permitted direct association with beings or things or places that were *ra'a*.

In some other Pacific Island societies where comparable practices of male–female segregation prevailed, the inherent *noa*-like attribute of females was based on belief in and male fear of the pollutive nature of menstrual blood, but the Tahitians of this era displayed little if any anxiety about the process of menstruation.

In any case, whatever the rationale of the Tahitian rule of male-female segregation at meals, and granting the likelihood that the rule was bent in families where strict adherence to it was too burdensome to bear, several reports attest that observance of the rule was very widespread, especially in families of the upper class. Why then was it ignored, on board the *Providence*, by members of the society's very highest class?

One possible answer lies in the personality of 'Itia, whom many Europeans characterized as 'imperious', to say the least. Another may be sought in the cultural context of the ship: the Pomares may have reasoned that Tahitian rules prevailed only in Tahitian settings, and *Providence* was an alien, English, setting where such rules need not apply.

Wednesday, April 18th

Westerly Winds all the Morning and dark Cloudy Weather at Night Calms and smart Rain favorable to my Plants. Thermometer from 81 to 77 degrees.

Employd Caulking the Starboard Bends & in restowing the Main hold.

About 30 Cannoes were about the Ship today, which I consider a very small number when compared to the Multitude of People I have been accustomed to. We have very sufficient supplies of Hogs, Fruit and Tarro. I have only seen 3 She Goats, which I bought for my Sea Stores.

Otoo sent me a handsome present of Hogs and Fruit, and gave others to the Officers at the post.

This day we completed 83 Pots with Plants. The Weather is very favorable, and I have got every duty going on <every duty goes> with *regularity. It is always <takes> some time before this can be effected, coming <when we arrive> among Indians; but <it is> a material point to be gained. Mr. Smith & Mr. Whiles the Gardeners ['Mr. Smith & Mr. Whiles' crossed out in ML] have every assistance, some of their Men [i.e., Tahitians] were employed by me in my last Voyage, which is of considerable advantage to them.*

A fine Child about 12 Months old was brought to me today <it is> a Daughter of George Stewart Midshipman of the Bounty. [marginal note: 'Its Mother is the Woman that Stewart always kept on board the Bounty.'] It was a very pretty creature, but had been so exposed to the Sun as to be be very little fairer than an Otaheitean.

Tynah with his Friends still remain at Oparre, debating on their capability to carry on the War.

From the most authentick account I can get, I find the Otaheiteans have got from different Ships, Musquets etc as follows:

	Musquets	Pistols
Belonging to Oparre—	8	5
At Oaitepeha [Vaitepiha]	5	5
At Iteeah [Hitia'a]	1	0
Attahooroo [Atehuru]	0	5
Matavai	5	0
Paparrah [Papara]	8	6
. . . [?] One Swivel		
Total	27	21

The 'Multitude of People' referred to in Bligh's third paragraph must have been those that thronged around the *Bounty*; so far during the present visit the numbers had been fewer, owing to the absence of the Matavians.

George Stewart, Midshipman, the father of the 'very pretty' little girl whose mother introduced her to Bligh, was killed during the wreck of the *Pandora*, aged about twenty-three.

Bligh's listing of the forty-eight firearms known to be in the hands of Tahitians may appear to be an exercise in triviality, but to the island's leaders it represented a situation fraught with deadly political possibilities and risks. For, as matters then stood, against the Pomares' eight musquets and five pistols were forty other firearms in hands of their opponents, whether outright foes or unreliable 'friends'.

Lieutenant Portlock on this day had nothing of interest to report beyond the usual shipboard routine, but Tobin, in his serendipitous manner, continued to see and report on the native scene:

Visiting the Post this morning, my messmates seemed comfortably settled, except being dreadfully tormented by flies which are very numerous at the Island. I did not hear of any mosquitos, which is rather singular in a tropical country.

The Botanists were busily employed in bringing in plants and forming a little garden. Young Otoo was about the post all day, but never dismounted his towtows shoulders, who alternately relieved each other of their princely burthen. Pearce has given him a scarlet jacket, of which he was not a little vain, making him in return a present of some cloth, fruit, and a hog. His young majesty without much ceremony asked for everything that particularly pleased him, and had all his requests been complied with, some of us would have been left Sans Cullottes. Of his privileges he seemed to an inconvenience tenacious; it rained heavily the major part of the day, yet he did not condescend to enter any habitation, taking shelter under the umbrage of a bread fruit tree; and we were informed that, he never on any account entered any house but his own. He had the happy facility of pronouncing many English words, particularly those expressive of his wants.

In the young Kings retinue was a native of a colour disgustingly white. Similar instances have been met with in many Indian [South Sea ?] countries. He was of a weak frame of body, and by no measure equal to his countrymen in figure. The O'tahyteans have dark penetrating hazel eyes, but those of this poor wretch, who seemed to have been ushered into the world imperfect, were of a light grey colour, and so weak that it was with difficulty he kept them open. His hair and eyebrows, though equally strong with the other natives, were of a white flaxen colour. His skin was sorely blistered by the sun which encouraged the flies to incessantly torment him. The sight of this man perplexed our seamen considerably, nor was it without much perswasion they were convinced he was not a European settled on the Island.

Strolling not an hundred yards from the Post the Matavai river came suddenly on my view, on the banks of which clear and beautiful stream, the bread fruit, Cocoa nut and avee [vi, Tahitian 'mango'] were growing in the most luxuriant state; amid which, it was mortifying to see most of the houses deserted, and many totally destroyed by the war. In crossing the river, which was on the shoulders of a native, there was a friendly conflict among them for this post of kindness and attention. To have refrained from dispersing the few beads (poeys) in my pockets, among this more than willing group, would have argued a heart callous to every grateful sensation.

Thursday, April 19th

During the fore noon the Wind was steady from the ESE, but the remaining part variable with Calms, and the whole day so Cloudy as made the Air Cool and pleasant. The Thermometer from 76 to 77 Degrees.

Employed <in> Caulking the Starboard Bends. Airing Sails. Salting Pork and Cleaning Ship.

This Day we filled 149 Pots with Plants, the Weather very favourable for the Work.

We have a great abundance of Fruit & Roots, but no Hogs to day.

In the evening Tynah & his Wives returned from Oparre, they brought with them a Hog and a quantity of dressed Breadfruit as a present to me. As they remained on board, I was obliged as usual to give <up> the Cabin to them, where three Men Servants, their King & his Wives, after eating a hearty Supper, slept upon the same floor, & by the side of each other.

It surprised me to find, that both Iddeah & Tynah were called Pomarre, & on enquiring into the Cause of it, I find it owing to their having lost their Eldest Daughter Terreenaoreah of <by> an Illness called by that name, <and> which they describe to me by coughing. [marginal note: 'Pomarre is compounded from Po Night & Marre the name of the Disease.'] Whenever a Child dies the Parents or relations take the Name of the disease—if a dozen Children die of different diseases, the Parents have as many different Names, (or give them to their Relations) and may be called by either, but commonly by the last. It is common to all Ranks of People.

Among a Number of Plants which I have brought here from England, the Cape of Good Hope & New Holland, consisting of Oranges, Pines, Guavas, Pomergranates, Quinces, Figs, Vines, Firs, Metrocedera and Aloes. The Natives only have a desire for the three last, the Firs & Metrocedera because I assured them they would grow to very large Trees, & were fit for building Ships; and the Aloes on account of <its> being a very fine Flower. No Value is set upon any of our Garden productions, <and> it is really taking trouble to no purpose to bring them anything that requires care to get it to perfection. A fine Shaddock Tree I saw Yesterday very nearly destroyed by Fire, and the Fruit of it they told me was good for nothing. Some Trees in the Country as I have remarked in my last Voyage bore Fruit, & a few very fine ones were brought to me in the Evening from the same place. This is just the time for them to be ripe, or in the course of this Month or next.

Bligh's 'surprise' about the name 'Pomare' reflects the circumstance that Tahitians' ways of naming persons can drive the historian, especially the genealogist, to despair; once unraveled, however, such names can provide useful insights into social structure in general, into the histories of particular dynasties, and into the lives of individuals. We have already touched on the crucial distinction between personal names and kin-Titles—but should add here that in some cases (such as that of 'Pomare') the former eventually became the latter. Even with such mutations however, once established (i.e., for a particular set of rights and duties) a kin-Title tended to endure through several generations of incumbents. In contrast, an individual's personal names were frequently replaced or added to, as Bligh had described in his *Bounty* Journal:

The People here as well as in England have several Names, and being differently used, it is frequently perplexing when the same person is spoke of, to know who is meant. Every Cheif has perhaps a dozen Names in the course of 30 Years, so the Man or Woman that has been spoken of by one Navigator under a particular name, will not be known by another, unless other causes lead to a Discovery. (Bligh 1937: I 384)

As in the case of 'Pomare', most changes, or additions, of personal names were made to commemorate unusual events. Thus, the man who was chief of the Papara District during Cook's visits was then known as 'Winker' ('Amo) because of his infant son's habit of winking. Bligh's *Providence* Journal entry of June 6th contains more on this subject.

Bligh's effort to introduce new kinds of 'useful' plants to Tahiti was just one more chapter in a series of failed noble experiments (which attempted to introduce some domestic animals as well, including the three goats mentioned in a previous entry). It was only after decades of European visits and residence that Tahitians began to use and nurture some of the alien species—or to deplore the introduction of others, such as guavas and goats.

During the morning of this day, Portlock supervised the moving of the *Assistant* to a position nearer shore, and during the afternoon he went on shore:

I *accompanied Captain Bligh in shore to the Post were we found Everything in Good order we Crossd the River and in our walk about the District of Matavia we saw one well grown Shaddock tree and Several Pumpkin Vines, our walk although through a most beautiful country did not afford much pleasure, as the district was Intirely deserted in consequence of the war the appearance of Numbers of uninhabiatated [sic] houses together with the Ruins of others and the Silence of What we usd in former times to Esteem the merry and happy district of Matavia could not avoid giving serious reflections and Pain for the fate of these poor people with whom we were once so happy, I am sure Captain feels accordingly for them and takes every step in his power to reconcile the Parties in which benevolent act I hope most Earnestly he may succeed.—About 6 in the Evening we returned onboard the Providence where we found the King his Wifes and Attendants, they had brought some presents for Captain Bligh and took their lodgings up onboard for the Night.*

Both Bligh and Portlock reported the presence of Tina *et al.* on board but refrained, due to circumspection or otherwise, from going into details—for which, again, we turn to Tobin:

Numbers of Chiefs came on board early in the morning, their Towtows bringing a quantity of Yava root ['ava] for their recreation . . . Edeea drank nearly a pint of this deleterious beverage, but it seemed that the effect, and not the pleasure while drinking it was alone cultivated, as no child ever evinced more disgust at a dose of rhubarb than her majesty and the whole party did as it passed their lips. It soon spreads its baneful influence on the human frame. In ten minutes my Tayo [i.e., 'Itia], scarcely able to support herself, begged permission to recline her tottering limbs on a bed, which was no sooner reached, than she unavoidably sunk into a profound sleep for several hours. Another of their courtly party came reeling into the Ward Room with all the symptoms of epilepsy or affection of St Vitus's dance; this man was also found necessary to support to another couch. Yet so violent is the attachment of these people to Yava that, it is among the few plants cultivated in the lower grounds, and however averse the O'tahytean is to exertion, he thinks his labour well repaid by bringing from the distant mountain this pernicious root, where it grows in abundance. Like many other opiates, it is succeeded

Plate 9   Point Venus, with distant view of shoreside Post
Watercolor by George Tobin

Plate 10   Point Venus, with close-up view of shoreside Post
Watercolor by George Tobin

by the most enervating effects to the whole body, and when taken to excess affects the skin with a rough scaly appearance.

Guthrie and myself, however disgusting the preparation, were willing to follow the example of our visitors. About half an hour after taking a large tea cup full, which was but a moderate dose, its narcotic effects were very perceptible, a pleasurable giddiness succeeding, which soon terminated in an undisturbed sleep of about three hours. The small quantity taken, was probably the reason why I suffered but little after awaking, a slight uneasiness over the temples, which subsided in about an hour, only taking place; but so sweet is the sleep promoted by Yava, that were it now within reach of your friend, it would be sought with avidity, even with the certainty of a subsequent head ache, or shattered frame, sometimes experienced by taking too copiously of Yava no Pretaney (English Yava).

My messmate experienced similar effects with myself. It is not within my recollection whether the Yava plant was taken on board the Providence at Otahytey, but it certainly never reached the West Indies. The root from its powerful nature might probably be of use in medicine.

Bligh described the preparation of the beverage in his *Bounty* Journal:

. . . the operation of making ['ava] is as filthy as the Use of it is punicious.

This Ava is made from a Strong pungent Root which few Cheifs ever go without, it is chewed by their Servants in large mouthfulls at a time, which when it has collected a sufficiency of Saliva is taken and put into a Cocoa Nut Shell. This is repeated until there is enough chewed, it is then squeezed and given to the principall Men, each of them taking nearly a pint wine measure. What remains is mixt with water and again squeezed and Strained, it is then delivered to the inferior Cheifs, or those of the highest class if they prefer it diluted, and it frequently undergoes a second and third mixture if there is not enough to supply everyone. (Bligh 1937: I 382)

Tobin's description of the preparation and consumption of 'ava differs somewhat from Bligh's:

The root, fresh from the ground, the earth not being washed off, is first masticated by the Towtows for about two hours, The juice expressed from it, being discharged by the mouth into a wooden tray—at this time it becomes of a consistence similar to the cud of an oxe, the remains of the root being with it. Milk from the Cocoa nut is now added, and well beat up together. There yet remains to eradicate the coarse and stringy parts, which is effected by rincing a bunch of grass which collects it, leaving the Yava a liquid of the colour of muddy water. It is now portioned into Cocoa nut shells for drinking, and no sooner swallowed than every one eats immoderately of bread fruit, plantains, or Mahee [mahi], a preparation of the first [i.e., bread-fruit] by fermentation.

Friday, April 20th

Calms with light Easterly Breezes. Thermometer from 78 to 81 Degrees.
Employed <in> Caulking the Starboard Bends. Salting Hogs. Unbending Sails, Washing Ship, and Clearing Hawse.
Moderate Supplies of Hogs Breadfruit, Cocoa Nutts and Plantains, but as much as we are in need of.

Everything is now going on well at our Post, and the Natives behave in a very orderly and good natured manner. I have now my Shed for the Plants completed, and the Botanists <Gardeners> accustomed to the Work. 111 Pots of Plants were Potted to Day.

I had another Visit from the Young King, and made some presents to him. I could do nothing to <not> induce him to come on board, or to get off his Man's Shoulders, where he rides as easy as any of us would do upon a Horse. About 20 or 30 Young Men attended <attend> him, and he shifts from one to the other without the least inconvenience as they become tired. I cannot get Tynah, or any one to tell me the exact time when he will be permitted to Walk (any other way) <otherwise> than by saying, when he is a Man. At Home he runs about as other Boys.

It is about the same time that Tynah will perform the Ceremony of Oammo or Oammoah to all his Children, and become free to feed himself. I have given an account of this Ceremony in my last Voyage Page 271 which I cannot improve.

Whatever Men were taken in their Wars, are killed. They share the same Fate with those who fall in the Battle, and remain on the Field. Their Eyes are taken out—one is presented to their God Oro, and the other to the Erreeahigh, and the Man is then put into a Grave and buried. In presenting the Eye to the King it is put on a leaf, and the person who presents it, on being near him calls aloud Hammamah my [hamama mai, gape or yawn towards here]. The King then Gapes wide, and the Ceremony ends. He does not even touch the Eye, much less to eat <eat it>, or smell to <of> it.

Hammamah signifies to Gape, we may turn the Phrase therefore to Threaten to Devour—or Gape to me.

The Men belonging to the Matilda who have lived at Oparre, brought me word, that they had seen a White Man at times who would not speak English to them, but had spoken at one time to a Boy of theirs, and therefore they suspected he might be one of the Bountys People. They asserted also, that he had been attempting to disfigure himself by tying a String around his head across his Nose to flatten it. They told me the Story clear <clearly> and distinct <distinctly>. The Oparre People denied the fact. All our friends there, declared there was no such Person, and I was beginning to suspect their fidelity, when Iddeah said 'perhaps they mean Taow [Taoro?]'. The affair was now unravelld, and like a Sailors Story, there was not a word of Truth in it—for the Person was an Otaheitean, but one of those Lapses of Nature, it is not possible to account for <for which it is not possible to account>—his Skin and hair being <are> White; & <he> is the same person I have spoken of in my last Voyage. Strange it is <to me> that these Seamen <people> were not content in <with> representing the case to me as the appearance of the Man had impressed <it> on their Minds; but they would willfully add <without adding> to it, that he had conversed with the Boy.

*Such is the determined desire of most Seamen to tell unbounded falsehoods, that I
fear their fancy often misleads them in cases of the most serious consequence. [Note:
This last sentence is crossed out in ML.]*

The particular 'ceremony of Oammo' that Bligh refers to here was
probably the *fa'atoira'a*, Coming-of-Age. The earliest recorded description
of this ceremony is that of the English missionary, John Orsmond, who
resided in these islands from 1817 to 1856, and whose copious notes on
Tahitian culture were assembled and 'edited' by his granddaughter, Teuira
Henry:

When the young heir apparent became of age a feast, called the *fa'atoira'a*
(becoming-of-age), was given at which he or she for the first time appeared officially
among the dignitaries of the land. On this occasion was offered a human sacrifice
called the *amo'a-tapu* (putting aside of restriction). For the firstborn of under chiefs
there was also a *fa'atoira'a*, and their *amo'a-tapu* consisted of a fine hog offered at
the local marae of their district.
    As the Tahitians had no method for recording the years, coming of age
depended upon the maturing of the child. (Henry 1928: 188)

It is not reported when this ceremony took place on behalf of the 'heir apparent' Tu, but it may have been in 1797, when he was fifteen, and when his
father sponsored a very large feast at Papara, which was attended by leaders
from all of the island, and which included human sacrifice. (And after which
the younger Pomare began more actively and overtly to wrest secular authority from his father.) Clearly, the criteria for 'maturing' in such cases had as
much to do with politics as with physical maturation.
    Bligh's observations about human sacrifice are treated much more
fully in his entry of April 28th. As for the fate of men killed and captured in
battle, his summary of the matter is accurate only up to a point. In fact, when
fatalities were numerous the victors usually subjected only the bodies of the
enemy's leaders and famous warriors (*aito*) to sacrifice; the rest of the enemy
slain were left on the battlefield, after their conquerors had hacked them to
pieces and collected their skulls or lower jawbones as trophies. As for living
captives, there were seldom any except those too disabled to flee, and most
of those were killed on the spot. Of the few left alive, they were indeed
usually sacrificed—the more prominent ones at the time; the others on later
occasions, when need for sacrificial victims arose.
    Tobin's entry for this day records a visit to the *Providence* of some
'Chiefs' from Mo'orea (where, it will be recalled, Tina had several relatives
and other allies):

*Several Chiefs from Moorea visited the ship, Pomaurey being very assiduous in pointing out
her different parts. Although a dull man, he gained much in our esteem by his uncommon good
nature. I again met him at Captain Blighs table, where Edeea and Whhyereddy joined the party*

and eat in his presence, notwithstanding a forbearance of it was strictly observed on shore. His younger wife shared the honour of his bed on board.

Tobin's account of this day's events also notes the presence on board of several girls, who collected on the quarter deck ('as usual') to perform the heiva, a dance that is described in Bligh's entry for April 23rd and my accompanying comments.

To top off the events of this day, a remark by Portlock serves as a reminder that even paradisical Tahiti had its serpent, namely, that 'colic' can strike anywhere:

Several of the Ships company according to the surgeons report very much Gript and panged [purged?] he thinks it owing the fresh provisions and fruit which we get in Abundance.

Saturday, April 21st

Strong Sea Breezes in the Day at ESE and much Swell on the Dolphin Bank. During the Night Light Winds off the Land from the SSE. Thermometer 80 to 81 Degrees.

Number of Plants Potted 196. I mean so many Potts were filled, many of which had two Plants in them.

Employed Caulking the Starboard Side, Cleaning Ship, and Mending Cloaths. Very few Canoes off to us.—but we have nevertheless sufficient supplies.

Tynah, as usual, is generally on board with me. No Strangers have been yet to see us, and we are remarkably quiet and free from bustle, both here and at the post. Our Plants are taken up very advantageously, from the Soil being Moist and adhering to the fine fibrous Roots, and I have every thing going on <every thing goes on as well> as I could possibly wish.

[Marginal note: 'Total Pots, 571']

Despite Bligh's official report that 'everything goes on as well as I could possibly wish', Portlock, who accompanied him onshore, recorded the Captain's 'recommendation'—command?—regarding desirable improvements:

Captain Bligh in seeing that the plants were taken up rather too late in the day, recommended it to the Botanists to be on the spot for gathering by dawn of day in the Mornings by which means the Plants might be gatherd and brought in before the heat of the day came on, he also recommended it to them to be exceedingly particular in procuring the different kinds of bread fruit plants as there is a great variety of them and some kinds grow much larger and finer than others, they adopted this plan.

Sunday, April 22nd

Moderate Sea Breezes at ESE and Land Winds at SSE in the Night. Calm in the

Morning and hot untill the Sea Breezes set in about 10 OClock. Thermometer from 79 to 81 Degrees. Completed 166 Pots with Plants.

Cleaned Ship and Mustered the Ships Company. Performed Divine Service. Gave leave to Six Men at a time to go on Shore. I find the Venereal disease is still common, one of our Men at the Post having Complained of being infected.

Very few Natives about us, but we have very sufficient Supplies. Some Shaddocks were sent to me, they were very large, and of a fine sort, but not sufficiently ripe. They were brought about 4 Miles out of the Country near Pearoah, where Mr Nelson Planted three Trees, that are now loaded with Fruit. The Natives do not value them.

Mr. Portlock picked up a lump of lava to day near the Post which had every mark <appearance> of being thrown up from a Volcano. I made several enquiries among the Chiefs about it, who assured me it came out of one of their Ovens, where, by the heat of the Fire the Stones frequently take that change. Sir Wm. Hamilton says that the materials of Lava are common matters to be found every where in the Earth (Viz) Stones, metallic ores, Clay, Sand &c. and that the hottest furnaces would not by any means be able to bring them into any degree of fusion, since the materials of Glass cannot be melted without a great quantity of fusible Salts, such as alkalies, nitre &c. mixed along with them. I found it would attract the Magnetic Needle.

Tahiti's 'shaddocks' were very familiar to Bligh, and evidently much on his mind. These large grapefruit-like citrus fruits (*Citrus decumana*), which grow on small trees, are native to tropical Asia. Cook collected some plants on Tonga in 1777 (the expedition which Bligh accompanied), and had his gardener, David Nelson (of Kew Gardens background), transplant them in Tahiti, for the benefit of the Tahitians and of visiting Europeans. Unlike most of the other food plants introduced by Cook, a few of these shaddock trees survived, largely through the care given them by the faithful Anglophile mentioned by Tobin in his Journal entry for this day (see below). Nelson, who was also Bligh's principal gardener on the *Bounty*, saw the trees in a flourishing state in 1788, and Tobin again on this day, during an excursion that will be presently described.

Bligh's reasoning concerning the 'lump of lava' was of course correct; Tahiti and all the other high islands of this archipelago were of volcanic origin—a suggestion recorded by Joseph Banks in his *Endeavour* Journal (Beaglehole 1962: I 308), which Bligh had probably either read, or learned about in his conversations with Banks.

Sunday being 'liberty day' for those not needed for household or other duties, Tobin set out with three of his quarter-deck mates (Edward Harwood, surgeon; Richard Franklin, midshipman; and James Norris, surgeon of the *Matilda*) to attempt to follow the Matavai River to its source. I reproduce in full his account of the excursion, along with one of the watercolors of the scenery he subsequently painted, this having been the only exploratory episode that took place during the *Providence's* single-minded, bread-fruit focussed visit to Tahiti. Tobin and his friends were not, however, the first Europeans to explore the course of the Matavai; in 1769 Joseph Banks and another member of Cook's *Endeavour* expedition had gone upstream just as far. (Beaglehole 1962: I 306–8) Tobin's lack of mention of that earlier excursion suggests that he had not read Bank's Journal.

Tobin's account confirms what is now generally believed to have been the geographic extent of native habitations on Tahiti. Except for a few of them in the larger, level-floored valleys, such as Papeno'o, most households were located within about four miles from the coast, and mainly in the adlittoral plain—i.e., the most extensive part of the coastal plain, which extends from the littoral to the bottom of the mountain slopes and into the lower reaches of the valleys. Remains of stone structures have also been found along the water's edge and a few on hillsides and plateaus outside the adlittoral zone; but most of those belonged to non-residential structures: temples, council platforms, archery platforms, and fortresses, most of which were purposely distant from residences. This is not to say that Tahitians did not venture farther inland (as Tobin's account may seem to suggest). That they did so on occasion was described by the *Bounty* crew member, James Morrison, who was on Tahiti for about twenty-three months, including eighteen spent living nativestyle ashore:

When they Go into the Mountains, which they often do in Companys to Cut Timber, Gather Herbs & sandal wood for their Oil, Cut rafters for their Houses, Paddles for Canoes, &c. and for the Purpose of dying Cloth [bark cloth] which takes them up several days, they subsist themselves on Birds, fish &c. Using the Mountain Plantain and Wild Roots for Bread, the land producing plenty of Birds and the Springs plenty of fish . . . (Rutter 1935: 217)

And now for Tobin's adventurous day:

Having made a party in the hope of reaching the source of the Matavai, we left the Post at early dawn. Its direction for a short distance was parallel with the beach, then from the East about a quarter of a mile, when it again took a northern course from the mountains.

About a mile and a half from the Post, after passing the low land which in most parts girts the Island, we entered a valley about half a mile across the hills rising gently on each side richly clothed above half way to their summits, with bread fruit, cocoa nut, Avees [vi; Spondias dulcis, native 'mango'], Eratta (a large kind of chestnut) [i.e., rata, also mape; Inocarpus edulis, Tahitian 'chestnut'] and many other trees whose names were unknown to us. The soil was here very rich. We passed many houses, but in general they were injured and deserted in consequence of the war. The valley however was not destitute of people, and, as is

*ever the case with the european traveller at this Island, our party increased as we went along.
[Plate 11]*

Advancing up the stream bread fruit and cocoa nuts became scarce, and the valley more confined. After walking about three miles, having crossed the river several times on the natives shoulders, we came to some inhabited houses, contiguous to which was an offering to the Eotooa *[atua] (or God) on account of the war. The oblation consisted of twelve hogs placed on four stools, three on each, about five feet from the ground. Near them was a square pavement of about twelve feet, and one high, with twenty long stones standing upright on it, ornaments at thier tops, about two feet high, with the common bonnet (Tawmowtow) [taumi upo'o?] worn by the women. Ignorance of the language denied our getting any information, but that everything was sacred to* Eotooa, *and that the offering was for his protection in the war. The hogs were in a dreadful putrid state, giving the air of this part of the valley by no means a fragrance. A little higher up, three very fine shaddock trees attracted our notice, two of them teeming with fruit. The natives estimate this fruit but lightly, though they call it* Ooroo no pretaney *[uru no Peritani, bread fruit of Britain]. They were brought from the Friendly Islands.*

These trees were planted in 1777 by the late Mr. Nelson, who was with Captain Cook in his last voyage. An old man whose habitation received shade from them spoke with affection and the warmest gratitude of our countryman, and with unfeigned sorrow lamented his death when informed of it. Here, we sufficiently understood one anothers language; little indeed was there to explain—Nelson died at Timor in 1789. The country soon became more wild and picturesque. In many places the current being impeded by huge rocks, where it did find a passage, was very rapid. Bread fruit and cocoa nuts were no more to be seen, but there were plantains the whole of our walk, and the soil, where free from rocks, productive. On either side many beautiful cataracts from a great height suddenly caught the eye, yet not without a warning as we approached, by their roar in forcing a passage among the woody cliffs to the stream below. At this distance no more habitations were observed. [Marginal note: 'not of Areoyes'—i.e., not even sheds constructed by members of the Arioi sect, who used to retire to the wilderness for riotious 'vacations'.]

Our guides now became urgent for returning, but 'though every foot became more difficult, we were not willing to leave undetermined the object of our pursuit; another inducement also, the hope of reaching a cascade called Peeir, by the natives, made us journey on. Extending our rugged walk about two miles we were indeed rewarded for our labour. It is formed by a perpendicular basaltic rock of above an hundred feet, extending at its base, on the right bank of the river, more than two hundred. The margin above projects a few feet, the water falling in a broad sheet without meeting resistance until it reaches some detached rocks, whence by several channels a still deep pool receives it. The pillars are closely connected, but in many parts broken. Similar rocks were observed in the course of our walk. The Drawing of the Peeir was from recollection on returning to the Post, perhaps the pillars may not be critically correct, but the general appearance is all that is attempted. The weather had been dry for some days previously to our excursion up the Matavai; doubtless after the rain the fall acquired an additional degree of beauty and grandeur.

Above the Pe-eir the river became very confined. In some places it was a clear deep pool, while in others it rushed amid the rocks with great force and rapidity. Our Island friends

*had by this time quitted us in numbers, being reduced to about a third of the party gleaned in
the valley. The day advanced so fast, we were under the necessity of returning, much chagrined
at not having reached the source. A rock in the midstream served as a resting place, where we
sat down to refresh ourselves with Cocoa nut milk, of which fruit some had been brought from
the lower grounds. There could not be a more delightfully retired spot. Every surrounding object
disposed the mind to quiet contemplation. On the one side a lofty mountain richly clothed with
various trees to the summit, whose branches nearly reaching a stupendous bald cliff opposed
to it, overhanging the river full of threats, scarcely allowed a glimpse of the blue canopy of
heaven; yet through the playful foliage was a faint view of the purpled summit of the Isle (Otoos
Horns) far above the fleeting clouds along its side. The Tropic bird, the Sheerwater, and other
sea fowl, as if weary of their watry element, were ranging high in the air above these craggy
steps, in whose recesses they rear their young. Here no animal, no reptile with envenomed fang,
as in most tropical countries, is to be found checking the ardent researches of the traveller. Not
even the soaring rapacious kite, the trembling dread of the smaller feathered tribe was here ever
seen.*

*From so interesting a spot, it was not that we returned to the boisterous scenes of
nautic employment without reluctance. It was night ere we reached our encampment, not a little
fatigued, yet highly gratified with the excursion.*

*In many parts of the river the natives were procuring small fish by making a dam
across it with stones where it was shallow. To this dam the fish were driven by people coming
down the stream and beating it with bushes, interstices being made [presumably, in the dam]
to which baskets were applied. It is hardly credible what numbers are taken in this simple way.
Others were caught near the bottom by introducing a small 'landing net' under them.*

Tobin's description of the place—the temple—where the offerings
of hogs were displayed, is better postponed to a discussion of Bligh's journal
entry of April 26th, which contains remarks about temples in general. And
Tobin's remarks about the absence in Tahiti of reptiles 'with envenomed
fangs' and of 'the soaring rapacious kite' (i.e., hawks) were correct—but not
of course based on his own researches.

Portlock's entry for this day adds that the natives who accompanied
Tobin *et al.* were Matavians, who:

*. . . expressd much happiness on the meeting with their friends of Bretania, behavd in the
most friendly manner Imaginable and lamented much that the present troubles prevented them
from being nearer to the ships. They walked part of the way to Matavia with these gentlemen
but could not be prevaild on to Enter the Post for fear of their enemies the people of Oparre,
they took a friendly leave retired to their places of security . . .*

Portlock also describes another encounter with Tu, this time at the Post. Tu
was

*. . . much pleasd to see us, he appeard (notwithstanding his scruples the other day in receiving
presents with his own hands) fond of [. . . (illegible) . . .] searching the pockets for knives.
His father with most of the other chiefs are at Oppare. Otoo remaind with us a few hours was
highly pleasd with the treatment he receivd and returnd to Oparre in high spirits.*

During this visit to the shore Post with Bligh, a nearly daily occurence, the two of them

. . . made a short Excursion up the Valey of Matavia w[h]ere we saw several Opparre familys building houses on the spots w[h]ere houses in war had been pulld to pieces or burnt [a rather unusual practice; war victors seldom occupied permanently the lands of their victims] . . . in this short walk we saw a Number of fine breadfruit and Ava or Apple trees [vi] quite destroyd by being Notched all round the trunck, this practice we found was adopted by the Oppare people to destroy the Matavians and I suppose is the general practice between parties at war.

Monday, April 23rd

During the Day from 10 OClock fresh Sea Breezes at E b S the Night and Morning. Light Land Winds and Calms. Thermometer from 79 to 84 Degrees. Wind ENE at Noon but at Sea about East.

Employed Caulking the Starboard Side. Salting Pork and Tradeing <Trading> with the Natives. Plentiful Supplies. «Condemned per Survey 1593 lbs of Bread.» I took a Walk to day over the greatest part of our Neighborhood <which> I found «it» altered very much for the worse, occasioned by <in consequence of> the late War, few Houses remained; and all those places that swarmed with Inhabitants had scarce <scarcely> an Individual to account for the calamity. At this time Peace is said to be established; but the Matavai Chiefs do not wish to send to me either the Money or Arms, and therefore keep in the Mountains; notwithstanding they send to me fair promises that the Money shall be returned. On this account we have but few Natives about us, only the Oparre People Visit us.

Otoo again paid us a Visit at the Post where a Heiva was performed by one Woman and four Men in their common Interlude Stile. In the Cool of the Evening our Marines exercised, and the Natives were exceedingly delighted, particularly with the Sergeant who played so many tricks with his Musquet, that they said he was Mad.

Tynah with his Wives, Father and Brothers dine with me every Day. A Canoe with a Party came over from Moreah to see the Ship, these were some Friends of Whyerreddee for whom Tynah had recourse to my lockers, to satisfy <them> with presents. Tynah is a perfect Fool to this Woman. She rules him as she pleases, while Iddeeah quietly submits, and is contented with a moderate share of influence. Since I sailed in the Bounty, Tynah has had another Child (a Boy called Oroho) by Iddeeah—by Whyeereddee he has none. His children now, are,

Otoo—Errerahigh [Tu, Ari'i Rahi]
Terreetapanooai his Brother [Teri'i Tapanuai]
Tahanydooah his Sister (see 28th May) [Tahanitua]
Oroho his Brother
Huheine [Vahine] Moyere, the Wife of Oreepyah, arrived to Day from the district

of Itteah [Hitia'a] where she had been at the Burial of her Father and Brother. To my surprise <I found> she would touch no victuals, but what was put to her Mouth by the hands of another person. I have accounted for this in my last Voyage in one instance, and now I find from Tynah that the loss of relations is another cause of not feeding themselves <cause of being fed>. It is a degree of mourning that lasts three Months.

It is extraordinary to see how fond our Friends here are of Liquor. They speak of Brandy and Strong Spirits with delight, and are Mad to get as much as will render them stupid. I have done all in my power to prevent them. With me they are orderly and contented with their Wine, but wherever they can get it about the Ship they are sure to get drunk.

<Whydooah humorusly calls Rum, Avah Tyo ['ava tai'o], or friendly draught. He says altho he has lost the use of his legs by drinking it, he had always the use of his tongue; whereas the Otaheite Avah took away the use of both.>

Completed 80 Pots to Day with Plants.

In listing the currently living offspring of Tina and 'Itia, Bligh was building on information gained during the *Bounty* visit:

As it requires much attention and care to get a real knowledge of any thing from these people, I have ever since I have been here, been particularly anxious to know for a certainty, the situation of Tynah, and how many Children he has; with respect to the first he is certainly Erreerahigh of all the Island, but as he is only Regent during the Minority of his son Otoo, his Regal power will end at that time. In regard to the last, a perplexity arose I could not for some time unravel. On asking Tynah how many he had, he said five, this astonished me and his Wife and some others confirmd the report, altho universally I had never heard of but four before. The fifth Child I therefore asked the Name of, they said it had no name for it was killed, showing that they twisted its Neck as soon as it came from its Mother. As this is a matter which I never heard of before, I became more particular in the investigation of the truth of it, and it was confirmed to me in every respect that the first born child was killed. Now I could not find out, if in the case it had been a Boy, instead of a Girl which it was, whether or not the Boy would have received the same fate. I cannot speak of this with certainty, but the Answer I got respecting it was, that the Boy would not have been killed & yet they all agreed that the first born, or Moah [mua, in front of, first] as they called it, was always destroyed. (Bligh 1937: I 387)

And two days later:

Oreepyah unravelled to me the account I have given on the 6th respecting the first born Child of Tynahs being killed. His account to me was, that when Tynah married Iddeah, he was an Eree-oy [Arioi] and continued so untill nearly the Birth of his second Child, but before that took place he renounced the Society among whom is that horrid and detestable crime of killing their Children, and of course was the cause of Tynahs destroying his. (Bligh 1937: I 389)

And still later:

I do not often speak of Otoo, for his being a Child and kept out of our way we have of course no intercourse with him. I however see him perhaps once a Week and the other Children, but we never come nearer each other than 30 or 50 yards. At those times I carry them some little present and by this Means they are always rejoiced to see me. The River separates their dwelling from the part we are at, and it would be considered as a great violation were we to cross it near their dwelling. There are two Brothers and two Sisters but they do not eat or sleep under the same Roof. On that account the Girls have a House about ¼ of a Mile from their Brothers. Each of them are situated on the side of a pretty River which has its source out of a Rock on the side of the Hill near Otoo's House. The Parents sleep every night at the Girls House, but are mostly absent from them in the day. The Childrens names are Otoo, about 6 years Old, Tereenah-owah, about 4, Terreetapa nooai, a Boy between 2 and 3 years Old, and an Infant Girl about a twelve month, Tahamydooah. There was a Child before Otoo but it was killed as the Mother was delivered of it, Tynah at that time being an Erreeoy.
    Two Children of Tynahs sister by a Man called Modaurro live with the others and have similar marks of Attention & respect paid to them. (Bligh 1937: II 56)

Of the four offspring of Tina and 'Itia alive in 1789, one—the girl 'Tareenah-owah' [Teri'inavahoroa ?]—had evidently died, and the boy born after *Bounty*'s departure, 'Oroho', was perhaps given her name (or kin-Title?). Concerning the un-named firstborn, the girl killed at birth, the cause of that killing—because her father 'was an Eree-oy'—invites attention.
    'Arioi' (Bligh's 'Eree-oy') were a focus of Europeans' interest—and puzzlement, and misinterpretation—from Cook and Banks onwards well into the nineteenth century (when missionaries succeeded in bringing on the demise of the sect). Georg Forster described them as a society of warriors (1777: II 128 ff); Cook and Anderson, as young libertines 'of the better sort', and likened them to Freemasons (Beaglehole 1961: 415; Cook 1784: 157); James Morrison, as a 'set of young Men of Wild, Amorous & Volatile disposition, who from their Infancy devote the youthful part of their lives to Roving, Pleasure & Debauchery' (Rutter 1935: 234)—and the missionary John Orsmond, as 'Players . . . the most obsessed and wicked creatures conceivable'. (Orsmond n.d.: *Arioi*) Bligh's first direct encounter with them was in 1788, when he witnessed Tina making a ceremonial gift of food to a visiting party of them. After that occasion he wrote that 'the Eree-oys were people highly respected' and that 'great trust and confidence reposed in them'. (Bligh 1937: I 383) Bligh had had other encounters with Arioi during his *Bounty* sojourn; based on those and on his verbal inquiries he concluded that they were a 'Society', which he described as follows:

This Society was certainly in the beginning formed under a View of Celibacy through fear of too great a population, the establishment therefore for the good of the Country, whereby the Members were deprived of the pleasure of having Children, had great honor, and the other part of the community granted them peculiar privileges. But as a security to the grand object which unhappily they only kept in view, it appears they fixed as a guard to it, that should any of the members transgress and break through the law and produce Issue, such Issue should instantly be Strangled on being born. Hence what was intended to preserve Celibacy without blemish proves the source of constant transgression, and as Custom or Religion did not prove to them a Crime what equally secured to them the object of the Institution, and prevented the Evil they so much feared, the Society of the Erreeoys has become disgraceful to human Nature, altho it may be said to have been founded in wisdom. Custom therefore has produced a law that their Issue is to be destroyed, altho the Primary motive of the Institution was, that it never was to have been begotten.

It is allowable that after a person has been sometime an Erreeoy he may quit the Society, marry and have Children; or he may distroy his Children. If he does the latter he enjoys most of the privileges of the Society but not the whole, as Marriage was certainly a Violation. If he preserves his Children he is no longer of the Society, altho he retains their Name & is called Erreeoy Vahnownow [*fanaunau*, 'parentaged', one who has sired or borne offspring].

It appears however that the Erreeoys from leading an Idle and gay life have among them the finest Women of the Island. They have luxuriant and fine situations where they have their Meetings and live with all the disipation imaginable, and they vary the enjoyments of their lives with the Seasons of the Year. As for Example the Island of Teturoah [Tetiaroa], which is a few leagues to the Northward of this, they resort to in Crouds in the Season when the Fish is plenty, and at other times to some Charming places in the Mountains to enjoy other peculiar dainties. They are always in large Parties. Always drest with the greatest profusion of the best Cloth and are generally fat and Saucy.

Wherever they travel they are fed by the Cheif of the district with abundance, who calls them his Man-nee-innees or Erreeoy Friends [*manihini*, guest, visitor].

These are perhaps only a few of the Advantages of the Erreeoys, they however seem sufficient to establish a large Society, and are equally well calculated to effect, what may be wanting to render permanent the Grand design of the institution.

. . . The Erreeoys are Warriors and yet have the most frequent use of Women . . . (Bligh 1937: II 77–79)

Since the Arioi were 'discovered' by members of Cook's *Endeavour* expedition many visitors have described their activities, etc., and have attempted to explain them. Putting all these observations together, and viewing the sect—for such it was—within the context of other facets of Tahitian society, here in brief summary is what I have been able to glean about it.

It was a characteristic feature of Tahitian society that nearly every social unit, of whatever type—kin-based, territorial, occupational, etc.—was at the same time a religious congregation. But there were some social units made up of persons whose only, or most notable, common attribute was their homage to a particular spirit. One such unit was the Arioi, whose members were divided into local chapters that were distributed throughout the archipelago, one to almost every district. The principal activity of the Arioi sect was worship of the god 'Oro. As we have seen, 'Oro was also the primary tutelary of the dynasties of *ari'i* claiming derivation from Opoa, in Ra'iatea, but because of this god's supposed efficacy in warfare, he was the focus of widespread supplication by other leaders as well. In fact, reverence for 'Oro had become during the eighteenth century so extensive and so paramount that it attained the character of monolatry—i.e., belief in the existence of several gods but worship mainly of one of them. As previously noted, temples dedicated to 'Oro—i.e., those in which human sacrifice was chartered—were located on several islands and shared the name of *Taputapuatea*.

For its leaders the Arioi sect was a full-time and in some cases a lifelong vocation; the facts are not clear in this matter but it seems that most other members spent up to several weeks of each year in sect activities and the rest of their time at home in ordinary pursuits.

Those activities consisted mostly in travelling about from place to place (including island to island) and performing ceremonies and entertainments in exchange for lavish hospitality and within the context, mainly, of 'Oro worship. In some cases a single chapter went on tour by itself; more usually the chapters of several neighboring districts assembled and travelled together. Before arriving at some place, usually at a host chief's residence, they dressed in their distinctive costumes and approached their destination (most often in canoes) with great clamor, proceeded to the temple (one dedicated to 'Oro, if nearby), paid their respects to their tutelary, and then settled down to a few days of dancing, theater-performing, feasting, and—according to some European observers—sampling the sexual wares of their hostesses and hosts (there having been female Arioi as well as male). While many types of dancing and theatrics of the Tahitians contained sexual allusion, those performed by the Arioi seem to have been expecially explicit in this regard. In addition some of their plays were farcical satires containing biting social critique, including mockery of the characters of their principal hosts—a remarkable licence in this society, where acts of *lèse-majesté* were at most times sternly punished. A week-long visit by a crowd of Arioi clearly was a drain on the host community's food supplies, and perhaps a strain on many marital relationships as well, but at the same time such visits were regarded by many in the host communities as pleasurable breaks in their ordinary day-to-day routines.

Because of the emphasis upon sexuality in many of their performances, the sexual licence that attended their tours, and the promiscuity that obtained among the Arioi themselves, some writers have characterized the institution as a fertility cult—a grandiose rite of sympathetic magic designed to encourage natural fertility, of humans and of supplies of food. Be that as it may, the sect did also serve to curb warfare somewhat, fighting having been interdicted at any place where Arioi performances were taking place; and when on tour the Arioi themselves were immune to attack. And while the sect's principal tutelary was the war-god 'Oro, the aspect of the latter specifically worshipped by Arioi was "Oro-of-the-laid-down-spear'—in other words, the war-ending, peace-making side of the god. (In Tahiti every high-god spirit had several, functionally different, personalities.)

There are no credible head counts of Arioi members, but during the era now under discussion there were certainly hundreds and possibly thousands of them, and male outnumbered female members by about five to one. Nearly every district had its own distinctively named chapter, headed by a Master Arioi, whose office was also distinctively named. Three types of members were distinguished: active, 'parentaged', and 'retired', along with two or three categories of persons who regularly assisted the members in their activities. The distinction between 'active' and other members was based on the fundamental requirement, that full participation in the sect's activities was dependent upon a person's having no living offspring. Constraints were however not placed on copulation—far from it; in fact, active Arioi were notoriously avid and promiscuous, among themselves and with non-members. The rule was against allowing a member's progeny to survive, which was accomplished by abortion and infanticide. (Whatever may have been the basic reason, or the rationale, for this rule, it had the practical effect of enabling members to carry out their sect activities free of domestic responsibilities.) If, then, an active member bore or sired a child that for some reason or other happened to survive, the guilty parent (now called 'parentaged') was thereby disgraced and thenceforth forbidden full participation in sect activities. The status of 'retiree' was, however, entirely honorable; it was reserved for members who had spent years in active membership and then, upon reaching 'middle' age, had deliberately dropped out of touring, etc., and had married and settled down to domesticity.

Active members were divided into seven or eight grades (observers differed concerning the number), from novice (po'o) to 'Black-leg' (avae parai). In most cases an individual became a novice by 'application': he (or she) attended a sect performance, and in a state of nevaneva (spirit-possession, presumably by 'Oro himself, who thereby selected the applicant for membership), proceeded to dance and sing along with the performing members. If the applicant's dancing, etc., revealed sufficient talent, and—most crucial—if he (or she) was physically well-formed and unblemished, he was invited by the chapter's Master Arioi to join. (Physical perfection was a hallmark of Arioi-hood, along with such other aspects of youthfulness as skill and ardor in dancing, singing, and sex—along with freedom from the burdens of parenthood.) At the end of the period of novitate (how long it lasted is not specifically stated) the novices were tested by full members—in dancing, etc.,—and either accepted or rejected by them. After that, members were promoted to higher grades according to progress revealed in Arioi skills (including, according to some sources, deepening knowledge of unspecified sect 'secrets'). Advance up the grades was marked by changes in costume and by different designs and body placements of tattoos. Thus, the lowest-grade member wore a headdress of colored leaves, while the highest-grade member (the 'Black-leg', a status achieved by very few) wore a red-dyed bark-cloth loin-girdle, and was tattooed solidly from foot to groin (in addition to all of the other torso and arm tattoo marks acquired in the intervening grades). And as is to be expected, rise in grade-level was accompanied by increases in privileges, including command over the services of lower-grade members.

As previously mentioned, each local chapter was headed by a 'master' and in many cases by a 'mistress' as well, both of these having been appointed to their offices by the local district chief and from the chapter's active membership. In addition, the offices of master of the separate chapters were graded in terms of ceremonial precedence, etc., for those not infrequent occasions on which two or more chapters joined together on tour; not surprisingly, the highest-graded office was that of the master of the chapter at Opoa. As for the general membership, when they were not busy trying to kill one another as citizens of separate and frequently warring political units, *all* Arioi were supposed to behave towards one another amicably and hospitably. To behave otherwise was grounds for expulsion.

Despite the paradox represented by sect universality alongside district separateness, there were positive correlations between sect membership and the Tahitians' class hierarchy in general, and with the Opoa-derived *ari'i* dynasties in particular. Regarding the former, while membership in the sect was not limited to persons of upper-class status—even commoners (*manahune*) were admitted if they were otherwise acceptable; a remarkable flexibility in this class-stratified population—it transpired that when young persons of upper-class status joined the sect, which many if not most of them did, they were excused from the novitiate and admitted directly into a higher grade. As for the sect's connection with the Opoa-derived dynasties of *ari'i*, that, as already mentioned, was signified by its devotion to 'Oro, by the pre-eminence of the Opoa chapter's master, and by the loin-girdle worn by the Black-legs—which, although made of bark cloth and not feathers, was nevertheless dyed red.

Another large subject touched on by Bligh in this entry was dancing. Tahitians danced on many occasions, from carefree informal gatherings of a handfull of neighbors, to solemn assemblies of thousands. Dancing took place at welcomings and departings; at births and deaths; before, during, and after battles; as preludes, interludes, and postludes to contests, theatricals, and religious ceremonies. They danced for sheer pleasure or to vent rage, to express happiness or grief, to invite or defy, to entertain or terrify, to worship their spirits or humble their opponents. Another dimension of dancing's diversity was its instrumental accompaniment and number of participants. This varied from single performers dancing to a single instrument—or with no accompaniment—to large troupes of males *and* females, or males *or* females, with full accompaniment of flutes, drums, gongs and vocal choruses. And finally, there was a wide variation in body movements: some were slow and regular, others rapid and wild; some involved the whole body, others only the arms and shoulders; some were stately and 'innocent', while others were characterized by their observers as being so 'lascivious' or 'obscene' as to elude description or demand reticence.

In some cases there was matching between occasion and body movement and personnel, as in the case of the *ponara*, which Bligh described as follows in his *Bounty* Journal:

The Women divide into parties about 30 or 40 Yards apart and perform a kind of recitative accompanied with a Stamping of the feet and claping the hands with many wanton odd motions. A Breadfruit is then taken by a person of one party, and being placed on the foot is thrown over to the others. If it is caught, that party performs the dance and the others look on, but if it is not caught, the Party who threw it has the dance in token of the Victory, and the ball is thrown by turns from side to side. (Bligh 1937: I 412)

What Bligh did not record about the *ponara*, or perhaps did not see, was its customary finale, as described by Morrison:

. . . after they have Playd at this for some Hours they Kick the Ball to one side and both Partys strike up together, when each, to draw the Spectators to their exhibition, produce two or three Young Wantons, who stripping of their lower Garments Cover them selves with a loose piece of Cloth and at particular parts of the song they throw Open their Cloth and dance with their fore part Naked to the Company making many lewd gestures—however these are not merely the effects of Wantoness but Custom, and those who perform thus in Publick are Shy and Bashful in private, and seldom suffer any freedom to be taken by the Men on that account. (Rutter 1935: 225)

During the visit of the *Bounty* Bligh witnessed and recorded several other kinds of dance, one of which was lascivious enough to shock him—but not to constrain his reportorial conscience. The occasion was the visit of a troupe of itinerant entertainers (whom Bligh calls 'Strollers'), who like others of the same vocation were a customary, and much appreciated, feature of Tahitian life. (And although they resembled the Arioi in their roles as entertainers, the latter had other roles and purposes as well.)

Teppahoo [Te Pau, Chief of Fa'a'a District] and his Family left me to day to go to Tettahah [i.e., Fa'a'a] where their presence was necessary at a Grand Heivah which was to be performed as soon as they arrived.

These Heivahs are performed by People who travel round the Island,

Plate 11   Lower bed of Matavai River
Watercolor by George Tobin

Plate 12   View of Taputapuatea canoe
Watercolor by George Tobin

like a set of strolling Players in England, and in every District where they perform all the principal people make presents of Cloth to them with provisions and every thing they are in Want of.

A Small party of these Strollers past here this morning and in compliment (for they were hurrying down to Tettahah by appointment) they sent me word, that they would perform a Heivah before me. I therefore immediatly attended. The Party consisted of four Men and two Girls, the Youngest a mere Child. Their dress was in the Common Stile but not so prettily Ornamented as I have hitherto seen it. What was new however, at least what I have not seen this time of my being here, was Wood drums beat with two Sticks in time with their others. These were nothing more than a log of Wood about three feet long and about 10 Inches Diameter hollowed out and cut through in the side; they made a clattering noise. The Girls had twisted fibres of Grass about a foot long with a Ring at one end which fitted the fingers and one of them had a Small ring of Feathers which gave an appearance of more motion in the fingers than they really had. The Part of these Girls was very short, when they dropt all their dress suddenly before me, as a present (for it was tyed conveniently for that purpose) and went off without my seeing them any more. The Men now began their performance which of all things that was ever beheld I imagine was the most uncommon and detestable.

They suddenly took off what cloathing they had about their Hips and appeared quite Naked. One of the Men was prepared for his part, for the whole business now became the power and capability of distorting the Penis and Testicles, making at the same time wanton and lascivious motions. The Person who was ready to begin had his Penis swelled and distorted out into an erection by having a severe twine ligature close up to the Os Pubis applied so tight that the Penis was apparently almost cut through. The Second brought his Stones to the head of his Penis and with a small cloth bandage he wrapt them round and round, up to-wards the Belly, stretching them at the same time very violently untill they were near a foot in length which the bandage kept them erect at, the two stones and head of the Penis being like three small Balls at the extremity. The Third person was more horrible than the other two, for with both hand seizing the extremity of the Scrotum he pulled it out with such force, that the penis went in totally out of sight and the Scrotum became Shockingly distended. In this Manner they danced about the Ring for a few minutes when I desired them to desist and the Heivah ended, it however afforded much laughter among the Spectators. (Bligh 1937: II 34–35)

Another performance witnessed by Bligh during his *Bounty* visit was on the occasion of his having been dubbed (Honorary!) *Ari'i* of Matavai:

In the Morning [of December 15, 1788] I had an early Visit from Tynah to take me on shore to the Tent, where he had directed a Hevah to be performed. I accordingly went with him and by the time we got there a great number of People and all the Cheifs were collected on the occasion. This Hevah was different from any we had yet seen. The performers were eleven Men habited in that singular dress called Parry. They were placed in three files, and each Man had two Mother of Pearl shells in his hand, which by the Manner they were Strung on a peice of cord, and about an Inch asunder, with a small motion of the fingers made a clinking kind of Noise. As is very common, before the performance began a Priest pronounced a long oration or prayer, which being done a Man came running towards me, sometime stopping suddenly, and then advancing again with many odd motions, holding between his hands some twisted Cocoa Nutt leaf, which at last was laid at my feet, and I was cloathed with a peice of cloth, during this the Men in the Par-ry dress were all sitting on their heels not unlike kneeling, but as soon as the two peices of Cocoa Nut leaf were laid down they got up and made a few Motions with their Feet at the clinking of the Shells.

This being over, another prayer was given by the Priest, and the Man who had placed the two peices of Cocoa Nut leaf at my feet took one of them away and carried it to him, which being done, a few sentences were spoke by a person in front of the performers, and the whole inclined their bodies to one side with the Arms extended towards the ground, another Sentence then took place, and they all regularly leaned in the same manner to the other side, and from that position they suddenly sprung up and making a few Strange Motions at the clinking of the Shells the ceremony ended.

This Hevah I was told was in favor of me as being acknowledged Erre of Matavai, that the Cocoa Nut leaf which they called Ha-hyree was never presented but to a principal Cheif, and whose wellfare depended on his agreement with the Eatua [Atua, god] which was supplicated by the Priest on the return of the other peice of leaf. I have had this ceremony and compliment paid to me before, and on an occasion which one would imagine, sacred or religious ceremony had little to do with, but then Tynah received the same, which at this time he did not.

The Par-ry [parae] dress is certainly not used but on particular occasions, and is so strange and odd of itself that by description there is scarce a possibility of giving anyone an Idea of it without a drawing, one of which may be seen in Captain Cooks Voyage.

Having highly satisfied the performers with a Toey each & some Nails, I returned to the ship with all the Cheifs to dinner, during which I was very anxious to get more information about what I had seen, but I could only learn it was about myself and the Eatua and I gave up my enquiries in despair. (Bligh 1937: I 1421–2)

On May 25th Bligh witnessed another dance performance, which will be described by him in his Journal entry for that day, but in far less detail than those recorded in his *Bounty* Journal. Meanwhile, Tahitian dancing also made an impression, of a predictably different kind, on young Tobin; the occasion here described was the one mentioned earlier, on April 20th:

About Sun set the girls collected on the Quarter deck to dance the Heeva as usual. No sollicitation was required, as they took great delight in their amusement. The party on these occasions, consisted generally, of from ten to twenty. The chief study of the performers seemed to be in keeping exact time with their feet and hands, clapping the latter together with great regularity and a sharp noise; at the same time repeating short sentences with an arch look, chiefly the scandal of the day, where our names, as well as those of our Island friends were frequently introduced. The dances were of short continuance, but often repeated, the performers exhibiting their pliant well formed limbs in the most sportive postures; at times, full of the most encourag-

ing invitation; when suddenly, as if anger or neglect gave birth to it, the coy repulsive movement succeeded—but of short duration—as, at the winding up of the dance, every look, every motion, solicited the warm admiration of the gazing spectators. And may ye, my good and cheerful girls, long dance the Heeva, unconscious that among us, it would be deemed full of danger to the morals of our refined damsels. 'Tis the custom of your favoured Isle, and in doing it, you are as free from turpitude as the City Miss, who, under the strict observance of her Mamma's eye, stiffy paces at Lord Mayors ball the laboured minuet; or rustic red cheeked lass, who, in the hoyden revel, receives the eager pressure of her partners lips with more than half met joy.

Even the laconic Lt. Bond was moved to comment on Tahitian dancing:

In their Haivas they represent with great humour the follies of their visitors, as well as their domestic scenes; for mimickry is acquired by them with great facility, and much genius. Their dances are graceful and lacivious—those of the men by wonderful contorsions of the body & limbs, and most extravagant gestures of the countenance. The drum & flute their chief music; the latter highly pathetic and Plaintive.

The new personage to appear in Bligh's Journal entry of this day was Vahine Metua (Bligh's 'Huheine Moyere' and Tobin's 'Ena Madua'),who was wife of Tina's brother, Ari'ipaea. Her birthplace had been in the district of Hitia'a; her pedigree is not recorded but it evidently was superior enough to merit her marriage to the high-ranking Ari'ipaea—and she herself was powerful enough a personality to command widespread respect. The reason for her self-feeding restriction on this occasion was her situation as a mourner, a custom explained above, under the entries for April 17th. In addition to this sign of mourning, Tobin's entry for the day records about Vahine Metua that 'in her ear she wore a lock of the hair of the deceased [i.e., her father], her own being cut in ridges as a mark of sorrow.'

Tobin also records another aspect of Vahine Metua's visit that was perhaps not known to his Captain:

Orepaia with his wife Ena Madua, and her sister were on board most of the day; the latter, Orepaia presented to his Tayo [i.e., an English officer], nor could the laws of hospitality admit of his refusing the boon of this generous Chief.

Another noteworthy person to appear aboard the *Providence* this day was Ari'ipaea Vahine (also known as Tetua te Ahurai, and Fataua), the second of Tina's elder sisters. This jolly woman had been residing on Ra'iatea but returned to Tahiti in September 1790 with a fleet of canoes, perhaps only for a family visit but in time to assist her brother in his armed conflict with Atehuru. Then and afterwards she proved to be a useful ally to Tina in his efforts to maintain and extend the Pomares' authority, but to Tobin her main attraction was her personal charm and her dancing ability—even at the advanced age of about forty-two:

The sister of Pomaurey was always remarkable for her gaiety, and is mentioned by Captain

Cook as excelling in the Heeva, nor indeed had she forgotten it, frequently mingling in the dance with the younger damsels on the quarter deck of the Providence. As the O'tahyteans do us the honor of imitating some of our manners, no little pains were taken to please her, in the assurance that, our english ladies never felt old, that being Grandmothers rendered them more lovely in the eyes of our Chiefs, and that five-and forty was the criterion of beauty, while the warm blood mantled but in vain, on the vermeil cheek of neglected sixteen. Where James, did our countrymen acquire this strange, this unseemly propensity? Is fashion, as in the cut of our coats, to influence us in an election where nature should alone guide? Surely, such ought not to be.

Meanwhile, in the midst of all these distractions, Lt. Portlock continued to supervise the mundane activities of his ship, including the administration of a bit of quarter-deck justice to:

Mulberry marine on board under charge of Corporal Rea with a complaint from the Officer Lieut Guthrie of his having lost a full Cartridge out of his Cartouch box, and one of his shirts and that there was every reason to suppose that he had sold them to the Indians, we have had several Instances at the Post of the chiefs attempting to procure ammunition from the Marines and as the Penitence of leting them have it and saying it was lost might be a pretence very Easily adopted by others (much to the Risk and disadvantage of the Whole) it became highly necessary to make an example of this man particularly as it was the Opinion of the Officers that he really had sold these things to the Natives, I therefore punishd him with 18 lashes for these crimes and returnd him on shore again to his duty.

Tuesday, April 24th

Fine Weather. Sea Breezes at E b S and Land Breezes at S b E & SE. Thermometer 81 to 83½ Degrees.

Employed <in> Caulking the Starboard side. Got the Spare Anchor up out of the Main Hold, and put the Guardian's Anchor down in its place. Got the Coals up in the Wake of the Hatchway, and got on board two load of Ballast about 4 Tons. It is a difficult thing to be got here, as the Stones lye at the wash of the Beach w[h]ere is, at most times, a very great Surf. Plentiful supplies of Cocoa Nutts, Breadfruit, Plantains, <Tarro> & Hogs.

This Day we Potted 95 Plants. [Marginal note: 'Total Pots—912']

The Ereerahigh, Otoo, changed <the place of> his residence to Day from Oparre to this Place, this is a pleasant circumstance as I have now all the Chief People about us—Otow lives on Point Venus, Tynah and Otoo about 500 Yards within the Point, and Oreepyah on the Beach towards Tarrah. In this manner they prevent a number of worthless fellows lurking about the Post and committing Thefts.

The quantity of Old Cloaths that has been left among these People is considerable. Any article of Dress they set the highest value on, they wear such rags and dirty things as are truly disgusting, and deform themselves in a very

great degree. It is a rare thing to see a person dressed with a neat piece of Cloath
<Cloth> [i.e., bark cloth], which formerly they had in abundance and wore with
much ellegance. Their general habiliments are now a dirty Shirt, an Old Coat, Jacket
or an Old Waistcoat, so that they are no longer the clean Otaheiteans, but in
appearance a set of Raggamuffins with whom it is necessary to have great caution
in any intercourse with them.

Bligh's regrets over the changes in Tahitians' clothing is the familiar, and
correspondingly unreasonable, one of: 'If only these natives would adopt our
absolutely rightful customs, such as monogamy, respect for contracts,
sobriety, Christianity, and the like, and retain their innocently exotic ones,
such as picturesque palm-thatched houses and colorful and simple
garments . . .'. As a matter of fact, the disapproving Captain was certainly
overstating the case. His remarks may have applied to the Tahitians he actually saw in the vicinity of Matavai Bay, but arithmetic argues against the prop-
osition that most other Tahitians at that time had adopted European
clothing. Up to the *Providence* visit less than about two thousand Europeans,
man and boy, had visited the island—hardly enough to have outfitted the
twenty to thirty thousand Tahitians who had thus far survived. But while
Bligh's sample was small (and hence his arithmetic wrong), there is much to
be said for his aesthetic judgment.

Tahitian children went naked until they were, by European reckon-
ing, five or six years old. After that persons of both sexes were accustomed
to wearing clothes at all times except when asleep or on a few ceremonious
occasions (such as in some of the dancing previously described).

The basic garment for males was a breech clout (*maro*), for females
a short underskirt (*pareu*). Over these, both sexes wore a wraparound (also
called *pareu*), which extended from waist to knee in males and from above the
breast to below the knee in females. In addition both sexes sometimes wore
a long, open-sided poncho (*tiputo*) belted around the waist with a girdle
(*tatua*); and on top of all these, women occasionally donned a loose cloak
(*'ahu*). The garments were made of bark cloth or mats (ie., plaited leaves or
plant fibers); some girdles were made of plaited hair. The fabrication of mats
and bark cloth (as will shortly be described) were complicated and lengthy
processes, but making them into garments was a simple and often
extemporary job.

Everyday headwear was of four types: bark-cloth turbans, caps,
braided head bands, and wreaths of many shapes. The only kind of footwear
consisted of sandals made of bark cordage and worn usually for protection,
when fishing, against sharp coral and shell.

In his nostalgic remarks of this day Bligh seems to have implied that
the Tahitians were no longer 'clean'. In this he could only have been referring
to their European garments; the traditional body-cleanliness of the Tahitians

111

has survived two centuries of European contact, and is unlikely to have lapsed temporarily during Bligh's visit.

Recorded descriptions of the eighteenth century Tahitians all agree on their body cleanliness. Their mornings usually began with an all-over bath and this was followed by other baths during the day. Fresh water was greatly preferred for bathing; even after immersion in salt water, people customarily bathed in a freshwater stream. So addicted were these islanders to bathing that it sometimes led to their undoing; no matter what the kind or stage of their infirmities the sick or wounded made every effort to bathe in fresh, flowing water. Observers have referred to the swarms of flies that often accompanied Tahitians; that however was due more to their between-bath sweat and to the fish and other things they carried, than to any long-lasting grime.

Bark cloth, *tapa*, the textile used for most Tahitian garments, turbans, and bed covers was made of the inner bark of several kinds of trees, principally of the Chinese mulberry (*Broussonetia papyrifera*; Tahitian *'aute*), a variety of breadfruit called *pu'upu'u* (*Artocarpus altilis*), and a figlike tree (*Ficus prolaxa*; Tahitian *aoa*). The first of these, the most widely used, was cultivated mainly on plantations near residences; one such plantation was described by Georg Forster:

The next day we took a walk up one of the hills, which is every where planted with bread-trees, pepper [the shrub whose root was used for making kava] and mulberry-trees, yams and eddoes. The mulberry or cloth-trees were cultivated with particular attention; the ground between them was carefully weeded, and manured with broken decayed shells and coral, and the whole plantation surrounded with a deep furrow or channel, in order to drain it. In many places they had burnt away ferns and various shrubs, in order to prepare the ground for future plantations. (Forster 1777: I, 118–19)

Cloth differed somewhat in strength, texture, and color, according to the variety of tree, but the method of manufacture was much the same for all varieties. Only young saplings were utilized, and the stems of the young plants were kept free of branches to insure that the bark was not punctured. After the bark was peeled off the straight and unmarred young saplings, or in some cases limbs, it was soaked in water, the rough outer layer scraped off, and the inner bark placed on a flat board and beaten thin with wooden mallets. The width of the strips was increased several times by beating; to make them longer and wider numbers of strips were felted together by further beating, helped by the resinous substance in the bark. Or, to thicken or repair the cloth separate layers were pasted and beaten together. Tobin has given a brief description of the process, but the best description is provided by Morrison:

Their Cloth, of which the General Names is Ahhoo [*ahu*], is of Different sorts and made from the Bark of different trees but the process of all is the Same.

The Best and finest white Cloth Calld Hoboo or Parrawye is made from the Yowte ['*aute*] or Cloth Plant and is made thus—The plants having to their proper length (10 or 12 feet) are cut by the Men and brought in by them which is their part of the work, the Weomen then Strip off the bark by entring a pointed Stick between the bark and the Plant and ripping it the whole length on one Side, & the Bark peels off. After they have Stripd all the Plants they take the Bark to the Water where they wash it, [and] spreading it on a board for the Purpose Scrape it Clean, taking off the Outside rind with a large Cockle shell and having freed it from the Sap and Slime it is wrapd in plantain leaves and covered with Grass, where it remains for two three or four days when it becomes Clammy and glutinous, & is then fit for working, it is then spread of a regular thickness of several strips forming a band of 7 or 8 inches broad and of what length the piece is intended to be and Ground where they intend to work is spread with plantain leaves to keep it from the dirt—the Beans [beams?: i.e., of wood] are then placed at equal distances about 6 feet asunder & at each of them two weomen work, having the Piece between them, beating it with square beetles [i.e., mallets] to its proper breadth; this they perform by a Song given by one & Chorous'd by the rest and keep regular time and Shifting the Piece backwards and forwards till it is all beat out to a regular Breadth and thickness—it is then spread in the sun to Dry for one Day, after which it is bleachd in the Morning Dew till it is perfectly white, being kept from the sun till it is sufficiently bleached, and then it is spread one or two days in the Sun to dry it and put up for Store or Use.

They make another sort of several Thicknesses which are not placed regular or above half beaten, this is Calld Marro; of this they make their Upper Garments by Striping from one part and pasting on to another till they bring it to a reglar breadth & thickness and trim the Fragments off with a piece of split bamboo which answers the purpose of a knife. (Rutter 1935: 160–1)

Some bark cloths were used as is, others were soaked in or painted with dyes, of which there were several kinds. A favorite red dye was made from the berry of the *Ficus tinctoria* mixed with the leaf of the *Cordia subcordata*; other colors—yellow, brown, and black—were obtained from parts of other plants.

Bark cloth not intended for immediate use was usually rolled up and stored. Some such strips were up to four and more yards wide and dozens of yards long, wealth sometimes having been reckoned in these terms.

Every household produced some bark cloth, for the use of its own members or for 'taxation' and gift-exchange. Manufacturing it was customarily the work of females, but males, including upper-class and chiefly ones, were known to take a hand in its manufacture when occasion demanded.

After bark cloth, the Tahitians' most common textile was plaitware, of numerous kinds of raw materials, plaitwork patterns, thickness, overall shape and size, form of decoration—and use. The principal raw materials used were the inner bark of some plants, bamboo stalks, arrowroot, certain grasses, midribs and stems of certain ferns, and the leaves of coconut and pandanus palms. The products ranged, in form and use, from fine-grained and softly pliable pieces used for clothing, to course ones used for flooring. As with bark cloth, plaiting was mainly the work of females, but men could and sometimes did engage in the craft. And, like bark cloth, fine mats figured frequently in exchange.

Wednesday, April 25th

Fair Weather during the Morning, but the Latter part of the Day Cloudy with Rain in the Mountains and a sprinkling below. Wind E & SE. Thermometer 81 to 83½ Degrees.

Employed in the Hold and Caulking Ship. Plentifull Supplies. Received one Load of Ballast about 2 Tons.

Our Friends here have some weighty deliberations in their hands which I cannot yet account for. The Cause of Otoo having moved to Matavai is on some busyness respecting the late War. Some concessions are made by the Matavai Party. The Temple of Oro their God, which is always kept near the residence of the Erreerahigh, was brought up in a Cannoe with him, it is to remain here untill tomorrow, when after a meeting of the Parties, Otoo returns with it to Oparre, but all the other Chiefs remain here. Tomorrow Morning I am to have a sight of it, and to hear prayers performed by Tootaha the Priest. This Man is a great Orator among them, and highly respected for his abilities, as well as <for> being a Chief of consequence. He <u>has</u> <is> always been the Prime Minister of Tynah, is their Oracle, and Historian of this Country, and possesses a great fund of humour. He is now called Hammene,manne [Ha'amanemane], but was spoken of in my last Voyage by the Name of Too-taha [Tutaha]. He is remarkable for speaking English, and could he write is capable of forming a Vocabulary of near a thousand English Words.

I have mentioned the Death of Teppahoo [Te Pau] the Chief of Tetaha [District, also called Fa'a'a] and now find he is succeeded by Teppahoo (the youngest Brother of Tynah) his Nephew by Marriage with Terranoo [Teranu], the Sister of Oberreroah [Peroa, also Tetupaia] who is his Mother.

We filled 71 Pots to Day and the whole are doing exceedingly well as far as we can judge. [Marginal note: 'Total Pots 983']

The large subject of 'temples'—i.e., *marae*—touched on by Bligh in this entry, will be discussed in connection with his entry of the following day, when he was permitted a view of the 'Oro temple stewarded by the young Pomare, Tu.

Old Tutaha-Ha'amanemane, who appears in Bligh's Journal entries of April 9th and 11th, was indeed a remarkable man, and in several respects: as sage, orator, linguist, high-priest, 'Prime Minister', political broker, sorcerer—and possessor of a powerful *libido* (as reported by the newly-arrived English missionaries in 1797):

Mannemanne, who though nearly blind with age, is as libidinous now, as when thirty years younger; and, in order to gratify his lust, has frequently upwards of a dozen females with him, some of them apparently not above twelve or thirteen years of age . . . (quoted in Oliver 1974: 1292)

As noted earlier (entry of April 9th), he was a younger brother of Tina's mother, Tetupaia, and had been both highest-ranking kin-Titleholder and secular Chief of Ra'iatea, until forced to flee from that island by the conquering forces of Borabora. Like Tu, who was the son's son of his elder sister, Tetupaia, Ha'amanemane was entitled to preside over human sacrifices to the god 'Oro, and he was evidently closely attached to the young Tu. (He appears to have regarded Tu as *his* own successor to his Ra'iatean heritage; having remained an *active* Arioi throughout his life, none of his own progeny had been allowed to live.) During Bligh's *Bounty* and *Providence* visits, although Ha'amanemane seems to have acted as 'Prime Minister' to Tina, his closest personal attachment was to the latter's son, Tu. In fact, within a few years after departure of the *Providence* Ha'amanemane sided with Tu in an armed bid to hasten the transfer of Tina's secular authority to Tu.

The political machinations of the Pomares were well exemplified in Bligh's report of the Title succession in the small neighboring district of Tetaha-Fa'a'a—from the deceased Te Pau, who seems to have had no surviving offspring, to his wife's sister's son (and Tina's youngest brother) about whom Vancouver wrote:

Although in the possession of a very considerable property, Tapahoo seems little regarded by his family, and less esteemed by his people. This want of respect is greatly, and possibly wholly, to be attributed to a natural imbecillity of mind; as, to all appearance, he is a young man of an exceedingly weak and trifling character. (Lamb 1984: 432)

Bligh's reference to the outcome of the recent war between Pare-Arue and Matavai can be supplemented by a fuller, and wisely prophetic, one by Portlock:

. . . *about 6 in the morning we [he and Bligh] again went on shore to the Post where we found Otoo, he had slept the last night in the district of Matavia as had done his father and several of the Principal chiefs from Oparre, who now appear to think themselves quite Secure in the Possession of the Matavians houses and Plantations, and beside the chiefs many others of the midling class from Oparre are now gathering about Matavia and building themselves houses on the spott were the houses have been burnt or otherways destroyd during the war, how long they may keep Possession of the situation after our departure is very uncertain for there is little doubt but the Matavians will make an attempt to regain their Estates and perhaps aided by some other districts (the people of which led forward with a hope of geting a part of the Oparre peoples riches [i.e., their European goods]) may soon Accomplish the point Establish themselves again in Matavia and perhaps turn the Tables upon the Oparre people, this seems the more likely as its thought the Matavians are of the two Districts the best warriors and there are several smaller districts to the Eastward that seem disposd to join the Matavians, one of two had Indeed Joind and others would soon have followed their Example but were no doubt prevented by our arrival in the Bay—knowing Captain Blighs friendship for the Otoo family and people of Opparre.*

Thursday, April 26th

The high point of this day's happenings was Bligh's (and Portlock's) visit to the temple of 'Oro, which on this occasion was located on a double canoe anchored about a mile to the east of Point Venus. But before discussing that occasion, and that very special kind of temple, some comments are called for about temples—*marae*—in general.

In Tahitian cosmography the universe consisted of two separate 'rooms' (*piha*) or spheres: the *ao*, which was the sphere of mortals (and also meant 'daytime'), and the *po*, which was the sphere of spirits (and which also meant 'nighttime'). During sleep the souls of living humans often wandered into the *po*; correspondingly, spirits entered into or continually moved about in the *ao*. In addition, at an early stage in the mythical evolution of the universe, fixed structures, *marae*, were built where humans could interact with spirits in a more regularized manner—i.e., by means of prayers and offerings presented through properly qualified intermediaries, namely, priests (*tahu'a pure*, specialists in praying). This arrangement did not wholly supercede other kinds of interaction between humans and spirits, such as a spirit entering and speaking through a human, or such as human souls wandering into the *po* during sleep. It did however provide fixed locations for most other kinds of interaction between humans and spirits—not for any and all humans with any and all spirits, but rather for certain groups of humans (e.g., households, districts, fishermen guilds, religious sects) to interact with their respective tutelars. Some temples—*marae*—were temporary in use and construction, as for example, a small and nondescript altar set up before a corpse, or a stage built on a large canoe. Most however were meant to be fixed and permanent, and these latter consisted of at least four components: an *ahu*, i.e., a resting place for the visiting spirit(s); a place for the priest(s) in front of the *ahu* (typically one or more stone uprights against which the priests leaned while officiating); an altar (commonly a wooden platform) for offerings; and a place, behind the priests, for other members of the congregation. All but the smallest of such temples were paved with flat stones or coral rubble and some were enclosed by low stone walls.

Permanent, land-based temples varied in size from less than a hundred to many thousands of square yards. Correspondingly, their component *ahu* ranged in form and size from a small and rough pile of boulders, to carefully constructed multi-level stone pyramids, the largest having been about 85 yards long and 15 high. (Some of the temples in the Leeward Society Islands differed from those of Tahiti and Mo'orea in having long rectangular *ahu* faced with hugh slabs of coral, but their functions were the same.) Many land-based temples contained additional elements, such as stone or carved wooden pillars set into the top of the *ahu*, for spirits to rest upon; a 'bed' near the *ahu* for a spirit's image; cist repositories for human bones (although only

116

a few of the temples served as cemeteries, and those for important personages and for human sacrifices); wooden huts for the storage of priests' vestments and other items used in religious services. And in a few—a very few—temples there were gods' houses (called 'arks' by some Europeans) in which were deposited images of the temple's most powerful tutelar deities.

In the commentary of April 9th, reference was made to the Cult of 'Oro (the tutelary deity of the Ra'iatean Opoa dynasty), who of all deities was most widely and obsequiously venerated during the era now under discussion, mainly with respect to his supposed influence over the outcome of martial conflict. As noted earlier, 'Oro's 'home' temple was the one in Opoa named *Taputapuatea*, and, by a line of reasoning not difficult to follow, the only other temples at which humans could interact with him were those that also bore that name. (By the same logic, it would not be reasonable for, say, Lutherans, to perform their services in a cathedral or synagogue.) Also, it will be recalled, the full support of 'Oro could only be secured by offering of human sacrifice, and the only persons qualified to preside over such sacrifices were those holding feather-girdled kin-Titles of the Opoa dynasty. During the *Providence* visit it appears that Tu and Ha'amanemane were the only persons on Tahiti so authorized; Ha'amanemane, who was the elder brother of Tu's paternal grandmother, was entitled to *conduct* such services, but seems not to have had the right, or duty, as has Tu, to *receive* the human sacrifice— i.e., to simulate eating it on behalf of 'Oro.

At the time of the *Providence* visit there were four permanent, land-based temples bearing the name of Taputapuatea on Tahiti, and one on Mo'orea, in all of which human sacrifices could be performed—but only with the active participation of a person authorized to receive the sacrifice on behalf of 'Oro, and, what is most important, only in the presence of the deity himself. As noted previously, most spirits resided most of the time in their own sphere, the *po*, and had to be invoked, with prayer and offerings, to enter the sphere of humans, the *ao*. Moreover, when invoked, most spirits required specific tangible resting places during their sojourn in the *ao*, and these consisted mainly of the temple *ahu* just described. In the case of 'Oro, however, something more than a general-purpose *ahu* was required, namely, a special avatar-idol (*to'o*), in which the great god reposed during his rare and fateful visits. According to legend there were three 'Oro idols on Tahiti-Mo'orea during the second half of the eighteenth century, but only one of those figured in historically authenticated events, and that was the so-called 'Papara Idol', possession of which had been fought over for decades. During the *Bounty* visit it had reposed in a *marae* in Atehuru (specifically, in the Paea District temple), but before the arrival of the *Providence* some subjects of the Pomares, with the indispensable assistance of their *Bounty*-mutineer supporters, had seized it and deposited it in their own temple in Pare, thereby re-uniting the three elements needed for invoking 'Oro: the god's own idol-

avatar, the red-feather girdle associated with the highest-ranking kin-Title of 'Oro's nascent temple at Opoa, and the person best qualified, by birth, to don the girdle—namely, the young Tu. The Pare-Arue temple itself had not previously been a Taputapuatea one—i.e., one dedicated mainly to 'Oro. That, however, was not indispensable; the god could be invoked wherever the other three elements were assembled, and wherever that was, was *ipso facto* called *Taputapuatea*. In fact, during the *Providence* visit, as was described by Bligh, the name *Taputapuatea* was given to the canoe on which the relevant god-house and red-feather girdle were transported.

Tobin and Harwood were the first of the *Providence*'s company to see that canoe-based temple, about which Tobin reported:

In the afternoon [of April 24th] I accompanied our worthy Doctor in a walk to the Eastward of the River. Our notice was soon drawn to a double canoe hauled up on the beach near to which was Otoo's house. Here, for the first time, I saw him sit down. Being desireous of examining the Canoe, as we approached it the young Monarch evinced much displeasure, his attendants repeating Eotooa, Eotooa, (the god, the god); not wishing to give any offence we proceeded no farther, but it sufficed to observe that on one of the prows there was a roasted hog with the head of another, besides bread fruit, plantains, and sugar canes. The other prow supported a large bundle about five feet in length covered with red european cloth. Several bunches of feathers were hung to different parts of the canoe, and on its fore part was erected a stage three feet in height, supported by a railing on which was a long box in the form of a coffin covered with a canopy of reeds and network. It was understood that this box was to protect the Eotooa, (who was wrapped up in the red cloth,) in bad weather. The canoe had recently arrived, decorated in this manner from Oparrey, Otoo coming in her. On the beach were two Island drums ornamented with european cloth. The provisions were for the Eotooa's consumption. Otoos house was nearly full of the different finery with which he had been presented by officers of the various vessels that had visited Otahytey. [Plate 12]

Bligh and Portlock made an 'official' visit to the canoe-based Taputapuatea temple on April 26th:

Fair Weather with Land and Sea Breezes. Thermometer from 81 to 83½ Degrees.
Employed in the Hold, and Caulking the Starboard Side of the Ship. Very plentiful Supplies to Day. Filled 99 Pots with Bread Fruit Plants and one of Vees. [Marginal note: 'total Pots 1082']
At day light this morning I walked with Tynah and Hammennemanne (for so I shall now call him) to see the Great Temple Tebbootabooataiah. I found it on a double Cannoe, about a Mile from Point Venus to the Eastward, near the small Island called Modoo,ow, in the harbour called Taipippee. It was hauled up on the Beach. On the prow of the Cannoe was a baked Hog, the Head of a Dog & a Fowel, with a piece of Sugar Cane. Being seated in the Cannoe Hammennemanne began a Prayer in favor of King George, Myself and

Mr. Portlock, who was with me, the principal purport of which was, that we might never want or be overcome by our Ennemies. His chanting was accompanied by two Drums, one was beat by a Native and the other by one of my People who was with me, so that it cannot be supposed there was much harmony in it <between them>. There was an interval in the Prayer, when the Priest took off all his Cloaths and lifted a bundle like an Egyptian Mummey covered with red Cloth from under its Vault into a kind of Trough on the Top of it. It contained (he said) the Etuah [atua, god], & Worrow te oorah [marginal note: 'many Feathers'], and some other sacred things. I requested to have it opened, which at this time he did not like to comply with, but assured me I should see it tomorrow at Oparre, where it was to be sent in the course of this Day to be ready at a Ceremony which I was to be at <at which I was to be present>.

    This senseless lump and Cannoe <of> which my drawing [Plate 13] will give a just Idea of, and <which> has been spoken of with so much wonder and respect, is about 6 feet long and 4 feet wide and 5½ feet high. They call it the Ephare no t'Etuah [e fare no te atua] or Ephare Tuah, the House of God [marginal note: 'see 12th July']; and his Temple Tebbootaboo, ataiah [Taputapuatea]. The Wooden Arches which are 18 Inches high are cut hollow in Ribs and are called Avy [avae] or Legs. There are three Arches which support the Morai [marae], but the Ephare Tuah has the interstices filled, so that it forms only one Arch. On the top of these arches are fastened two Troughs (like mangers) one has a narrow shed over it and is called the House of God, the other with four rude ornaments is called the Morai. The Trough however is called Erro'ee [ro'i, bed]. On the top of the Morai are represented two Birds. There is in no part of it, ingenuity or Workmanship to recommend it to notice; but its duties and the sacred Rights [rites?] performed to it, among which are the human sacrifices, induced me to be particular in the description.

    Otoo slept under a small Shed near the Morai, he had most of the things with him that we had given to him, and a St. Georges Ensign which was left here by Captain Cook. This Ensign is always carried with the Morai, and it was displayed in sailing past the Ships to Oparre, with a small Red Flag. [Marginal note: 'This place is Sacred to the Chief no person ventures near it. He always Sleeps here when it is too late to go to Oparre.']

    Peace is established. Poeeno and Tynah have had a meeting, and it is agreed that Poeeno shall live again at Matavai. They have promised to return C[aptain] Weatherhead's Money, but I am in doubt about their sincerity. I however dare not involve myself in any trouble with these People to get either one part of his property or the other, altho I will do my utmost to regain it by every fair means I am capable of.

    The Harbour of Taipippee is but small, and nothing about it to induce any Person to Anchor a Ship there.

> *A Shark 7 feet long was caught along side the Ship. Many Porpoises were in the Bay.*
> *The Native name for the high forked Mountain which I have called Otoo's Horns is Orohee,nah, or Orooenah [Orohena].*

Portlock's account of the visit to Taputapuatea complements somewhat that of Bligh:

. . . after walking about a Mile we came to a large Double Canoe that lays on the beach this they made us understand was their Sacred Canoe and made use of to carry their God in when it was found Necessary to remove it from place to place over the fore part of the Canoe was built a kind of shed and in the shed was laying a large parcel which appeard to contain Matts and feathers and I suppose many other things all wrapt up in a piece of fine Scarlet cloth and held in great respect and Estimation by them, the old high Priest approachd it with much respect and ceremony and as well as I could understand they imagine their God hovers about this Parcel and their presents of red feathers and other Valuable things offerd to the God are all deposited in it the high Priest caried with him a few red feathers made up and fastned neatly to the end of a piece of rush or Bamboe and deposited it in the Canoe, he then began his prayers in a Singing tone of voice, accompanied with two drums and as he was short of a drummer he seemd desirous that a man belonging to Captain Blighs ship who had attended us should beat one of them, the man readily comply'd, performd very well and gave great satisfaction to the high Priest—we continued here about half an hour and then returnd the way we came.

Bligh was afforded a closer view of the sacred objects on April 27th, when he witnessed their use in a full-scale religious rite, but as a prelude to that account two items in the April 26th entry will receive comment here. One was the action of Ha'amanemane in undressing before handling the sacred objects, the other has to do with the use of feathers in religious rites.

The antithesis, noted earlier, between *ra'a* (sacred) and *noa* (secular, profane) was especially sharp in the context of formal religious rites. Persons (without exception males) who played active roles in those rites were required to be 'de-sacralized' before resuming their everyday lives: the attribute of sacredness that clung to them as result of their close contact with powerful spirits would have been dangerous to other persons, especially females. Special rites were sufficient to remove that sacredness from the individual's own body, but in most cases the clothes worn by him in contact with spirits had to be kept at the temple, for future use, or destroyed. For the latter purpose there were pits dug within the precincts of many temples into which such clothes, along with the remains of offerings, etc., were thrown. In light of the above it seems likely that Ha'amanemane had removed his clothes before handling the sacred objects so that he could continue wearing them afterwards, the rite Bligh witnessed on this occasion having been an informal and relatively trivial one.

The place of feathers, especially red ones, in Tahitian religion was central and extremely important. Red feathers, above all other tangible instruments, were used to induce spirits to grant supplications (such as to abate a storm at sea, or reverse the course of an illness, or empower a weapon to kill or a canoe to float). It is impossible to conclude whether they owed their powers to coercive magic, or to the liking spirits had for them. (The latter rationale is argued by the circumstance that some deities were imagined to have integuments of feathers.) But, whatever the cause, feathers, and especially red ones, were (prior to the introduction of firearms) perhaps the most valuable commodities in Tahiti, both as repositories of wealth and as articles of exchange—among humans and between humans and spirits.

A final comment of this day's journal entries concerns the 'end' of the Matavai versus Pare-Arue war. According to Bligh, 'Peace is established'—although he doubted the 'sincerity' of the peace pact. Portlock was even more dubious:

This day Poe'E'noe [Poeno], Chief of Matavia came in [and] sued to the King for Peace which was granted on condition of Poe'E'noe's bringing in the fire Arms and Money that he had in Possession, belonging to the Commander of the late Ship Matilda, he consents to these terms, and the King and him have touched Noses as a mark of friendship for each other, for my part I think they cordially hate each other and that Poe'E'noe does not mean to comply with the Conditions of Peace.

Friday, April 27th

Moderate Sea Breezes at East and E b N Land Winds at Night from the SE. Thermometer from 81 to 83 Degrees.

Employed <in> Caulking the Larboard Side. Fitting up a place on the Quarter Deck for Extra Plants. In the Hold and other necessary Duties. Sufficient Supplies of Cocoa Nutts, Plantains, Tarro, Breadfruit and Hogs.

[A marginal note records the following plants having been collected through April 26th: breadfruit, 1082 pots and 4 tubs; plantains, 12 pots; Tahitian chestnuts, 6 pots; Tahitian 'mango', 2.]

Tynah and his Friends got very much intoxicated with their Ava this Morning and were not able to perform their promise of going with me to Oparre. Towards Mid day they recovered and were a little ashamed of their conduct, and our excursion was put off untill the Morning.

On my enquiring the cause of the Marro Oorah [maro ura, red-feather girdle] being removed from Attahooroo where it was kept in Captain Cook's time, and when I was here in my last Voyage; they told me that after Christian had left <part of> his Villains <crew> at Otaheite, Otoo made War against <the> Attahooroo People, and by the Aid of the Bountys Men, overcame them. The Marro, the Etuah [Atua] and Tebbootaboo,ataiah were then seized and brought to Oparre where they will remain.

The seizure and transfer of the *maro ura* and other sacred objects from

Atehuru to Pare was mentioned in the commentary of April 26th. A detailed account of that destructive conflict, including the role played by the 'Bounty Villains' in it, would lead too far from the focus of this book. However, for anyone interested in that (cyclic) turning-point in Tahiti's perennial wars the Journal of James Morrison, one of the Bounty crew participants, can provide a vivid description. (Edited by Owen Rutter, London: The Golden Cockerel Press, 1935) Or, for excerpts of Morrison's Journal dealing with that conflict, and placing it within the context of the whole era 1767–1815, see Oliver 1974, vol. 3, 'The Rise of the Pomares'.

Portlock's entry for this day confirmed the end of (or, as was characteristic of Tahitian armed conflict, a temporary truce in) the Matavai–Pare-Arue War, in noting the return to Matavai of Poeno and some of his supporters. Bligh however refused Poeno's request to meet with him, until the latter had returned all the money and firearms taken from the Matilda people. Portlock also noted in this day's entry: 'a Custom we now see prevail which I believe has not before been Observd, and that is the Queen E'dea drinking quantities of Gava ['ava], I have not observed any other woman follow the practice.' And finally, Portlock's entry recorded the appearance of a new face at the Providence's officers' mess:

About 1 PM Maa'hoo a friend of the Kings came onboard the Providence, he had Just arrivd from Morea of which Island he is principal Chief and what I can learn he had been sent some days since to Morea to kill a man and bring him to Opparre and there to be offerd up to their Gods as a thank offering for their success in the late war with the Matavians and another part of his Errand was to d . . .[?] the people of Morea to come over with their Hogs &c for sale to the ships, Maa'hoo the King and his two wives dined with us and afterwards went on shore to the Post.

This 'Maa'hoo' (probably, Mahau) is something of a mystery. In his entry of May 3rd Bligh identified him as a 'Nephew' of Tetupaia, i.e., Tina's mother—who, it will be recalled, was daughter of Ra'iatea's Ari'i Rahi, Tamatoa III, and through whom the Opoan red-feather girdle kin-Title had passed, first to Tina and then to the present Tu. I am unable to discover this Mahau's specific kin links to Tetupaia, but his credentials were evidently distinguished enough for him to have been named Regent—but not 'principal Chief'—of at least part of Mo'orea (see Bligh's entry for May 8th). Along with that, he seems to have been a supporter and emissary of his 'cousin', Tina. The main purpose of his recent mission to Mo'orea is described in later journal entries.

Saturday, April 28th

Fine Weather with Land & Sea Breezes. Thermometer from 81 to 83½ Degrees. Cleaned and Washed Ship. The remainder of the day the People employed <in> mending their Cloaths & washing. Received one load of Stone

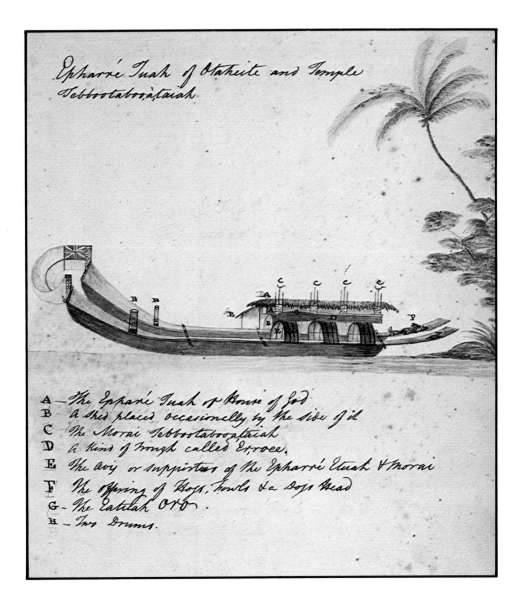

Epharré Tuah of Otaheite and Temple
Tebbootaboo,taiah

A — The Epharré Tuah or House of God
B — A shed placed occasionally by the side of it
C — The Morai Tebbootaboo,taiah
D — A kind of trough called Er,roee.
E — The avy or supporters of the Epharré Etuah & Morai
F — The offering of Hogs, fowls &a Dogs Head
G — The Eatúah OVO .
H — Two Drums.

Plate 13   Bligh's sketch of Taputapuatea canoe

Plate 14   The inland *marae* at Pare Point
Watercolor by George Tobin

Ballast per Launch about 2½ Tons. Sufficient supplies of Fruit, but no Hogs.

      [Marginal note: 'total pots as of Yesterday—breadfruit-1086, plantains-12, ratahs-25, mallies-6, vees-16, ettow-1']

      At Sun rise I set out in my Boat with Tynah & Orrepyah for Oparre, where Hammenne,manne was waiting our arrival at the Morai at the entrance of the Harbour. [Plates 14 and 15] He was at Prayers at the Temple, the Etuah laying before him, wrapt up in Red Cloth as I had seen it at Tepippee. To the right of it lay the body of a dead Man wrapt up in the Platted branch of a Cocoa Nutt Tree, and tied to a Pole by which means the Body was carried about. To the right of the Priest were two Drums very different in size, & at the distance of 20 Yards in the same direction was the Eva'tah [fata], or Altar, on which were twenty nine dead Hogs, and a middle sized Turtle. [Plate 16] On nine stout Posts was erected an Ephare Tuah [fare atua, house (of a) god], & there were two others on Cannoes. Two other Priests assisted Hammennemanne besides two or three inferior People of that Order [the Priesthood?]. I had scarce <scarcely> been seated a quarter of an hour by the Priests, when the Sun having risen above the Trees, caused such a violent stench from the dead Body, as forced me to quit the place and take a Seat out of the direction of the Wind, where our Friend Tynah had placed himself under a spreading Tree. Otoo was carried about on a Man's Shoulders talking to us & playing his tricks during the whole time of the devotion. After the first Prayer upon our arrival, the Bundle which they called the Etuah was untied & exposed. The Marro oorah, or feathered Belt, was also taken out of another bundle & spread out, so that I had a view of every sacred thing that belonged to them. Hammennemanne now began another Prayer, it was very long, but had many repetitions in it, so that it is not so extraordinary, as Strangers imagine, the retentiveness of this Mans Memory <the retentiveness of this Man's Memory is not so extraordinary as Strangers imagine>. Taking up his prayer <his prayer being considered> in all its various changes and repetitions, the whole amounted to this. We have sacrificed a Man—we have presented his Eye unto thee as a token of they [sic] power, and unto our King, because it is thy will <that> he reigneth over us, and knowing <we know> that every thing belongeth unto thee. We display our Feathers. We present our Hogs; and all this we do oh Oro', for we know thou delightest in it—our hope & wish is to do as thou desirest, prosper us therefore in all our undertakings, let us conquer our Enemies and live in Plenty.

      After this prayer, a Hog which had been strangled was scorched his hair taken off, and the entrails taken out and burnt except the liver. After smearing the Hog over with its blood, and broiling the liver, the whole was brought to the Morai, (or Temple) the place of Prayer. This appeared to me to be particularly the offering of my Friend Tynah, & Hammennemene pronounced another Prayer, which was in favor of King George, Myself and all the People who were with me in the Ships. The Drums were beat at intervals, and the Hog being laid on the Evatah, & the Corps [sic] buried by the side of the Morai; the Marro was made up in one bundle, & the Eatuah in the other, carefully covered over with a piece of English Red Cloth (as I have observed before) and the Ceremony ended.

There were not many people present, and among those that were, I saw no grave or serious attention. The Priest himself the moment he had done prayers began to joke & create fun in an obscene manner.

Tynah requested I would not return immediately to the Ship, as he had ordered a Turtle to be killed for us; it was about 20 lb Weight and baked as they do their Hogs. While it was dressing we went to the Morai [marginal note: 'called Wow,ooreah'] on the Point of the Harbour [Plate 17]; & there I observed that two Bodies had recently been deposited under the Coral Rocks, <of> Men who had been sacrificed in the beginning of the War. The dead Body we saw was brought from Moreah four or five days back—it was a sacrifice made by the people of that Island and sent to Otoo. The Ceremony of presenting the Eye was not performed at this time, it was done when the body was first landed.

In War time these Sacrifices are common,—on being defeated; a Man is Sacrificed <they sacrifice a Man> to their God to implore assistance and success. On a Victory, <it> is their most sacred way of returning thanks. The Wretch on whom the lot falls is of no estimation, and is always called a bad Man. On my return to Tynah, the People showed me a large Drum in one of their Houses, that Christian had brought from Toobooi [Tubuai]. It appears that this Wretch [in ML 'this Wretch' has been replaced by 'he'] had gone to Toobooi to settle, but on finding the inhabitants inimicable, he was forced from <to leave> it, and returned to Otaheite, where part of his Gang [in ML 'Gang' replaced by 'Crew'] left him as I have before related.

The Turtle being near <nearly> ready, our repast was to be taken on the Ground which was covered with fresh leaves for that purpose under the Shade of a fine Tree. When we were all Seated, Tynah desired the Priest to perform a Ceremony called Errow,wow,ah. This Ceremony is a token of Friendship and intercourse with all those who <whom> the Ereerahigh shall be pleased to Name—it gives all the Chiefs great pleasure to know of it being performed, and <they> feel themselves highly honored in having their Names called over. It is <was> performed thus—The Priest collected a number of leaves and standing up, he called every name as Tynah directed him or <as> he knew to be his <Tynah's> wish, and each set of names he numbered with a leaf. These leaves were then given to Otoo, (who was by on a Mans Shoulders,) and he held them untill all the Friends were called over, among whom were ourselves & the Ships. Part of this Ceremony Myself, Mr. Bond, & James Harwood the Surgeon who was with me assisted in, by the help of Tynah, who told us alternately what we had to say. The first Word was, Errow,wowah, which signifies the Kings good Wishes to the person whose name follows.

124

The Morai or Temple where the Ceremony was a*t* <performed>, is an oblong pile of Stones about 10 Yards long & four feet high [marginal note: 'A Pavement was in the front where the Priests Sat & leaned their backs against Stone Posts for that Purpose'], on the top of which was, stuck about fourteen rude Ornaments, on some of which was a resemblance of a Man & on others a Bird. The whole range of them they called Tebbotaboo,ataiah, as they did also similar Ornaments [marginal note: 'See 26th'] on the Ephare Tuah's that were in the Cannoes. The only interpretation I can give to Tebbotaboo ataiah is, that it is their Great Temple or principal place of Worship.

The Red Bundle their Etuah (which they called Oro) was nothing more than a number of Yellow and Red feathers, and four rolls about 18 Inches long platted over with Cocoa Nut fibres, to which they gave the Name of some inferior Deities. Captain Cook calls this lump of superstition the Ark.

The Marro Oorah, or feathered Belt, which is put on the Erreerahigh when the Sacrifice is first made and the Eye presented, is about 12 feet long, and about 14 Inches wide, one half is made of Yellow Feathers stitched on Cloth, and the other half is some Red English Buntin without any feathers. The Ends are wrought, with feathers, in divisions, which give a change to the form of it, and are the parts which hang as ornaments when worn by the King. The Yellow-Feathers are diversified by narrow stripes of red feathers, it is however not remarkably ellegant or neatly made. [Plate 16, top]

We took our repast very heartily, and with <experienced> the most attentive and kind Welcome ever Men had. [In ML 'ever Men had' is crossed out, Bligh evidently having tempered somewhat his earlier enthusiasm.] Our conversation turned various ways. They spoke in a very reprehensive manner of Christian, and said they were very happy that Captain Edwards had carried so many of them <his People> away. Coleman the Armourer they said cried when he spoke of me and had told them that he was not concerned in the busyness, and <that he> had declared so to me when I was d*r*ove <driven> away from the Ship, on this account they said they had considered him as a good Man, and were glad to hear I had forgiven him. Churchill & Thompson they said lived at Tairraboo, where being jealous of each other, Churchill induced the Chiefs to Endeavor to steal Thompsons Musquet and Pistol, The Friends of Thompson informed him of it, he therefore on the first sight of Churchill shot him through the Body. This produced an utter aversion in the Chiefs to Thompson, they laid hold of him in return and beat his Brains out, thus these two Villains <unfortunate Wretches> affected their own destruction, and avoided the punishment that <otherwise> awaited them.

I was particular in my questions to know how it was, that <why> the Marro which we had known to be kept at Attahooroo, together with the God Oro and Temple Tebboo-taboo,ataiah, should be now at Oparre. The

General answer was, that they had been at War with the Attahooroo People, and had seized their God and brought him to Oparre. This I find really to have been the Case, and that the Bounty's People assisted with their Musquetry.

Before the present Otow's [marginal note: 'The Father of Tynah'] time, it appears that Attahooroo was the principall residence of the Erreerahigh. In my last Voyage, I have given an account of the Principal People as far back as Otow's Father, which I find perfect, and from this and the information these People give me, <it appears that> the Power of Tootahah, who was a great Chief, and Otow's Uncle, was the Cause of the Marro and Tebboo, tabooataiah remaining at Attahooroo; but as he had been a long time dead, and those people having <had> injured them, they went to War and Conquered the whole District.

The Moon was now nine Days Old. I asked the Name of the Month and Tootahah told me as he had done in 1788 that it was (Ahounoonu or) April.

About Noon we all returned to the ship.

This was an eventful day, for Bligh, and consequently for the student of Tahitian culture. Bligh's description of the visible proceedings of the *marae* ceremonies is characteristically succinct—so much so that a number of his points require explication; first, the plan and architecture of the *marae* itself.

In fact, the area comprising Bligh's 'Marae Point' (called Utuhaihai by Tahitians) contained two large and at least two small stone-built units, and a number of other less permanent ones (for example, wooden altars, platforms for the sacred objects, a round-ended storage house, etc.) (For a detailed description of this *marae* complex and of the major ones of Atehuru, see Green and Green, 1968) The first of the two large stone-built units seen by Bligh—the one at which the principal ceremony took place—was located about a hundred yards inland. On May 21 it was visited by Tobin, who sketched it (Plate 14) and described it as follows:

As we approached the Morai, the eastern breeze wafted to us no very odorous perfume from numbers of hogs that had been sanctified as an oblation to the deity. These were on a stage about forty feet in length; supported by three rows of pillars eight feet high; long rushes nearly reaching the ground from each side of it—close to the stage were two tables on one of which was a single hog. Those on the stage amounted to about fifteen. The Morai was a pavement about a foot high, sixty four long, and forty two broad; at one end indeed, it was raised four or five feet, like two steps which part was decorated with carved wooden figures, some of them representing Heeva dancers, birds, and lizards. A few upright stones were fixed in different parts of the pavement, three or four feet high, and bread fruit and Cocoa nut trees were growing among them. A human skull, and one of a hog were hanging to some carved figures near the Morai, and another skull was brought to us which our guides said was kept with great care at this place, it being that of Thompson, one of the mutineers in the Bounty.

A case for the Eatooa nearly similar to the one seen in Otoos canoe at Matavai was near, supported on a platform, about six feet high, by nine pillars. Close to it, was an uninhabited house, but for what purpose we did not learn.

126

The second of the two large *marae* units, visited briefly by Bligh, was located at water's edge. It was also sketched by Tobin (Plate 17), and described by him as follows:

As well as the pavement already mentioned, there was, on the eastern point of Oparrey harbour, not an hundred yards distant, a large pile of stones in the form of a base of a pyramid, regularly placed in four stories. Many carved figures in wood, similar to those on the pavement, were here placed upright, and the Toa [Casuarina equisetifolia] was growing luxuriantly among the coral rocks, though its roots were washed by the ocean. The windward side of this projecting coral point was sheltered by a wall, inside of which were several human skeletons laying in different directions.

Now to comment on the above topics:

Tahitian drums (*pahu*) were made of a sharkskin head fastened over the hollowed-out end of a section of the trunk of some close-grained tree. The heads were stretched tightly over the openings by means of sennit (i.e., cords of braided coconut-husk fiber). Drums varied both in height and in diameter and were beaten either with sticks or by hand. Tones varied mainly with the size and shape of the drum, although, according to Joseph Banks, 'they know also how to tune two drums of Different notes into concord' (Beaglehole 1962: I 350)—presumably by varying cord tension *before* a performance (but not, according to another observer, *during* one—i.e., not by means of slides).

Turning to Bligh's remarks about priests, there was in fact what he referred to as a priestly 'Order'—not a society-wide one, however, but a number of them attached to each of the more important *marae*. While there were few full-time priests (in addition to some part-time ones who were too decrepit to engage in other activities), some men, such as Ha'amanemane, spent most of their time in priestly or related activities. Moreover, most of those belonging to any one *marae* 'Order' played specialized roles, which were learned during lengthy novitiates.

Priests in general were called *tahu'a pure*, 'specialists (in) praying', as distinct from *taura* (shaman, human oracle), and from sorcerers of various kinds—although some priests also engaged in shamanism and sorcery as well. The defining activity of a priest was to communicate between humans and spirits, which usually consisted of inducing the latter to enter a *marae*—into some image or 'seat' within the *marae*—and listen to the priest's verbal supplication, usually backed up with offerings of food and other objects and of services considered pleasing to them (including praise). In many, perhaps most, *marae* all of the various jobs comprising this activity were carried out by one all-round priest, with perhaps one or two general-purpose assistants; but in *marae* associated with a whole district the jobs were distributed among priestly specialists, including an officiating 'high priest' (such as Ha'amanemane), image bearers, novices, and attendants (called 'Big-bellies'!).

The offices of high-priest were usually hereditary, but most incumbents underwent arduous training as well—as indeed was the case with all priestly specialists directly engaged in verbal supplication, inasmuch as errors in delivery were believed to be punished by the spirits in question. Consequently, although specialists in priestcraft were well compensated materially—e.g. with frequent rations of food delicacies, and were rewarded socially—e.g., with prestige and influence, their calling was usually onerous to acquire and sometimes dangerous, spiritually, to engage in.

Bligh's translation of Ha'amanemane's prayer may have been a bit too 'free'—and suspiciously suggestive of the Common Book of Prayer!—but his characterization of its structure was quite accurate. (A structure that is still evident in the formal, and typically interminable, deliveries of modern-day Tahitian pastors and other orators. See Oliver 1981: 31-2.)

The remarks by Bligh about the mood attending the principal *marae* ceremony—the inattentiveness of the onlookers (including the ever-playful Tu) and the jocosity of Ha'amanemane as soon as it was concluded—are confirmed by the accounts of other European observers of that era. Notwithstanding, those behaviors contrast sharply with what we are told, in some other accounts, about the actual performance of the rites *per se*—which was required to be word- and gesture-perfect, and unprofaned by alien (i.e., *noa*) intrusion, such as the presence of a female. (In other words, the action of *pure*, of prayer and supplication, seems to have contained an element of magical coercion: another example of the hazards of scholarly classifying!)

The image (*to'o*) of the Deity (i.e., of the *Atua* 'Oro) used in the ceremony was probably the one that has come to be known as the 'Papara Image', to distinguish it from two other 'Oro images reported, in fairly credible legends, to have been in Tahiti at that time—one at Taiarapu, the other in Paea. Also credible is the legend that the Papara Image had been fabricated at Opoa (Ra'iatea) and transferred—why, is not fully known—to Papara in about 1760, along with a feather-girdle named Teraiputata. From there the Image was moved to the 'Utu'aimahurau *marae* in Atehuru, and in 1791 (as mentioned in the journal entries of April 26th and 27th) from Atehuru to Pare. Bligh's characterization of the Papara Image as 'nothing more than a number of Yellow and Red feathers' was fairly accurate—although the feathers were not simply loose but probably attached to a wickerwork frame. It was certainly not an 'image' in the sense of an anthropomorphic likeness to 'Oro—nor, it seems, was it intended to be so. The more powerful spirits, such as 'Oro, were conceived to be tegumented with feathers, and were attracted to them *per se*. Besides, the 'Bundle' was not the Deity himself, but rather his temporary seat during his sojourn in the *marae*.

As for the particular feather-girdle that figured in this ceremony (Plate 16, top), that too had had a checkered past. Cook saw it in 1777 and described it as follows:

. . . it was about five yards long and fifteen inches broad, and composed of red and yellow feathers but mostly of the latter; the one end was bordered with eight pieces, each about the size and shape of [a] horse shoe, with their edges fringed with black pigeon feathers; the other end was forked and the ends not of the same length. The feathers were in square compartments ranged in two rows and otherways so disposed as to have a good effect being first paisted or fixed to their Country cloth [i.e., bark cloth] and the whole sewed to the upper end of the English Pendant [that] Captain Wallis [of the *Dolphin*] had displayed, and left flying a shore the first time he landed at Matavai . . . (Beaglehole 1967: 202)

The origin of the original part of this *maro* (i.e., before the Wallis pendant had been added to it) is not entirely certain, but it is likely to have been the one that accompanied the Papara Image from Ra'iatea. In any case, there are good reasons for thinking that the Wallis pendant had been added by Purea—Wallis's famous 'Oberea', who was the wife of Amo, Papara's Chief at the time. Purea happened to be at Matavai during Wallis's visit, and her commanding presence and imperious manner led the English to identify her as Tahiti's 'Queen'. Shortly after the English pendant had been added to the original segment, thereby enhancing its emblematic authority, and perhaps also its religious efficacy, the *maro*, along with the Papara Image, were captured in a war against Papara and moved to Atehuru, where they remained until 1791, when—as previously noted—they were captured again and taken to Pare.

Our—and Bligh's—concern with this 'lump of superstition' and with this 'Belt' (which was 'not remarkably ellegant or neatly made') may strike the reader as tedious, an exercise in triviality, until it is realized how absolutely indispensible the two objects were to the exercise of supernaturally sanctioned ritual pre-eminence in the Tahiti of that era. Bligh appears to have understood that well. He also understood the difference between ritual pre-eminence and secular authority, as indicated in the second-last paragraph in this day's entry, and in the *Bounty* Journal account to which he refers. The latter states, in effect, that 'The King'—i.e., the incumbent of the kin-Title associated with the Wallis *maro* and the Papara Image, who in this era was a Pomare—possessed 'great honors' but no secular authority over people outside his own district. In fact, at the time of Cook's visits, the present Tina, whom the English labelled 'King', exercised little secular authority over even his own 'subjects' in Pare-Arue. The person who did so was Tutaha (Bligh's 'Tootahah'), who was brother of Tina's paternal grandfather and who by all accounts was an imposing figure of a man (Bank's 'Hercules'), a respected war-leader, and an effective administrator and diplomat. So great, indeed, was his authority and influence that Cook described him as 'the Chief man of the Island'. (Beaglehole 1955: 85) Conventionally, Tina's father, Teu (Bligh's 'Otow'), was Regent during his son's minority, but it was Tutaha who exercised the authority of that office. And it was Tutaha who led the forces that defeated the Paparans and transferred the Papara

Image and the Wallis *maro* to Atehuru. In doing so he acted on behalf of his grand-nephew, the present Tina, but why Atehuru had become his 'principall residence' and why he installed the sacred objects there, and not in his (and Tina's) own *marae* in Pare, is not known. (Perhaps he wished to extend Tina's potential secular authority to include Atehuru, inasmuch as the Atehurans would have required Tina's presence there in order to invoke the assistance of 'Oro.)

The ceremony witnessed by Bligh was a sequal to one that had been held a few days previously, when the human sacrifice being celebrated had actually taken place—i.e., when one eye of the victim had been presented to 'Oro directly—i.e.,to his Image—and the other to Tu, as vicar of 'Oro. The victim was the one brought from Mo'orea by Mahau, the man mentioned in Portlock's entry of April 27th. (In most recorded instances the formal ceremony of human sacrifice had no sequel. Why this one took place is not entirely clear; perhaps the formal one, which Tina *et al.* had been too hung-over to attend, had been unalterably scheduled.) Whatever the explanation, the climactic action of formal rites of human sacrifice was, as described by Bligh in his entry of April 20th, the symbolic eating of one of the victim's eye-balls by the Deity's vicar (in this instance, Tu). As Bligh reported, the latter did not eat it, or even sniff at it; he merely gaped open his mouth *as if* to eat it. This, the only conventional practice in Tahiti suggestive of cannibalism, is viewed by some scholars as a relic of an earlier era when cannibalism actually took place there. (Cannibalism is known to have been practised in some other Polynesian societies, so—it is reasoned—why not in Tahiti as well?) Be that as it may, the Tahitians of the era now under discussion were vehement in their abhorrence of cannibalism—although their eschatology included the belief that the souls of some humans were devoured by deities, and then regurgitated, in order to 'purify' them.

Persons selected for sacrifice were of three types: (1) war captives, some of whom were sacrificed immediately and others held for future sacrifice; (2) persons who, deliberately or unwittingly, had violated religious taboos—such as interrupting solemn religious rites; and (3) persons who had incurred the animosity of leaders by, for example, thievery or acts of *lèse majesté* or seduction of females of higher social class. Or, as Lieutenant Bond wrote in his Journal: 'the chief who makes the offering causes some of his domestics to lay in ambush and knock in the head one of his subjects who is most obnoxious to the people'. In the case of war captives, who were called *titi*, some of them went on living for years before 'execution'—or in fact may never have been executed; nevertheless, they and their descendants remained indefinitely in jeopardy (or, as sometimes happened, moved to another district and a new social identity). With respect to the other categories of victims (who were called *ta'ata ino*: Bligh's 'bad man', or rather, 'despised person'), they were not always executed immediately after their crimes or infractions, and may not have been apprised of their jeopardy at the time, but when a victim was needed for sacrifice were executed without warning.

Most of the victims selected for sacrifice were adult males and, except in times of war (when some of the sacrificed captives were maimed), the preference was for victims without crippled limbs or disfiguring scars, particularly scars that had been inflicted by women (for example, scratches, in the heat of passionate embrace). The need for unblemished bodies usually led to the victims being executed by a blow on the skull.

The adjunct ceremony, in which Bligh and his officers participated, was nearly identical to those performed at professedly friendly meetings between politically equal leaders, or between leaders and their principal—and often unreliable—'supporters'. The closest Tahitian word I can find to Bligh's rendition of the name of this ceremony (i.e., 'Errow,wowah') is *aroha* (which was translated by early nineteenth century missionaries as, 'to have pity or compassion; to shew mercy, love, sympathy'—Davies 1851: 38, but which has now become banalized to meaninglessness).

Also appropriate for such an august assembly was the *pìece de résistance* of the meal—turtles having been the choicest of Tahitian delicacies and reserved for upper-class males. (In fact, anyone else capturing a turtle was required to hand it over to his district chief.) And finally, the use of leaves in this ceremony was typical, leaves having been used as tallies whenever listing took place.

Tobin was not present at the human-sacrifice ceremony. Instead, his Journal entry for the day recorded a theft, and a continuation of the unashamedly public dalliance between Tina and Vaereti:

Until this day, the natives only interrupted us by kindness in our excursions; but Mr Whyte, one of the Surgeons mates wandering too far without a guide, was plundered of his handkerchief by a man whom he met in the woods. The thief displayed some address and ingenuity having offered his friendly services to conduct our countrymen to the hills, while his shoulders bore him safely over many a stream until far from the busy 'haunts of man,' when being by far the strongest of the two, he without ceremony rifled the doctors pockets, nor did he leave instructions which was the shortest way back to the post.

With Pomaurey, Orepaia, Edeea, and Whyhereddy, I had the honour of dining at Captain Blighs table to day. The King Regent had scarcely finished his meal when he betook himself to toy with the false Whyhereddy, who, heedless of our presence, was reclining her finely turned limbs, not too much enveloped in drapery, on the cabin floor.

There was a disparity in the years of Pomaurey and Whyhereddy, which at Otahytey is by no means uncommon. It has before been observed that his Majesty is of the numerous fraternity of Cuckolds, but like many among ourselves, seemed not aware of what he was robbed, or else, was indifferent about it. Yet did he doat on his younger wife, who with an art, inseparable from her sex, managed this amorous infirmity, to her own benefit and amusement.

The whole day Orepaia was very indignant in consequence of several articles having been stolen from our shipmates at the post, giving every assurance that strict search whould be made to discover the thief.

Sunday, April 29th

A quiet and uneventful day—except perhaps for the crew members who were permitted shore leave, 'for exercise', but who have left no written evidence of their activities. Bligh's entry is as follows:

Fair Weather with Land and Sea Breezes the Thermometer from 81 to 83½ Degrees.
Mustered the Ships Company. Saw them all clean Dressed. Performed Divine Service. Gave leave for Six Men to go on Shore for exercise.
Plentiful supplies. Broached a Puncheon of Spruce Beer for the People.

And Portlock:

AM) *a Moderate sea breese, very few Canoes about, no hogs and but few Cocoanutts at Market gave a part of the Ships Company leave to go on shore.* PM) *a Gentle sea breeze with fine weather I this Afternoon had a visit from the King and his Wifes, they each of them made me a present of a large Hog a Quantity of Bread Fruit and Cocoanutts and some pieces of Otaheitian cloth. I made them a proper return and in the Evening they departed very much pleasd with the Attention shewn them towards Night I accompanied the Commodore on shore to the Post were [sic] we were Joind by the King and other chiefs we found all perfectly quiet and the Natives behaving in the Most friendly manner, the liberty men all onboard and during the Night we had light winds and hot weather.*

Monday, April 30th

Ditto Weather [i.e., same as yesterday] Employed in the Hold. Carpenters Caulking the Larboard side and making Extra places for the Plants on the Quarter Deck. Cooper repairing Casks and making Tubs. Received 3½ Tons of Stone Ballast.
Plentifull supplies of Fruit, Roots and Hogs.
Our Post is little incommoded by the Natives. In the Evenings they collect to see the Marines go through their M̲anovies <Manouvres>, but at Sun down they retire and all becomes quiet. The Plants are doing well. I have this day 1194 Pots filled and 4 Tubs <filled>, 1094 Pots and 4 Tubs have Breadfruit Plants in them.
I have forgot on the 28th to give a description of the Great Evatah, or Evatarow [e fata roa, it is an altar large; Plate 16, bottom] as it is called, on which the Hogs were lying. This famous Altar is formed by three Rows of stout Posts about 8 feet high, thirty six in number aranged regularly, so that the whole space of ground it takes up, may be nearly forty feet by ten. From the Top of one Post to the other, Poles are secured to form a Platform which is covered with small branches and leaves to receive the Offerings. Round the sides the Evatah is prettily ornamented <ornament> with a Curtain of Cocoa Nutt leaves.

The 'Great Evatah' observed by Bligh was seen by Tobin on May 21st; his description of it was reproduced in the entry for April 28th and his watercolor sketch as Plate 14.

In his Journal Lieutenant Portlock recorded the following incident for the forenoon of this day:

Light winds and Variable procurd a small supply of Hogs Employd some hands in salting Pork, loosd Sails to Air, got water off for present use and Employd the Ships Company about the Necessary duty of the ship. Messrs Tobin, Harwood, and Frankland overset in a Canoe going on shore I sent a boat to their Assistance no lives lost.

At this point in Portlock's Journal the handwriting changes (to his clerk's?) and the entries become brief, and concerned almost entirely with housekeeping aboard the *Assistant*, until the departure from Tahiti on July 19th. Tobin, however, continued throughout the visit to record his observations and reflections, including his account of an excursion made on this day:

Early in the morning Harwood and myself quitted the Ship for the post, with an intention of walking to Whapiano, five or six miles eastward of Point Venus, first calling on board the Assistant for a gentleman who was to be part of the party. The Canoe in which we were going on shore, was a single one [i.e., a single-hulled one] very small, and heavily freighted, nor was it long before she overturned; sousing us all completely. Had not our good Doctor [Harwood] effected a fast grip by the outrigger, where he clung magnanimously, the 'number of our mess' would have been reduced, and the world have lost a truly estimable character, as he could no more swim than one of his own coins. To the rest, it was rather a ludicrous affair, as a boat from our consort soon landed us in safety.

This disaster did not frustrate the excursion, and getting our clothes dried at the Post, we proceeded with two confidential natives.

We soon passed a quantity of Tarro, a kind of yam or eddoe, with which the Island abounds, it being issued daily to our crew as one of the substitutes for bread. This root delights in a moist soil; in many places, it was in a luxuriant state nearly half a foot in the water. Some pains had been bestowed in enclosing it against the destruction of their hogs.

The surf along the beach broke high, though sheltered by a reef, an opening in which appeared about two miles from Point Venus, as well as others as we walked eastward.

The path along shore was nearly obstructed when about four miles from the Post, by a high cliff, forming the western boundary of Whapiano. [Plate 18] As well as their language would admit, our guides described that when Captain Wallis visited the Island in 1767 there was no travelling, even at low water, at the foot of these cliffs, and that there had been a gradual secession of the sea on most parts of the Island.

Tupira [Poeno's principal supporter in the recent war] had taken up his residence in this district, to whom we paid a visit, being received with much civility, yet with a reserve that seemed to arise from an apprehension our views might be hostile to his party. He was surrounded by Matavaians and his own family apparently prepared for an attack.

The whole conduct of this Chief evinced a spirit of enterprise and dignity of Character, superior to any one I had yet seen. Most of his front teeth were missing from the blow of a stone, in defending what he deemed his right, and he had still an unhealed wound in his knee from the same weapon [i.e., a sling-shot]. In our conversation pistols were mentioned, which instantly caught his attention, while it animated a countenance in which suspicion could not but be perceived that he still doubted his visitors. This it was our study to remove, when he anxiously requested to see them. Thinking he would be gratified I fired at a mark, which more from accident than skill, took place exactly, gaining me so much applause that I had prudence not to risk losing it by a second attempt. Being our host, we said nothing, from a point of delicacy, of the Matildas muskets, but were afterwards informed that he kept them under his sleeping mat.

The usual refreshments of fruit and cocoa nut milk being taken, the walk was continued about two miles further eastward, when the river presented itself after our having crossed several smaller streams.

The mouth of the Whapiano is above an hundred yards across, its bed being formed of large dark pebbles. The view up the stream is singularly grand and picturesque, but it was rendered imperfect this day by the distant mountains being enveloped in clouds. A sketch I made [Plate 19] will give you a faint idea, and but a faint one—of this beautiful landscape.

The usual mode of crossing the rivers on the natives shoulders, placed us on the eastern bank but after heavy rains, this is not to be effected but in canoes.

Whidooah [Vaetua], the Tayo of Harwood, who had a house in this district received us cordially, instantly ordering the slaughter of a hog (Boa) [pua'a] but as time would not admit of the whole being baked, a limb was cut off and put in the oven.

As usual we were surrounded by men, women, and children, from all parts of the plain who without any deference to the mansion of a prince of the blood [i.e., Vaetua] soon compleatly filled it.

While the joint was baking we strolled up the stream to a place sacred to the Eotooa (God) in a large enclosed square of railing. Near to it was a stone Morai, (burying place) and, as at the Toopapow in Oparrey, a small table with different kind of provisions. All information was denied us by our ignorance of the language, except that, everything was sacred to Eotooa, even a musical instrument formed of a large conch shell with a bamboo pipe to it. Apropos, there is one of them in our collection, at home.

The shoulders [of the hog] was served up on our return, and cleanliness, if not elegance; was as conspicuous as at the most fashionably appointed table in Europe. Leaves, fresh from the tree, served for a table cloth, the appetite had been assisted by exercise, and we had the cheering looks of our host—when awake—with those of his pretty wife Tai Aiva—the Belle of the Isle—to crown the whole.

Whidooah during our walk had taken a moderate portion of Yava, and we found him reclining on the lap of his wife, much disposed to sleep; nor was it long before the somnific effects of the Yava, aided by the operation of towrowmey, (in which Tai Aiva and the Towtows were employed,) fixed him in a sound nap for an hour or two. After fatigue, I have experienced the most delightful relief from the custom (towrowmey) of rubbing and compressing the different parts of the body, and so sensible are the natives of its salutary effects, that we never entered a house after a long walk but that it was offered to be administered, which I can assure you was ever eagerly embraced by your friend. Pomaurey was generally encouraged in his afternoon nap by the operation of towrowmey, nor was it uncommon, to see it persevered in, after the drowsy god had taken possession of his Majesty.

Taking a friendly leave we returned towards the Post.

134

Tai Aiva crossed the Whapiano in simple nudity, unconscious of her hitherto hidden charms, for the translucency of the stream but ill served, however in some places deep, to envelop them.

Tupira's served as a resting place, where every thing was prepared for our refreshment.

It was flood tide, and many of the natives were fishing for mullet with rod and line in the same manner the fly is used for trout. [Plate 18]

Reflecting the wide variety of topics touched on in Tobin's entry, the following commentary will treat them in the order of their recording.

First, the political geography of the area visited. Unlike the more populous western sides of Tahiti's larger land mass, which was divided into several autonomous chiefdoms, its eastern side was thinly populated and its major territorial units less sharply distinct, politically. Geography had much to do with this contrast, the eastward (hence windward) side having narrower coastal plains and fewer offshore protective reefs. The five units comprising this area were, from north to south, Ha'apape (also Mahina), which included Matavai; Ha'apaiano'o—Tobin's 'Whapiano' (also called Papeno'o and Vavau); Tierei; Mahaena; and Hitia'a. The name 'Te Aharoa' was used to refer collectively to the inhabitants of all five units, but little is known about their political inter-relationships beyond the fact that Hitia'a's principal people figured more prominently in events elsewhere on the island than did the leaders of the other four units.

Tobin's 'Tarro' was of course 'taro' (*Colocasia esculenta*), the root of which vied with breadfruit in being Tahitians' most favored staple plant food (their other cultivated vegetable staples having been *taru'a* (*Xanthosoma atrovirens*), *fe'i* (plantain, *Musa fehi*, which also grew wild), *'ape* ('giant taro', *Alocasia macrorrhiza*), *'umara* (sweet potato, *Batatas edulis*), *uhi* (yam, *Dioscorea alata*), *pia* (arrowroot, *Tacca pinnatifida*), *to* (sugar cane, *Saccharum officinarum*), and, of course, coconuts (*niu*, *Cocos nucifera*). The mature tuberous root of the taro is 10 to 12 inches long and contains about 50 per cent starch; the tender young leaves and stems of the plant were also cooked and eaten. Taro grew only in well-watered soil, either in naturally marshy areas or in artificially irrigated patches. Along with saplings of the 'paper mulberry' (*'aute, Broussonetia papyrifera*), the principal source of bark cloth, and with the shrub, *Piper methisticum*, from whose root kava was made, taro was perhaps the most carefully cultivated plant of the Tahitians, all others having required a minimum of labor after planting. Thus, in Bond's view:

Abundance has made this a Luxurious and indolent nation, for most of their time is spent in sleeping and feeding. The Taro . . . Ava, and Paper Mulberry demand some attendance, and are laid out with great regularity, but very few other plants need the least assistance, and grow spontaneously throughout the island.

The reader will remember Tupira, Tobin's first host during this excursion, as having joined with Poeno, at the cost of his front teeth, in opposing the Pomares' attempt to 'recover' the *Matilda* firearms. In view of Bligh's deliberate unfriendliness towards himself and Poeno, Tupira's suspicion of Tobin is understandable.

Tobin's next host, 'Whidooah', was of course Tina's youngest brother, Vaetua, earlier described as a bold warrior, but a 'very impudent, dissolute young man', much addicted to kava. His residence in this place, somewhat distant from the Pomare domain of Pare-Arue, and even beyond the eastern boundary of Matavai (which was a sometime dependency or ally of Pare-Arue) may have been consequent upon his marriage to the delectable 'Tai Aiva' (Taeva?)—if indeed their present residence were her natal home. (Although Tahitian married couples tended to reside in the neighborhood of the husband there was no rigid rule to that effect, most couples having resided where they perceived their greater advantages to be.) Whatever the reason, in several of the eye-witness reports about this era, Vaetua has been described as 'chief' of his present residential district, Ha'apaiano'o—not merely the holder of a 'Royal' (i.e., Pomare) kin-Title, but the local secular leader as well.

In Tobin's judgment 'Tai Aiva' was not only beautiful and tantalizing but an expert in the Tahitian practice of massage (*rumirumi*). In his *Bounty* Journal Bligh reports having undergone this refreshing and therapeutic treatment, but the best account of it is provided by James Cook:

. . . when they [Tina's mother, his three sisters, and eight other women] got to the ship they told me they were come to sleep on board and to cure me of the desorder that I complained of, which was a sort of Rheumatick pain in one side from my hip to the foot. This kind offer I excepted of, made them up a bed in the Cabbin floor and submited myself to their direction, I was desired to lay down in the Midst of them, then as many as could get round me began to squeeze me with both hands from head to foot, but more especially the parts where the pain was, till they made my bones crack and a perfect Mummy of my flesh—short after being under their hands about a quarter of an hour I was glad to get away from them. How[ev]er I found immediate relief from the operation, they gave me a nother rubing down before I went to bed and I found my self pretty easy all the night after. They repeated the operation the next Morning before they went a shore, and again in the evening when they came on board, after which I found the pains intirely removed and the next Morning they left me. This they call *Romy* an operation which in my opi[ni]on far exceed[s] the flesh brush, or any thing we make use of of the kind. It is universally practiced among them, it is some times performed by the men but more generally by the Woman. If at any time one appear languid or tired and sit down by any of them they immediately begin with Romy upon your legs, which I have always found to have an exceeding good effect. (Beaglehole 1967: 214–15)

Having met with Tahitian drums in an earlier journal entry, we are now introduced to the conch-shell 'trumpet' (*pu*), another of their sound-making instruments (the others having been bamboo gongs, nose flutes, castanets, and dance rattles). The most detailed description of their trumpets is that of the missionary, William Ellis:

The sound of the trumpet, or shell, a species of murex used by the priests in the temple, also by the herald, and others on board their fleets, was more horrific than that of the drum. The largest shells were usually selected for this purpose, and were sometimes above a foot in length, and seven or eight inches in diameter at the mouth. In order to facilitate the blowing of this trumpet, they made a perforation about an inch in diameter, near the apex of the shell. Into this they inserted a bamboo cane, about three feet in length, which was secured by binding it to the shell with finely braided cinet [sinnit]; the aperture was rendered air-tight by cementing the outside of it with a resinous gum from the breadfruit tree. These shells were blown when any procession marched to the temple, at the inauguration of the king, during the worship at the temple, or when a tabu, or restriction, was imposed in the name of the gods. We have sometimes heard them blown. The sound is extremely loud, but the most monotonous and dismal that it is possible to imagine. (Ellis 1829: I 283–4)

Tobin's brief mention of rod fishing is, inexplicably, one of the few descriptions in any of the expedition's journals of the large number of methods utilized by the Tahitians in what was their most technically skillful subsistence activity, namely, marine fishing. In comparison with many other Pacific Islanders—for example, those of New Guinea's Western Highlands—the Tahitians were indifferent horticulturists; as salt-water fishermen, however, they were (and still are) superb. Not only did ocean and lagoon fishing supply most of the savory—the animal—supplements to their bland vegetable foods, but it was to them a pleasurable pastime, sometimes a most exciting sport.

Small nets, sticks, spears, traps, or even bare hands were used for collecting crustaceans, sea urchins, molluscs, and gastropods on the reefs or in the lagoon shallows. Poisoning was also resorted to in quiet lagoon waters, the bruised leaves of several plants having been used. Lures were employed to catch octopus and torches for night-time fishing within the reefs. The nets used for fishing within the lagoons varied from small one-man scoop nets and throw-nets, to seines up to forty fathoms long and twelve fathoms deep. In addition, in some shallow waters weirs were constructed—of stones, coral, leaves, nets, or combinations of these. Spears were used mainly for fishing in quiet waters; hooks and lines both in lagoons and open sea. (Plates 18, 20)

But of all their methods of fishing the Tahitians were at their best in the dangerous art of offshore fishing. In their quest for albacore, bonito, dolphin, shark, sword fish, and other pelagic fish they worked singly or in groups, sometimes staying out for days at a time. Moreover, the various types of hooks used in that fishing revealed a reservoir of knowledge about the prey, and an ingenuity in capturing them, that was matched in no other of their enterprises.

——Curious, that the men—the *mariners*—aboard the *Providence* and the *Assistant* paid closer attention to, for example, temple architecture, bark-cloth manufacture, and tattooing, than to the Tahitians' matchless methods and skills in catching fish!

Tuesday, May 1st

Fine Weather with Land and Sea Breezes at SSE and East. Thermometer from 81 to 84 Degrees.

Employed Caulking the Larboard side, making places for the Plants on the Quarter Deck, and in the Hold. Repairing Casks. Received 3½ Tons of Ballast per Launch.

We continue to have Plentifull Supplies and have Salted 13 Hogsheads of fine Pork. A few families are now getting to Matavai, and we have a great <greater> number of People collecting, Peace being established. Poeno is also come in, and has intercourse with Oparre People as usual, but I have forbade him to see me, untill the Property of C[aptain] Weatherhead is returned. They say it is at Teturoah, and shall be brought in as soon as the Wind will permit them to send for it. This will be more than I expect, for today Mr. Bond bought two Dollars for a few trifles he had about him, it is probable therefore that no one person has it in his possession.

Tetiaroa (Bligh's 'Teturoah') is a coral atoll some thirty nautical miles north of Tahiti. In the era of the *Providence* visit it had little natural vegetation but supported a large number of coconut palms. Potable water was supplied by rain catchment and by a fresh-water spring on one of its ten islets. These resources, along with great quantities of fish in its lagoon and surrounding waters provided subsistence enough for a permanent population of two to three hundred. Morrison, the *Bounty* crew member, provides the best available account of the atoll's economic and political conditions:

[The coconut palms] are the Property of O Toos [Pomare] Family who keeps the Inhabitants in subjection by keeping them from Planting the Breadfruit or other Trees and suffers nothing to grow there except a few Tarro for His own use under the Charge of one of His favorites—and as these Islands cannot be Approached by large Canoes He makes them His Magazine for all His riches; a Number of Canoes are kept there for Fishery and Near 40 Sail of small sailing Canoes which they Haul over the reef are kept constantly plying between them & Taheite; they bring Fish for the Kings household, and return loaded with provisions—and besides these the Dolphin Canoes trade there when the Dolphin Fishery is over, Carrying Provisions and Returning With [coconut] Oil which they Make in large quantitys, a Variety of Fine Fish and a Sauce Made of Ripe Cocoa Nuts Calld Tyeyro [taioro], the Nuts being gathered before they are too old and [are] Grated in the same Manner as for Oil, which being Mixed with Shri[m]ps and left a day or so to ripen becomes like Curds and is excellent sause for Fish, Pork or Fowle. (Rutter 1935: 201–2)

138

Plate 15   Bligh's sketch of part of inland *marae* at Pare Point

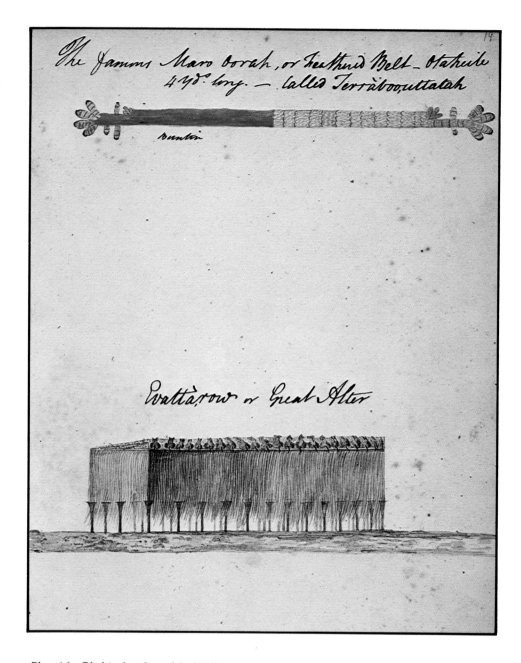

Plate 16   Bligh's sketches of the Wallis *maro* (*top*) and the 'Great Altar' of the inland *marae* at Pare Point (*bottom*)

In addition, the Pomares and their relatives and retainers used to repair to Tetiaroa for 'vacations',—to rest, amuse, and fatten themselves, and to recover health after heavy bouts of kava drinking.

All the above having been confirmed by other writers on the Tahiti of this era, it is curious, to say the least, that Poeno would have sent the captured *Matilda* objects to Tetiaroa in order to keep them out of the Pomares' reach! In fact, other entries in the *Providence* journals indicate that the firearms, at least, had never left Tahiti.

Wednesday, May 2nd

Cloudy Weather and Light Variable Winds and Calms. Thermometer from 81 to 83 Degrees.

Employed in the Hold. Carpenters making places for the Plants on the Quarter Deck, and caulking the Larboard side. Received 3 Tons of Ballast.

Very Sufficient supplies.

The People began to collect about Matavai, and particularly Women and Children. A Woman with a Child about 18 Months old, calling herself the Wife of McIntosh (late of the Bounty and gone home in the Pandora) came to me to day and told me, she had constantly lived with McIntosh, and he was the Father of the Child, a fine little Girl, she had then in her Arms.

This Woman with several others had been with Christian to Tobooai. [Marginal note; 'see 10th April'] She related that they stayed two Months there with the Ship. Christians intentions were to settle at that Island, and <he> had begun to build Houses, and a Battery to defend himself, with the Ships Guns. Teeneerow and Arrowytaihoah two principal Chiefs on the Island, on seeing their <this> proceedings objected to their <his> stay. Altercations insued, and at last War was declared on both sides, many of the Islanders lost their lives. Christian however did not find it safe to remain among them, and therefore Embarked with all his Party. They arrived at Otaheite two Days afterwards, when such different ways of thinking arose among them, and the principal Chiefs treated Christian with so much coolness that he determined to part with those who were discontented, and immediately to set Sail. It <this> took place in the course of 16 Hours, and the Bounty left Matavai with some Natives on board [marginal note: Tobooi Men Taheite Men Boys Women'] never to return again. The only knowledge of his proceedings in future was, he declared openly his intentions to look for some land that would Suit his plan of making a Settlement, and <that> then <he> would haul the Ship on Shore and break her up.

This Woman who calls herself Mary (and her Child Elizabeth, for she says all the Mens Wives had English Names) constantly remarked that McIntosh, Coleman, Hilbrant, Norman <Norman, Hilbrant>, Byrne, and Ellison, scarce <scarcely> ever spoke of me without crying. Steward and Haywood were *perfectly satisfied with their situation, as any two Villains could be, [in ML 'as any two Villains could be' is crossed out] and so were the rest of them. They deserved to be killed she said; but hoped those who had cried for me would not be hurt. She agreed with Tabbyroos [Tapiru] account that Coleman was obliged to swim from t<u>he</u> S<u>h</u>ip <Christian> by Stealth, for he was detained as being <a> Blacksmith and a usefull Man.*

So perfectly had this Woman been informed of the whole Story, that she told me of all the Men who came into my Cabbin and assisted to tye my Hands, and <said> that no Person beside myself were tied.

It appears that the Ship lay in an open Road at Toobooi, and Rode out some Gales of Wind.

Tynah, Otow, and Oreepyah with their Wives, are always with me at Dinner. We continue on the best footing with the Natives, and our Plants thrive so fast a<u>s</u> g<u>ives</u> <to give> me great satisfaction. Out of great a number a few are not so flourishing, and I have therefore, directed about 68 to be shifted.

Our Sick List consists only of Venereals, and the People unfit for duty owing to boils about their extremities, which the change of diet has occasioned.

Anyone choosing to read this far in a book about Bligh's *second* Breadfruit Voyage may be assumed, I suppose, to be well acquainted with the events and consequences of his *first*. Hence, I shall not burden this account with a repetition of the *Bounty*'s wanderings after the mutiny, including her ill-starred stay at Tubuai. Instead, I shall merely refresh the memories of those *Bounty* devotees who, like myself, are forgetful of names, that the ex-*Bounty* men mentioned in this entry met with the following fates:
——Macintosh, Coleman, Norman, and Byrne were eventually acquitted of complicity in the mutiny, the first three having been specifically absolved by Bligh, and the last by obvious circumstance (i.e., he was too blind and decrepit to enter the loyalists' launch);
——Hillbrant and Steward drowned during the wreck of the *Pandora*;
——Heywood and Morrison were sentenced to hang, but were paroled by recommendation of the Court (mainly due to the 'influence' of their families and friends);
——Ellison was found guilty, and having had no 'influence' was hanged. (Note: for an excellent résumé of the famous Mutiny Trial see Kennedy 1978: 162–75)

Thursday, May 3rd

Land and Sea Breezes SE and E by N with some Westerly breezes in the Morning. Thermometer from 81 to 82½ Degrees.

Employed in the Hold <and> Caulking the sides, and building places for the Plants on the Quarter Deck. Received 4 Tons of ballast per Launch.

Cooper repairing Casks and making Tubs for the Plants. [Marginal note: 'Stone Ballast in all taken in here 22 Tons. Ships Draught of Water 15 feet 8 inches abaft, 14 feet 5 inches forward']

Sufficient supplies of every kind.

No Chiefs of any consequence have yet come to see us, except the Otoo family. The Matavai People have begun to erect some Sheds, but a number of them have not yet returned, so that it is not clear to me, that good fellowship is yet established among them, altho Poeeno is here and is on very good terms with our Oparre Friends. I do not suffer him to visit me notwithstanding, but have given him permition to come on board on the Money being returned belonging to Captain Weatherhead. By Messages he assures me it shall be brought, I however doubt it being in his power. A Dollar w<u>a</u>s b<u>r</u>ought t<u>o</u> m<u>e</u> t<u>o</u> d<u>a</u>y <to day was brought to me>, «and» offered in exchange for a Knife, this is the third we have received—and I fear the whole is not to be got, it being in the possession of many Proprietors, at least among those who will think themselves so.

S<u>o</u>me <u>of</u> o<u>u</u>r G<u>e</u>ntlemen <Lieut. Tobin> made an excursion to day <accompanied by Mr Franklin, the Surgeon of the Assistant> which terminated in being outwitted by an Indian, t<u>he</u> l<u>o</u>ss <u>of</u> <and losing> their Jackets and a brace of Pistols.

I have taken the greatest pains to explain to my Officers and People in general how little they were to rely on the fidelity of Indians. Direct orders, that all those who had leave to go on Shore should return to the Post before Sun down <the Sun was set>. «I» informed them that if they took distant Walks without having a Chief with them, they were subject to be insulted and stript of their Cloaths <Clothes>, besides showing them the many consequences which would hurt the general good; yet these Gentlemen tired even of wearing their own Jackets, pulled them off with the only Arms they had, <being> in the Pockets, and gave the whole to a worthless fellow to carry, who had thought it worth his trouble to follow them. A short time after, gave him an opportunity to lead them into an intricate and blind Path, where without any ceremony he abruptly took his leave, and left his Benefactors to find the way home by themselves, which they did not accomplish untill 8 OClock.

I determined o<u>n</u> giving <to give> the Chiefs no uneasyness about the matter, and would not have them spoke <spoken> to about it. The Theft was very unfairly and unjustly thrown on a Servant of Oreepyah's, when the Fact was, t<u>he</u>y <the Gentlemen> had picked up a worthless fellow of Itteeah [Hitia'a], and had fancied him like a Man they had seen, who they were told w<u>a</u>s b<u>e</u>longing <belonged> to Orrepyah.

This day we shifted 68 Pots of Plants that were not so well looking as I could wish, and planted 16 Tubs and Boxes.

And here is the hapless Tobin's account of the excursion. Although he lost his pistols and jackets during it, as well as his picnic lunch, he retained and eventually colored a sketch made by him of distant Tetiaroa—a fair exchange from posterity's point of view!

Mr Frankland [i.e., Franklin], Surgeon of the Assistant, accompanied me early in the morning to explore the mountains toward Otoos horns (Orooynah) [Mt. Orohena] as far as the day would allow. In our way through the plain three natives attached themselves to us. The Hills above the plain rose gradually in ridges, being generally cloathed with fern, but nearly destitute of trees. The soil did not appear good, but higher up, it improved. A path was soon reached taking the direction we wanted.

About four miles from the post, in a southern direction, having passed the middle hills before mentioned, the country became more woody, as we continued along a ridge separating Matavai river from a smaller one eastward of it. The path was so narrow, our march was by Indian file. On either side was a valley some hundred yards beneath, in many places the descent nearly perpendicular. Two of the natives bade us farewell, but the one, on whom we placed confidence as a guide, journeyed on with spirit.

On the departure of his countrymen, a small piece of baked hog, a single cocoa nut, and a small pocket flask of brandy, was all our provender, and though surrounded with trees none offered any fruit that was eatable. The air was oppressively warm, and our limbs felt wearied in clambering these steeps. One now before us was so discouraging that it was with pleasure the almost lost path was observed to take a direction down its eastern side. Here were great forests of wild plantain trees, but not in fruit; we were however greatly surprised in meeting water in the hollows of the rocks. Of this we drank perhaps incautiously, rested awhile and followed the path, which brought us to the other side of the mountain, but only to present still higher rising to the view. Here they shut out the river to the eastward, but the natives beating of cloth lower down its banks was still heard. [See entry for April 24th, on the manufacture of bark cloth]

On a birds eye view of the Matavai from this spot there was a village of about a dozen houses on a spot of cleared land near the base of Otoos Horns. To this village the Aereoyes [Arioi] resorted at particular periods to indulge uninterruptedly, in unbounded licentiousness.

As, for want of time, it was found impracticable to further ascend the mountains, the guide promised to conduct us to the Aereoye village, giving an assurance that after surmounting a high steep in front, a path led directly to it.

It was about noon, and a refreshing breeze, hitherto attending us; began to decline. Our limbs courted rest, and on looking at the guide the cocoa nut was missing. All these drawbacks staggered our resolution, and it was determined instead of proceeding higher, to strike directly through the woods for the Matavai.

As nearly as could be estimated from the rate of travelling we were at this time about seven miles in a direct line from Point Venus, and five from (Orooynah) Otoos Horns, but it appeared impracticable to ascend their summit by the northern side. On looking about ere we descended, on all sides but to the North, where the ocean and the small Island of Tetheroa formed the limit, we were surrounded by mountains richly closed with wood to their very tops. Our elev-

ation was so great that the eye circumnavigated Tetheroa, from whence to the visible horizon was several leagues; and it was plain to determine, like many of the South sea Islands, that, it was encircled by a reef. The Providence and Assistant, at anchor in Matavai bay, 'though so much nearer, could only be distinguished as two specks on the blue surface of the water. [Plate 21] [Marginal note: 'In 1789 Mr Samuel, Clerk of the Bounty, saw from the mountains of O'tahytey the Islands of Huhahayney [Huahine] and Maiteea [Me'etia], which are nearly in opposite directions, seventy leagues apart.']

Our grand object was to reach the river, but for ten yards before us there was no answering, the woods were so very close; the guide however pushed on cheerfully, and by vaulting from tree to stone, and from stone to tree, with the vanity of sliding on a part which the climate did not require to be heavily covered, trusting frequently to unfaithful twigs, and mouldering rocks, we found ourselves an hundred yards lower.

While the O'tahytean continued in view all went on well, yet could we not conceal that our situation was not cordially relished, and we found too late that to inveigle us into it was a plan for the purpose of robbing us with impunity. Taking advantage of some thick underwood in front, he scampered of with the agility of a monkey, not more to be seen.

The ingenuity of our fellow traveller was great.

I had my pistols with me, which, to satisfy his curiosity had been frequently discharged in the course of our walk, and in return for this attention he very politely offered to carry them for the English Chief, who as simply granted it. Besides the pistols, he had both our jackets, and, direful to relate, the bit of pork, for which our stomachs now yearned. The brandy bottle was still left, with which we sat down on a projecting stump without a casting vote as to our proceedings. After a short debate, the same course was continued, not without execrating the Otahytean, and our own simplicity, until we came suddenly on the margin of a precipice, the bottom of which could not be seen for trees. However laborious the task, it brought us to the neccessity of again ascending, which short was the distance took nearly two hours to effect.

Journeying homewards by the old path it felt light in comparison, however much we were fatigued, but the want of water was indeed felt, nor did a frequent application to the brandy bottle give relief to your friend, though it had the wished for effect with his companion. At length reaching the water among the rocks, we almost deluged our parched frames, and to our great joy found the lost cocoa nut, which was swallowed with avidity. A single bunch of the wild plantain was here seen, but after the trouble of cutting down the tree, the fruit was so strong and course as not to be eatable. Ginger and Turmeric were growing in abundance; the latter indeed, is to be met in most parts of the Island, and is used by the natives as a yellow dye.

The moon assisted us to the post late in the evening after having lost our way several times. Nor, was the good supper and Yava no pretaney [brandy or rum] prepared for us by our Shipmates, at all unwelcome, yet could we have dispensed with the laughter occasioned by our disasters.

Though we did not reach Otoos Horns, it was ascertained that the Matavai was supplied by numberless falls of water from this mountain, which serpentining amid the woods had a picturesque appearance.

Many Fern trees, some above twenty feet in height, were in great beauty on the mountains; Yava was also observed, appearing to thrive best in a high situation.

Friday, May 4th

Light Winds at E by N SE, NW and Calms. Thermometer from 79 to 83 Degrees.

Employed <in> Caulking. In the Hold, the Rigging. Making Extra Places for the plants. Making Tubs and Boxes to contain them. Sufficient supplies of Breadfruit, Cocoa Nutts, Vees, Plantains, and Tarro. Finished Caulking the Sides and Bends.

In the Morning our old Friend the Queen Dowager, Oberreeroah, arrived from Moreah, and her Daughter. Nothing could exceed their joy and kind congratulations, in the midst of which they disavowed any friendly intercourse with Christian, and exculpated their whole family. It is remarkable the pains all the Chiefs have taken to prevent any stigma lying with them on that account.

On <as for> Oberreeroah, excepting that she has grown a little more corpulent than when I last saw her, time has made no alteration. Her corpulency has ever since I knew her, been a burthen to her, and as it creates indolence, she finds a difficulty in Walking. As coming up over our lofty sides was troublesome, I gave them great pleasure by hoisting her <them> into the Ship in a Chair.

Wowwo who is now called Whyerreddee, & <who> in my last Voyage was cured of a Scrofula by Mr Ledwards, enquired particularly after him, and acknowledged the great good he had done her. She was now in perfect health except an ulcer she had in her right leg about the Ancle <Ankle>, which she said was not the same disease as she had before, & requested the Surgeon to cure it.

All the Otoo family are now here.

Otow	*Father*
Oberreeroah	*Mother*
Toury	*Eldest Daughter & Child*
Tynah	*Eldest Son & 2nd Child*
Oreepyah	*Third Child & Son*
Wydooah	*Fourth D[itt]o—a Son*
Wowwo	*Fifth D[itt]o—a Daughter*
Teppahoo	*Sixth D[itt]o a Son*

Wowwo's Husband who in my last Voyage I mentioned was Ereerahigh of Moreah is since Dead. The present Chief is called Mahow [marginal note: 'See 8th May'] a Nephew of Oberreereah, he is always with us and very pleasant good Creature. He informs me that there are only Six Horned Cattle at Moreah. [Marginal note: 'Mr Norris saw 6 cows and one Bull'.]

Oberreeroah had only a few Attendants with her, who all shared in my good wishes towards her. Among the many things I gave to them, linnen Bed Gowns pleased them the most. Tynah, Iddeeah, Wyerreddee, and Hammennemanne dined with me, as in general they do every Day, but Oberreeroah and Wowwo eat nothing untill they got on Shore in the Evening.

An account was brought me to day, that Pooeno and all his

adherents had left Matavai and fled to Itteeah, the cause of this was owing to an
attempt of Wydooah (the younger Bro. of Tynah) to seize the Musquets which
Tabyroo had the charge of, and kept at a distance from Matavai.
     There has been a great deal of Art in this busyness which they
have nevertheless failed in <in which they have nevertheless failed>.
Hammennemanne was taught to tamper with me, and had artfully recommended to
me, as a thing between ourselves, to ask Poeeno on board, and then make a Prisoner
of him untill the Arms were returned. I would have done it had I been ready to Sail,
or my Plants safe, but at present it particularly behoves me to be quiet.
     This day we shifted 60 Pots and Planted 6 Tubs and Boxes.

    Bligh's notable visitor on this day was none other than Purea-
Tetupaia, the eldest offspring—the next elder having been Ha'amanemane—of Tamatoa III, Ra'iatea's highest-ranking kin-Titleholder and
sovereign Chief. It was Purea-Tetupaia who, upon her marriage to the Pare-
Arue Teu (Bligh's 'Otow'), had brought to his family dynasty the *maro ura*
that served to enhance greatly its rank—and to stimulate its members' appetite for more political authority. The first Pare-Arue person to be invested
with this *maro* had been Purea-Tetupaia's (and Teu's) son, Tina; the second
to inherit it had been Tina's son, Tu, whose investiture in 1791 had been witnessed by Morrison:

This day the Ceremony of Investing the Young King with the Marro Oora or Royal
Sash took place; the Sash is of fine Network on which Red and Yellow Feathers are
made fast, so as to cover the netting; the Sash is about three yards long, and each end
is divided into six tassels of Red Black & Yellow feathers, for each of which they have
a name of some Spirit or Guardian Angel, that watches over the Young Chief while
the Marro is in his Possession and is never worn but one day by any one King; it is
then put into the Sacred Box and with a Hat or Shade for the Eyes made of Wicker
& Covered with feathe[r]s of the same kind and never used but on the Same
occasion it is delivered to the priests, who put it Carefully by in the Sacred House
on the Morai, where no person must toutch it. (Rutter 1935: 116)

    Tobin's account of the Bligh–Purea reunion provides some details
not reported by the Captain (including a bit of bartering that the latter either
did not see, or chose not to report):

Obereroah, mother of the King Regent, this morning paid her first visit to Captain Bligh. The
old Lady was so very corpulent it was necessary to hoist her on board in a chair. She no sooner
reached the Cabin than a very curious scene took place. To express her happiness at meeting
Captain Bligh she threw herself on the floor weeping bitterly in loud lamentations. Her whole
suite soon caught the sad infection, and it was a full hour before this woeful ceremony closed;
when the Queen Dowager and her Court regained their wonted cheerfulness, visiting our different cabins, where they asked for beads and other articles.
    On her receiving a present from one of my messmates, she very graciously begged
his temporary acceptance of one of her 'maids of honour'. He was ever well bred, and incapable

of giving offence, so that however his philosophic disposition resisted it, the power was denied him of refusing the friendly offer of Obereroah.

The Queen Dowager appeared above sixty, yet with as fine a set of teeth as can be imagined. The teeth indeed of these people are in general desirably white and regular; perhaps the latter quality is occasioned by their mouths being larger than most europeans, which I am disposed to believe arises from the custom of extending and distorting it when dancing the Heeva. The quantity of vegetable diet used, no doubt preserves their colour, which it gives a purity to the breath, rarely is met with where too much animal food is taken into the stomach. After meals they seldom fail thoroughly washing their mouths.

In the evening Obereroah was lowered into her canoe and went on shore—her suite being reduced by the aforesaid 'Maid of honour'—which no doubt was it to reach the ears of many bearing the same rank in our red book, a degree of indignation would be felt at the frailty of the Otahytean Court.

Tina's sister, Aua (Bligh's 'Wowwo', new name 'Whyerreddee'), born about 1768, was the widow of Mahau, who had died in January 1792, during Vancouver's visit, and whose mummified corpse Tobin was to see. Mahau's connections with the Pomares had been doubly close, he having also been brother of 'Itia and Vaiareti. (One manifestation of the closeness was the circumstance that the two offspring of Mahau and Aua had spent their early childhood in the same exclusive household as the offspring of Tina and 'Itia.) In 1789 Mahau was characterized as 'a tall, stout, good-looking man, speaks but little, and seemed to be of a timid disposition'. (Mortimer 1791: 38) Timid or not, Mahau possessed a distinguished pedigree and held positions of considerable authority. On his mother's side he could claim succession to the chieftainship of most of Mo'orea—although it required the armed intervention of many of his Tahiti relatives (with some assistance from several *Bounty* people) to establish him in that position. And on his father's side he had claims on the chieftainship of the Tahitian district of Fa'a'a—but again, it required the assistance of his Tahiti relatives (this time of Tina) to install him in that office. Conversely, Mahau's death served to strengthen, if anything, the Pomares' claims to high positions in Mo'orea, inasmuch as Mahau's heir was Tina's nephew, and Mahau's daughter was affianced to Tina's son, Tu.

Aua's medical benefactor had been Thomas Ledward, *Bounty's* assistant surgeon, then acting surgeon. A 'loyalist', he managed to survive the launch trip to Timor, but then disappeared. Bligh surmised that he was lost with the Dutch vessel carrying him home but it is possible that he may have remained in Java. (Kennedy 1978: 130n)

Saturday, May 5th

Fine Weather and East Winds varying at Night to the SSE & SE off the Land. Thermometer 82 to 84 Degrees.

Employed in the Hold completeing the Ground Tier with
Ballast. Cooper making Tubs for Plants, and the Carpenters making Boxes. In the
Afternoon the People employed <in> mending their Cloaths.

Our supplies to day were not so plentifull, we are however able
to keep four or <and> five Days Hogs always in the Sty, & Fruit and Roots we
have sufficient.

Some of our Plants have already given fine Shoots, and <there
are> very few that have not evident signs of vegetation. A few were still
backward, we have therefore shifted 26 Pots and planted 14 Tubs and Boxes.

In my Walk today I found a few Matavai People in their
Dwellings, it appeared to me that those People were become attached to the Oparre
interest. Tynah took me to an Oopeowpah (or Concert) there were three Flutes and
two Drums. These performances do not want for harmony, there is notwithstanding
such sameness in the Airs, and dull heavy sounds, that we soon became tired of the
Performance, altho the Natives are delighted with it. These kind of amusements
were formerly called Haivahs, but the word Haivah being given to Tomarree Erree
of Papparrah as a name, they are now called Oopeowpah.

One reason for the food supplies having become somewhat less
plentiful was put forward by Tobin:

A scarcity of cocoa nuts was observed about this time in the public |i.e., ship's general| stock,
and other provisions were brought in but slowly. The eager demand |by the ship's individual
crew members| for shells ornaments and other curiosities, however publicly discouraged |i.e.,
by Bligh| occasioned this scarcity.

Like most other European visitors, Bligh was not entranced by
Tahitian instrumental music, and he may have erred in stating that such
concerts—i.e., without dancing—had formerly borne the name of *heiva*,
which most other European visitors during that era identified as performances that included dancing. Right or wrong—and without better evidence
it is fruitless to speculate about what Tahitian words 'really' meant two centuries ago—he invites our attention in this entry to the intriguing, and
etymology-obscuring, custom of *pi*. Since Bligh discusses the custom in a
later entry (June 5th) it will suffice here to note that it was the practice of pro-
hibiting general use of a word or syllable which had become 'sacred' by its
having become adopted as the name of some highly exalted personage. Thus,
in the case of 'Pomare', *rui* had been substituted for *po* when speaking of
'night', and *hota* for *mare* when speaking of 'cough'.

Sunday, May 6th

Land and Sea Breezes with Calms. The Thermometer from 81 to 83½ Degrees.
Sufficient Supplies.

Mustered the Ships Company after Washing & Cleaning Ship. A more healthy set of Men were never seen. The Sick List contains three Venerials and one Man with a Fever which he caught by coming on Deck in the Night without his Cloaths, very severe Cramp has seized his limbs. Performed Divine Service.

Oreepyah to day brought back the things that had been taken away from Mr. Tobin and Mr. Franklin. His attention and diligence on the occasion deserved praise, and I promised him not to forget it. <Made him a present of a Shirt and some Iron.>

I saw a Dwarf about Eight Years old. The Boys head was very large. The Body tolerably proportioned, but the thighs, and Legs particularly, were very short. His Height was 31 Inches, and all the People agreed that he would never be any taller. His name was Tommah, but he was commonly called Hai,ah, (or Dwarf.) He was without four of the upper fore teeth, all the rest were perfect.

Since my account of the 30th we have Completed (as per daily account) with Breadfruit Plants 26 Boxes and 13 Tubs each having 3 and most of them 4 Plants. The number of Breadfruit Plants that we have shifted amount to 154.

Total of Breadfruit		Other Fruits &	
Pots	1090	Pots of Vees	25
Tubs	17 + 7 See 26th May	Do. of Rattahs	25
Boxes	26	Do. of Ayrahs	25 +
		Do. of Oraiahs	12
		Do. of Pee,ahs	9
		Do. of Ettow	6
		Do. of Mattee	6

Tobin formed a different, and probably correct, view of Ari'ipaia's 'diligence':

Orepaia was on board at early day bringing the pistols that had been stolen in the mountains. He said that, his brother Whidoooah intercepted the thief at Whapiano when making his way to Teairaboo, the windward peninsula of the island. It was more than probable the pistols had been carried to Orepaia, but that the apprehension of Captain Blighs displeasure, in the event of a discovery, had induced him to return them, and that the story of the thief being taken by his brother was a fabrication; the more so, as in some recent transactions Orepaias veracity had been doubted. I could not however help making some acknowledgment for his exertions, which he at first declined, but a little perswasion soon conquered this delicacy. He was loud in condemning the thief, calling him a bad man, (Eno de Tata) [ino te ta'ata, wicked the man].

In fact, Tobin continued to see another side of Ari'paia—which Bligh either did not see, or was reluctant to express in his official Journal. According to Tobin:

Ena Madua, his [i.e., Ari'ipaia's] wife, felt amazingly jealous of him, and spoke this day in anger but affectionate terms of his incontinence. It was that meretricious 'Queen', Whyreddy, who tempted Orepaia to wander from his own home. Of this I had occular demonstration, yet did it seem charitable to aim at perswading this neglected wife that her fears were groundless; but, it was in vain, the 'green eyed monster' had taken too strong a hold.

For Tobin the events of this day also led him to expatiate about pigs and women, which according to some of his shipmates were Tahiti's principal attractions, and which, to many Tahitians, were the main reason for European visits:

In return for a present, Edeea sent me an amazing large hog, with a quantity of fruit, and a promise of cloth. The music of these cloven footed animals was no little annoyance to the nerves of your humble servant. To prevent irregularity, trade was only allowed to take place on one side of the ship, and this, unfortunately was where my six foot apartment was situated, so that from the 'rising of the sun 'till the going down of the same' did the ceaseless lamentations of these poor half strangled grunters din my ears, nor without an apprehension of their finding a passage through the port in their struggles, while dragging up the side from the canoes.

Boa [pua'a] (a hog)—(Waheeney [vahine], a Woman, must not be forgotten)— seems to be one of the first words our countrymen understand. It is indeed the staple commodity of the Island; and what I verily believe these good people think, brings us among them. Both indeed have been said—and perhaps with great truth—to be of a very delicate flavour. Yet so affectionate were the terms, some within the sides of the Providence had been on, with the latter of these good articles, they were sorely lamenting they had not confined their researches to the former.

Monday, May 7th

Fair Weather with Land and Sea Breezes SSE and East. Thermometer from 81 to 83½ Degrees. At Night we had a light Shower of Rain. Sufficient Supplies.

Carpenters Employed making Extra places for the Plants. Hauled the Launch ashore to repair ⟨her⟩ and to raise ⟨her⟩ a strake higher. Hands going on with such parts of the Rigging as it is not necessary to have exposed to the Weather. We continue on the best footing with the Natives, and our Plants promise to do well.

An account was brought to me to day from Tabyroo, that the Money was come from Teturoah, and he only wanted some person to come for ⟨fetch⟩ it, lest by sending it with ⟨by⟩ any of his own people some accident might happen and prevent my getting it after all his trouble. In consequence I directed Mr. Norris with the Matilda's People to go for the Money to morrow.

Again, Tobin's version of this episode is fuller than Bligh's:

A message came from Tupira importing that, if Captain Bligh would send for the Matildas money it should be given up. Mr Norris in consequence, and some of her crew, proceeded to Whapiano with instructions to first secure the money, and then request the arms. The Messengers acquainted us that Tupira had retreated to the Whapiano mountains, an attempt having been made by Whydooah to secure him.

Tuesday, May 8th

Fair Weather with Land and Sea Breezes at SE & E by N. Thermometer from 81 to 84 Degrees.

Employed the Carpenters making Extra Places for the Plants, and at Work on the Launch. Some hands going on with the Rigging.

Early in the Morning I had a Visit from Toeepoee [Toipoi ?], the Wife [now widow] of Poohaitaih Otee, a Chief of Itteeah. He was a fine active young Man and highly respected. I have mentioned him in my last Voyage as a Person who was fed in the same manner as Tynah. Nothing can exceed the vehemence with which his Wife expressed herself against Capt. Vancouver's Ship,—'it was there he caught his illness as did many others.' I endeavoured to do away the belief she had of the disease originating with the Discovery [i.e., Vancouver's ship], but it was to no effect, she continued firm in her opinion. She described the disease as every person has done before, to be a flux and some Vomiting. I made her up a Present of every article I had.

Tynah was called away suddenly this Morning to Oparre without my knowledge. On his return he told me he had been to Pooray [pure, marginal note: 'to pray'], for he had ordered a Man at Tiarraboo to be sacrificed and sent here to be presented to the Etuah. About 12 OClock, Iddeah who was on board, showed me a Cannoe going past the Ship with a human sacrifice from Wannah a Chief of Happy,ano, this was not offered to the Etuah, but to Otoo the Errerahigh. I was unwell all this day and did not dare go to Oparre where I must be exposed to the Sun, from the accounts however, it was of no consequence, as I should not have seen any thing more than I have remarked on the 28th April.

These Sacrifices are truly Shocking and Savage, and I am sorry to say I find they are made not only on solemn occasions, but on the most trifling differences between great & inferior Chiefs, & upon the Erreerahigh's sudden whim or desire of praying to his Etuah.

The Cause of the <This> Sacrifice from Wannah was owing to his not having assisted Whydooah, his Brother Chief, in getting the Arms from Tabyroo; but <he was> the Means of their being carried off. [Marginal note: 'See 4th'] This gave great displeasure to Tynah & Otoo. Wannah sollicited forgiveness & permission to live on the footing he had done before with them, but they refused untill after many concessions, they agreed to take him into favor again on his presenting a Sacrifice to the Erreerahigh. Upon any of these occasions it is sufficient for the dead body to be sent to the Erreerahigh, wrapt up in a platted Cocoa Nutt Branch fastened to a Pole to carry it by <by which it is carried>. The body to day was in a Cannoe with only «one» man to conduct it.

I cannot arrive at <discover> the Cause, to my satisfaction, of the sacrifice from Tiarraboo, all that I can make of it, is <I believe it was> solely an act of Devotion.

In my last Voyage I have given a particular account of the Principal Families of this Island (See Folio 327) From a connection in the female line, the present Otows Grandmother being Sister to the then King of Tiarraboo, his grand child [marginal note: 'Tynahs 2nd Son Terreeapanooai'] is now become Erree of that place, the Heirs of Whaeeahtuah in the male line being extinct. The late Whaeeahtuah whose Wife [marginal note: 'Whyerraddee'] Tynah is now connected with, died without any Children, and on his death (since my last Voyage) Terreetapanooai Tynah's second Son was sent to Tiarraboo to be elected, or more properly, acknowledged Eree of that part of the Island.

The Tiaraboo People always insisted that Whaeeahtuah was Erreerahigh of that Country, & Otoo Erreerahigh of the Western part of the Island, but all the Otoo family & <their> connections, say there is only one Erreerahigh. Their power however has not marked any superiority over the Tiarraboo People since our time, and the present Terreetapanooai, has taken the Name of Whaeeahtuah. We may date the birth of the Boy in the Year 1787 and his being acknowledged as Erree in 1790.

It is a remarkable thing, that Otow and Oberreroah with all their Sons should be perfectly free of the Evil [Kings' Evil; struma, goiter] or any Scrofulous disease & that their Daughters should be infected with it. Tynah and Iddeah also perfectly free, <and> with every appearance of the most healthy people, have their only Daughter Tahamydooah infected with it about the Glands of the Throat. But in Iddeahs Children there is an exception of <to> the disease following the female line, for her last Child Oroho (a boy of 18 Months Old) has the disease broke out in his Groin. May <not> this be owing to Iddeah having intercourse with too many different Men? I am of opinion from the great number of different Men who cohabit with one Woman in this Country, originates the Venerial disease which it is infested with in a dreadful degree <the Venereal disease which prevails very much originates>.

I find that Otoo is betrothed to his Cousin Tarroaheinee a Child of His Aunt Wowwo, born since 1789, so that I have observed before, first Cousins marry. This is a very fine little Girl about 12 Months Old, and is to all appearance free of any disease, altho its Mother is Scrofulous in a high degree. The father Moduarro Chief of Moreah when I was here in the Bounty, is dead, & his Son Tettoo,anovee elected in his stead. Mahow who <whom> I have mentioned on the 4th last [actually, on May 3rd], has only an honorary title on account of the great esteem that Moduarro had for him. I imagine Tettooanovee is about 4 Years Old.

The recently deceased 'Poohaitaih Otee' (Puhaitai-oti?) whom Bligh met during the *Bounty* visit and whom he identified then as son of 'Marre Marre', a 'chief' of Hitia'a, is a mystery. He would have had an upper-class pedigree in order to qualify him for the self-feeding restriction, 'in the same manner as Tynah'. And his widow behaved in an 'upper-class' manner;

women of lesser credentials would hardly have presumed to 'visit' the Captain of the *Providence* and to have displayed 'vehemence' in his presence. Yet, I can find no other information about either of them. Poohaitaih may indeed have been *a* 'chief' of Hitia'a. In the notes recorded decades later by Orsmond, and reproduced in Teuira Henry's *Ancient Tahiti*, the traditional name—probably kin-Title—of Hitia'a's 'Chief' is given as 'Teri'itua' and that of the 'under-chief', 'Fanaue'. Writing in 1769 Cook characterized the district as having two 'chiefs', 'Orette' (Reti) and 'Teemehinnee'. (Beaglehole 1955: 105) Of the existence of Reti there is ample evidence (for example, in the journals of Bougainville, Cook, and G. Forster); he was indeed a powerful leader and an ally of the leaders of Pare-Arue. But of Hitia'a's other and later leaders nothing is known, save these off-hand references by Bligh.

Loyal Englishman and naval officer that he was, Bligh evidently did his duty in attempting to absolve Vancouver and his people of responsibility for introducing the disease—probably a dysentery—which had resulted in widespread illness and many fatalities after *Discovery*'s departure. In fact, three other European vessels had visited Tahiti between *Discovery* and *Providence*—the *Matilda*, the schooner *Jenny* and the *Prince William Henry*—but the Tahitians explicitly blamed their ills on *Discovery*, and so probably did Bligh.

In the days now being chronicled the Pomares were clearly in a triumphant and expansionist mood, encouraged by their capture (with the help of the *Bounty* people) of the Papara Image and the Wallis *Maro Ura*, by their 'victories' over Mo'orea and Matavai, by the catalytic presence of Ha'amanemane—and doubtless by the presence of their friend Bligh. Moreover, recent events in Taiarapu had created a leadership vacuum there into which the Pomares moved swiftly to fill.

The vacuum in Taiarapu had been created by the death, in March 1790, of Vehiatua III, without issue. For a brief interregnum it was filled by the election of Churchill to the office; but when that worthy was slain by his fellow mutineer, Thompson, the Taiarapuans elected a four-year-old 'nephew' of Vehiatua to be district chief. The exact relationship of the nephew to Vehiatua is not known, but his pedigree cannot have been distinguished enough to discourage Tina from asserting his own family's claim to the office—which, as Bligh (partly) explained, was based on the pretension that Tina's paternal grandmother, Tetuaehura, had been daughter of an earlier holder of the Vehiatua kin-Title. (In addition, although it provided no *conventional* grounds for the claim, Tina's present—*ever* present—second wife Vaiareti, had been married to Vehiatua III.) As Bligh reports, Tina took it upon himself to appoint his second son, Teri'itapunui, to the kin-Title. (A year or so earlier Tina had attempted to *persuade* the Taiarapuans to bestow that kin-Title on Tu, but they declined, giving as their reason that Tu was a bastard, having been sired by one of 'Itia's commoner paramours.) Not all of the Taiarapuans accepted the pretension of the new appointee, as shown by the fact that he himself remained in Pare, while his uncle, Ari'ipaea, resided part of the time on the border of Taiarapu in order to support the youth's interests there.

Notwithstanding—or perhaps because of? —all the remaining uncertainties, about the Taiarapu sovereignity and the *Matilda* firearms, Tina evidently felt that the times required more human sacrifices—one in the form of a petition of forgiveness from a Ha'apaino leader who had not been supportive enough of the Pomares' attempt to recover the *Matilda* firearms; the other as an offering to 'Oro, in gratitude for past favors and those yet to come.

And now, focussing on the last paragraph in this entry, the 'Moduarro' referred to is none other than the 'real' Mahau, who had been both husband of Tina's sister, Auo, and brother of 'Itia and Vaeareti. The Mahau mentioned here, a 'nephew' of Tina's mother, was serving as Regent for Mahau's son and successor, the four-year-old 'Tettooanovee' (Tetuanui?).

As Bligh remarks, 'first Cousins [did] marry' in the Tahiti of that era, but such marriages were very rare. For all but a few Tahitians marriage with a 'close' consanguine was strictly proscribed; as far as I can discover there were no stated 'biological' reasons for that proscription and no religious sanctions against it—no punishment by spirits—but abhorrence of it was widely expressed. It is not possible to discover the consanguinous limits of this ban on marriage, and on sexual intercourse in general, but it is likely to have included *all* consanguines, on both parental sides, believed to have been linked by ties of tertiary or closer degree, including second cousins. (A person's *primary* consanguines comprise his father, mother, siblings, sons, daughters; his *secondary* consanguines comprise those other relatives who are the primary consanguines of his own primary consanguines. And so on.) Such at least was the rule that applied to *most* Tahitians—i.e., to those of the lower and middle classes. For persons of upper-class status, however, the rule was not only bent but, in some instances, ignored. Some 'abhorrence' may have remained, but it was clearly a less important consideration than the political advantages that could be gained by uniting in one offspring the pedigrees of two parents of high kin-Title rank. In fact, in the game of status-rivalry, of kin-Title ranking, that was being played at the time, some of the principal players (such as the Pomares) were left with few choices for mates—few persons whose kin-Titles were considered exalted enough to approximate their own. This game of course could have drawn its rationale from the notion of genetic 'sanctity' mentioned earlier, but I expect that the motives for playing it were mainly political.

(A similar game was played among Hawaii's Polynesians but there the preference for close-in marriages among highly-ranked kin-Titleholders was even stronger, and supported by a more explicit 'sanctity' rationale, culminating in some instances of brother–sister marriage, which, as far as I can discover, did not take place in Tahiti in the era under examination.)

As usual, Tobin's entry for this day dealt with a matter of less political import, namely, a clever theft of his own bedsheets:

While at dinner in the ward room a native took the opportunity of stealing my sheets through the port. Mideedee [Hitihiti] who was upon deck, observing a canoe paddling on shore with unusual exertion suspecting something wrong, pursued and overtook her just as she reached the beach. The thief offered to share the booty, but this worthy Islander, was not to be corrupted, and being the most powerful man brought the sheets back.

Wednesday, May 9th

Fine Weather with Land and Sea Breezes and Calms. Thermometer from 80½ to 83½ Degrees.

Employed <in> making places for the Plants repairing the Launch <and> fitting Blocks and other necessary parts of the Rigging. Sufficient Supplies but not abundance <abundant> as in the beginning.

I have always Tynah and his Relations about me. They dine with me every day. A few People from different places of little note have been to see us, to whom Tynah has according to his usual custom distributed Toey's, Knives Etc. Etc.—this little power which I have always accustomed him to, pleases him exceedingly, and I must acknowledge he has never abused the indulgence but on the contrary acted with the greatest frugality.

About Noon Mr. Norris returned from Tabyroo who has now retreated far back into the Mountains complaining of the treachery of his People—a number of them having left him. With a few trusty fellows he however kept possession of the Musquets & were <was> determined not to give them up.

All the Money that was in his power to procure we <he> had now got, which was delivered to Mr. Norris, and Mr. Marshall the Chief Mate [of the Matilda]; it was 172 Dollars and three half Crown pieces—ten other Dollars were received at the Post which made 182 Spanish Dollars in the whole, and a Watch belonging to the late Chief Mate No 3827 Makers Name Jan Henkels Amsterdam. This was a Silver Watch Value about 30 Shillings. Here ends our Negotiation with Tybyroo for Money, as he has declared he can get no more, it is however not half of what the Captain [of the Matilda] States he left behind him. [Marginal note: 'See 10th April']

Otoo Visits us every day at the Post and returns to Oparre in the Evening as soon as the Sun sets. He sits the whole day on the Shoulders of some one of his Servants for he has a number with him who shift every quarter or half hour. He amuses himself with childish tricks and going among our people. I date the Year of his Birth 1783.

Plate 17   The *ahu* of the seaside *marae* at Pare Point
Watercolor by George Tobin

Plate 18   View from Ha'apaino'o district towards Point Venus
Watercolor by George Tobin

Tobin's version of this latest *Matilda* episode adds some details:

Mr Norris returned with the major part of the money. The remainder, Tupira informed him, was a long way distant in possession of another person.

This persevering Chief was found a long way up the Whapiano [River] surrounded by about an hundred of his faithful Matavaians. It was in vain, he said, to expect the musquets, as with his life he would only yield them, he repeated as he had before, that, in case of an attack he would retreat to a narrow pass in the mountains and defend it until his ammunition was expended. He reprobated in contemptuous terms the pusilanimous conduct of his brother who had deserted him and was at Matavai with the females of his family, who, not withstanding the quarrel had remained unmolested by the Oparreans. It appeared that one of Tupira's party had treacherously deserted, giving Whydooah intelligence of his retreat, who under shelter of a dark night made the unsuccessful attempt before mentioned. His five 'stand of arms' were constantly kept under his bed; that is, his sleeping mat.

Thursday, May 10th

Fair Weather and Cloudy, with Calms and Variable Winds. Thermometer from 80 to 82½ Degrees.

> *Sufficient supplies of every article.*

> *Employed building extra places for the Plants. Cooper making Tubs for D[itt]o. Carpenters about the Launch. Hands about the Rigging.*

> *Mr. Ridgeway, <The> Surgeons 1st Mate brought a Guinea to me to day which was offered to him by one of the Natives for a Knife. It is <a> part of Captain Weatherheads Money.*

Tobin's entry for this day reveals, among other things, that Bligh, for all his friendliness and generosity to the Pomares and other Tahitian notables, insisted on maintaining his dignity and social distance, as befitted a commanding officer in the Royal Navy. Tobin's entry also reveals that there was no limit, in some instances, to Tahitians' appetites for European goods:

In the afternoon Pomaurey begged permission to take a nap on my bed. He had once before enjoyed that privilege, but unfortunately left two of his attendants behind, which my bed maker (the officers in the Providence, that it might not weaken the crew had no established servants) found in solemn march upon the pillow, and to use his own expression, swore they came from the head of his Majesty by 'their colour'. Captain Bligh though truly friendly to the Chiefs, kept them in such excellent order that they never took any liberties with him, by which means he enjoyed some degree of retirement. However fraught with danger, it was not in my power to refuse Pomaurey the boon he asked.

Such were the fears of a trembling unmellowed damsel as the sun sunk behind the distant hills and the hour of dedition [?] approached, that, unequal to the contest she leaped into the briny element and reached the plain, undeprived of that—she was urged on board—to lose. Thine own friends my good girl, with an Eree no pretaney, (an English Chief) had formed a compact against thee. Hadst thou come free and uncontrolled, like many others who sought

155

the Providence for English finery, I might have felt for the disappointment of him, who with meretricious longing, coveted thy wrapped charms.

Friday, May 11th

Calms and Variable Winds with very Cloudy Weather and a little shower of Rain. Thermometer from 81 to 82½ Degrees. Sick List 9 Venereals.

  Employed as Yesterday. Punished James Combes Marine [the Drummer] with 12 lashes for having disobeyed my orders, and having connection with a Woman while he was infected with the Venereal disease. Nothing but severe punishment or <not> even that will prevent these Wretches from committing this infamous act among these poor people.

  Every thing remains quiet, and but few of the Natives about us—we have however sufficient supplies.

  In addition to my constant Guests Tynah and his Wives, & Brother Oreepyah, I had my old Friend Moan,nah or Monah, spoken of in my last Voyage. He then quitted me from a fear of my displeasure in not getting the Deserters.

Tobin's comment on the lashing contains a surmise, and an observation about Tahitians' 'tenderness':

The Drummer was this day punished, in the presence of a number of the Islanders, for forgetting, in his amours, that he was under the care of our messmate the Doctor. The beater of parchment perhaps thought retaliation no crime and that as the Otahytean fair ones had given him a warm token of remembrance, he had a right to return it 'in kind.' But whether he reasoned so or not, the dozen he received was properly and justly inflicted. With the tenderness inseparable from them, the natives pitied his sufferings, but acknowledged that he deserved punishment.

  Moana ('Moannah') had been a good friend to Bligh during the *Bounty* visit. Identified then as 'a chief' of Matavai (Poeno having been identified as 'the' chief of Matavai) he, along with Tina and Poeno, were frequent, almost daily, guests aboard ship. And on shore Moana assisted greatly in setting up and maintaining the breadfruit nursery, having moved his sleeping quarters nearby in order better to guard it. The deserters referred to in this entry had been William Musprat, John Millward, and Charles Churchill (the same who was to become 'Chief' of Taiarapu, until murdered by his fellow mutineer, Thompson). On January 5th, 1789 the three left the *Bounty* and escaped to Tetiaroa. Moana and Tina's brother, Ari'ipaia, agreed to go there and capture them, but due to bad weather (and some fear of the firearms the deserters had taken with them) they delayed reaching the atoll and failed to capture the deserters when there. The latter returned—'voluntarily'—to Tahiti, where Bligh himself captured them. After his own failure to capture them Moana had kept clear of the ship, evidently fearing that Bligh would confine him there. His fears were based on his memory of Captain Cook, who under similar circumstances had confined Tahitian leaders as hostages in order to force their cooperation in recovering deserters and thefts. During the desertion now referred to, Bligh had indeed resolved to use what Gavin Kennedy (1978: 75) calls the 'hostage gambit' in order to force Moana and others to proceed more vigorously with the capture, but postponed doing so because of the possible danger to the breadfruit nursery. Then, as during his present visit, the plants were the most important consideration: 'the most material Circumstance I have to attend to'. (Bligh 1937: II 13)

Saturday, May 12th

Cloudy Weather with Variable Winds round the Compass & Calms. Sea Breeze a few Hours in the Afternoon. Thermometer from 80 to 82½ Degrees.

Employed Working and Cleaning.

While I was at Van Diemans [sic] Land I procured a quantity of Plank of the Metrocedera, to enable me to make Boxes and extra places for my Plants, this has given me an opportunity to remark, that the Wood which Strangers would imagine was fit for the common purposes of building is not, in fact, worth any thing or valuable for any purpose, but Fuel, when sawn into Plank, it is so inclinable to Warp and Split. Small Spars however we find strong and usefull for such purposes as do not require them to be cut out of their natural shape.

Oreepyah, with his Nephew Otoo, (the King) & Hammennemanne came to take their leave of me on their going to Paparrah to see their Relation Tomaree the Chief of that place, who lies very Ill and is expected to die; But their principal object is to see what can be done; to take <whether they can bring> away some Musquets which the People of that District are in possession of from the Seamen of the Matilda's Boat who put in there. Nothing can equal the rage these people have after Arms. There is nothing they would not sacrifice to procure them, but the Parties who have them in possession I believe are too wise to part with them. Could the Otoo Family get Arms I have no doubt but they would govern the whole Country—a Right which they say is inherent in themselves.

Before they set out on their expedition it was necessary to consult me. Tynah therefore came with the party to give <exert> his interest for them to be so equipped <that they might be provided> with presents of different kinds, as would <to> insure them a welcome reception.

I indulged him in the most <things> he asked for, and they left us with light hearts, dressed in European Clothes, and <with> a large quantity of Iron Work and Trinkets in their bundles.

We have now so few people about us that I have no new circumstances to relate—the day passes over in quiet, and the busyness of the Ship <is> carried on without interruption as we have seldom fifty of the Natives on board at any one time. A few cannoes are generally passing and repassing, and those supply us with as much as we are in need of.

Matavai still remains a deserted Village [i.e., neighborhood], some Families however are come in, and the Women and Children have their little amusements as I have described (common to them) in my last Voyage.

Towards Tarrah (which divides Matavai from Oparre) a great deal of injury is done to the finest of the Trees—numbers of them are barked all round and are in a dying state, but others have been considered of such Value, <that> the Natives have endeavored to save them by laying on a bandage of plaster <plaister> of clayish kind of soil round the wound, and wraping <wrapping> it carefully over with leaves. Here we find among a set of People, (whose minds are uncultivated,) what has lately been extolled in our own Country as an ingenious devise <invention> of Dr. Fothergill; with this difference, <that> I cannot assert there is any Cow Dung in the composition.

Not far from this spot, was the evidence of Peter Haywood the Villain who assisted in taking the Bounty from me. His House was on <at> the foot of a Hill, the top of which gave him a fine look out. He had regulated his Garden & <the> Avenue to his House with some taste, the latter was made conspicuous by a Row of fine Shaddock Trees, which, like other favourite things, suffered in the late War. The care with which all the Villains <Mutineers> regulated their domestick concerns, and the account I have <received> of them, give the clearest proofs they enjoyed <that enjoyed they> their Situation, if it was possible, burthened with the heinous crimes they had been guilty of—happily, perhaps it was ordained they should be entrapped through their own seduction. <If it was possible for them to do so, burthened as their minds must have been with the recollections of the Injustice and Cruelty they had committed against me and the people whom they forced out of the Bounty.> [Note: This revision in ML is in a hand different from that written by Bligh himself in his ML Journal—perhaps by his clerk Hatfell ?]

The occasion has arrived for some particulars about Papara, the district twenty-five miles to the South of Matavai that the Pomares were preparing to visit.

Previously, and in times yet to come, the principal people of Papara contended vigorously with those of Pare-Arue regarding the relative ranking of their respective kin-Titles—a contest that (as readers will, I trust, have come to see) was of crucial importance in Tahiti's overall polity. In approaching this commentary the reader may need reminding that the seeming advantage enjoyed by the Pomare side in this contest was due in part to the decision made by the commanders of English ships to anchor in Matavai Bay. Had they chosen instead to anchor in one of Papara's embayments, or even in Taiarapu's Vaitepiha Bay (as Cook did, but only briefly, in 1773), Tahiti's political history would likely have been different, including the outcome of the kin-Title contest.

The area of Papara is somewhat larger than that of Pare-Arue, as was its population when Wallis 'discovered' Tahiti in 1767: about 4500 in Papara and about 4100 in Pare-Arue. The Papara chiefs of that era exercised more authority over their (eastern) neighboring districts (Ati Maono, Mataiea, Vaiare) than did those of Pare-Arue over theirs. Moreover, the earlier phases of the Paparans' kin-Title pedigrees were somewhat higher-ranking, and certainly more localized, than those of the Pomares' forebears, whom the Paparans derided as originating in the Tuamotus, hence of 'commoner' status.

(The Paparan side in this status-rivalry was elegantly espoused by the historian, Henry Adams, in his book, *Memoirs of Arii Taimai*, privately printed in Paris in 1901. Adams spent a lengthy vacation in Tahiti in 1891, during which he recorded and transmuted the verbal memoirs of that elderly lady, who was a Paparan 'princess' and the divorced wife of the last reigning Pomare—and for that and other reasons no friend of the Pomare 'upstarts'. For a delightful, though understandably biased, exemplar of dynastic pride *Memoirs* is highly recommended. And for a searching critique of it, see Pierre Lagayette 1973.)

Rivalry between the two dynasties became more explicit with their acquisition of Opoan kin-Titles, and their associated *maro ura*, at about the same time. The Pare-Arue one had been brought by Tetupaia and later used to invest her son, Tina (and later, *his* son, Tu). The Papara one had been brought there in about 1760 by the son of an Opoan kin-Titleholder and his Paparan wife; the objects that accompanied this kin-Title were the so-called Papara Image of 'Oro and the original part of what later became the Wallis *Maro Ura*. (See April 28th) However, it required more than the mere presence of these symbols to win the status contest; it required that their superiority be *asserted*. An attempt to do this was made by the famous Purea (Wallis's 'Queen Oberea') mentioned in the entry for April 28th. As wife of Papara's Chief, Amo, she determined to celebrate the investiture of their son, Teri'irere (known also as Temari'i), by building a huge *marae* to 'contain' the youth's numerous kin-Titles, including the recent Opoan one, those of his father, and her own distinguished pedigree. The *marae* was built—Tahiti's largest, which included a nine-stepped pyramid—but was not used. During its construction Purea and her husband, but mainly Purea, attempted to establish its supremacy, and that of their son, by imposing a widespread prohibition that among other things forbade the reception of distinguished guests with the usual grandiose hospitality—a gesture of utmost arrogance and contempt in Tahitian eyes. The first to challenge the prohibition and its explicit assertion of the son's Island-wide supremacy, was a delegation from Fa'a'a. When that attempt failed (to the deep humiliation of its leaders), the leaders of other districts—i.e., the guardians of other high-ranking kin-Titles, including especially those of Pare-Arue and Taiarapu—took up the challenge and invaded Papara. The Taiarapuans arrived there first and routed the Paparans, including Amo and Purea, after killing scores of them. Then arrived the Pare-Arueans under the leadership of Tina's grand-uncle Tutaha, and made off with the Papara Image and the Wallis *Maro*, as has already been described. This debacle put an end to Purea's pretensions, but her son, Teri'irere-Tamari'i, retained the Paparan chieftainship, and while he and his supporters continued to assert his equality with Tina, and later with Tu, no further attempt was made by them to assert his superiority over them (an accommodation that was not reciprocated by the Pomares). Aside from matters of kin-Title ranking, however, Teri'irere-Tamari'i and the Pomares became friendly, albeit uneasily so, to the extent that he became married to Tina's eldest sister—although such marriages as often as not represented truce rather than alliance. At the time of the *Providence* visit Teri'irere-Tamari'i was about twenty-eight years old, and as Bligh recorded (July 11th) he had been 'discouraged' by the Pomares from visiting him. And while the present excursion to Papara was announced as one of sympathy for the sick Teri'irere-Tamari'i, its main object, as Bligh notes, was to recover some other *Matilda* firearms—and by a strategm that Tobin describes:

Preparations were making at this time by Orepaia and their chiefs for an expedition to Paparra on the South West part of the Island. The Chiefs of this district were in possession of a few fire arms, and an attempt to get them by strategem was to be made by Orepaia, by his going round laden with presents that no suspicion might be entertained of his intentions. Of this he made no mystery to his English friends, attaching no dishonour to such a proceeding.

    The absence of most of the 'Principal People' left Bligh free to devote full attention to ship housekeeking and the collection of his precious breadfruit, but it deprived him of some of his informants on matters Tahitian and, more importantly, of opportunities to attend extraordinary events ashore. And he had neither the time nor the health—nor, more decisively, the curiosity and inclination—to engage in the kind of slogging observation of the commonplace, which distinguishes the commited ethnographer from the observant traveler, no matter how shrewd and open-minded the latter may be.

Sunday, May 13th

Cloudy Weather at times and a few Showers of Rain in the Night. Wind E by N. Thermometer from 80 to 82 Degrees.

    Saw every Person clean and as usual on this Day I performed Divine Service. This being the Po no t Etuah [po no te Atua, night of the God], as the Natives call it, we have fewer of them about us, as they see we observe to keep it without <it by not> doing any Work.

Monday, May 14th

Light Variable airs and Calms most of the day and a Sultry heat. Wind at East towards the Evening. Thermometer from 80 to 84 Degrees.

Employed <in> building Extra places for the Plants and repairing the Launch. Moderate supplies.

This Morning examined all our Plants, and arranged all the doubtfull ones <so> as to be ready for shifting after another Weeks tryal <trial>. Happily I have but few that will require it and on the whole every thing turns out as my anxious mind wishes it.

Tuesday, May 15th

This day we had light Westerly Winds and Calms. The Clouds hung heavy about the Hills and promised Rain, but it did not reach the low land. Thermometer from 81 to 84 Degrees.

We have now but very few Natives about us, we have nevertheless sufficient supplies.

As I now happily found my Nervous complaint much removed, I got my Observatory up and my Astronomical Quadrant ready to make some observations for the Rate of my Time Keepers, which I have hitherto examined by daily altitudes in the afternoon, and horizon being open to the NW.

Wednesday, May 16th

We had mostly Calms to day except a few hours in the afternoon when a light Easterly breeze backing the Clouds that had been driven from the Westward, produced a fine refreshing Rain which not only benefited our Plants but the whole Country. The Thermometer from 78 to 81 Degrees.

I find that the cause of our having but few People about us, is their being gone to Papparah. Only Tynah and his Wife Whyerreddee remain with us <me>. Our supplies are sparing, but we are generally provided against such times, by keeping a sufficient Stock in hand. Our Carpenters are Employed <in> making places for the Plants and the Boatswain about the Rigging.

In the Morning I had the Seine hauled near the East Head of Tarrah, and caught 190 lbs of fine Fish—Cavallys from 2 to 10 lb. Weight—fine Mullet—Horse Mackerel—kind of herring—a number of small Fish something like a Gurnet and a few other sorts not known. Served an allowance to each Man.

Thursday, May 17th

Untill 4 O'Clock this afternoon it was generally Calm, the remaining part of the day light Winds, at E by N & ESE and Cloudy Weather throughout. Thermometer from 79 to 82 Degrees.

Employed repairing the Launch, and about the Rigging.

Very few Natives about our Post, or Ship, and our supplies today confined to Breadfruit, Vees, and Plantains. The Venereal list is now increased to 10. Two of them have been under care ever since we left Terariffe.

Our Plants benefit by the Cloudy Weather and are in general in a thriving State.

Friday, May 18th

Light Winds, Calms and Cloudy Weather. At Sea Wind generally at ESE. In <the> Morning and Afternoon some smart Showers of Rain. Thermometer from 78 to 81½ Degrees.

Employed repairing the Launch, fitting extra places and stands for the Plants. Refitting the rigging.

Very few Natives about us, and excepting my Friend <Friends> Tynah and Monah no person of consequence, so that we have no bustle or anything passing curious or interesting. We still have a sufficient supply of Provisions to enable me to continue an allowance of 1½ lbs of Pork per Man with as much Breadfruit, Cocoa Nutts, Plantains and Vees as can be used.

Some of our People who have sent to the River for Water have lately been insulted by some worthless fellows, who threw Stones and dirt at them, and endeavored to take away their Cloaths. I thought it proper to punish such unfriendly behavior, and one of the offenders appearing at <on> the Post, I ordered him to be seized and put in Irons. I had little difficulty to explain to the Natives the cause of it, when they all exclaimed 'You have done right kill him'—indeed they seemed not to interest themselves about him, altho they told me he was a person belonging to Oreepyah.

Saturday, May 19th

During the Morning Calms with light Winds and much Rain. Towards Noon the Weather came fair with light East Winds but at Sea it appeared very Squally and Wind to the S.E. Towards Midnight it blew fresh from the ESE. <Thermometer from> [incomplete]

Employed cleaning Ship, Washing and mending Cloaths.
Moderate Supplies.

AT 2 O'Clock this Morning a Native under cover of a thick Squall of Rain opened the Port of the first Lieutenant's Cabbin, and took from him the Sheet that covered him in his Bed, which was not discovered untill the last Inch of it was pulled from him. Boats were sent after the Native but to no effect, the Night was so dark it favored his escape. Whether this Man had hid himself at Sun set when all the natives are turned out of the Ship, or had Swam off, we cannot determine—it appears however that he had made an attempt on the same Article about Midnight; but Mr. Bond not suspecting the twitches he had felt and had <which he felt and which had> awakened him, to be real; went to sleep again. What is remarkable, I found on enquiry, that the Centinels on Deck, and the one at my Cabbin Door (whose walk is before Mr. Bond's & guards each equally) and the Mate and Midshipmen of the Watch were all attentive to their Duty.

Tynah as usual dined with me. After Dinner I told him I had a man in Irons who <whom> I intended to punish for insulting my officers and People. He agreed with me that the Man deserved it, and I ordered him to receive 36 lashes on his posteriors <back sides>. He received the punishment without moaning, or winsing, for it was not in the power of the Boatswain to make him beg forgiveness. <I have observed that no impression can be made on their [?] and therefore this [? ?] but this man received the punishment without mourning or whining> It must be owing to the bodies of these people being constantly exposed, their feeling <that they feel> so little of a punishment which is exceeding <exceedingly> severe, in all other cases they are as susceptible of pain as we are. I ordered the prisoner again into Irons.

In the Morning we were so successful with the <our> Seine as supplied every Person <that every person was supplied> in a plentifull manner. They <the People> Caught 300lbs Weight of fine Cavallies.

Sunday, May 20th

Strong Winds and Fair Weather ESE. Thermometer 78½ to 81½ Degrees.

Mustered the Ships Company and saw them all Clean Dressed. Performed Divine Service. Gave leave to a Party to go on Shore.

Another Complaint was made to me to day of a Native beating one of the Seamen and giving him a black Eye. The Parties happened to be on board, I could therefore here <hear> the Story on both sides which went so much against the Native that I ordered the Seaman to take his own satisfaction. A few strong blows made his antagonist jump into the Sea.

In my general orders I forbid either Man or Officer to redress his own grievance with a Native, or to strike him upon any pretence whatever. Many worthless fellows have taken an advantage of this; I however expect I have prevented it happening in future, if the <they> Chiefs have done as they have promised me, to warn <warned> all their People of the Punishment that will attend them.

Monday, May 21st

Strong Breezes at ESE Moderating at Night and the Wind at Sea at SE. Thermometer from 77½ to 81½ Degrees.

Sent the Fore Top Sail on Shore to repair. Carpenters about the Launch and others completing places for the Plants. Hands about the Rigging.

Sufficient Supplies, but very few Natives about us.

After Dinner Tynah sollicited me to forgive the Man who <whom> I had in Irons. He promised ardently not to behave ill again. I therefore forgave him and he was dismissed.

Tuesday, May 22nd

Moderate Breezes at E. and ESE and fair Weather. Thermometer from 76 to 81½ Degrees. Some light Rain.

Employed as Yesterday.

Our Plants appear to thrive. We have very few in a doubtfull state. Up to this day, the total number of Plants that have been shifted amount to 270. See 6 May. I have now got the most of my Plants that I brought from England and the Cape of Good Hope, planted in such places <places>, where I hope they will be taken care of. The principal dependance I have is with <upon> an Old Man in the Country who I have spoken of as Mr Nelson's Friend for the care he has taken of some Shaddock Trees.

Our supplies are brought off so scantily to the Ship, that I am now obliged to send a Boat, about the Shore between this and Oparre to trade for Hogs. I never saw so few People about us, as at this time. Tynah and Monah are the only People of consequence who dine with me generally every day. Nothing new occurs. The day passes with me in attending to the different duties of the Ship <and> the Welfare of the Plants, and it <which> fully occupies my time. The Matavians are all absent, the Plain is destitute of Inhabitants except a few Strangers or people who do not consider it their fixed place of abode. Poeeno and Tabyroo are fled, and every thing respecting the War is over and peace established.

Tobin also expressed appreciation for the new-found quiet:

The departure of the chiefs for Paparra gave us considerable relief; it is true, nothing could be more cheerful and amiable than their demeanour, but the ship was so constantly crowded with them that little rest was allowed us.

The numbers of day-time visitors on board the *Providence* is nowhere specifically reported, but some idea about them may be had from statements to the effect that 'the ship is quiet today with scarcely fifty natives aboard'.

During periods of quiet on board Tobin continued to report on incidents that Bligh either did not witness, or considered too trivial or unseemly to record. For example, Tahitians' reaction to the siring of the ship's nanny goats:

My pen is frequently obliged to touch on subjects, which the purity of him who guides it would rather avoid, yet, this would be witholding from you some simple facts strongly indicative of the manners of these Islanders.

Among other good things required for the passage home, were some kids. Assistance from the shore was necessary on the occasion as our Nannettes were living in a state of celibacy. If a congregation of the O'tahytean fair did not withdraw from the consummation of their nuptials, habit must acquit them of indelicacy. There are scenes which the english maiden has been taught to close her eye lids on, the uninstructed peery peery [piripiri] (Virgin) of this Isle views with indifference. Yet, if she is familiar with that, doubtless, as well concealed from her, she owes not her knowledge to aught but simple nature. That, which is acquired under the broad shelter of art, or affected mystery, belongs not to the O'tahytean.

As noted by Tobin, but unreported—perhaps unnoticed?—by Bligh, another *Bounty* 'widow' visited the ship during these days of relative quiet:

In the morning a woman came on board with her child, whose unfortunate father was a mutineer in the Bounty, and had been taken by Captain Edwards of the Pandora, with many others, about a twelvemonth before. There were on the Island three or four children of this description, besides one belonging to Brown, a man left by Captain Cox of the Mercury Brig in 1789. Brown it seems left O'tahytey in the Pandora.

The mother of the child was sensible of the fate that awaited the unhappy mutineer, yet without expressing much sorrow on the occasion, so little does serious reflection intrude on their thoughtless dispositions. An O'tahytean may be tenderly affected for a short period, but it would appear that, no circumstance whatever, is capable of fixing a lasting impression on the mind.

As the children of the mutineers have been mentioned, an enquiry naturally follows, why, after the many visits to the Island, more children are not to be seen partaking of european blood. It is certainly a fact that, until recently, not a single instance has been noticed, from the time of Messieurs Wallis and Bougainville in 1767 and 1768. The fathers of the children brought to the Providence resided on the Island above a twelve month and were individually attached to the mothers, which may account for the children being born; and yet, no proof, I believe has reached us of the females, under any circumstances, using means to promote abortion. The Aereoye [Arioi] Society it is known destroy their children instantly on their birth without the least reproach or stigma attending it. This may have been the case with the children of the casual visitors to the Island, from the conviction of the mothers that they were left fatherless on the departure of the ship to which such father belonged; whereas it most likely was not calculated on by such women as had connected themselves with the mutineers of the Bounty. Indeed, had the mothers felt any disposition to destroy the children of the latter, no European father—it is to be believed — could have consented to it.

On May 21st Tobin and Harwood went ashore, partly to sight-see but mainly, it appears, in search of 'Curiosities'. During their tour they viewed a corpse on display (of which more later) as well as some *ti'i*:

In our walk we saw several of the carved figures called Etee. [Plate 22] The most remarkable one was about twenty feet in height, consisting of sixteen figures, the base being of the female sex, about three; the others decreasing gradually according to the size of the tree. They are carved without the tree being cut down, and it must be a tedious undertaking. The Etee was observed in various parts of the Island, distant from as well as contiguous to Morais and Toopapows, the distortion of the mouth as when dancing the Heeva seemed to be imitated, and in some of the male figures the distinguishing mark of the sex was most preposterously evident, affording no small degree of giggling to some O'tahytean damsels, who retreated not from their God of Gardens.

Ti'i was the general term for, among other referents, carved figures, whatever their size or function. The one described (and pictured) here had nothing to do with 'Gardens', as suggested by Tobin; rather, it served as a *boundary-marker* for an area in which was located the house of a person having one or more very highly-ranked kin-Titles, high enough to require all other persons nearby to display respect behavior, such as baring one's shoulders. In passing such a marker and into the area so restricted, people were required to bare their shoulders as if in the actual presence of the exalted personage, and keep them bared until outside—such areas having had *ti'i* on all paths leading into and out of them. The area here demarcated was doubtless identified with Tu; no other individual in Pare-Arue, and indeed few others in all Tahiti, warranted such homage. Moreover, there were probably other such areas similarly reserved for Tu. As described previously, Tu's sanctity was such that he could enter no building other than his own, lest he render it supernaturally dangerous for others, thus, in moving about the country he required more than one sleeping house—hence more than one reserved area marked off by *ti'i*. And the sacrosanct character of such areas remained in force whether or not Tu was in them at the time. Persons entering such areas without paying the required respect, whether by deliberate refusal or forgetful neglect, were believed to be subject to punishment by the spirits investing the *ti'i*. And, if word of the act of impiety reached the ears of the sanctified personage, the transgressor would likely have been killed and sacrificed at the time, or, unknown to himself, reserved for future sacrifice.

As for Tobin's statement that such *ti'i* were carved from standing trees, that seems quite unlikely; no such technique is reported in any other known source.

During their excursion Tobin and Harwood also witnessed a 'private' fight:

In our way home, a quarrel having taken place at Matavai, we found two of the natives fighting. The weaker man had a fast gripe of the others hair, nor could he be disengaged the whole conflict. Kicking and every advantage was taken, and one gave the other such proofs of the sharpness and strength of his teeth that the blood gushed out amain. It did not continue long, but the wounded man brought a handful of hair from the head of his antagonist ere he 'gave in'. The women of the combatants were weeping and lamenting bitterly in loud shrieks the whole time.

Wednesday, May 23rd

Wind at East. Fresh Breezes and Cloudy Weather lessening at Night with some Calms. Rain in the Mountains and a light sprinkling at the Post. Thermometer from 76 to 81½ Degrees. These three Weeks past we have had no swell in the Bay or Surf on the Shore.

So very little is brought to the Ship that I am obliged to send the Boat to Oparre [Plate 23] for Provisions of every kind. Sailmakers repairing Sails, Carpenters about the Launch and fixing a new Trussel Tree to the Main Topmast the Old one was carried away at Sea. On examining it I found it had been Sprung before we left England and the Shipwright at Woolwich had disgracefully attempted to secure it by nailing.

Hauled the Seine. Caught 50 Weight of Fish which was served to the People.

The cause of our being scantily supplied with Provisions I find to be owing in some measure to curiosities being brought on board. Most of our People and Officers have their Tyos, and these are the most wealthy of the inhabitants, they therefore while they [the Tahitian taio] find their Friends [the English] pleased with trifles [i.e., 'curiosities'] neglect to bring supplies, and are incouraged in it as they [the English] value the curiosities more than any thing eatable, while they conceive it must be found them, altho every person [Tahitian?] receives the Market price, from the People who are authorized to Trade, when he brings any article of food which has been brought on board to by his Friend. I forbad anything but food to be brought on board the Ship. The next Month and the latter part of this is considered a scarce time for Breadfruit.

One possible reading of the first part of the lengthy sentence in the last paragraph of this entry is, that the seamen encourage their native friends to sell them 'curiosities' rather than food, knowing that food will be supplied to them anyway. The meaning of the rest of the sentence eludes me.

For the enlightenment of landlubbers, including myself, a 'Trussel tree' (i.e., Trestle tree) consists of 'two strong pieces of timber fixed horizontally fore-and-aft on opposite sides of a mast-head, to support the cross-trees, the top, and the fid of the mast above'. And a 'fid': 'A square bar of wood or iron, with a shoulder at one end, used to support the weight of the top mast and also the topgallant mast'. (*Oxford English Dictionary*)

Trussel tree aside, Bligh's main concerns of the day were with the supply of provisions—hogs, breadfruit, taro, coconuts, etc.—and his men's craze for 'curiosities', the two having been intertwined.

Only very rough estimates might be made regarding the amounts of native provisions consumed daily by the expedition's members — either what was actually consumed or the amounts purchased to constitute a 'sufficiency',

The usual rations of salted beef, seabiscuit, dried peas, etc. were discontinued the day after arrival, when Bligh wrote, 'I had . . . a sufficiency of Hogs, Breadfruit and Cocoa Nutts to feed every Person sumptiously', and while the daily quantities of rations thereafter varied—from 'sumptious' and 'more than he can consume' to 'sufficient' or 'moderate' or 'scanty'—the four- or five-day reserves of provisions maintained ruled out the necessity of reverting to sea provisions while at Tahiti and for several days thereafter at sea.

One large breadfruit a day is stated by Portlock (April 17th) to be the usual ration of that staple. At first the fruit was acquired raw and cooked on board but later it was purchased 'dressed'—i.e., baked in the native earth ovens. Wrote Portlock, 'we incourage their bringing the Bread fruit dressed as they certainly by their method of baking make it much more palatable than we do'. (April 23rd) Breadfruit is a seasonal crop, ripening two to four times a year in Tahiti. In the Matavai area the time of greatest plenty is from the end of December to about the middle of May. Such timing doubtless occurred also in 1792, although that seems not to have resulted in any subsequent reduction of supplies from neighboring districts; there was a considerable variation in times of ripening, depending upon location around the island, and canoes were always available—and Tahitians always eager—to carry them to Matavai and the ships.

Plantains were another native staple issued, sometimes native-baked, as a substitute for seabiscuit, and the same was true of taro. Of the local fruits available, native 'mangoes' were frequently acquired and apparently much enjoyed. On the other hand, there is no mention of yams or native manioc or sweet potatoes having been regularly served aboard ship—the first having been too fibrous and the second too bland, for English tastes, and the the third unpopular even to Tahitians.

As for coconuts, according to Tobin (May 19th) the English consumed about one thousand a day. In supporting his Commander's order to issue grog only three days a week, Portlock wrote: 'Grog is an Article that can be well done without here where every man gets as many fine Cocoanutts as he chuses to make use of . . . and the Milk of the Cocoanutt before the kernal becomes hard and firm is exceedingly pleasant to drink'.

And then there was pork. As Tobin wrote in his entry of May 6th, the word for pig, *pua'a*, was one of the first two native words his compatriots learned upon reaching Tahiti (the other having been *vahine*, female). In fact, he added (as was previously noted), so eager were his fellow countrymen for those two delicacies that Tahitians had come to believe them to be the reason for their coming there.

The earliest European visitors to Tahiti reported that the native pig was, 'a chaines [Chinese] breed, non of them above Eighty or a hundred pound weight'. (Carrington 1948: 179) And in the opinion of the Spanish

Andia y Varela, writing in 1774–1775, it was, 'a very small breed [but] plump and well flavored'. (Corney 1915: 272) Subsequent expeditions introduced European breeding stock, so that by 1797 the newly arrived English missionaries reported having acquired a pig weighing 340 pounds exclusive of head and entrails. (Wilson 1799: 60) None of the *Providence* nor *Assistant* journals records actual weights, but as their visit was only five years prior to that of the missionaries' ship, *Duff*, and no other ships between them, it is almost certain that many of the pigs acquired by them were of the larger mixed breed. And enough of them were obtained to permit daily rations of pork (which according to Bligh's entry of July 2nd averaged 1½ pounds a day), plus large enough amounts left over for salting, for issue during part of the journey home. In this connection, there is no mention in any of the expedition's journals of the purchase and issue of dog flesh. To Tahitians the native dog was a delicacy, and while some of the earlier European visitors, such as the experimental Banks, sampled dog flesh and pronounced it edible ('like mutton'), the animal never became acceptable to the average English palate—for reasons probably more sentimental than gustatory. (Also, there were far fewer dogs than pigs to permit widespread eating.)

All the above concern provisions acquired for the general store and the regular daily issue. In addition, many of the visitors acquired some provisions, probably mainly coconuts and fruit along with some cooked porked, for their separate personal consumption. And while this was discouraged by their Commander, the practice seems not to have ceased, nor to have been publicly punished.

In Bligh's 'Orders for establishing an amicable intercourse with the Natives . . .', reported in the entries for April 8th, one of them read: 'A proper Person or Persons will be appointed to regulate Trade and barter with the Natives & no Officer or Seaman or other Person belonging to the Ship shall trade or offer to trade for any kind of Provisions or Curiosities without my Leave.'—Manifestly, an unrealistic decree. Person(s) were in fact appointed to trade 'officially' for provisions both on shore (probably at the Post) and on board the ships, and doubtless most or all of the general-issue provisions were acquired in this way — why should an individual barter his own belongings for food for the *general* store? But the rule did not and could not stop individuals from bartering for *some* provisions, much less for curiosities, for their private use. Moreover, every man jack had his own *taio*, and although the items exchanged in this relationship were conventionally labelled 'gifts', they nevertheless were obliged to be reciprocated. (It is likely, however, that most of the larger 'gifts' of provisions received by Bligh and his officers were added to the general store.)

Besides 'gifts' (whose exchange values would be impossible to calculate on the basis of available data from the journals) there appear to have been fairly fixed values attached to most of the provisions acquired for the general store. The only journal to provide such figures is that of Portlock, who reported the price of ten to twelve breadfruit or coconuts to have been one sheathing nail, and of six to ten breadfruit, or eight to ten coconuts, one one-and-one-half inch nail (prices that he characterized as being cheaper than those prevailing in 1777, when he was there aboard the *Discovery*). In his *Assistant* Journal of April 15th Portlock also reported having purchased 'a fine hog' of 150 pounds for 'a hapenny or a Eightpenny hatchet'.

All very orderly and satisfactory—until May 23rd (or a little earlier, according to Tobin and Portlock), when so few provisions were brought for sale to the Post and the ships that Bligh had to send the launch to Pare in search of them. And on the 23rd, as recorded, he attributed the scarcity to his people's bartering for curiosities. Tobin as early as May 5th had remarked the scarcity and had attributed it to the same cause, but persisted (doubtless like many others) in the popular pastime. Thus, on May 21st:

Harwood was kind enough this day to accompany me on a visit to the Morai at Oparrey. Our pockets were filled with different articles to exchange for any thing curious which might be met with. It was soon circulated through the plain that two Erees from the ship were in search of curiosities. The natives ever laughed at the avidity with which such collections were made and to shew their contempt some brought a stone, another a feather, and so on, being highly delighted with the tricks they were playing on us. One fellow really deserved much credit as a sharper. I had bargained for four of the beautiful little blue paroquets called Veneys, with a promise to call for them on returning. In about an hour after, he came lamenting that, two had escaped from the cage. As I did not doubt his veracity he received the whole price, which was no sooner done that a boy brought two more and sold them, but we soon discovered by the looks of those around that the whole was a scheme to get double pay for the birds.

The most common items sought by the English were stone adzes, which, wrote Tobin, had been so depleted by a succession of European visitors, 'that nine tenths of those brought home in the Providence were purposely made for sale'—portent of Airport Art! Tobin himself coveted rarer items, such as the *taumi*, the warriors' demi-gorget, a wickerwork breast covering decorated with shell, shark's teeth, and feathers. He and some of his compatriots also were eager for *tamau*:

My Tayo [i.e., 'Itia] brought me a present of plaited human hair, about the thickness of a double thread and . . . [?] yards in length. [Joseph Banks saw some that were 'above a mile in length'] It is worn by the women as an ornament round the head in the manner of a turban, and called Tamow. The superior sort of dancing girls generally decorate themselves with it. This was the only present brought to me by Edeea for a considerable time, which occasioned our being rather on cool terms. She had reproved me for not being more bountiful, which in some measure was a true charge, but as I wanted some articles difficult to be procured in the neighborhood of Matavai I still thought it politic to withold any gifts until she brought them; at the same time making as great a display of my riches as possible, which had the desired effect of soon placing me in possession of a War mat (Tawmey) [taumi] and some other curiosities.

Plate 19   View of Ha'apaino'o River
Watercolor by George Tobin

Plate 20   Scene of fishing, in Tetaha-Fa'a'a
Watercolor by George Tobin

To get such kind of articles there was no little difficulty, from the eagerness with which we sought them, and from the introduction of european implements having rendered many of them nearly useless.

The desire for curiosities, wrote Tobin, was not onesided:

Though very profitable to them, the natives laughed at the avidity with which we coveted all their household and other goods. Yet have they at O'tahytey their collectors, and their cabinets of European curiosities, and you will hardly credit it, that old Hammaneminhay [Ha'amanemane], the High Priest was in possession of a volume of the 'Statutes at large,' which he procured from a vessel that had touched at the Island, on which he placed as much value as some among us do, on a brass Otho [?], a petrified periwinkle, or even (as you and I once heard a showman say) a 'stuffed baboon from the mines of Golconda.'

Most of the European goods sought by Tahitians were more prosaic: cloth, clothing, hatchets, knives, scissors, needles, nails (mainly for fish hooks), mirrors, and the like—plus brandy and firearms, especially the latter two. Continued Tobin:

Walking up the river with my gun many natives attended, and it is impossible to describe the pleasure they evinced at seeing a swallow shot [while] flying. So great is the estimation these people place, on all kinds of fire arms and ammunition that a dozen or them were anxiously employed in picking up the few shot that fell on the ground in charging my gun, and but a few days before, one of the Chiefs offered the Sergeant of marines some curiosities in great demand, for four balled cartridges.

The traffic at first so acceptable to these altered people now bears little value when compared with weapons of any kind, and there is but too much reason to dread the sad consequences of vessels, particularly trading ones, touching at this and the neighbouring Isles. For a dozen Muskets and a good proportion of ammunition a large vessel could procure an abundant supply of provisions. Strong liquors are also sought with avidity. These, among too many others, are acquired evils at O'tahytey; unknown happily, until introduced by the visits of civilized nations. What does the future promise? Does the avaricious trader much heed what misery his destructive articles produce among untutored indians? He wants refreshments and supplies to enable him to prosecute, in this distant quarter of the globe, his greedy scheme of gain—and if Gunpowder, or pernicious enervating brandy, should be demanded in preference to the useful Axe, or ornamental bead, will they not be given without reflecting on the consequences?

Thursday, May 24th

Fair Weather with some Showers of Rain. Wind at E. and E by S. Thermometer from 80 to 82 Degrees.

Employed about the Rigging, Launch and repairing the Main Top Sail. In the Morning hauled the Seine and Caught 150 lbs of fine Cavallies, Horse Macral and Ribband Fish (having brilliant stripes that characterises them). Washed and Cleaned Ship.

This Morning I was informed that an Indian had got by Stealth into our Post last Night and stolen several articles of Cloaths—several

171

circumstances occurred, which if f<u>act</u> <true>, prove these people to have such wonderfull expertness in theiving as exceeds all belief.

In the Night a fellow was seen about the Assistant with a design of doing some mischief, the Boats were immediately sent after him, but the Night was so dark he escaped. I have frequent conversations with Tynah respecting the want of power or order in his government to prevent thieving. He has told me that only good people could be governed by advice, Townahs [taona] (or Rogues) he said would at all times when it was in their power, do mischief and commit Thefts and could only be guarded against by a strict Watch, and <he> desired whenever we had it in our power to put them to death, that an example might be made to deter others. I cannot discover that they have any custom or law which inflict punishment for particular Crimes by Trial. The Strongest Man, or the most powerfull Chief decides in his own cause, but there is an appeal from the inferior people of every District to their superior Chief who judges fairly of the matter in dispute.

One can sympathize with Bligh for his perplexity over the matters touched on in this entry. The English system (or systems?) of law and order—of definition of breaches, of judicial procedures, of the execution of penalties, etc.—were in some respects doubtless also obscure to a man of Bligh's calling; but he evidently shared the popular belief in its straightforward nature, as a system consisting of Parliament-made laws, trial by jury, and punishments that fit the crime. Needless to say, the analogous Tahitian practices differed in many respects from those of England, but deeper study would have revealed to Bligh some similarities as well, including some widely-shared definitions of breaches, and some near-universal customs concerning punishments—even, in some cases, 'trial by jury'. Perhaps the widest differences between the two sets of practices lay in the nature of the breaches that were held to be 'official'—i.e., of direct concern to 'officials', and in the roles those officials played in judicial processes. The subject is far too large to cover in a few paragraphs, but here are some points that, had he known them, might have reduced Bligh's perplexity somewhat.

As in all known human societies there were in Tahiti some widely held views regarding right and wrong ways to do things, and along with those views there were widely shared convictions about how wrongdoing should be dealt with. Generally speaking, it was held that, say, 'unauthorized' adultery (as defined locally), or breach of an exchange understanding, ought to be dealt with by the principals themselves and according to their own judgments (unless the punishments were harsh enough to enrage relatives of the culprit—which then might have led to wider and protracted feuding). But what about theft, the matter that led Bligh to his inquiry?

The Tahitian attitude towards theft was complex. Except for those, such as Tina, whose own connections with them might be thereby imperilled, most Tahitians probably regarded theft from Europeans as hazardous and profitable but certainly not disgraceful. As for theft *among* Tahitians, their attitude was evidently ambiguous. On the one hand, a proven thief could be killed by the victim with impunity—one of the few kinds of personal 'executions' among equals that did not usually lead to feuding. If detected and overpowered the thief was either killed on the spot, or was taken out to sea to drown or be devoured by sharks. Also, the victim had the licence to plunder the thief's property. Nothwithstanding all this, there prevailed a widely shared admiration for clever—i.e., undetected—thieving, including some emulous veneration of Hiro, God of Thieving. However, there could be too much of this good—i.e., clever—thing: individuals who were widely believed to be recidivist in their thieving, even if undetected in specific acts, were commonly selected by their neighbors when a body was needed for human sacrifice. This, in a way, did constitute judgment and punishment by 'trial', hence in this respect Bligh was incorrect. But in the sentence in his entry following that, he was at least partly correct: *might* did make *right* in many instances.

As will be noted, there were some constraints on arbitrary acts on the part of even the most powerful of chiefs, but those bounds were very wide. They were able to confiscate the property and the women of lesser men quite arbitrarily, and to levy services for their own projects in return for little or no compensation. And they punished harshly any act they believed to be offensive to their own persons, property, or positions. Moreover, when, as usually happened, such an offender was slain, he was disposed of as an offering to a god, thereby reducing the inclination or possibility of revenge. But, as said above, there were limits to the power of any chief. The power of assassination was always present, but more constraining than that was the opposition, often exercised, of disgruntled under-chiefs—either through their combined strength alone or through their temporary alliance with rival district chiefs. (Such coalitions were commonplace and subject to continual reshaping, having been nourished by political ambitions and implemented through extensive kin networks.)

Finally, what of Bligh's statement concerning the role of the Chief as Judge? Evidence on this point is conflicting, partly as result of differences in personalities of chiefs. Some of them did occasionally intervene in this way in their subjects' affairs but, as remarked earlier, most disputes, including those arising from offences, were settled more directly by the subjects themselves—unless of course the chief's own interests were directly or indirectly at stake.

Bligh's reaction to the thefts committed or attempted on this day was to ask large questions about law and order; Tobin's was to expatiate on the Tahitians' swimming skills:

We were again alarmed at night by a thief near the ship, yet, notwithstanding the shore party were posted along the beach, and the boats in pursuit, his activity in the water was so great he effected his escape. But they are so early habituated to this element, and remain so long under its surface that our pursuits on such occasions were always tedious, and frequently in vain. When nearly within grasp they dive, nor is it possible to tell in what direction they will rise. Most likely you have been shooting, or rather shooting at, loons, and divers, on some of the 'American waters', if so, you may form a tolerable idea of an O'tahytean in the Sea. From the gangway of the Providence, I have frequently seen children eight or nine years of age leap into the sea for beads, fifteen or twenty feet below the surface, scarcely ever failing to Rise with the reward of their exertions. Their vision under water must be astonishingly clear, as when the smallest beads have been thrown into it, several yards assunder, after securing some, they have returned with the same success to others in a different direction. Doubtless the Sea among these Islands (which indeed is the case in most tropical latitudes) being so translucid, greatly aids the distinguishing of objects in it.

While speaking of the agility of these people in the water it is impossible to help reflecting how little the qualification of even swimming, is cultivated in our own country. To sailors and soldiers it is particularly useful and should be encouraged by every means. Yet even among the former, who may be said to live on the deep how small the proportion of those who can swim!

Friday, May 25th

Light Breezes Easterly and Calms with some light refreshing Showers of Rain. Thermometer from 78 to 83 Degrees.

At Day light I had the Ship unmoored to examine the Cables, which we found not at all injured. By 2 O'Clock we shifted our Birth a little more to the NNE and moored with an open Hawse to the East Winds as I now considered no Winds of any consequence to be expected from the Sea. Bearings. The End of the Reef N 23 [degrees] W Point Venus N 23 [degrees] E Distant a Mile, from the nearest beach ¼ of a Mile. The Heads of Tarrah S 10 [degrees] W to S 27 [degrees] W. The Small Bower [anchor] in 10 fathoms and the best Bower in 14 ½ fathoms.

After Dinner Tynah and his Wives requested I would accompany them to a Heivah. They are remarkably fond of these amusements, and as my presence is sure to produce some <always produces> additional exertions and more mirth among the People, from the presents I distribute among them, if any thing is going on I am sure of being <to be> acquainted of it. Including Children the number of Persons collected were about two hundred. The Performers were two Men who did the interlude and a Women and a little Girl <did> the dancing part. The Airahyree or platted Cocoa Nutt leaf was as usual brought to me, but not any thing <nothing> new in the performance.

In the Evening we gave great entertainment to the Natives by setting off a Dozen Sky Rockets. We have ever found them highly delighted with our Fire Works.

Besides confirming the obvious, that *ai-rahiri* was the name of the plaited coconut frond presented to notables before dance performances, there is nothing that this commentator can add to Bligh's account, nor did Tobin record any noteworthy happenings for this day.

Saturday, May 26th

Fresh Breezes and fair Weather. Wind E by N. The Thermometer 78 to 83 ½ Degrees.
    Employed <in> Mending and Washing Cloaths as usual on this day. Our supplies are sufficient, but we have very little more than we absolutely want. Our Venereal List is increased to 20.
    I received a parcel of fine Breadfruit Plants to day from Tiarraboo which are reckoned vastly superior to any at this place. I had heard of this kind, and had such reports confirmed to me by the Chiefs, that I employed two Men to go for them. Our Number of Plants are now increased by 7 Tubs containing 3 to 5 Plants each, 7 small Pots containing One and two each, and 7 extra Pots of Ayyahs (the Jambo of Java). I have taken some small Bread fruit Trees [marginal note: '7 feet high'] in very large Tubs such as half Halfhogsheads [?]. I expect they will stand the Sea if none of the others do. All the Plants are now in charming order, spreading their leaves delightfully. I have completed fine airy <convenient> places for them on the Quarter Deck and Galleries, and shall Sail with every inch of space filled up. My anxious moments have been hitherto <anxiety hitherto has been> to complete my Numbers, they are now <it is now to provide> for their security. The greatest circumspection is observed at the Post, which is well guarded to prevent any vicious designs of the Natives, altho I have no reason to suspect them.

—The plants 'in *charming* order, spreading their leaves delightfully': elegant words for an old sea dog. Bligh's engrossment with the welfare of his precious breadfruit plantings was evidently deep and personal. And why not? Clearly, they were to him the means of demonstrating his ability to complete his assigned mission despite the failure of the first attempt (for which, he well knew, many persons held him responsible notwithstanding his official clearance). Loyalty to his patrons, especially Banks, and concern for career advancement, were undoubtedly factors in his single-minded determination, but in addition one should not overlook his intrinsic, hard-driving, self-immolating sense of duty, and his immense personal pride.

But leaving Bligh to contemplate his beloved plants, we turn to Tobin and accompany him on another of his eventful excursions:

In the morning Guthrie and myself left the Post for Whapiano, to examine a War Canoe, of which, great praise had been given by Pomaurey. As usual in all our walks, several natives joined us, and it was with difficulty we prevented the party being too crowded.
    A spot was pointed out to us where one of the recent battles had been fought, and many of the trees exhibited deep marks from the stones of slings. These weapons in the hands

of a resolute people would occasion sad destruction. The O'tahyteans use them with great skill, but their timidity, which seems excessive, prevents any warfare being carried on with energy.

In our way we called on Whidooah, who instantly ordered a hog to be prepared for the oven. Tai-Aiva his wife was breakfasting on fish barely warmed, according to the custom of the Island, alone, in a small shed about fifty yards from the house.

Whidooah, next brother to Orepaia appeared about seven and twenty. His counten-ance was handsome, and figure elegant, both of which had been much injured by an unre-strained use of Yava. As a warrior he was esteemed the best in the Island, and had killed Maheeny, a chief of Moreea. It is true, the manner of his death gave nothing heroic to the conqueror, as he was seized by several Towtows while Whidooah beat out his brains with a stone. Much confidence however seemed to be placed in this prince by the state, but he appeared a complete voluptuary and from the account given us, his indulgences were so various it was difficult to believe them true at O'tahytey.

He was among the few who entertained jealousy of his wifes conduct. Tai Aiva was considered as the Belle of the Island, as well by the English, as her own countrymen, and the temptations to seduce her from the 'right path' were various, and often repeated—but in vain. Ruffled, or unruffled, she was still the same cold, repellent fair one. Had Tai Aiva been more yielding, the ward robe of many an English Chief, would have been expended, and this kindly . . . [?] far richer in various sorts of foreign drapery. Little credit was given her by her own sex, this sturdy denial being alone attributed to the dread she entertained of offending her Lord, to whom she was very inferior in blood. In this surely there was some merit due to her. Let us at the same time soften the guilt of others, whose husbands and relations rather promoted than suppressed a more complying conduct.

Tobin's cursory reference to the killing of Mahine ('Maheeny') points to one of the largest, longest and most fateful conflicts in these islands' recent history, and one of the most tangled ones.

Although little is known about the political geography of Mo'orea (also called, Eimeo) during the 1870s, Mahine, of Opunoho, was certainly the most powerful and perhaps the most influential chief in that island. And as another measure of his political importance, he was a hated but respected enemy of the chiefly dynasties of Taiarapu, Fa'a'a and Pare-Arue. The reasons behind the Taiarapuans' hostility are somewhat obscure and need not con-cern us, but his enmity with Fa'a'a and Pare-Areu involves some of our fam-iliar *Dramatis Personae*, and warrants a closer look.

Mahine had no offspring of his own (he was an Arioi, and evidently a fully active one); for reasons unreported he appointed his foster-son, whose kinship link to him is not recorded, to succeed him, thereby by-passing his only surviving nephew, his sister's son, the original Mahau, whom we have met with before (May 6th). Deeply resentful of this substitution (which was however not altogether unusual) were 'Itia (Mahau's own sister) and Auo (Tina's sister and Mahau's wife)—and hence Tina himself. Equally resentful, on the Fa'a'a side, was Mahau's father, Teihotu, who was brother of Fa'a'a's chief, Te Pau. The leaders of Atehuru were also against Mahine in the early

176

stages of the conflict, probably because of their connections with the leaders of Fa'a'a.

Such was the line-up when *Resolution* and *Adventure* were in Tahiti in 1774, when Cook observed a huge armada drawn up off Pare in preparation for an assault against Mahine: 160 large double canoes armed for fighting, plus 170 smaller canoes with sail. By Cook's estimate this fleet contained no less than 7760 men; another 40 canoes from Fa'a'a subsequently joined it, and further reinforcements from Taiarapu were expected (but not observed to have arrived).

Cook's expedition sailed before the assault took place but Cook learned of its inconclusive outcome three years later. After the failed assault an uneasy truce had prevailed until this time, but at the time of Cook's last visit, in 1777, preparations were under way for another naval expedition, including a contingent from Atehuru, against Mahine. The assault took place while *Resolution* and *Discovery* were at Tahiti, and once again the encounter had been a stand-off, largely because of the timorous—the journals say 'craven' and 'cowardly'—Tina, whose fleet had not arrived in time to supply the needed reinforcements. Needless to say, the Atehurans and Fa'a'ans were enraged, and more with Tina than with Mahine, with whom they concluded a peace pact that, it may be inferred, served to confirm Mahine's choice of a successor (i.e., his foster son), which was unfavorable to Mahau, and hence to Tina. Moreover, the Atehurans, especially their co-chief and the fleet's 'Admiral', Te To'ofa, felt so vengeful against Tina that Cook was moved to try to protect the latter:

The terms [of the truce] were disadvantageous and all the blame fell upon Otoo [i.e., Tina] for not going to assist Towha [Te To'ofa] in time. The current report was now, that Towha assisted by the forces of Waheatua [Vehiatua, Chief of Taiarapu] would, as soon as I was gone, come and fall upon Otoo; this called upon me to support my friend by threatening to retaliate it upon all who came against him when I returned again to the island, if there was any truth in the report at first this had the desired effect, for we heard no more of it.' (Beaglehole 1967: 214)

Thus was formulated a more or less 'official' British policy, and Cook's threat evidently worked—but only for a while. When Bligh returned to Tahiti in 1789 he reported:

He [Tina] said that after five Years and three Months, from the time of our sailing [Bligh having been with Cook], counting 63 Months, the Imeo [Mo'orea] People joined with Tettowah [Te To'ofa], (the noted old Admiral called by Captain Cook Towah) and made a descent at Oparre . . . that after some resistence by which many Men were killed, he [Tina] and all his People fled to the Mountains. The People of Imeo and those of Atta-hooroo under Tettowah now being masters of all their property, destroyed every thing they could get hold of, among which were the Cattle, Sheep, Ducks, Geese, Turkeys and Peacocks left by Captain Cook in 1777 (Bligh 1937: 378)

It may seem surprising to see Mahine and Te To'ofa as allies, but it appears that the antagonism shared by the two chiefs against Tina overrode their former feelings against each other.

The end of this chapter of dynastic rivalry took place in April 1790, when a war party from Pare-Arue went to Mo'orea to attempt to put an end to the 'rebellion' against Mahau. This time however they took along firearms, which had been put in good repair by some of the *Bounty* people, and under the leadership of the English-trained, musket-wise Hiti Hiti, forced Mahine's foster-son successor to flee, and installed Tina's brother-in-law Mahau in his place. Alas, as will be recalled, the pawn-like Mahau lived to enjoy his position only until January 1792, when he died of illness, leaving his four-year-old son to succeed him. (See May 8th)

Meanwhile sometime between 1777 and 1789, Mahine was captured by some of Tina's people, who—according to Tobin's version—held him while Vaetua beat out his brains. According to Bligh, writing in December 1788, the killing took place 'at the time of the Imeo War'. (Bligh 1937: I 411) The only battle between Mahine and the Pomares known to have taken place during that period was the one just described, hence Mahine's death may (must?) have taken place then, despite the final victory of his forces and the routing of the Pare-Arueans. Thus, this particular victory that Vaetua had snatched from the jaws of defeat was of benefit only to his legendary reputation as a great warrior.

And speaking of this great warrior: his wife's beauty evidently accounts for her husband's possessiveness. Had Tai Aiva been older and less beauteous he would doubtless have followed his brothers' paths. And, as Tobin reports, had she been of upper-class family, she would probably have behaved more like 'Itia and Vaiareti. Faithful wives were to be found among Tahiti's upper-class women, but accounts of them—being less interesting?—are far fewer than those about adulterous ones.

But let us accompany Tobin throughout the remainder of his excursion:

The Whapiano was crossed several times, as usual on mens shoulders before we reached the Shed under which the canoe was building. Its dimensions were as follows:

Extreme length	*70 feet*
Extreme breadth at about one third from the stern	*3¾*
Height at the Stern	*17*
Height at the Head	*11¾*

Like the common canoes it was formed of a number of pieces sewed together, the seams being payed [?] over with a black composition, not very unlike pitch. On the head and stern, was the rude figure of a man. It [the hull] had seven knees, or timbers of a single piece of wood. About the sides, head and stern, were carved figures of turtle and lizards, and on the fore part was placed an Efarrey no Eootooa [fare no te atua], *the wooden case which has been before mentioned to shelter the deity in. It also serves him as a sleeping place. I never saw a Canoe decorated for any religious occasion, without an Efarrey no Eoatooa being affixed to it.*

In a shed near at hand was a piece of carved work twenty feet in length, to be erected as an ornament on the stern, and a conical helmet formed of bamboo, decorated with cock feathers, to be occasionally worn by the priest. The Canoe was a full quarter of a mile from the Whapiano, yet, when finished, was to be carried to it by the means of poles on mens shoulders. We were informed that it was small when compared to some in the Society Islands [i.e., Huahine, Ra'iatea, Taha'a, Borabora, Maupiti]. Mahau told us that at Orieteeah [Ra'iatea] he had seen one that employed several men to steer it. This one on the stocks, and another smaller at Oparrey, were all we heard of in the neighborhood of the ship. How different the state of Otahytean Navy when Captain Cook describes the armament at Oparrey in 17[74].

Tupira, who was at his stronghold some distance up the river, learning we were in the neighbourhood, soon paid us a visit; and what seemed rather inexplicable, accompanied us to the house of his enemy Whidooah. The two Chiefs hardly noticed each other, but this coolness did not prevent Tupira assisting us to demolish the hog of his antagonist with a good appetite, while he informed us that the greater part of the furniture we were using, had been taken from him in the late attack. We could only conjecture that our presence was a protection to Tupira. Yet, could Whidooah have made him prisoner on his return from accompanying us part of the way to Matavai, had such been the object.

The hog was served up whole with baked breadfruit and plantains. Milk from the Cocoa nut was our beverage, and salt water the sauce to our meat. From having frequently used it as a substitute for salt, so easily are our prejudices surmounted, I found it equally palatable.

Pahraihea, a chief of Whapiano behaved with much kindness, insisting we should not return to the ship without a live hog, and our friend Tupira loaded our attendants with a variety of fruits.

Tupira's 'safe passage' at Vaetua's could be explained by the presence of Tobin and Guthrie, or by the over-riding conventions of Tahitian hospitality —or by the widely prevalent circumstance that family loyalty (in this case, Vaetua's to Tina) quickened only when the individual's personal interests were directly involved.

Sunday, May 27th

This Day terminated with heavy Rain, Wind Variable. Thermometer from 78 to 83 ½ Degrees.

Mustered the Ships Company and saw every person clean dressed and performed Divine Service.

I went on board the Assistant, where I found everything so much <much> to my satisfaction as <which> gave me great pleasure, and a continuance of satisfactory <I had continual> proofs of the Commanders good conduct.

Our supplies of Breadfruit are worse every day as are the Plantains, but <of> Hogs, Vees and Mahie we have sufficient.

179

Tynah with his Wives dined as usual with me to day, he had however taken such a dose of Avah before he came on board, that his common allowance of Wine made him very drunk. While the height of the Fit was on him, he was so convulsed as to require Six People to confine him to the Cabbin Deck. Iddeeah, altho the cast off Wife, took more pains to assist him than Whyerreddee, and after she had got him free of <recovered him from> the convulsions, put him to sleep untill the morning, when at Day break he rose <was as> well as he had ever been in his life.

A Towtow [teuteu] [marginal note: 'Slave or Servant'] in this Country can never get permission to be connected with a Woman who is above him in situation, & to live <with her> publickly as Man & Wife. There are many however who fall <many an one however falls> in love desperately where they <he> can never expect any return to their <his> affections—not even <and where> the inclination of the Woman bears the least in his favor <is not in the least favourable>, yet <in this case> he will wander about and meet her <his mistress> at every turning in a disconsolate manner, at last comfortless <till being comfortless at last> he is left without any resource except an unnatural one which suggests itself—the beastly Swain follows the <gratification except a very extraordinary and beastly one, he follows his> Lady and deprives the earth of that which she meant to be deposited in it. Of this strange and unnatural liking <practice> I never heard before. I remember an account however of Muller's in his History of Siberia and Russian Discoveries, that among the Kamchadales or Korjacks, (I forget which) when a Stranger is introduced into a Family, the Master offers to him the prettiest of his Daughters or Women as a companion to him for that Night,—on his expressing his approbation, he has presented to him a bason of the Womans Urine made in his presence which he is obliged to drink, or forfit the hospitality and protection of the Tribe he is among.

In the beginning of the Night Tarrah Hill [Plate 24] was beautifully illuminated with Flambeaus to light Tynah over, who had stayed late at Oparre, perhaps a prettier sight was never seen than the effect it had upon the smooth Water about the Shore, for the lights were brilliant and numerous. When any of the Royal Family pass over the Hill they have it lighted, as the Road is bad and a fall likely to be attended with bad consequences.

Notwithstanding the rage the Otaheiteans have for our clothes of evry kind, yet we find some of them so honest that the People in general have given them their Linnen to wash—no losses have yet been experienced, but every thing returned in good order.

I have endeavored by every means to get a knowledge whether Marriage has any common and general ceremony attending it, to give legality to the Man and Woman living together, and I find from the best collected accounts among *those People who are capable of giving me information, that any ceremony attending Marriage is not general—the Women <there is no general ceremony attending Marriage. With Chiefs and particular persons the Parents of the Woman> are sollicited for their consent, and untill they give it the Man dares not to take the Woman away. When the Parents approve of the match, there is a ceremony of Prayer at a Morai and the Parents perform AAmo to the married Couple. [Marginal note: 'See 20th April'] (This Aamo or Aammoah, as it is called, is a Ceremony performed by Parents to their Children when they are supposed to be able to look out <provide for>, and take care of themselves). The Parties may separate whenever they chuse <choose>. A Man may have as many Wives as he pleases, and a Woman may have as many Gallants as her husband has different Wives.*

The Woman who bears Children has greater priviledges than those who do not—they always abide by the property of the Husband, while the others have little or no share.

The infidelity of a Wife, any further than <beyond what> the husband permits or aproves, is considered whoredom and punishable by himself; but while [if] he approves of the Man she is connected with, they may Sleep under the same roof, so that it is not uncommon for a Husband with his <who has> three Wives to sleep on the same floor, and they with <with them and> their Gallants.

It is remarkable that the ceremony of Prayer is only performed to the first Woman, and might reason from thence <one might thence conclude> that the others were Concubines and not Wives.

A potpourri of topics in this day's entry; first, Bligh's remarks about Portlock.

Anyone who recalls Bligh's drumroll of complaints against his *Bounty* people (e.g., 'such neglectful and worthless petty Officers I believe never were in a ship as are in this.' 'If I had any Officers to supercede the Master and Boatswain, or was capable of doing without them, considering them as common Seaman, they should no longer occupy their respective statuses.' 'As this affair [a desertion] was solely caused by the neglect of the Officers who had the watch . . .' 'I have such a neglectful set [of Officers] about me that I beleive nothing but condign punishment can alter their conduct.' etc. etc.), will be struck by his praise of the *Assistant's* Commander. And fans of *The Mutiny* will doubtless wonder about the contrast. Was it due to the inherently better qualities of his present people, or to Bligh's greater experience in managing men, or to what?

In the case of love-sick *teuteu*, if by 'connected' Bligh meant 'married', as he seems to have done, he was certainly correct (see the commentaries for April 9th and 16th). But if he implied, as could perhaps be inferred, that *teuteu* in general could not and did not engage in sexual affairs with women 'above [them] in situation', he himself knew that not to be so, even in the case of a woman as high-ranking as 'Itia (see his entry for April 17th). As for his generalization about the bizarre behavior of rejected *teuteu* swains, it could be true, but this is the only mention of such a practice that I have come across, and I suggest that it may have been one of the tall tales which Tahitians of that era—and of today!—delight in telling credulous Europeans.

Street lights on Tarrah—One Tree—Hill! Bligh evidently saw the beauty of it but Tobin is fuller in his explanation of their being there:

Pomaurey, with other chiefs, having in the evening to pass One Tree Hill and it being extremely dark; had sent their Towtows to prepare fires at different parts of the road; these had communicated with a quantity of high reeds, causing a brilliant illumination over the whole bay. It was the only instance during our stay of the Chiefs being assisted in this way in their journeys; indeed, travelling by night rarely happens, nor is an Otahytean often seen out of his house after the day has closed.

Tobin should have added that the main reason why Tahitians rarely travelled over land at night was their fear of spirits, which were believed to be more active during darkness, as was audibly manifest in squeaks (of rats) and cries (of night birds). The belief that some of those were ghosts of relatives seems not to have been entirely reassuring. Even indoors at night, they preferred company to being alone.

In writing about nuptial ceremonies Bligh was correct in stating (or implying?) that they did not occur at the beginnings of all 'marriages'. In fact, usually only those marriages through which valued heritages—kin-Titles, offices, specific land rights, etc.—devolved upon the offspring, were legitimized by a formal ceremony, which, as Bligh remarked, was also an *amo'a* rite, another step in the sanctity-neutralizing series.

In considering the rest of Bligh's statements about connubiality it should be recalled that most of his information came from or concerned upper-class persons. Like most other European visitors writing about the Tahiti of that era (with the possible exception of James Morrison) he had not the opportunity, and perhaps not the inclination, to observe the domestic lives of the middle and lowerclass.

Divorce, as he wrote, was a matter of choice by either spouse, and was marked by no formalized procedure; moreover, such was the case with persons of any class.

Bligh's next statement is however problematic, depending upon what he meant by 'priviledges'. While 'Itia, the mother of Tina's children, certainly had more decisive influence over dynastic and district affairs than did her sister and co-wife Vaiareti (partly because of 'Itia's personality and partly because of her maternal ties with her influential children), Vaiareti clearly—openly, almost challengingly—enjoyed the privilege of Tina's attention and sleeping mat. As for a child-bearing wife always abiding by the property of her husband, etc., it must be noted that the only 'shares' a wife acquired in the properties of her husband—and vice versa—were userights, and those only during the duration of the marriage—although many widows continued to enjoy such rights, by consent of their in-laws and/or through their children, to whom the full-rights devolved. As for childless widows, the continuation of their use-rights in their husbands' properties depended entirely upon the consent of their in-laws, which involved factors too situational to try to list.

The next paragraph in Bligh's remarks was certainly true of some of the upper-class marriages known to him. It may however not have been true generally of most middle- and lower-class marriages, and, according to Tobin's entry for May 26th, it was also not true of upper-class Vaetua's.

And finally, Bligh was generally correct in stating that nuptial rites were performed only with the first wife, that is, with the first woman agreed upon by both families as socially eligible to transmit their respective heritages—a corollary of the broader propostion regarding birth-order.

On the other hand, if a first wife had borne no children after some time (*how* long a time is not reported), and if the husband's heritage was highly valuable, another woman of suitable pedigree (and of likely fecundity) was chosen to wife, and the marriage also established with a formal nuptial ceremony. As for Bligh's conclusion that only the first woman married was a 'wife' and the later ones only concubines, an attempt to deal with that semantic problem was made in the commentary of the entry of April 16th.

While Bligh's thoughts were focussed on larger, more sociological matters, Tobin had his distracted by a second but nevertheless highly 'privileged' wife:

The O'tahytean seldom loses an opportunity of bathing in fresh water. Whyhereddy in the middle of the rain surprised our frail nerves by suddenly emerging from the cabin in a state of nudity. She was a wicked jade, and we should all have been much more pleased, had it been Taihiera or Warrianow.

After getting thoroughly soaked, and playing numberless tricks and sportive gambols to a congregation that, of course encreased on such an occasion; she as suddenly disappeared to enrobe herself in the cabin; but, and without leaving us in admiration and wonder, at the ingenuity with which she disposed of her pliant and beautifully molded limbs; yet seemingly accidental and unstudied—while they scarcely presented, a shade, of what she aimed at concealing. Edeea took leave of us for a few days, having heard of the death of her child in its passage from Paparra to Oparrey.

We are, alas, given no further information about the identities or charms of Taihiera or Warrianow. And it will require more ingenuity than this commentator is capable of to unravel the complexities of Tobin's prose in his comments about the tartiness of 'Whyhereddy'.

183

Monday, May 28th

During the Morning frequent hard Rain which about Noon <at about Noon it> began to clear up and remained fair with very Strong Winds from the WSW at Night and Moderate Westerly Winds the other parts <part> of the Day. Thermometer from 78 ½ to 80 Degrees.

Employed at the Forge. Carpenters at the Launch. Sailmakers about the Main Top Sail.

We have <Have> sufficient supplies of Pork, Cocoa Nutts, Plantains, Vees, Tarro and Mahie, but Breadfruit not to be got except a few heads which are brought from the Country.

Accounts were brought to Iddeah and Tynah that their Daughter Tahamydooah was dead. They cared very little about it, particularly Tynah, but Iddeaeah at last shed a few tears. The people who had the care of the Child had been at Papparah with it to see some Heivahs. It there caught a violent cold which terminated in a Fever, and <it> died in the <on its> way back to the Parents.

'Ideeah at last shed a few tears'—implicit in this statement is a charge made by many other Europeans about the shallowness of Tahitians' emotions (including their feelings for each other), as manifested in the seeming artificiality and transience of what in other peoples—especially Europeans! —is grief. I must leave to other, better qualified specialists* the delineation of Tahitians' inner 'emotions' and reproduce only some eye-witness accounts of outward expression of them. First, a record of Tobin's, who was present on the previous day, when news first reached Tina and 'Itia about their daughter's illness:

Edeeas feelings were put to the test at dinner by our Commander expressing his surprise that she thought so little of the illness of one of her children left at Paparra. She, for a few minutes wept bitterly, exhibiting every symptom of unfeigned grief, when drying her eyes, laughter soon succeeded, and the child no more intruded on her thoughtless disposition.

Bligh reported similarly in his *Bounty* Journal:

. . . I was suddenly surprized at a violent degree of distress by some one at a little distance off, where I saw a Toopapow [*tupapa'o*, a bier on which a partly-embalmed corpse was kept until decomposition]. As I expressed a desire to see the distressed person, Tynah took me to the place, but we no sooner came in sight than the Mourner burst into a fit of laughter at seeing me. This person was the Mother of a Young female Child that lay dead. Several Young Women were with her, but they all resumed a degree of chearfullness, and the tears were immediately dryed up. I told Tynah the Woman had no sorrow for her Child, as her greif could not so easily have subsided if it was the case that she regretted the loss of it. When with some humour, he told her to cry again; however we left her

* For example, Robert Levy in his *Tahitians* (see Bibliography).

without any visible marks of its return. These are nevertheless funeral rites which are paid to the deceased at certain times after his death, but it is extraordinary that the great degree of sorrow and distress that these people are susceptible of can be changed in an instant to an opposite extreme, and unless it can be proved, that as impressions are most violent they are the least lasting, I see no way of accounting for it, as they are fond Parents and in general affectionate and friendly to one another in the highest degree. (Bligh 1937: II 18)

On another occasion, after the *Bounty* had been buffeted by alarmingly huge swells Bligh was visited by Poeno and his wife:

These kind people had no sooner left me than Poeeno and his Wife came of[f] with another supply of fruit. This Woman has on many occasions shown that she is possessed of great Sympathy, and now marked it with such excess of Greif for the danger the Ship had been in, that would have affected the most dispassionate creature existing. The strongest and only established proof among these people of their sincerity on those occasions is the Wounding of themselves on the Top of the Head with a Sharks tooth untill they bring on a vast profusion of blood, and having a knowledge of this I was prepared to prevent this Woman from doing it; but I had no sooner come to her than the Operation was performed before I was aware of it, and her face covered with blood in an instant. This circumstance however frequently happens upon trifling occasions, and with the drying up the Blood all feelings of the mind subsides it is allways a proof of great joy as well as excess of greif, but at this last time it was a lasting token of the latter, and this affectionate creature could not be brought to resume any kind of chearfullness for two hours that she remained on board. (Bligh 1937: I 416)

The self-bleeding referred to was standard practise, as described by the Captain of the ship *Duff*, which carried the first contingent of missionaries to these shores in 1797:

When a woman takes a husband, she immediately provides herself with a shark's tooth, which is fixed with the bread-fruit gum on an instrument that leaves about a quarter of an inch of the tooth bare, for the purpose of wounding the head, like a lancet. Some of these have two or three teeth, and struck forcibly they bring blood in copious streams; according to the love they bear the party, and the violence of their grief, the strokes are repeated on the head; and this has been known to bring on fever, and terminate in madness. If any accident happens to the husband, his relations or friends, or their child, the shark's tooth goes to work; and even if the child only fall down and hurt itself, the blood and tears mingle together. (Wilson 1799: 340)

Self-bleeding was practised more frequently as an expression of bereavement, but it served also to express, or at least display, great joy, as upon the return of a close relative after a long or dangerous voyage. In other words, the practice was meant as an expression of intense—or deep, or strong—emotion, over loss *or* gain. That in itself should have been no surprise to Europeans, who were accustomed to people shedding tears both for sorrow or joy; what

185

most surprised them, understandably, was the drastic, mortifying (and messy!) form of the expression. The social rationale of the practice is quite evident: to demonstrate to others that one 'feels' strongly. It may also have had a religious rationale (for example, *bloody* bodies, of pigs or of humans, having been considered highly acceptable sacrifices to some spirits), but that is a surmise unbacked by any recorded statements of the Tahitians themselves.

The final rites for little 'Tahamydooah' are described in Bligh's next Journal entry.

Tuesday, May 29th

Land and Sea Breezes. Thermometer from 72 to 79 Degrees.

Employed as Yesterday. No Bread Fruit to be got, and am obliged to send on shore after other supplies, the Natives being indifferent about bringing them to Sale.

This Morning I went to Oparre to look after some Plants I had ordered to be planted in the Hills at Tynahs Country Seat. I found them all in good order and taken care of, but I have little hope they <the People> will persevere in guarding them from accident, as not one article <that> I left here last Voyage is remaining. I have now planted here 59 Orange and Citron Plants, and 12 Pine Apple, besides <beside> many seeds, and 8 Fine Young Firs which the Natives value the most, as they are likely to produce plank and Masts.

Upon any part of those Hills the situation is delightfull. This place of Tynahs is charmingly diversified and shaded with Cocoa Nutt Trees and Breadfruit. He has a few old People to look after it whose only Stock is a few Fowles and half starved Hogs. Whenever Tynah goes there himself, he takes food with him, such as Fish or Pork, Cocoa Nutts and Breadfruit are <is> all else that is required. Our repast was a Baked Fowl.

Teturoah bore N 7 [degrees] W.

On my return I found Iddeeah attending her Dead Child at a distance from her friends, and in a meloncholy manner. The Child was laid out under a neat Shed with her hands laid over her breasts as our custom is—a piece of European Scarlet Cloth besides some very neat Country Cloth [probably bark cloth] covered the Body. A man attended dressed in a clean manner to show the Child to the Friends, and while remarkable silence and but very few people to be seen <a small number of people>, gave a Solemn cast to every thing about us, the Scene was rendered more affecting by a view of <by> the Servants preparing the Tupapow or Teapapow. On this Stage which is elevated about 6 feet above the ground, fenced round with reeds and neatly ornamented with coloured Cloth, leaves and Flowers, the Body remains untill all that is perishable is gone, the Friends then order the

Plate 21   View of Matavai Bay and Tetiaroa
Watercolor by George Tobin

Plate 22   Boundary-marker *ti'i*
Watercolor by George Tobin

bones to be put in the Earth, but it sometimes i̲s̲ t̲h̲e̲ ca̲se <happens>, that a particular Friend of the deceased will seize the Scull and present it to his God in the Morai.

It is only with Erees that the Body remains so long on the Tupapow [marginal note: 'Teeapapow']—with the lower orders of the People it is put into the Earth after a short time allotted for the Friends to mourn.

Our Friend Tynah was not at all concerned at the loss of his Child, he would not however return with me to the Ship, for he seemed to consider it but decent to remain with Iddeeah. They told me their mourning would be over in two days, and they would then return to the Ship.

In my last Voyage I have spoken of the Natives embalming their Chiefs. There are particular People whose o̲ffice <busyness> it is to e̲ffect t̲h̲i̲s̲ p̲urpose <perform this office>, called Meereetuappapow [miri tupapa'u]. They are similar to undertakers, and lay the dead Bodies out in the same manner. When the Chief is to be embalmed, the near Friends are said to know nothing of it—after three, four, or five days t̲h̲at <during which> the Body has l̲aid <lain> on the Tuapapow, the undertaker comes in the Night and begins his Work̲. The first thing he does, is to clear the body of its outer sk̲in. This is done easily, from the putrefaction which has taken place, b̲y̲ t̲h̲e̲ <by> help of a Wood scraper. The effect of this operation is, that the body becomes perfectly white with an entire skin as it had before, but the whiteness lasts only for a day or two, during which time the Head is ornamented with Flowers; and the body anointed with Oil exhibited with some pride.

After the Body is thus cleaned by scraping, the bowels are taken out, (by introducing the hand at the Anus,) and buried—the inside is dried by the same means, and a Wash is in the mean time prepared with which it is thoroughly cleaned, and <of which it> imbibes a considerable quantity. The Mouth and Throat are not less attended to, and the Eyes are carefully washed, and the lids closed. The Wash is made from the leaves of certain plants or Trees which are in the Mountains, known only to the undertakers. They are bruised, and the juice e̲xpressed <being pressed> from them without any mixture of Water, preserve the Body in a very firm state.

Tahamydooah [the dead child] they say will not be embalmed.

In the résumé of Tahiti's social structure given in the commentary of April 9th were described the society's two most common territorial types of domains: the neighborhood, which was owned corporately and residually by members of its occupying kin-congregation; and the district, whose chief enjoyed certain rights over all its constituent neighborhoods, including a portion of their produce, authority to restrict harvesting, and in extreme cases, confiscation—all that in addition to the more direct, proprietary rights he had over the lands of his own kin-congregation neighborhood.

In addition to the above, some individuals—mainly chiefs (along with members of their immediate families)—possessed full and undivided rights over certain tracts of land from which they obtained some or most of their daily food. Most of these specifically 'chiefly' lands were parts of a chief's kin-congregation territory, and had become identified with his own lineal ascendants by continuous use over time, but some had been acquired by conquest, or by confiscation from a subject—most typically as punishment for acts of *lèse majesté*.

Tina's 'Country Place' was I believe the latter type of estate, although he evidently used it more as a quiet retreat than as a source of food. Its location must have been fairly high up in the hills, since Bligh was able to see from it the distant Tetiaroa.

Returning to the dead 'Tahamydooah': the ghost-house (*fare tupapa'u*: *fare*, house, *tupapa'u*, ghost; Bligh's 'Tupapow' or 'Teapapow') under construction was the conventional type of structure in which some corpses were kept, on display, for varying lengths of time prior to interment (Plate 25) As Bligh states, that time varied according to the class-status of the deceased. It also varied with sex and age—males longer than females and adults longer than children. The element comprising all ghost-houses was a bier roofed over by an open shed, its size and elaboration and decoration also having differed with the class, etc. of the deceased. Associated with some ghost-houses were an altar (for food offerings to the spirits hovering nearby); a pit under the bier (for receiving the corpse's body fluids as they drained); a place for depositing the blood-soaked rags of self-bleeding mourners; in some cases, weapons or other possessions of the deceased; and fragrant leaves, to help neutralize the stench. The most interesting—most obscure — element just listed has to do with the corpse's body fluids, which were believed to contain the deceased's *hara*.

The underlying meaning of all the many usages of the word *hara* seems to have been some kind of social-relational error, such as disobedience to a superior, unfriendly acts towards a *taio*, and, especially, wrongful acts, of omission or commision, *vis à vis* spirits (for example, irreverence, failure to offer sacrifices when called for, mistakes in performing ritual). Much of Tahitian religious ritual consisted of *tarae-hara*, measures designed to 'untie' (*tarae*) *hara*. The concept is a profound and multi-faceted one, and still somewhat obscure; the facet of present relevance consists of the Tahitians' belief that at least some of a person's *hara* accumulated within his body in a physical form. While alive, people took religious measures, by *tarae-hara*, to discharge their *hara*, but, in adults at least (Tahitians reasoned) some of it remained, and must be allowed to drain away after death. (Needless to say, the hole into which it drained had to be eventually covered and ritually neutralized.)

Embalming was performed largely, perhaps solely, in order to lengthen the time for displaying a corpse. During one of his excursions Tobin saw, and sketched, such a corpse about four months old (Plate 26); it was that of Mauaroa, a younger brother of Teu (and hence Tina's uncle), who had been a leading Arioi and one of Bligh's most learned informants in 1788–89. Tobin's description of the encounter reads as follows:

Understanding it was in the neighborhood we visited the exposed corpse of the late Chief Mow-oroah. We were informed that he had been dead about four moons, and that every evening the body was placed under a shed. The Corpse was in a sitting posture on a stage about four feet high, but different from the common Toopapows. Except a bandage of white cloth over the middle, and another around the temples, the body was in a naked state. It was more tatowed than any I had seen on the Island, the legs and thighs being marked so as to leave no remains of the natural colour of the skin. The arms were in circular ridges from the shoulder to the wrist, and under the left breast was the broad mark of the Eareoye Society. The stage was decorated with a quantity of striped red and white cloth, a rail at the back of which supporting the body from falling, being hung with the same. The whole of this, and the shed was enclosed in a bamboo fence, of about eighteen feet by six, partly open at one side for the attendants on the corpse to enter by. It was the only body I saw exposed in this manner. Several inferior Toopapows were in the neighbourhood, nor would it seem that any particular spots are appropriated for them, which is the more remarkable in so cleanly a people, as the stench from them is very offensive; yet the inhabited houses were quite contiguous to many, without any annoyance being felt, or apprehension of disorders being generated by the putridity of the air around. It is customary when a corpse is exposed in this way, to first remove the intestines.

In 1777 Cook reported having visited the ghost-house in which the twenty-months-old remains of a Taiarapu chief were still being kept, but did not comment on the state of the corpse. (Beaglehole 1967: 190-1)

Bligh's entries for the next four days require no editorial comment, except to confirm that in this northwest part of Tahiti the season of breadfruit ripening had evidently passed, this being the beginning of the island's 'winter', marked by less rain.

Wednesday, May 30th

Land and Sea Breezes and fair Weather. The Thermometer from 73 to 79 Degrees.
Employed Tarring the Rigging. Armourer at the Forge.
Carpenters about the Launch. Sailmakers repairing the Fore Sail. Cooper making Tubs for Plants. Cleaned Ship and Aired below with Fires. Water let into the Ship twice a Day and the Pumps worked as usual.
We have still sufficient supplies to allow every Person one

pound and half of Pork per Day. No Breadfruit to be got for common use. Plantains Tarro Mahie and Vees are all we can get for <of the> Bread kind.

  Oreepyah with his Wife arrived to day from Paparrah, Otoo the Young King with <and> his Father <grandfather> Otow are gone to some other districts, and will not return to us for some time. When I enquired of Oreepyah how many Musquets he had taken from the Paparrah People he felt hurt, I therefore did not banter him with < upon > his project.

  I got a few large Plants or rather young Trees into Tubs to day in addition to those < what I had procured > on the 26th—these I expect will stand the Sea Air even when exposed, for they must take their chance upon Deck as I have no place else < other place > to put them <in>. They are all flourishing delightfully.

Thursday, May 31st

Land and Sea Breezes and Fair Weather. Thermometer from 75 to 79 Degrees.
  Employed as Yesterday.
  Unhappily to day I had a severe attack of my Nervous Head Ach. I attributed it to my making some Astronomical Observations, and the extreme heat of my observatory. I am never thoroughly clear of the Head Ach, but when these dreadfull fitts lay hold of <seize> me I am almost distracted. My mind being constantly on the stretch will I fear never let me <suffer me to> be free of these complaints untill I return into a Cold Climate.

Friday, June 1st

Moderate Breezes at East and Calms with Land Airs at Night. The Thermometer from 78 to 80½ Degrees. The Air however felt as if the Thermometer had been at 84 at least.
  Nothing New—a few Natives about us bring a few scanty supplies of Plantains, Cocoa Nutts, Vees and a few Tarrow.
  My Head Ach not so bad, but I can bear little Noise.

Saturday, June 2nd

The Morning and Night Light Breezes from the Land at South. During the day Strong Breezes from the WSW. Thermometer from 74 to 80 Degrees.
  Employed <in> Washing and cleaning Ship, airing below with Fires and mending Clothes. Served Tobacco.
  Carpenters finished the Launch, and have made a very fine Boat of her. All Men of War Boats are a Strake too low.
  Got a few very good Breadfruit to day from the Country. The

Trees about the low Grounds have a fine Show of Green Fruit about ¼ grown and in some places more forward.

I find my Nervous complaint much better to day, which I attribute to bathing in <the> Matavai River at Sun Rise <where the water is fresh>. /It/ is remarkably cold and may have a better effect than the Sea Water.

«We have» several of the Natives applying <apply> to the Surgeon to cure them of Ulcers and Sores <boils> about different parts of the Body, and his opinion, like my account last Voyage is, the disease is the Scrofula.

A few infected with a Gonorrhea have applied, but we have seen none who are remarkably bad in that disease.

My Plants are doing wonderfully well and I have added two small Trees to the number to Day.

Sunday, June 3rd

Light Winds at Night, but strong WSW Winds during the Day.

Mustered the Ships Company and saw them all clean dressed. Read the articles of War and Abstract. Performed Divine Service, and gave leave to a party to go on shore.

Got a Moderate supply of Tarro and Breadfruit—a sufficiency of Hogs, Cocoa Nutts and Vees.

Tynah and his Wives as usual dined with me to day. He took an opportunity to sollicit the attendance of the Surgeon on his Youngest Child Oro,oh [marginal note: 'see 8th May'], who he said was very ill. We found it under the care of an old Man, for what <which> is strange, Women are not permitted to be attendants on any of the Royal Family, so that Male or Female, the Children are unnaturally nursed by Men. ['unnaturally' appears also in ML but has been crossed out, probably by Bligh] The Complaints <Complaint> of the Child was said to be in his bowels, <and> the belly was much distended; but the Scrofula seemed the most <more> alarming symptom <disorder>, for in one groin it had broke out, & in the other were swellings which convinced us of the deplorable state this poor infant was in <of the poor infant>. I told Iddeeah to take better care of her Child, and altho I disputed the propriety, she insisted that Whyerreddee's attention should be engaged towards it & not particularly hers. It is not extraordinary that Tynah is not remarkably fond of his Children, for he is in some degree weaned from them, by the accursed Custom of their becoming <his> superior in rank. ['accursed' appears also in ML but has been crossed out] On that account no one approaches them but the Mother to give <who gives> them suck, and the Man who is the Nurse. The Moments therefore that <in which> the paternal feelings would be delighted with <gratified by> the little tricks of its Offspring, and view with pleasure the infant *progress of the mind <in which the progress of the infant would be observed with delight>, are here lost to the Father. When he sees or speaks to his Child it is at a <the> distance of ten or fifteen Yards, and the Man who brings it is often cautioned not to come too near, thus untill the Children become Men and Women, and He has performed the Ceremony of Oamo [marginal note: 'See 20th and 27th April'] do they mix together like other people.*

It is happily different with the lower order of the People. The Father and Mother have mostly their flock of little Children about them, they nurse them with great care and tenderness, and receive returns of Affection and respect. In short no Parents can regard or attend on <to> their Children more than they do, and but few more engaging and pretty Children are to be met with, could we divest ourselves of the dislike to the Colour.

The sick boy, 'Oro,oh' (spelled Oroho in Bligh's entry of April 23rd), was about eighteen months old at this time. In the May 8th entry referred to Bligh surmised that his disease was venereal and congenital, 'owing to Iddeeah having intercourse with too many different men.'

As recorded in his *Bounty* Journal and reproduced in our editorial commentary of April 23rd, the offspring of Tina and 'Itia resided in households not only isolated from the general populace but, the boys at least, from their parents as well. ('The Parents sleep every night at the Girls House [which was about one quarter mile from that of the boys], but are mostly absent from them in the day.' Bligh 1937: II 56) That arrangement was in part occasioned by the greater 'sanctity' of the children, which, it will be recalled, would become progressively neutralized through the series of *amo'a* rites, and in part by the society-wide separation of males from females during meals. As for Bligh's sentimental complaints about the 'accursed' custom that weaned upper-class fathers from their children, it would have been interesting—but hazardous!—to ask how he felt about the Royal Navy custom that weaned English sea-going fathers, including especially himself, from *theirs*.

Bligh's arcadian view of parent–child relations among 'the lower order of the People' was evidently based on a few fleeting glimpses and a rosy imagination. There may indeed have been some families of the kind he imagined, but closer and more numerous observations would have revealed also other kinds, as for example, some of those seen closer-up a few years later by the English missionaries (as recorded in Oliver 1974):

The natives are sinfully & very injuriously indulgent to their offspring now. I have often seen a child cast stones at his parents while they only laughed at it. (John Orsmond, Journal, 22 November 1826)

Their children [are] under no restraint from their parents: and are allowed to gratify every appetite without leave of any person. (Gyles to Sleigh, 23 November 1818, LMS Archives)

Savage ignorance and brutal freedom are [the children's] delights. The children cannot bear to have their desires crossed, their actions prohibited & their wild ramblings controuled. (Jefferson, Journal, 23 April 1799, London Missionary Society Archives)

Monday, June 4th

Light Variable Winds round the Compass and fair Weather. Thermometer from 75 to 79½ Degrees.

In commemoration of <the Birthday of> our most Gracious and Good King we held the <this> Day as a Festival. At 8 <OClock> in the Morning both Ships were dressed to the great delight of the Natives. At Noon the Marines were drawn up under Arms and Fired three Vollies, and the Indians <Natives> joined <in> with us in three Cheers. At One O'Clock the Ships fired 21 Guns each. To every person was served an allowance of liquor, and the day was spent with great chearfullness and good humour. At Night I had a Dozen Sky Rockets set off, and Mr Tobin having made two small Balloons the whole were successfully displayed to the great pleasure and satisfaction of 600 Persons. Mahannah no tErree Brettanee, King George. (The King of Englands Birth Day—King George.) was repeated every minute by Men Women and Children. All the Chiefs were collected about us, and drank to His Majesty's good Health, and afterwards dined with me. Tynah got drunk, but the other Chiefs were the better for the Wine. They are all very fond of Rum, Brandy or Wine, and will generally get drunk if permitted. Twice a Day is the course with their Avah, so that some of them have but few hours of the twenty four when they can be considered sober. Whydooah [Vaetua] [marginal note: 'the Brother of Tynah'] remarked <as usual> to me that the English Avah was better than the Otaheite; for if it took away the use of his limbs it never did <that of> his tongue; it always made him feel very bold.

Our custom has been to overhaul the Plants every Monday morning. They had a very fine appearance to day, and I have the pleasure to think every Plant has firmly taken root. Our Account now stands thus —

Pots of Bread Fruit	1099	two Plants in most of the Pots
Tubs of Ditto Ditto	34	four and five Plants in each
Boxes of Ditto Ditto	26	Ditto Ditto
Pots of Rattahs	25	four Plants in each
Ditto of Oraiahs	12	
Ditto of Vees or Avees	25	two and three in some of them
Ditto of Oahighyahs	32	Ditto Ditto
Ditto of Peeah	7	Ditto Ditto
Ditto of Mattee	6	Ditto Ditto
Ditto of Ettow	6	Ditto Ditto

'Mahannah no tErree Brettanee, King George' (more likely, 'mahana no te

Ari'i Peretane, Tini Tihoti') would have been totally meaningless to Bligh's 'Indians-cum-Natives'. *Mahana* meant *day*, i.e., the period from one sunrise to the next, within which was the period of *ao*, daylight, and a period of *po*, darkness. The *ao* was divided also into *po'ipo'i*, from the rising of the Great Star (i.e., Venus) to: *avatea*, a little before noon to: *ahiahi*, mid-afternoon to: *po*, dark, or *poiri*, totally dark. There were also conventional phrases for refer-ring to numerous phases of the *ao*, mainly with reference to the sun: for example, 'the sun is mostly revealed', etc. 'the sun is over the crown of the head', etc. 'the sun has dipped', etc. 'twilight', 'indistinctness', etc. Other ways of referring to stages in the *mahana* included, 'the opening of gardenia blossoms' (which occurred about noon), 'the singing of thrushes' (just before sunrise), and, of course, the crowing of cocks.

Clearly, sunlight was all-important to the Tahitians; most outside activities—except for reef-fishing, by torchlight—took place during the *ao*, whereas spirits were believed to be most active during the *po*. As noted earlier, *po* was also the name given to the sphere—the 'room'—of spirits as such, the distinction, if any, between *po*-darkness and *po*-spirit sphere having been vague.

In addition, the Tahitians perceived and reckoned 'time' by means of several other 'natural' phenomena: a lunar month (*marama*) of twenty-nine days—or rather, 'nights'; an annual (*matahiti*) cycle of twelve to thirteen lunar months; an annual cycle based on weather conditions at sea and on other conditions having to do mainly with fishing; a seasonal (*tau*) cycle based mainly on the visibility of the Pleiades; and an annual cycle, marked by large festivals, based mainly on the ripening of different varieties of breadfruit. In fact, Europeans found some Tahitians capable of time-placing past events with considerable accuracy.

But no *birthdays!*

Although *some* Tahitians had the conceptual and linguistic means for doing so, they did not reckon an individual's chronological age in years, etc. Furthermore, while the birth of some of them was formalized by ritual, the day of its annual—or lunar, or seasonal—recurrence was ignored. As for what they made of King George's birthday, Tobin supplies a part-answer: 'This loyalty [to our King] when so remote from our native Isle gained us the unqualified approbation of these good people, not without their participat-ing in it most cordially as our Allies.'

Returning to the first sentence in the paragraph above, it is necess-ary to emphasize the word 'some': as Bligh recorded in his *Bounty* Journal:

To get a certain Knowledge of their division of time has given me much trouble, for altho many people pretend to know it, Yet I have found them so contradictory in their Accounts as convinced me they were not acquainted with the particulars of it. [Welcome to the company of ethnographers, my good Captain!] Tynah assured me only a few Old People could give me any

194

information and that he knew it but very imperfectly himself, he however has always referred me to Toota-ah or his Uncle Mowworroah and from those people, who were exceedingly clear and distinct, I got the following information. [There follows a detailed lists of months, seasons, etc.] (Bligh 1937: II 45)

Tuesday, June 5th

Fine Weather with some Calms. Wind East. Thermometer from 74 to 80 Degrees.

Employed at the Forge. Got on board the Launch, and hauled the large Cutter up to to repair. Sailamaker Employed about the Jibb and Main Top Stay Sail. Carpenters making railings for the Sky lights to prevent «any» things falling on the Plants.

Hauled the Seine and caught about 150 lbs of Fish.

Sufficient supplies except of Bread Fruit, only a few Baskets <of which> are brought on board. Tarro and Plantains, we have instead of it, <but> not in great altho sufficient abundance.

The indolence of the People in our neighbourhood is so great, that now the Breadfruit is not to be had, they have very little to eat. No Country in the World would produce greater plenty of Ground Provisions, yet these lazy wretches cultivate scarce a yam nor Potatoe. In the whole district of Matavai and Oparre I have not seen half an Acre of Ground Provisions, if I except about that quantity of Tarro at Oparre, but their late broils joind with their natural indolence has <have> most likely been the cause of the present scarcity.

Bligh's remarks about native horticulture and work habits will be discussed following the next entry, in which he records more about these matters.

Wednesday, June 6th

Moderate Sea Breezes at East. Land Winds at SSE—fine Weather. Thermometer from 73 to 80 Degrees.

Employed at the Forge. Mending Sails. Repairing the large Cutter. Making Railings for the Sky lights. Washing Ship and Airing with Fires.

As Tynah engaged to go down to Tettaah [Fa'a'a] to get some Plantains & other provisions for the Ship, I sent him away in the Boat by day dawn with sufficient presents to have purchased a large quantity, but he was not successfull, for he returned about 3 OClock in the Afternoon with only a few Plantains and Cocoa Nutts. I never saw a regular Plantain Walk [i.e., regularly spaced orchard] in Otaheite. A few trees are stuck about their Houses, and others are dispersed arround the Hills in the same manner—this is all the trouble taken with them, or with any thing else that requires regular planting—cleaning <clearing> and keeping their Grounds neat and free from Weeds is beneath the care of an Otaheitean. They have as little neatness about their dwellings. An Otaheite Village, if their mixt Dwellings may <can> be so called, is the dirtyest place *immaginable, every thing is thrown before and around the House, even if they fix their Sheds upon the Sea side they will not take the trouble to throw the filth into the Sea, if they have <only> ten yards to carry it—yet no People in the World are cleaner in their Persons. So much sloth and indolence may be attributed to the vast support that Allbountiful Nature has given to them in the use <possession> of the most valuable of all Fruits of the Earth, the Bread Fruit and Cocoa Nutt.*

 I asked Iddeah to day if her Name was to be changed on account of her late Child dying, she said no as the name was given to the Childs Aunt, Wattowaw, who in my last Voyage was called Towry. It is very extraordinary the shifting of Names in this Country <the changing of Names in this Country is very extraordinary>. Upon the permition of the Erreerahigh a Chief may take any name he likes, and if it happens to be the name of any particular Article —of day —night, or any other known thing, another is thought of for it to be called by <by which it may be called>. Example—Pomarre, (the name of Tynah & Iddeeah,) is from Po, night, and Morre the Name of the disease the Child died of. To make up for the loss of Po, in the language, Ooarroo,ee is substituted.

 Oreepyah has fancifully taken the name of Apopo [?]. In the language it means To morrow, but it is very odd, that in supplying the want of this Word they have substituted Ahnonnahigh [ananahi], which before, and does <even> now mean Yesterday.

 Since my last Voyage, Heivah, the common name for all their Dances, has been taken by Terrederrie [Teri'irere] [marginal note: 'Chief of Papparah and son of Oamo; this was his first name next to Tomaree & now Heivah or Heivahrow'], and it [dancing] is now known by the term Oopeowpah.

 Tynah also took the Name of Mattee [mate], which signifies to kill, and Po,ee [pohe] was ordered to be used instead of it, which was strictly attended to. I remember Iddeah scolding at the People when they inadvertantly made use of the word Mattee.

 I should imagine this mode of changing Names must be attended with many disadvantages to the language. The alteration in the course of a Century must be very great it <and> makes it difficult to be understood.

Clearly, Bligh disapproved of 'laziness' in general and of slip-shod gardening in particular.

With regards to the latter, he evidently liked all gardens to be discrete, with their crops segregated by type and set out in orderly rows, as he had found their bark-cloth trees and kava plant gardens to be:

I saw no care taken of anything that was planted except the Cloth Plant and the Ava, both of these were kept free of Weeds. The Cloth Plant is taken great pains with, the bank on which it is planted is ditched round and fenced with Stones. (Bligh 1937: I 424)

He would have found food-plant gardens more to his liking had he travelled

196

to, say, New Caledonia or Highland New Guinea, or even to the Polynesian Island of Tikopia, but in most of the high islands of tropical eastern Polynesia he would have seen foodgrowing arrangements just as 'untidy' as Tahiti's— and like Tahiti's as capable of producing enough to satisfy their peoples' food requirements most of the time. Tahitians' heavy dependance upon breadfruit—and why not?—and the seasonality of the breadfruit's ripening resulted in a seasonal variation in type as well as in quantity of food staples eaten, but periods of even short-term food shortages were rare, and periods of widespread and prolonged hunger practically nonexistant. The shortage that Bligh remarked upon in his June 5th entry was probably due in part to the destruction that accompanied the recent war. And in contradiction to his charge of never having seen 'a regular Plantain Walk in Otaheite', there is a statement in his *Bounty* Journal that reads:

The Plantations for Yams & Plantains are upon the High grounds and Hills that are near to the Flat Land, and from the large plats we have seen them clearing by fire they certainly plant considerably, as well as from the great quantity of the latter we see them make use of and the abundance they bring us. (Bligh 1937: I 425)

Perhaps he had not actually seen them; or if he had, they did not conform to his idea of a regular 'walk'. This *Bounty* entry goes on to say:

I have seen but very few Yams, and these are Small, which I am told is because they are not in season, scarce any Tarro either have I seen, and perhaps they care little about it as they have plenty of Breadfruit which answers every purpose. (Bligh 1937: I 425)

It would appear that the Bligh who wrote those words, in 1788, was less irascible on that day—evidently better provisioned—than the Bligh of June 5th, 1792.

Bligh's mood on the latter day is also revealed in his judgment about Tahitians' dwellings, when compared with that of Tobin, who wrote:

The house[s] are of various kinds, some being enclosed from the eaves all round with a railing of bamboo, having a door on one side. Others are left entirely open, supported by three rows of pillars like the long one before mentioned at . . . [?]. The leaf of the Wharra [fara, pandanus] tree, a species of Palmetto, is generally used as a thatch, being very durable. None of them are floored, but the Chiefs houses have generally a carpet of cut grass, laid regularly, which, as it decays, is supplied by fresh. The furniture consists of a sleeping mat, a small wooden pillow for the head, and sometimes a larger of the same form to sit on. These are made in a neat manner, chiefly from a hard wood of a mahogany colour, and previously to the introduction of european tools, must have been a work of much time and labour, as the logs are carved from the solid block. Gourds are in use to contain water, and the cocoa nut shell to drink from. Besides a few other cooking utensils, little else is to be seen in an O'tahytean mansion. All these are kept remarkably neat and clean . . .

Bligh's charge about Tahitians' 'laziness'—one that was made by most other European visitors of that era as well—is easy to speculate about

197

but difficult to document. One specific basis for Bligh's slur was the Tahitians', to him, haphazard planting practices; another was their failure to weed. But behind those criticisms there was a general attitude about 'work', which in his view, I suspect, was something that every physically capable person ought to engage in lengthily, regularly, and industriously. The Tahitians were undoubtedly industrious in many of the things they did that Europeans would call 'work' (for example, fishing, carrying heavy bunches of plantains down from the hills, manufacturing bark cloth). And they sometimes 'worked' continuously for long periods of time (for example, building large buildings, shaping canoe hulls, processing breadfruit for preservation, preparing feasts). But they most definitely did *not* work with European-style regularity, except perhaps in cooking their main daily meal, and except insofar as periodic conditions required them to do so (such as the seasonal ripening of surplus amounts of breadfruit, and the seasonal spawning of fish).

The custom of word-replacement, *pi*, was discussed in the commentary of May 5th. Bligh was correct about its effects on the rate of language change—but one question is: how durable were such changes? For example, when Tina later on became *Pomare* was it simply an addition to *Mate* ('Mattee'), or a total substitute for that former name? And in the latter case, did *Mate* thereupon revert to permisable use as the word for 'dead'? Another question about the matter is political: When Tina assumed the name *Mate* did *all* Tahitians (including his enemies in Taiarapu) begin to call him that? And if so, did they also substitute *poe* for *mate*, as the Pare-Arueans did?

The first of these questions is unanswerable because of the absence of written texts going back far enough in time. The second cannot be answered because of the almost exclusive preoccupation of those Englishmen who have left records, with Tahitians ruled by or otherwise associated with the Pomares. This was also true of the English missionaries, who arrived on the scene in 1797 and who provided the lexical material from which the first comprehensive dictionary was compiled (i.e., John Davies's *A Tahitian and English Dictionary*, Tahiti: London Missionary Press, 1851). Moreover, by means of that dictionary, and of the Tahitian version of the *Bible* that accompanied it, the most recent *pi*-induced changes became 'frozen' in print, not only for all the natives of Tahiti but for those of the rest of the Society Islands as well. And although the language has since then continued to change in many ways, the *pi* process has long since ceased to be a factor in that change.

Thursday, June 7th

Fresh Breezes at East and some Calms, in the Night Winds from the Land at SE and S by E. Thermometer from 75 to 80½ Degrees.

Employed about the large Cutter. Fitting the Ports—mending Sails and Hauling the Seine.

Sufficient Supplies of Hogs, Plantains, Tarro and Vees, but Breadfruit only a few heads. Caught very few Fish.

Found a few of of Plants attacked by a kind of Weavel which entered the Rinds, and made thir doing well very doubtfull. I therefore directed them to be shifted, lest the other Plants might be injured in our Voyage home. We have but very few People about us, and no person but Tynah and his Wives of any consequence who dine with me every day. Otoo with his /grand/Father otow, are still absent. Whydooah is not a constant Visitor, as the most of his time is devoted to drinking Avah, and «he is» in a state of Stupefaction. The Erree Women are now become fond of this «that» pernicious root, and are generally drunk once a Day.

Friday, June 8th

Fresh Westerly Breezes in the Day, and very Cloudy threatening Rain—at Night Cloudy and Wind from the land. Rain in the Mountains. Thermometer from 78 to 82½ Degrees.

Employed at the Forge. Repairing the large Cutter.—Sails—and about the Rigging. A Party on Shore cutting up a Tree that Tynah gave to us. Sufficient Supplies of Hogs, Plantains, Vees, Mahie and Tarro.

Saturday, June 9th

Light Breezes and Fair Weather with Calms in the first part of the Morning. Land Winds at Night. Wind East and SE. Thermometer from 74 to 80 Degrees.

Employed as Yesterday in the Morning, but the remainder of the Day the people had to themselves to mend & Wash their Clothes. Hauled the Seine without any success.

Sufficient Supplies as yesterday, but no increase of the Natives about us, scarce ever more than a Dozen on board at a time. The Young Breadfruit are in abundance upon the Trees, and I get a head or two brought to me almost every day.

Sunday, June 10th

Light land and Sea breezes E and SE. The Thermometer from 75 to 80½ Degrees.

Washed and cleaned Ship. Hauled the Seine. Mustered the Ships Company and saw them all clean dressed. Performed Divine Service. Gave leave to a Party to go on Shore.

Sufficient Supplies of Hogs, Plantains, and Tarro, and abundance of Vees and Cocoa Nutts.

Monday, June 11th

Calms and Winds at West and WSW—and the Thermometer 77 to 81 Degrees.

Employed at the Forge—Mending Sails—about the Rigging—

Carpenters about the large Cutter, lining and fitting the Ports. Cooper repairing Casks and making small ones for the Boats.

About a half past 10 at night Mr Guthrie informed me an Indian <a Native> was discovered thieving at the Post, and that the Centinel had fired at him.

These People are become so troublesome in <the> dark Nights, that it requires <required> our utmost exertions to prevent them from taking away all we have. I fear very much some of them will be shot, for I have been under the necessity to give orders to that effect, in order to deter them in their attempts. One Viscious [sic] fellow may destroy all our Plants, and cut our Ships adrift. Every Man, Woman and Child, know they dare not come near the Post or Ships after dark, and the Chiefs are so sensible of the propriety <of the prohibition>, that their constant reply <to my complaint> is 'Why don't you kill them.'

The following paragraph appears in ML but has been crossed out:

This evening on my coming on shore I was informed by Mr Pearce the head of the Marines that the Serjeant was under arrest for insolence and contempt to him. He said the charge was, that in asking the Serjeant why he had not employed a party of men as he had directed, & on investigating the cause of his neglect, the Serjeant had with contumacy and disrespect uttered the words 'I know my duty as well as any man can show me' & on being threatened to be complained of to me, said with great indifference, 'Sir no person can prove I have said so to you,' for no one was present. That in addition to this charge against the Serjeant Mr Pearce declared he had proof of very great neglect, but that he had hitherto not brought it before me with a hope that the man would behave better in future.

I desired the Serjeant might be continued under an arrest untill the Morning when I should enquire into the affair.

Tuesday, June 12th

Light Westerly Winds and Fair Weather until Noon when the Wind came very strong in Squalls from the West WNW and NW with a smart Shower of Rain. At night Calm.

Employed mending Sails—repairing Boats—Armourer at the Forge—Cooper repairing Casks—Refitting the Rattlings and about the Rigging. ['rattling', small cordage used to strengthen edges of sail]

Sufficient supplies of Hogs, Plantains, Tarro, Vees, Cocoa Nutts, a few yams and heads of new Breadfruit.

We have very few Natives about us, and no Strangers. Tynah and his Wives dine with me every day, and occasionally as it suits their convenience, Monah and Orepyah with his Brother Whydooah. The three Brothers [i.e., the latter two and Tina] are become very drunken, and the Women not much *better for they all drink Avah. Tynah has been so bad lately, that I have been obliged to forbid any person giving him «any» liquor. Wine is no longer palatable to them, they call for Spirit, and have given it the name of Avah Tyo ['ava taio], or friendly draught. It is difficult now to get any information respecting their manners or Country, they seem suspicious of every enquiry.*

I passed in my Walk to day a Morai which was called Rooahaddoo—it consisted of a few Stones about three feet square, pieces of plaited Cocoa Nutt leaves (called Tepaow) [marginal note: 'Evahighree [e vahi-ri'i, a place-little ?] when presented to a Chiefs feet'] placed before it with some small pieces of Tarro and Cocoa Nutts. The Evatah [fata] or Alter of Offerings, was a Palm Stump with a small Stage on it, on which was a Cocoa Nutt Grater [marginal note: 'a piece of Coral'], «and» some Cocoa Nutt, Mahie and an empty Basket. The whole was fenced in, and I found it was just erected to ensure success to a kind of Ware [weir] or Dam which Tynah has made with Stones without Point Venus to catch Fish. Prayers have been performed, and the Deity supplicated by Persons of the Priesthood.

I heard <that> the Thief that <Man who> was fired at last Night was wounded—Shot through the Shoulder, and had sett of [off] for Tettaha [Fa'a'a]. He was traced about 200 Yards by <some drops of> his Blood. It seemed to give pleasure to our Friends here <but I am much concerned at the necessity I had been under of giving orders to fire.>

In addition to the extraordinary variety of practical measures used by them to catch fish (see April 30th), the Tahitians employed numerous measures of a religious kind. For example, proprietors could set up spirit-enforced signs to restrict fishing in their areas of lagoon—or a chief could do the same for all his district's lagoon waters (done mainly to protect fish during spawning). Also, some family lines owned *puna*, spirit-imbued fish-shaped stone images that were believed to influence the movements of fish. By pointing the image's head inland the fish along that coast were induced to move shorewards, hence easier to catch; by pointing it seaward the fish moved out to sea—the latter having been done to spite fishermen who had not given the image's owner his due part of previous catches. The many other religious devices utilized to catch fish included: petitions, with sacrifices, to spirits—nearly every variety of fish had its own tutelar spirit; the use of red feathers and prayers to calm stormy waters; rites of various kinds—e.g., to consecrate new fishing implements (especially, large seine-nets and fishing canoes), to preserve lines from breaking, to guide fish spears, to lure octopus, to keep away sharks, etc.; and more permanent structures—*marae*—on shore, such as the one described by Bligh in this entry.

The next four daily entries will be reproduced without editorial comment, since, as Bligh wrote in one of them, 'we see no strange People of any consequence, or does any thing pass interesting or worth notice.'

Wednesday, June 13th

Light Variable Winds and Calms. Much Swell in the Bay. Thermometer from 76 to 81½ Degrees.

Employed as Yesterday. Cleaned Ship. Sufficient supplies and more Bread Fruit.

Our Plants are doing remarkably well and <I> expect that in the course of a Month at farthest they will be fit to bring on board.

Our Sick List consists <only> of Venereals—19 out of 20 who were in it still remain under cure.

Thursday, June 14th

Light Westerly Winds and Calms with much Swell in the Bay. Thermometer from 77 to 80 Degrees. In my Observatory on Shore it was 90 Degrees.

Employed Breeming the Bends. ['Breeming'—clearing the ship's bottom of shells, slime, etc.] Mending Sails. Cutting Wood. Armourer at the Forge. Carpenters repairing the Boats, and fitting the Ports. A few hands completeing the Rigging.

Sufficient Supplies of Hogs, Plantains, Tarro, Cocoa Nutts and Vees—a few Yams and heads of New Breadfruit.

<But> Very few Natives about us, they regard us with very great indifference, <so that> we see no strange People of any consequence, or does any thing pass interesting or worth notice. Tynah, Oreepyah, and their Brother Whydooah so completely stupify themselves with Ava every day, as have affected their faculties. They have however faithfully promised me to drink less of it in future.

<The sick list are all Venereals. It contains at this time 20. Four have been cured.>

Friday, June 15th

Light, Easterly Winds and Calms the Nights and Mornings are generally Calm with light Land Airs.

Employed as Yesterday. Supplies sufficient but am frequently obliged to send People to Oparre and about these Districts to purchase them. The Natives seem indifferent to any intercourse of Trade with us. We have now scarce <scarcely> twenty Persons on board in a Day, and not more who come to the Post at Sun down to see the Marines exercised; where we have had several hundred since we have been here, and many hundreds every Evening of my stay at Oparre last Voyage.

Saturday, June 16th

Light Breezes Easterly in the Day, with Land Winds and Calms during the Night.

Employed Cutting Wood in the Morning, better <latter> part of the Day Washing and Mending Clothes.

Plate 23   View in Pare district
Watercolor by George Tobin

Plate 24   Tahara'a (Tarra) Heads (One-Tree Hill)
Watercolor by George Tobin

Supplies more than we can use of every thing but <article except> Breadfruit, several Cannoes having brought off fine bunches of Plantains, Tarro and several Hogs. Cocoa Nutts we have in abundance. We speak comparatively when we say Moderate supplies. Sometimes we have a quantity that spoils <which is spoiled> because we cannot make use of it. Not one day have we been without a perfect sufficiency.

Sunday, June 17th

Light Variable Winds and Calms. Thermometer from 72 to 80 Degrees, on Shore in the Air 82 Degrees.

Mustered the Ships Company and saw them all clean Dressed. Performed Divine Service. Gave leave to a Party to Walk on Shore. Hauled the Seine but caught no Fish.

Tynah had a Visit to day from some of <the> Tiarraboo People—they were of no consequence with respect to Rank, as is common, however, <commonly the case> he found himself engaged for the day to direct proper supplies, and to amuse them. A Maownah [ma'ona] or Wrestling Match gave a change to the dull scene we experienced every day, but as the Tiarraboo people had only a few Champions; a number of fine active Boys gave us more amusement than the Men. The Strangers were rather uneasy at every Victory they gained for fear it would displease me, and to the last I could not convince them that I was disinterested. There were several knock down blows between some of the Parties before they grappled. My Account last Voyage of this exercise, prevents my saying any thing particular of it, <as> I have not seen anything new.

No one has provided a better description of Tahitian wrestling than Bligh himself, in his *Bounty* Journal:

A great number of Natives were about the Bay this afternoon, and Tynah informed me it was on account of a wrestling match that was to take place on our going on shore. I accordingly set off with him and several Cheifs to see it, and they were all ready by the time we got to the place which was about a quarter of a mile from the Tents. We found here an amazing concourse of People, at least 1500 formed into a Ring under the cool and refreshing shade of the Breadfruit Trees.

As a prelude to this performance a dancing Heivah was performed by two Children and four Men, which lasted an half hour. Tynah then produced a long peice of Cloth and the Queen, Iddeah, and myself taking the two first corners of it, the remaining part of it being supported by many others, we carried it to the performers and gave it them. Several other Cheifs did the same and I had the like ceremony to go through six different times. I found this was a payment to the performers who were people that went round the country like Strollers in England.

No longer than this, remained any regularity or order, the place became

203

now a scene of riot and confusion and the challenges for Wrestling was made from one Man to an other.

After a quarter of an hour a Ring was again made but the combatants were so numerous within it, that every thing was in confusion and uproar. These people in their challenges lay one hand upon their breast and in the bending of the Arm at the Elbow, with the other hand they strike a very smart blow, which as the hand is Kept hollow creates a Sound that may be heard a considerable way off, and at this time there being so many Men, the sound resembled a number of People in a Wood felling of Trees. This is the general Challenge; but when any two Combatants agree to a trial, they present their hands forward, joining them by the extremities of the fingers. The striking and bending of the Arm is so frequent that the flesh becomes exceedingly bruized and the Skin being torn off bleeds exceedingly.

Near half an hour past before I saw any thing but a number of Stout Men parading about the Ring striking the challenge, when at last five or six couple by turns began. The onset was made by sparring, each endeavoring to take an Advantage, when at last they closed, and seizing each other by the Hair they twisted about for some time and was then parted. Only one couple performed anything like the part of Wrestlers and as they were an equal match it lasted longer than any of the others, but they were also parted. Upon the Whole this performance gave me a poor opinion of these people. They have strength enough but they are very deficient in skill and equally so in courage.

The Queen Iddeah was the general Umpire and no murmers were made at her decision. As her person is large she was very conspicuous in the Circle, but Tynah took no part in the Management of the business. (Bligh 1937: I 390–1)

No social-class line prevailed in wrestling, nor was it confined to males:

In the Afternoon I was detained at a House a small distance from my Post to see a particular Heivah performed by Women which Iddeeah told me I had never yet seen. I therefore waited the event which was only a Wrestling Match by Women of Attahooroo and those of Oparre. The manner of challenging and method of Attack is exactly the same as with the Men, but they differ from them in every other respect by being as savage as Wild Beasts; among the many degrees of Violence with which they endeavor to injure one another for life, is what is called gouging (in England but is now I beleive not practised) this is forcing the Thumb into the socket of the Eye and turning it out. My presence at this time prevented a circumstance of this kind, and as I could find no pleasure in such an amusement, I put an end to it and ordered them to leave off. When I spoke to Iddeeah and other principal people about it, that it was a disgrace to them, they laughed at me and said it was 'Myty Taheite'—it was customary in Otaheite [maita'i Tahiti: it is liked in Tahiti].

The Women not only wrestle among themselves but sometimes with the Men. Iddeeah is said to be very famous. (Bligh 1937: II 39)

Some injuries resulting from Tahitian-style wrestling were dealt with by measures as strenuous as the sport itself:

The Evenings are dry and I am always entertained with some of their amuse-ments. This afternoon a few Young Men were wrestling when one of them having an untoward fall his Arm was put out of joint at the Elbow. As instantly as the accident happened three Stout Men took hold of the Man by the wrist and placing their feet against his Ribs they put it in again. My Boat being waiting I sent off for the Surgeon but before he returned all was well, except a Swelling of the muscles from the Strain . . . (Bligh 1937: II 29)

Another wrestling match was held on the occasion of Bligh's instal-lation as (Honorary) Ari'i of Pare-Arue. After the solemn rite of acknowledg-ment a carnival atmosphere prevailed, which among other things calls to mind some dangerous parallels in Western athletic events:

The Men now divided, and there was a confused Wrestling Match, which soon after Old Otow, Tynahs Father, came and desired I would put a Stop to. The Sagacity of this Old Cheif did not counteract what I beleive he foresaw would happen in case they proceeded. There were many Strangers here, and not a particle of real friendship betwen them and [the] Oparre people. Otow was therefore Apprehensive they would quarrel, and it realy happened so, in an instant every Man was Armed and an Attack begun in a tumultous manner. . . . It however happened very happily that no Cheif was concerned [i.e., was involved in the brawl], their endeavors therefore were to quell the tumult among their own people, . . . [which they soon did]. (Bligh 1937: II 37)

Monday, June 18th

Light Winds at East and Calms. Thermometer from 79 to 81 Degrees. On Shore 83 Degrees at Noon in the Shade.

Very Sufficient supplies.

Employed Cutting Wood. Making Canvas coverings for the Greenhouses on the Quarter Deck. Painting the Ship's Stern & Head. Armourer at the Forge.

Our Old Friend Hammennemanne returned from his Tour round the Island. Otoo the Young King with <and> his Grand Father Otow will <would> still be absent for some time. It appears that the purport of this Old Man's journey is to collect Cloth, Hogs, and whatever he thinks will sell to the people of the Ships, and to make Friends of all his Chiefs before I Sail.

The Plants are doing exceedingly well, which is a peculiar happyness to me, as my time of Sailing draws so near it make their well doing anxiously interesting to me <my time of Sailing draws so near as to interest me very much in their well doing>. This with various other things respecting our <my> future wellfare [along with my?] Astronomical and Nautical Observations, keep me laboriously employed, and labouring <altho suffering> under a constant Nervous Head Ach which sometimes distracts me.

Our Sick List consists of 22 Venereals.

'Old Friend Hammennemanne' had evidently extended his visit to Papara into a 'Tour round the Island', and certainly not just to see the scenery. From the time of his arrival in Tahiti from Ra'iatea in 1788 this man of superior rank, commanding personality, and boundless ambition had schemed and fought to consolidate and extend the powers, both ceremonial and political, of his grandnephew Tu (the current incumbent of the kin-Title that his sister had brought to Tahiti from their Opoan home). Now that the feather-girdle and 'Oro image traditionally associated with that kin-Title had been restored to Tu, and in view of the renewal of English patronage represented by Bligh, the vigorous old priestly politician had very likely been making the rounds to drum up support for his further pretensions respecting Tu—and the Ra'iatean connection.

The same may be said of the journey of Ha'amanemane's brother-in-law, Old Teu ('Otow'). As for the latter's intent to collect goods for sale to the ships, that of course had a potential for familial profit, both economic and political.

It is not clear from this passage whether young Tu was accompanying his grandfather on the latter's journey. It is however unlikely that he was doing so: a tour by a personage of Tu's status would have occasioned an amount of show and solemnity that would have reached the ear—and Journal—of Bligh. Moreover, some districts, especially Taiarapu, contained leaders who were still, or again, unfriendly enough to the Pomares to render such a tour hazardous, to say the least.

The traditional procedure for testing political waters—for canvassing 'allegiance' to someone (the word is not entirely connotative of the Tahitian situation)—was to send the 'candidate's' banner, *vane*, on tour. That had been done a couple of years earlier on the occasion of Tu's inaugural ceremony at Pare-Arue. At that time, according to one of the *Bounty* men, the banner had been received appropriately—i.e., 'loyally'—in Taiarapu, but (it was reported by Tina, who had led the tour) the Taiarapuans had done so 'only for fear of [the *Bounty* people still on the island] and not [on account of] their regards to his [i.e.,Tina's] son'; and moreover, they 'had used him [Tina] very uncivil'. (Rutter 1935: 115)

Tuesday, June 19th

Light Easterly Winds and Variable with Calms. The Nights and Mornings finely serene and clear. Thermometer from 75 to 80 Degrees.

Sufficient supplies. Employed at the Forge. Cutting Wood. Sailmakers making covers for the Green Houses on the Quarter Deck. Carpenters painting the Ship Sides and cutting Scuttles in the Cabin Ports to give Air to the Plants when the Ports cannot be opened. Washed and Cleaned Ship.

A tolerable sized Chest was shown to me to day made in our

206

manner by an Otaheitean. It was really a curiosity—the hinges were made of Wood, the sides duftailed and put together perfectly square, and the lock was made like ours with a bolt all out of wood, with a Key made of a Piece of Iron. The whole showed so much ingenuity, that I made a present to the <this> Man as a reward, and he bartered his Chest away in exchange for an English one to one of the Gardeners.

I was sorry to hear again of a <an> human Sacrifice. Iddeeah informed me that the Chiefs of Waennah [Huahine] (called Ohaaine in Captain Cooks Map) had sent one to Otoo. I found it wrapt up in a platted Cocoa Nutt branch and Slung to a Pole as usual—it stunk <stank> very much, and on that account was hung up among the Bushes apart from any dwelling. The late disturbance and War between Matavai and Oparre People was the cause of this Sacrifice. The People of Waennah took part with Matavai, and the offence was not to be forgiven but by this melancholy claim <for pardon>. The absence of Otoo prevents any thing being done untill he returns, when the Eye will be presented, and the Etuah supplicated to continue the friendship between the two Districts.

I am now perfectly satisfied that Human Sacrifices are common and very frequent. If a Chief or Powerfull Man seriously offends the Erreerahigh he is obliged to obtain forgiveness by this means. It <sacrifice which> is not to be refused, so sacred is it as a pledge of faith and good will. It is evidently not confined to making Peace or declaring War, or supplicating the Etuah on an emergency, or any general calamity.

Huahine ('Waennah') lies about ninety nautical miles northwest of Tahiti, including an open-water gap of at least seventy. Canoes under sail could make the journey in two to four days—if the wind was right; if it was not it took them much longer, or sometimes they were never seen again. People occasionally travelled between the two islands for pleasure and for affairs of kinship and state. There is no record of large-scale military-attack expeditions as such between them, but boat-loads of warriors sometimes made the journey to join warring allies. The statement by Bligh is the first to record that Huahineans 'took part with Matavai' in the recent *Matilda* fire-arms war. Such support must have been small; it could not have been decisive. The question is: Why did it take place at all? What ties would have led residents of that distant island to take part in a parochial fracas on Tahiti? And why did their leader feel obliged to seek 'forgiveness' for having backed the Matavai side? I am unable to explain why those particular Huahineans sided with those particular Tahitians in that particular conflict, but can indicate the general nature of the ties that linked *all* these islands, from Maupiti to Me'etia, including Huahine and Tahiti, into a single society, whose members spoke the same language (with but little dialectical variation) and shared the same customs (except for a few small differences, mainly in craft work and temple architecture).

First of all, most of the residents of these islands derived from one group of pioneers, or from two or more closely related groups of pioneers. The evidence from archaeology is still accumulating; the findings so far indicate an earliest settlement at about 800 A.D., but that date could be—undoubtedly will be—pushed farther back. The ultimate source of all Polynesians in this eastern part of the Pacific was Tonga and Samoa. (That is to say, the linguistic and other indigenous cultural traits then shared, distinctively, by all native speakers of Polynesian languages took shape in Tonga and Samoa, and possibly also Fiji—but of course many of the elements of that amalgam originated not there but farther to the northwest.) In the course of several centuries some descendants of those pioneers came to populate all the high islands in the Society archipelago. At times during that lengthy period canoe-loads of other Polynesians from neighboring archipelagoes doubtless fetched up on Society Island shores, either deliberately or by chance, but because of their small numbers their descendants became, culturally, Society Islanders themselves.

In other words, all of the residents of these Society Islands shared a common cultural heritage, and they labelled themselves *maohi* ('native') to differentiate themselves from whatever other brown-skinned peoples they met up with, such as those of the Tuamotus (who, by the way, the Society Islanders considered 'barbarian', because of the latters' cultural differences from themselves). But, as we have seen, consciousness of a common cultural heritage did not serve to *unite* all the Society Islanders into a fraternal commonwealth; in fact, elaborately institutionalized and bloodily conducted warfare was a prominent and to many persons pleasurable part of Society Islands life. And while the situation did not resemble the kind that prevailed in, for example, some islands of Melanesia (where many neighboring communities lived in a state of perpetual and unrelenting hostility), there were several kinds of circumstances that could and often did lead Society Islanders to war among themselves. As was noted earlier, political more than economic factors were behind most of their wars, and that politics had to do mainly with dynastic aggrandizement, either sustained or opposed by ties of kinship.

I have already described some of the kinship ties between Tahiti and Rai'atea, more specifically Opoa: for example, the move to Papara in 1760 by an Opoan kin-Titleholder, bearing the so-called Papara Image of 'Oro and the original part of the Wallis *maro ura*; and more relevantly, the move to Pare-Arue, first by Tetupaia (Tina's mother), who was daughter of Opoa's Chief, Tamatoa III, and later on by her brother, Ha'amanemane. Tahiti's—more specifically, Pare-Arue's—kin ties with Huahine were less direct, but evidently strong enough to induce one of the chiefs of Huahine to intervene in Pare-Arue's affairs.

When James Cook visited Huahine in 1777 the highest-ranking kin-Titleholder there was Teri'itaria, a boy of about fourteen. His mother,

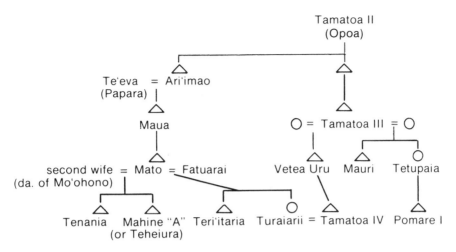

Figure 11 Genealogy of Opoa dynasty and close connections

Fatuarai, was daughter of Huahine's most prominent warrior-leader and her pedigree included high-ranking kin-Titleholders of Tahiti, Mo'orea, and Huahine. Moreover, the boy's father, Mato, identified as 'high priest' of Opoa, was related to the Tamatoa family, and thence to the Pomares. (Figure 11)

After siring Teri'itaria (about 1763) Mato left Faturai and married (the term is appropriate here) a daughter of Mo'ohino, identified as 'grand-priest of Huahine'. By this woman Mato sired two sons, Tenania and Teheiura. According to one account, Mo'ohino demanded that Fatuarai transfer sovereignity over the small island of Maia'o, then a dependency of Huahine, and when she refused, defeated her forces and transferred her son's kin-Titles to his two grandsons. Thus did Tenania, the elder brother, become ruler of Huahine. The first time his name appears in accounts about Tahiti was in the missionary records of 1804:

Sept 14. There was a report of a war having been kindled in Moorea or Eimeo, on account of the people refusing to acknowledge the King's [i.e., Tu] half-sister (daughter of Idia and [Tenania] as their governor, several were killed and the muskets of the people in general were seized by the Kings orders. Peace was however soon restored. (Quoted in Newbury 1961: 73)

Clearly, by this time 'Itia had severed all her sexual and domestic ties with Tina, although she continued to support him politically to the end. And just as clearly, her union with Tenania was one of marriage; otherwise their daughter would not have been eligible for the kin-Title that led her parents to pronounce her 'governor' of Mo'orea (which, it will be recalled, was 'Itia's birthplace). But the main point of this lengthy digression is that Tenania, the Chief of Huahine, had had a very close active (in contrast to latent) relationship with the Pomares by no later than 1802, and probably had had some, friendly or otherwise, relationship in 1792—in addition to the latent relationship inherent in his kinship ties with them.

Tobin, on this day, was concerned with matters less directly related to politics:

Edeea this day sent me a hog and some breadfruit, the latter being a great rarity. Boiled plantains and a kind of yam (Tarro) were issued as a substitute to the crew. Not an ounce of European bread had been expended since our arrival, and so familiar had our palates become to the vegetable kind [of bread], as not at all to feel the deprivation of the 'Kings own'. The supply of Yams was never bountiful, and of but an inferior quality; sweet potatoes were still more difficult to be procured. Tarro was generally in plenty, and Cocoa nuts were ever brought to us in amazing numbers. It was calculated that the daily expenditure of these fruit, on board the Providence, her consort, and at the Post, amounted to above a thousand, the milk from them being our common beverage. In our own colonies the Cocoa nut is not considered as by any means wholesome, but the conviction of its salutary effects on our people at Otahytey disposes me to doubt the truth of such an opinion.

Wednesday, June 20th

Light Variable Winds and Calms. Thermometer from 75 to 80 Degrees.

Employed at the Forge. Carpenters cutting Scuttles in the Cabbin Ports. Sailmakers making Weather Cloths for the Green Houses; Painting the Ship and blacking the Bends. Hands Wooding.

I went out to day to Sound about the Bay, & towards Oparre We found many Corral Banks, and some dangerous places for a large Ship if coming in with a Swell in the Bay. Three and four fathoms were <it was> in several places off Tarrah towards the Dolphin [i.e., the Dolphin Banks, where Wallis' Ship went aground]. On my landing at my second Station to take some bearings I was seized with a burning heat in my head and flushes in my face that I could no longer support myself. I was got <carried> under the Shade of <the> Trees, and by help of some kind Natives who brought me Cocoa Nutts and Apples I recovered, got into my Boat and returned on Board where the Fever happily went off. I left the rest <to day> to be done by Lieut. Portlock whose alertness and attention to his duty, and every thing I direct him to do, makes me at all times think of him with regard and esteem. I have now scarce <no longer> the power of bearing much fatigue. Many necessary duties however cause me to suffer a geat deal <and I am frequently overcome. The Surgeon Mr Harwood considers my disease Nervous>. [In ML this paragraph continues, as follows, but has been crossed out] <Besides a constant Head Ach, I have frequently in the day a sinking at the pit of my stomach, then a dreadfull heat flies up into my Face, which all but [a report?] seems to fly out at the top of my head, as if shot through me—a lowness and flurry of my spirits takes place. For a week past I thought I got the better of my complaint but this unfortunate busyness today has undone all again.>

Thursday, June 21st

Fresh Breezes and fair Weather. At Night Land Winds and Calms. Wind E, ESE–SSE. Thermometer from 76 to 80 Degrees.

Employed Cutting Wood. Painting the Ship. Sailmakers making covers for the Green Houses. Gunners Employed Airing their Stores.

Sufficient Supplies of Hogs, Plantains, Cocoa Nutts, Tarro, Vees and an increase of Bread fruit. All these articles are brought to us from a few People belonging to the District of Matavai and Oparre. About ten or a Dozen Cannoes are all we have <which come> off to us in the course of the Day.

The want of Breadfruit has freed us very much from being infested with the Flies. While the Fruit is plentifull they are a plague to us—<for as> it drops from the Trees when ripe, and the Otaheiteans taking <take> no pains to clear away the filth [i.e., of the rotting breadfruit], the Swarms of Flies <which are provided> are troublesome to us beyond measure.

I happily recovered from my Fever, but remained oppressed <occupied> with a dreadfull head Ach. I dare not <about midday> expose myself to the Sun. The shining of it upon any part where I am affects me in so violent a manner in my head that I cannot bear it. Before the Sun Rise I bathe in the fresh Water and return on board.—& after Sun down take my Walk, so that in a few Days I hope to be tolerably well again.

Friday, June 22nd

Ditto Weather. Thermometer from 75 to 80 Degrees. Employed as Yesterday.

I found myself much better to day <so that> I was able to protract off my Survey, and examine and rectify the Soundings about this Place. I continue to bathe in the River, which before Sun Rise is remarkably Cold and refreshing.

At intervals of ten Days, & a fortnight we have Fleets of 10 & 15 Sail of Cannoes passing and repassing to and from Teturoah—they bring a quantity of dried Boneto and other fish, which are considered dainties by the Otaheiteans, but by us not worth eating.

In the Course of the Night a Thief found an opportunity to pass the Centinels and Officers on Guard at the Post, and take from out of the House a Bag of Clothes belonging to Lieut Guthrie. It was a large quantity of dirty linnen to some amount—how the Thief could have got it out & pass the Centinels is incredible. At what time it was taken away was not known, we could not therefore fix the neglect on any particular Man. The Guard has hitherto been 3 Centinels, One Corporal to visit them and see they do their duty, and a Midshipman to superintend. The relief <superintend is> every two hours. I ordered another Centinel, so that we have now four Centinels to prevent Mischief.

211

Saturday, June 23rd

Moderate Breezes and fair Weather. Calms and Land Winds in the Night. Wind E by N–E by S–SSE. Thermometer from 76 to 80 Degrees.

Employed drying Powder and Gunners Stores. Sent a Party to Cutt Wood. Sailmakers making Hoses [i.e., flexible tubes formed of leather or tarred canvas, to conduct fresh water into casks]. Washed and Cleaned Ship. Cooper repairing Casks. Afternoon all hands repairing their Clothes.

Very sufficient Supplies and Breadfruit coming in Season again.

I suffered vastly in my head to day I cannot bear the sight of the Sun. In other respects I am terribly well—before Sun Rise and about Sun set I am able to see into all necessary duties, and regulate all busyness on Shore.

It gives me peculiar satisfaction to see my Plants thriving. I have now once more with unwearied Zeal and attention procured that great and valuable object, and hope God will grant my endeavours to <may> be crowned with success.

Sunday, June 24th

Very fresh Winds at E by S and extremely hazy during the Day, but fair in the Night. Thermometer from 79 to 82 Degrees.

Very sufficient Supplies. Caught 100 lbs of Fish with the Seine so that every Man had Fish and Pork for his Dinner. Mustered the Ship's Company and saw every person <one> Clean Dressed and Performed Divine Service.

My health much better to Day. My Friend Tynah and Oreepyah appear very much concerned at the theft committed on Friday Night, and have promised to do their utmost to discover the Thief and bring the Clothes back. To Morrow Tynah goes to Tettaha [Fa'a'a] under an escort of our Boat armed, and a Lieut. to accompany him, and I have determined on sending Lieut. Portlock to Attahooroo to bring away a Boat of the Matilda's which Monah has been after for me, and <which he> has sent word it <me word> will be forth coming on the arrival of my People. My motive for taking this Boat, if she is worth repairs; is to assist me in case of accident in my Voyage through <the Straight> between New Holland and New Guinea.

Monday, June 25th

Fresh Gale at East and E by S and Fair Weather. Thermometer from 77 to 81 Degrees.

Sufficient Supplies.

At dawn of Day Lieut. Portlock set off for Attahooroo, and I sent Tynah down to Tettaha with Lieut. Tobin to try his success to get Mr Guthries Clothes. They returned with a report that the Thief had gone to

Attahooroo, and <that they> were not able to get a single Article that <which> was stolen. I could not expect Lieut. Portlock back untill To-morrow.

[The following paragraph appears only in ML, where it is crossed out.]

<From Surmises of Mr Tobin we have reason to suspect the sincerity of Tynah and Oreepyah with respect to their professing themselves anxious to regain the Clothes.>

Employed getting Chests out of the Ship to destroy the Cockroaches. Cleaning below and Washing with Boiling Water to destroy the Nests and haunts of all manner of Vermine. The Ship is far from being pestered with Cockroaches or any kind of Vermine; but I consider it necessary to keep clear of them if possible, and therefore have adopted this Plan of Washing with boiling Water which destroys every offensive thing, and becomes a salutary operation to the Ship in general. The operation is performed thus. The Coppers and all Vessels are got ready with the Water—a select number of People with Quart Pots are stationed and on my giving the word every hole and crevise is so deluged that few Vermine escapes. The Men are Clothed with Jackets to prevent being scalded, and the Ship for an half Hour is a complete Vapour Bath.

Tuesday, June 26th

Moderate Trade Winds E by S. Land Wind SE at Night. Thermometer from 77 to 81 Degrees.

Sufficient supplies. Employed as Yesterday cleaning the Ship of Vermin by Washing with boiling Water. I first thought of this expedient when I commanded the Bounty. I recommend it as the most effectual and sure method of clearing of <cleaning> Ships of contageous diseases <if it be> followed by constant airing with large fires.

A little before Noon I had the pleasure to see Lieut Portlock arrive from Attahooroo, and with him the Whale Boat, which after some deliberation was given up to him, altho not to the general voice of the People.

Attahooroo is the largest County in this Island, it is divided into two Districts or Chiefdoms. The Northernmost, called Taigh <Pa,igh> [Pa'ea], was Governed by Poohaitaiah <Po,ahaitai,a,h> [Pohuetea; marginal note: 'Potatow when I was in the Bounty'], and the Southernmost called Paterre [Patea?] was governed by Tettowah [Te To'ofa], Men of great consequence when I was here in 1788 and in Captain Cook's time. These <The> Men are now dead, and Children are elected. Tettowah left a Wife and Son who naturally succeed to his power and influence, but Poohaitaiah left no Child, and I believe in consequence <of it> the present Minor Chief, some relation, is not firmly fixed in his Government.

It was at Paterre that the Boat was <The Boat was at

213

Paterre>. The Mob were for keeping <inclined to keep> it, but Tettowah's Wife ordered it to be given up, which after a few hours was effected upon Mr Portlock's declaring if he did not return with the Boat, I should in a day or two be round and set fire to the Country.

The endeavors of Tettowah's Wife were seconded by a very clever «young» fellow called Terraighteerree—his official capacity is that of a Priest and <he> had great weight among the People.

On the Boat being launched into the Water, Mr. Portlock made a present to the Chiefs which I had given him for that purpose. He relates that they received it with great eagerness, as if they had known the Value of Iron without ever having <had> the use of it, and withall expressed a thankfullness which gave him much <great> pleasure. They gave him cause to think the Matavai and Oparre People had prevented their having intercourse with us, and on his assuring them of my friendship it spread a general satisfaction. Tettowah's Wife with Terraighteerree; her second Husband Towryigno, and her Brother embarked to see the Ship, where they arrived in time for Dinner.

Tettowah's Wife they call Oweehee Vaheine ['ivi vahine, widow], a common Name to Women who have lost a Husband. She is a Stout good looking Woman.

I found a shyness about our Friend Tynah and his Wives to this Woman and her party. He had bantered me the Night before about my getting the Boat, and I now in my turn laughed at him. I also made a very large present of Valuable things to the Strangers, and made a great deal of them, so that they were truly delighted. The Men drank freely of all our liquors, and eat Cheese and drank Porter. All Strangers ask what the Cheese is made of, and it is a standing joke with our Friends here to call it Teeappapow, (Part of a Dead Body) [i.e., tupapa'u, corpse or ghost]. In the Evening they all went on Shore with Tynah who provided every thing for them. Owehee Vahiene eat nothing while with us, for no Woman except Iddeeah and Whyerreddee will ever eat before me, and on Shore as is their custom, they all eat apart from the Men.

Oporeeonoo [Poreonu'u] or Great Peninsula of Otaheite is divided into 12 Counties under these Names—Matavai, Oparre, Tettaha, Taaigh, Paterre, Papparah, Wyooreedee, Iddeeah, Whaennah, Tierrai, Happyano. They sometimes place another between Papparah and Wyooreedee called Atteemono. These Counties have different districts or Chiefdoms, each of those of Taaigh and Paterre is as large as any one County. There is however a mistake [marginal note: 'Capt. Cook does it'] in calling the whole Oporeeonoo, for I find there are three Grand Divisions, which include the subdivisions as follows. Under the Head of Oporeeonoo lie Oparre, Matavai, Happyano, Tierrai, Whaennah, Iddeeah. Under the Head O'Taiwyyootah [marginal note: 'or Tevvyyootah'] lie Paparrah,

Atteemono, Wyooreedee, Whyerree. Under the Head [of] Attahooroo lie Tettaha, Taaigh and Paterre.

Tieraboo [Taiarapu] makes a fourth Grand Division under the head Tevvyty, and the whole Land [island] is called Taheite,—Otaheite improperly, from no Taheite, of Taheite, the sign of the Genitive Case. Tevvyty is also divided into 12 Counties.

When the Island was formed into these four Grand Divisions it was governed by One King. I cannot consider it strictly so since I have known it. Each of the Divisions have a power which governs it independent of the rest. We have strong traits of it at this time. The Division of Tevvyootah is governed by a Person who certainly has had equal and like <similar> Power to Otoo. This is Tomaree—he had the Eye of the human sacrifice presented to him—wore the Maro, and every person uncovered to him. Every Person <every one> agrees that no other Chief had the power like Otoo & Tomarre, but this was before the present boy Otoo was born,—all the superior marks of distinction are now shown to him. Tomarre formerly called Terreederri [Teri'irere] is the Son of the famous Opureah [Purea; marginal note: 'Obereah according to former accounts']. He married Terreenaharoah [Teri'inavaharoa], Tynah's Sister, as I have stated in my last Voyage, and of course is the present (Boy) Otoo's Uncle.

The Division of Tevvyty has since our time been governed by one Chief of the Name Whaeeahtuah [Vehiatua]. This has been always the name of the Person who reigned there, and as Terreetapanouai, Tynah's Son, has become Heir to the late Whaeeahtuah, he has also taken the name.

The Division of Oporeeonoo is governed by Otoo, so that here we see something like three distinct Princedoms, and I believe Attahooroo was a fourth—how it has happened to be divided I cannot get informed <of>, for by the division, neither of the Chiefs, altho allowed to be people of consequence, have the Rank of the others, altho they have governed their respective Chiefdoms with equal power.

If it was not from the assertions of every one that Otoo was Erreerahigh; that no person else wore the Maro, or had the Eye of the human Sacrifice presented to him, I should pronounce it as a certainty that the Island was divided into four Princedoms totally independent of each other.

To know the exact state of the Government of the Island it would require a person to be some time in each part of it—a just conclusion might then be formed; but the information of any party is doubtfull, and the Strangers who visit /us/ are cautious to give intelligence that may offend.

There are two Words which they attach to the different Subdivisions of the Island. One is Manno, and the other Matynah. Oparre & Attahooroo have each two Manno's, but all the others, even Tiarraboo they say are

215

not Mannos but Matynahs. The People of Oporeeonoo are Matynahs no ['of']
Tynah. Those of Tiarraboo are the People [marginal note: 'manno'] of
Whaeeahtuah. Those of Tevvyoyootah are the People of Tomarre and those of
Attahooroo of Tettowah and Poohaitaiah—yet they say that the whole of them are
Matynahs no Otoo. This certainly implies he is their King.

Matynah [mata'eina'a] signifies a set of People belonging <to>
and governed by a Chief but I am at a loss to know what Manno means, unless it is
the place of resort or Palace of the King.

I conclude therefore that Otaheite is a Kingdom divided into four
Grand Divisions or Princedoms. Each of those are divided into Governments, and
these are again subdivided into parts which may be properly called districts or
Circuits of inferior authority—Counties, Corporation Towns & Villages.

Bligh's summary of Tahiti's political geography is the most nearly accurate one written during the first half-century of European visits. Of course, he had available to him the previous descriptions of Cook, Banks, the Forsters, etc., but in some ways those earlier summaries were obstacles to understanding—especially to Bligh, who was so respectful of Cook's and Bank's authority in most matters—or, for career purposes was so reluctant to criticize. Clearly, a great deal of 'interviewing' had been undertaken to acquire all the information he distilled in his summary; but the only clue he provides about how he had obtained it is found in his admirably unpretentious *caveat*: 'the information of any one party is doubtfull, and the Strangers who visit us are cautious to give intelligence that may offend'. By which he meant, that because of his close association with the Pomares some of his informants evidently believed he would not wish to hear any belittling of their pretensions.

Remarks about several of Tahiti's political units have been presented in foregoing entries and commentaries; the following paragraphs will attempt to place all of them in a summary—which, it should be added, draws much from Bligh's.

Tahiti's political geography of that era was in one respect like the present-day world as represented in the United Nations: it comprised a number of territorial units (Figure 9, p. 43) that were more or less autonomous but that varied widely in size, population, and structure. One way of comprehending them is in terms of orders of complexity:

First-order units   As set forth in the commentary for April 9th, next to households the simplest type of 'political' unit in Tahiti (and in fact throughout the Society Islands) was the neighborhood, consisting of one or more households. When these islands were being populated there must have been many autonomous neighborhoods, but long before 1767 (the arrival of

216

the *Dolphin*, marking the beginning of the era now being chronicled) all of them had become integrated into more complex units.

Second-order units (i.e., multi-neighborhoods)   The simplest autonomous 'political' unit larger than a single neighborhood would have been composed of two or more neighborhoods that were differentiated only to the extent that the headman of one of them exercised authority over all of them in events involving all of them (e.g., warfare against an enemy common to all of them).

Third-order units were those composed of two or more multi-neighborhoods each with its own headman but all subject to the ultimate authority of one among them. During the era under study this order of complexity seems to have been exemplified only by little Fa'a'a (also called Tetaha, Bligh's 'Tettowah'). Contrary to Bligh, Fa'a'a had managed most of the time to retain a large measure of autonomy despite pressures from its larger neighbors, Atehuru and Pare-Arue.

Fourth-order units were those composed of two or more third-order units, plus perhaps one or more second-order ones. The clearest example of such a unit was Pare-Arue, whose residents were known as *Te Poreonu'u* (Bligh's 'Oporeeonoo').

Fifth-order units   The exemplars of this order of complexity were Taiarapu and that composed of Papara and its eastern neighbors, Atimaono, Vaiuriri, and Vaiari. The people of Taiarapu (Tahiti's southern peninsula) had long been united under a single line of chiefs, i.e., the Vehiatua line (see May 8th), and were known collectively as *Teva-tai*, Seaward Teva. Those of the other combination, called collectively *Teva-i-uta*, Landward Teva, were also fairly firmly united and under the domination of Papara's line of leaders. (See May 12th)

Like most taxonomies, however well-meaning, this one is difficult to accommodate to that very large and populous unit known collectively as *Atehuru*. In fact, Atehuru consisted of two autonomous but consistently allied fourth-order units, Mano Tahi, or Puna'auia, in the north, and Mano Rua, or Pa'ea, in the south. (If Bligh is listening (!), *mano*—his 'Manno'—means 'one thousand', or 'numerous, while *tahi* means 'one' and *rua* 'two'.)

The other hard-to-classify 'political' collectivity on Tahiti was *Te Aharoa*, the string of territorial units—Ha'apape (which included Matavai), Ha'apaino'o, Tierei, Mahaena, and Hitia'a—that stretched from Pare-Arue to Taiarapu. As noted earlier (April 30th) little is known about their respective political natures, nor about their inter-connections, save that Hitia'a's leaders appeared more prominently than those of the others on the island-wide stage. Bligh notwithstanding they were *not* part of the Pomares' domain, Poreonu'u; and while Poeno, headman of Matavai, had an on-again off-again relationship with the Pomares, we have seen how off-again it sometimes was.

And while Tina's brother, Vaetua, the vaunted warrior, kava devotee, and jealous husband, doubtless exercised some authority in Ha'apape, it was not sufficient to recover the *Matilda* firearms, which were in possession of Tupira in another part of the district.

The meaning Bligh attached to *mata'eina'a* (his 'Matynah') is appropriately vague. Other visitors to Tahiti have used the word for neighborhoods, still others for (political) subjects, and still others for certain kinds of groups, as, for example, *va'a mata'eina'a*, 'the crew of a canoe'. In fact, the referents in the sources to this word are so varied that it would be pointless to try to select its 'real' meaning here. Also, it is to be hoped that Bligh's remarks about Tu's overarching 'power' and about his being Tahiti's 'King', will be read in the way he clearly intended, as referring to his religious-ritual status only; and the same applies to his remarks about Papara's Chief, Tomari'i.

Finally, as Bligh correctly concluded, Tina had done his best to keep the English, with their firearms and their largesse, to himself.

Wednesday, June 27th

Moderate Breezes and Cloudy Weather. Wind East. Thermometer 77 to 81 Degrees.

Employed overhauling Chests and Clothes on Shore to clear them of Cockroaches and Washing between Decks with boiling Water. Kept Fires in all Night to Air the Ship. Employed some Carpenters repairing the Whale Boat. Sailmakers about Boat Sails. Sufficient Supplies.

Thursday, June 28th

Moderate Winds at E by S and Calms in the Night & Morning. A Heavy Dew. Thermometer from 76 to 81 Degrees.

Sufficient Supplies but none to spare this Day. Our Attahooroo Friends left us with a promise of returning in five Days.

Employed in the After Hold. Began to Paint the Starboard Side of the Ship, and paid the Bends with Pitch and Tar mixed. Made Nettings to cover the Skylights of the Plants, and Employed the Carpenters Sawing Plank and repairing the Whale Boat.

Friday, June 29th

Land and Sea Breezes at E & SE by S with Calms in the first part of the Morning. Thermometer from 75 to 81 Degrees.

Employed repairing Boats Sails. Repairing the Whale Boat, Sawing Plank. In the after Hold, and Cooper repairing Casks.

Sufficient Supplies, but obliged to send about the Shore to purchase them, very few <being> brought of <off> to the Ship. No people of any

Plate 25 *Tupapa'o*
Watercolor by George Tobin

Plate 26   Mauaroa's *tupapa'o*
Watercolor by George Tobin

consequence about us but Tynah and his Wives who Dine with me every Day. I send the Boat regularly for them at Noon.

The Plants are coming on remarkably well. I still remain in an uneasy state in my head and cannot bear being exposed to the Sun, so that my shore busyness I execute early in the Morning & towards Evening.

Saturday, June 30th

Fresh Breezes at E by N and ENE which always brings a Swell into the Bay. Thermometer from 76 to 81 Degrees, on Shore about 3 or 4 Degrees hotter.

Employed in the Main Hold the first part of the Day. Afterwards the People had to themselves to mend and wash their Clothes.

Supplies as Yesterday. Very few Cannoes off to us, or about the Post. The Natives appear to care very little about us.

Sunday, July 1st

Fresh Breezes and fair Weather with Calms in the first part of the Day Wind E by S. Thermometer from 75 to 81 Degrees.

Washed and Cleaned Ship. Hauled the Seine and caught a few Fish. Mustered and saw every Person clean Dressed. Performed Divine Service. Gave leave to a Party to go on Shore to Walk.

[The following paragraph appears only in ML, where it has been crossed out.]

<Read a letter from Mr Pearce [the Officer in charge of the Marines] today requesting a Court Martial as soon as we came were [where?] it could be held on Sergeant _____ for disobeydiance of orders and neglect of Duty. This refers to my accounts on the 11th and 12th June. I ordered the Serjeant to be a Prisoner at large.>

We have Cannoes constantly passing and repassing in Fleets to & from Tetooroah on every favourable opportunity. In one of them to day arrived a Boy, who in my last Voyage I mentioned <as> being adopted by Teppahoo [Te Pau] and Teranno, the Chief of Tettaha and his Wife. He was a fine promising Child, but he is now diseased in the spine—his Backbone bends outwards to such a Degree that the Boy is obliged to be carried—he cannot sit upright. The Surgeon Mr. Harwood considers it owing to the Scrofula, as the Youth and all his Friends declare he had no hurt. The various appearances this dreadfull disease puts on is <are> truly Shocking.

Monday, July 2nd

Fresh Breezes and fair Weather. Land Winds at Night Wind E by S–SSE. Thermometer from 75 to 82 Degrees.

Employed in the Main Hold. Carpenters repairing the Whale

Boat and lineing and fitting the Ports. Armourer at the Forge making Hinges for the Port Scuttles. Sent Hands to cutt Broom Stuff. Sailmakers Repairing the Boats Sails. Served Tobacco to the People.

Sufficient Supplies but I am obliged to send People about the Country to purchase Hogs. Breadfruit still continues scarce, but the Trees have a very fine show of them about half and two thirds grown, and some we get perfectly fit for use. Plantains and Tarro is the Principal bread kind, for Yams have been neglected among those idle people of Matavai & Oparre. Cocoa Nutts and fine Apples we have in abundance, and I have not yet had a occasion to give my People less than one pound and a half of Pork per Day.

With my usual Visitors Tynah and his Wives, we had a few inferior Chiefs from the East part of Oporeeonoo. As customary <usual>, after Dinner they began to enumerate the Ships that have been here, and how far they liked one better than another. Mine <ours> they called the healthy Ships, but dwelled much on the Discovery Captain Vancouver for Disease. It appears now to me, that instead of giving the Chiefs Wine, they have accustomed them to drink Cape Brandy which has torn them to pieces and killed many, among whom is a celebrated Chief of Attahooroo called Poohaitaiah [Pohuetea] or Tootaha.

They describe the Jenny of Bristol as a Miserable Vessel and the Commander as a great Rascal.

'. . . inferior Chiefs from the East part of Oporeenoo'—meant here is the region collectively known as Te Aharoa, which comprised the districts of Hitia'a, Mahaena, Tierei, Ha'apaino'o and Ha'apape. As pointed out in the commentary for June 26th, those districts were *not* part of Poreonu'u—although the Pomares doubtless told Bligh that they were so. And the 'inferior chiefs' referred to were probably deemed inferior by the Pomares and their hangers-on because they were leaders of sparsely populated districts and, except for those of Hitia'a, would have held only inconsequential kin-Titles.

Pohuetea, who had been Chief of Puna'auia (the northern half of Atehuru), had indeed died shortly before the *Providence*'s visit, but there is no basis for Bligh's diagnosis of 'death by Cape Brandy'.

The *Jenny*, which had anchored in Matavai Bay for a week in March of 1792, was a mere schooner, hence smaller than most other European vessels seen by the Tahitians up to that time—and therefore, perhaps, 'miserable' in Tahitians' eyes. If her Captain, Baker, had been a 'great Rascal', he was only one of a long line of the breed that was to become familiar to the Tahitians.

Tuesday, July 3rd

Variable Westerly Winds and Calms. Thermometer from 78 to 81 Degrees—on Shore about 3 Degrees higher.

Supplies fully sufficient, but obliged to send about the Country for most of them, very few Natives take any trouble to bring provisions to the Ship.

I had the happyness to day to see my Plants so forward as to determine me to «begin to» fit out. I therefore began to Day to start [i.e., to discharge] the Water we have, and to take on board fresh. Every other person fully employed, and I sent Mr. Portlock to examine the bottom between this and Oparre, which I have not yet accurately assertained.

A Violent fit of the Head Ach, with the many things I have to attend to, confined me the latter part of this day. The pain I suffer when these fits seize me is beyond all description. Happily when oft [usually?] I am in tolerable Health, except a great contraction of the Nerves in the left side of my Face.

In the beginning of June I observed all the Cloth Plants [i.e., those whose bark was used for bark cloth] which were cutt down close to the Ground [during the recent war], beginning to shoot, and are now grown to considerable height. I now observe various other proofs of the effect of Spring. The Avee Trees are loosing their Old leaves by new shoots, and several other Trees that shed Annually their leaves are covering with new Garments <now beginning to vegetate>. The Natives give me an account of a number of Trees of this description. In one Month they say the Avees will be all gone.

Wednesday, July 4th

Fair Weather and Wind at East with Calms in the first part of the Morning and Land Winds at Night, which is constantly <commonly> the Case, and a fine Air. Thermometer from 76 to 80 Degrees.

Employed Starting [discharging] and filling Water. Cooper about the Casks. Carpenters lineing and fitting the Ports and Scuttles and repairing the Whale Boat.

My Friend Tynah undertook to go after the Thief who had stolen the Clothes from the Post a few Days since, for I find it was done by an inferior Chief of Tiarraboo (a Friend of his Brothers Oreepyah) who we had shown great attention to <to whom we had shown great attention>, and <whom> he calls ungratefull.

It is astonishing with what indifference these People speak of Death. It has ever appeared to me that they cared little how short their existence was, they are nevertheless affraid of the final stroke, when by War or accident they have reason to expect it, while in disease they are patient and not alarmed. They have no Idea of a future State, but <expect to> fall into a degree of nothingness without reward or punishment after Life.

'Starting and filling Water'—i.e., emptying the water casks of their old water and refilling them with fresh; this measure, in preparation for departure, received further comment from Tobin:

221

As the time approached for our departure, we began watering the ship from Matavai river [Plate 27] It has been observed that, her [the ship's] capacity for stowage was very considerable, which was indispensable, as we had a long and arduous passage to make by Torres straits to Timor before the necessary article could be replenished. The plants, it must be remembered, would require no small portion, every cask was therefore filled, which completed the stock to above a hundred tons.

Bligh's informants may have spoken to him of death with 'indifference' but we know from other sources that their ideas about it, including those about 'a future State', were myriad and detailed.

The Tahitians and other Society Islanders distinguished sharply between a human's body (*tino*) and his (or her: females were also considered human!) soul (*varua*). Most accounts placed the soul within the body during the waking state, dreams having constituted the experiences of the soul's wandering outside the body during sleep or trance. Humans also contained some of what I have called 'sanctity' (April 9th), but I have seen no assertion about where that was located. Some accounts place the soul in the head, and an association with breath is indicated in the belief that the soul left the body through the mouth. Taken with the belief that the heir of a dying person could acquire some of the latter's specialized knowledge by inhaling his expiring breath, this could signify either that such knowledge was considered to be an attribute of the soul, or that it was an independent entity associated with it. In common with most other Polynesians, the Tahitians treated the (human) head with much respect (except when bashing it in); but whether this had to do with the supposed location of the soul, I cannot say. In any case, the head was *not* held to be the site of thinking (*mana'o*) or of emotions (*horuhoru*), both of which were believed to be located in the stomach and intestines.

As just noted, it was commonly believed that the soul often left the body for short periods without effect upon the latter, but if it remained away longer—i.e., more than two or three days —the body began to decay and was considered no longer alive (*ora*), but dead (*pohe*). (There were legends, but only a few, about souls returning to their former bodies after decay had begun to set in.) Once having left the body 'permanently' the soul hovered around it for a short while and then entered the universe of spirits, the *po*, where it continued to exist for shorter or longer periods of time. (Belief was that the souls of premature infants entered periwinkles and those of some drowned persons sharks or dolphins, but none became part of another human body.) After entering the *po*, some souls remained there constantly but others returned occasionally to the *ao*, the sphere—literally, the 'room'—of living humans, in the form of ghosts ('*oromatua*).

Contrary to Bligh's assertion, the Tahitians and other Society Islanders held some very elaborate ideas about the After Life, including

222

'rewards' and 'punishments' therein. For the natives of Tahiti Island the Afterworld was believed to be in or west of Ra'iatea. The souls of Tahitians assembled on Tata'a Hill, in Atehuru, before taking off in a convoy of spirits. The journey was hazardous from the start. For example, on Tata'a Hill were two stones, one of Life and one of Death; if a soul, accidentally of course, touched the latter it was annihilated on the spot; if on the other hand it touched the former it was able to continue on its promising but still hazardous way. Near the end of its journey—if it had survived so far—it underwent a Judgment by a powerful spirit (who had never been a human) to determine which of two (three, in some versions) places it would then proceed to. Borrowing Western analogies, one of those places was a Paradise, one a Purgatory, and the third a kind of Limbo for purged 'sinners' and others not yet qualified for Paradise. In due course many souls were released from Limbo and permitted occasional visits to their earthly homes, while a fortunate few, presumably mainly those in Paradise, became apotheosized.

In the absence of any society-wide 'official' theological doctrines, ideas about the nature of the Afterworld differed from place to place (typically, from one temple 'school' to another), and, likely, from one generation to the next. Paradise —*Fragrant Rohutu*—was, not surprisingly, a place of abundant food, beautiful women, salubrious climate, eternal youthfulness, and amusements without end. Purgatory was a place where hapless souls worked unremittingly part of the time and sat around in utter darkness for the remainder. Meanwhile, according to one of many versions, the souls in Purgatory were occasionally eaten by a god, and then regurgitated; after a year or so of this misery most of them were permitted into Limbo, whence they returned now and then to their earthly homes, as ghosts.

Of greater interest than the *nature* of Paradise and Purgatory were the criteria by which souls were assigned to them. Entry into Paradise was reserved for Arioi and for all other persons who had behaved in an appropriate manner—that is, in an appropriate manner *to the gods*: namely, by prayer, by generous offerings (including compensation to the priests), and by correct behavior on religious occasions. Conversely, all those who, wittingly or not, had not behaved appropriately towards the gods were assigned to Purgatory—in which, by the way, a soul's sentence could be shortened somewhat by petitions, with offerings, made by his relatives and friends (who by similar actions could also reduce the hazards attending the soul's journey to the Afterworld).

The focus in the above on a person's religious behavior, together with the element of chance that attended the soul's journey to the Afterworld, seems to have ruled out social morality as a factor in determining a person's Afterlife—mostly, perhaps, but not entirely so, for the unloved and unlamented person would have inspired less generous religious offerings among the survivors than would the considerate and better loved.

Bligh's assertion that very ill Tahitians were usually stoical about the approach of death has been confirmed in the accounts of other Europeans. As for his conclusion about the Tahitians' fear of death when warring, or when exposed to lethal accident, the reports of some other eye-witness observers show that to have been a matter of individual temperament. Thus, while Tina was invariably described as timorous or fearful or even downright cowardly, he appears to have been an exception even among his 'Royal' siblings in this respect. Indeed, he made no secret of his fears, as Tobin relates concerning a trip taken with him in the ship's launch:

Pomaurey slept quietly by my side, until he was alarmed from his afternoons nap by my firing at a curlew, which produced a conversation on firearms. He had some time before accused me of being afraid (Matow) [mata'u] for not suffering him to navigate the boat inside the reef. It appeared a good opportunity to retort on him, but this he did not at all feel, making no secret of his want of courage; saying it was not necessary for a king to go into battle, and concluded by asking if 'Keen Yore' (King George) ever did. On being answered in the negative, he seemed more than usually pleased exclaiming Miti Miti [maita'i], (good) but he could not be perswaded that, it was not for want of personal courage in our Ereedahy [Ari'i Rahi, Paramount Chief].

The effect of early habit is particularly strong in the different characters of the Otahytean royal family. Pomaurey, from being taught that, a King should not appear in battle, is the most pusilanimous man possible, without feeling the least stigma attached to it, which Orepaia and Whidoooah, arrogate no small degree of consequence to themselves, as warriors, and are deemed the bulwark of the state.

Thursday, July 5th

Easterly Winds with Calms in the Morning. Lightning at Night and the whole day Cloudy Weather.

Sufficient Supplies by sending on Shore to purchase them. Very few Natives about the Ship or Post.

My Friend Tynah returned to Day with part of the Stolen goods. The Thief fled into the most distant parts of Tiarraboo, and escaped with the greatest part of the Articles he had Stolen.

Some of the Matilda's Men were round at Oaitaipeeah, and brought back an account, that a Leaguer [large water cask] and part of a Yard and Plank of the Matilda were drifted there. From the Captain's Account of the Shoal, it is distant 207 Leagues from this place in the direction of S 64 degrees W.

Busily Employed Starting and filling of Water. Carpenters about the Whale Boat. Received a Launch load of Wood. Hands Sawing Plank.

Friday, July 6th

Very Cloudy, Thunder and heavy Rain all Day. Wind in Squalls from the West NW & NNE, at times Calm. Thermometer from 78 to 80 Degrees.

The Rain to day a very uncommon circumstance. It swelled the River to a great degree. Only one turn [load] of Water could be got on board. At day break we hauled the Seine and caught 550 lbs of Fish all fine Cavallies weighing from 7 to 14 lbs each. Every Man had as much as he could eat, and I was able to make some presents to our Indian Friends.

During the latter part of the Day I ordered fires between Decks to prevent damps and ill health.

No Natives about us, but we have always three days supplies before hand, and <an> abundance for our use.

Saturday, July 7th

The Heavy Rain ended with the dawning of the Day, the remaining part was attended with very heavy Clouds, light Easterly Winds and Calms. Thermometer from 76 to 80 Degrees.

Employed repairing the Whale Boat—fitting up the Cabbin to receive the Plants. Starting and filling Water.

Some of our Officers to Day were successfull in Duck Shooting, as they have frequently been in their excursions to Oparre. They brought me an account that the Chief of Paparrah was in possession of many of my Books, and <brought me> one Volumn of Dampiers Voyage. [interlinear note: 'he gave them'] Some remarks which I have <had> written on it with a Pencil in the blank pages at the end of the Book were perfectly distinct. I have sent a Message to Tomarre, the Chief, that I shall be glad to see him. He has hitherto been prevented from coming by a dread of my not treating him well, and I have not been able to do away his fear. I attribute it to some underhand Work of our Friends at this place, who would consider him as a Rival, and «do» not like him to partake of the benefits they derive from us.

My Plants have received «vast» benefit from the Rains, & I hope in ten Days they will be fitt to be received on Board, as I am now anxious about my time.

Sunday, July 8th

Calms and light Breezes at East the first part of the Day; the latter pleasant breezes from the Westward. Thermometer from 77 to 80 Degrees.

As usual we relaxed from Work this Day. Performed Divine Service, and permitted Men to go on Shore for their amusement.

I suspected some of the Ship's Company might be infected with the Venereal and not inclined to complain of it untill we got to Sea, I therefore, after Mustering them, and examining their Cleanliness both in Person and Dress; ordered them to undergo an examination by the Surgeon. My Surmise was not Groundless, for I found two Wretches infected with the disease, and one of them *kept a Woman constantly with him. The Boatswain and a Midshipman were the two offenders.*

Otow and Oberreeroah came to see me to day from the alarm they had of the Ship going away. These old People are now infirm, the Old Woman is obliged to be always hoisted up in a Chair. They are happy in their Children, who show them every mark of affection and respect, and their filial attention is such a blessing to the Old Pair as delights me <us> on every occasion.

Very few Natives come about us. All in <is> peace and quietness, but most of the Matavai People are still absent. Poeeno is however permitted to return [i.e., to Matavai]. I never permit him to come to me on account of his behaviour to the Matilda's People, which I hope <and therefore I hope my conduct to him> will have a good effect.

On this day Tobin, as usual, adds color to Bligh's more routine remarks:

The major part of the Royal family dined on board, all of them, but Pomaurey, who seldom put aside his native dress for european finery, appearing in sumptuous apparel. Edeeas dress was truly ridiculous, being a crimson coat with gold button holes, brought purposely from England by Captain Bligh as a present for her husband. Whyhereddy differed from her sister in wearing blue. One had a sheet wrapped round her waist, and the other a table cloth. Orepaia exhibited himself in a Captains uniform coat which had been given to him by Captain Edwards of the Pandora.

They supped and slept on board. Their whole conversation was now, with great feeling, on our departure. We were told that the ceremony of wounding the head with a sharks tooth would take place, and A'row A'row Te Tye (a deal of crying) [araurau te tai, continuous the weeping].

Monday, July 9th

Untill Noon a very fresh Gale SW by W when it suddenly shifted to the East. The Weather fair but a considerable Surf in the Bay. Thermometer from 77 to 81 Degrees.

Received on board 5 Turns of Water and some Wood. Carpenters employed about the Whale Boat—Caulking the Cabbin Deck, and were ready to lay down the Stands for the Plants. Armourer <employed> at the Forge, and the Sailmakers making a Sail for the Whale Boat.

We continue to get sufficient Supplies by sending a Person on Shore to purchase them.

My Plants are now in such charming <great> forwardness, that the Botanists have determined <Gardeners are of opinion> I need not be any longer detained <detained longer> than a Week or two at most—every exertion is therefore made to be ready to their time. Our laborious work is watering. In this particular I had two things to attend too—the one to start all my Old Water, *«and» the other to take the new up at such a distance from the Sea Side, as to be sure no Salt Particles would be mixed with it. It was necessary for <that> this duty to <should> be done at the latest period I could allow «myself», that the Plants might receive the greater benefit from the fresh Water, and on this account we are now all bustle in getting ready for Sea.*

I find our Old Friends very disconsolate at our preparations, and it has been with no small trouble that I have resisted the sollicitations of Tynah to proceed to England with me. He has even considered himself slighted in <by> my not permitting him, and our friendship hinged on my complying with his request to take one of his Men, who he said would be of great service to him when I sent him out again, from the many things he could learn and see in England. He was sure he said <that> King George would not refuse him had he been here, and after enumerating <he had enumerated> the many ways <in which> he had served us, <and> particulising <particularised> his conduct to the Pandora, and I had viewed <considered> the Mans Character, I could not help thinking it was the least thing I could do for him, «and» that whether the Man returned or not it was <would be> no greater <great> burthen to our Country «than it should bear». I complied with his request and he seemed happy; but after all, he hoped King George would send out a Ship for him, as <for he thought> he would not have sent out so many things as I have given him <presents>, unless it was his wish to see him.

This Man's Name is Mydiddee [Maititi?], he is a fine Active Person about 22 Years of Age at most, and is considered above the common run of Men in all the exercises of this Country. He exceeds most of them in quickness of apprehension, which is the first excellence next to their natural <a naturally> good disposition that <for which> we could chuse a Man «for». He is a Servant, and therefore a more elligible person for the purpose of learning than if he had been a Chief, admitting his intellects equal. The School is common to all in this Country. There is no knowledge to be gained in the History of the Country but by tradition, and the only education being the Company of the Chiefs and Old People of distinction; wherever nature has planted good sense and a quick conception, the Individual whether Chief or Towtow, becomes informed and well educated. Such a Towtow is more likely to benefit his Country than a Chief who would be only led into Idleness and Dissipation as soon as he arrived in Europe, as was the Case with Omai.

'The School is common to all in this Country'—'The only education being the Company of the Chiefs and Old People of distinction': true, but only up to a point. There were in some districts Fare 'Aira'a upu, 'houses for assimilating prayers and chants', presided over by teachers ('Orometua) and attended by upper-class boys. One such school was at Ha'apape, where an 'Oro zealot is said to have 'established a school for the aristocracy of Tahiti and taught them the folklore of the mother land, Ra'iatea'. (Henry 1928: 130)

In addition, candidates for career-grade priesthood, and for higher positions in the Arioi sect, underwent lengthy and exacting novitiates that included instruction in cosmogonic mythology, practice in conducting ritual, and memorization of large numbers of prayers and chants. Unlike the Ha'apape School, and its parallels in a few other districts, training for the general priesthood seems to have been open to males of all classes.

As for 'Omai': for those readers unfamiliar with the name of that famous Tahitian, a few words from his biographer will serve to identify him:

Mai or Omai, as he was known to Europeans, was the first Polynesian to visit Britain. Picked up by one of Cook's captains, he was carried to England where he became a human curiosity and the lion of fashionable London. Under the patronage of Lord Sandwich and Joseph Banks, he was presented at Court, entertained by aristocratic hosts, examined by scientists, celebrated or satirized by poettasters, and painted by a succession of artists. He learned to skate and play chess, he developed a liking for the theatre, he acquired such social polish that he won praise from Dr. Johnson. At the end of two years he was taken back to the Pacific by Cook who left him at the island of Huahine. (From the frontispiece of McCormick 1977)

During the *Bounty* visit Bligh learned that some thirty months after Cook had left him off in Huahine, Omai had died of 'natural causes'. Before that the man had acquired some influence at Huahine, mainly on account of his firearms:

Tynah and his Brother Oreepyah with Odiddee [Hitihiti] and several others dined with me to day, and I took this opportunity to bring on a conversation about Omai in hopes to hear farther about him, and Odiddee gave me this short history of his life from 1777. Soon after Captn. Cook left Huahine there were some disputes between the people of that Island and those of Ulieta [Ra'iatea], in which also the Natives of Bola-Bola or Bora-Bora took a part. Omai now became of consequence from the possession of three or four Muskets and some Ammunition, & he was consulted on the occasion. Whatever were the motives, such was Omai's opinion and Assurance of Success, that a War was determined on, and took place immediately. Victory soon followed through the means of those few Arms and many of the Ulieta & Bora-Bora men were killed. The Ammunition only lasted to end the contest, and they were in such want for flints that the Musquets were at last fired by a fire stick. Peace was again established and Omai and Tyvarrooah died Natural deaths about 30 Months after Captn. Cook left them. [Tyvarrooah was the native youth recruited by Omai to be his servant when Cook's *Resolution* called at New Zealand *en route* to Tahiti in 1777.]

I asked if from this Victory Omai had gained any possessions or was of higher rank than we left him in. They said no, that he was just the same, which was only one Class above a Towtow. (Bligh 1937: I 394)

Tuesday, July 10th

Light Variable Airs and Calms. Thermometer from 76 to 80 Degrees.

Employed Starting and filling Water. Carpenters about the Whale Boat and fitting up the Greenhouse, which by night was completed.

Plentifull Supply from our old Friends of Oparre, but no Strangers about us.

My time <now> passes very anxiously. In the beginning of the Week I think the Botanists <Gardiners> can have no reason to hesitate to take the Plants on board, they are in a fine thriving state, some of them have made two and three inches shoots.

Wednesday, July 11th

Pleasant Sea Breezes from the East and Land Winds at SSE. Thermometer from 76 to 78 Degrees.

Employed Watering. Staying the Masts and setting the Rigging up. Reeving running Rigging and a variety of necessary duties preparing for Sea. Sufficient Supplies.

My Old Friends, the Otoo family particularly show their usual marks of concern at the approach of my taking leave of them. Tynah is almost disconsolate at being refused going to England, and Old Oberreeroah his Mother has expressed a degree of Grief which I have every reason to believe sincere.

In the Afternoon Otoo arrived from his Tour which was shortened by the News he had <heard> of the Ship's sailing. A few <of the> Papparah people came round with him; but Tomaree refused to accompany him from a fear of not being cordially received by me—by some means he has been made believe I am not his Friend. I do not believe he has any confidence, even among his Oparre friends, indeed there is a certain distrust which hangs among these People that marks them for abounding <discovers them to abound> in duplicity.

Tomaree has certainly many of my Books & Papers, as I am informed by some of the Matilda's People. He had the impudence to send me a Message yesterday, that if I would send him Cartridge paper he would deliver me a proportion of Books for it. It appears that he is in possession of all the Powder the Matildas People brought on Shore with them as well as the Arms, and the use he intends the Books for is to make cartridges of <he intends to make cartridges of the books>. All this information came too late to me to adopt means to recover any thing.

As soon as Otoo came round to the Post, I saluted him with Seven Guns, which gave <him> a high degree of satisfaction & fed his Pride not a little. On my going on Shore a Wrestling Match took place amidst five hundred People, & it ended without anything new. As the last leisure moments I would bestow among them, I diverted the Strangers with a few Fire Works at Night.

The Sacrifice I have spoken of a few Days since (see 19th June) is to be offered to Otoo tomorrow, and if I am well enough shall attend the Ceremony.

I bantered Iddeeah with <upon> the indifference her Son showed her after a long absence, <upon> which gave me a novel sight, her taking <she took> him in her arms (or rather on her Hip as they carry their Children). <This was a novel sight to me> She was however obliged to be uncovered as they always are in the Boys presence.

As recorded in the commentary accompanying the May 12th entry, Temari'i, known formerly as Teri'irere, was the young Chief of Papara, and along with Tu the holder of an Opoan feather-girdle kin-Title. He had at least two kinship links to the Pomares: his first wife, who had died without issue, was Tina's eldest sister, and his mother, the famous Purea, was sister of 'Itea's father's sister. During the *Providence* visit Temari'i's relations with the Pomares was friendlier than his parents' had been although there remained a residue of mutual suspicion, which was nourished by recent Pomare efforts to obtain the firearms in Temari'i's hands. (A few years after the *Providence* left, Temari'i became very friendly with Tu, and joined him in the latter's efforts to wrest secular authority from Tina.)

The books Bligh speaks of were from the *Bounty* and were probably given to Temari'i by some of the *Bounty* people who had resided in Papara for a while. It is tantalizing not to know their titles—for reasons set forth in my Introduction.

Thursday, July 12th

Fresh Breezes at East during the day and Cloudy Weather. Calm in the Mornings and Land Winds at SSE at Night. Thermometer from 75 to 79 Degrees.

Employed Completing the Holds, stowing away Wood. Bent all the Sails Carpenters about the Boats.

Plentifull Supplies altho but few Natives about the Ship. The Sails being bent has given a general alarm of my determination to go to Sea.

At Day break the Sacrifice which I have spoken of on the 19th June, was removed to a Double Cannoe which was likewise a part of the Offering of attonement by the Chief, Ohodoo [Hotu?], of Waennah [Huahine]. He was himself on the Cannoe with 18 Men. The Dead Body wrapt up as it had been brought from the place of execution, was laid across the fore part of the Cannoe, and by it were tied eight fine live Hogs. Near the Body were eight or ten long Rods connected by tyings. Each Rod had short «cross» peices about 8 inches long neatly tyed in form of a Cross. About these and the Tops of the Rods a few red feathers were fastened, «and» the whole is called Mannooteeah, a Temple belonging to their God, to which they likewise gave the common Name—Morai. It is always used on these occasions. The Cannoe was hung round with Course White Cloth, and proceeded towards Oparre with two Drums beating in the common way.

At 8 O'Clock I set off from the Ship accompanied by Tynah, Otow, Iddeah and Wyerreddee. The progress of the Cannoe was so slow, we got to

Oparre before them, where we found few People; but before the Ceremony ended there were about six hundred. Otoo received us on landing.

As soon as the Cannoe arrived, Hammenneemannee, the Priest, conducted us to the Morai called Tebbootabooataiah. (I find this Word is given to the Morai or Temple of Worship wherever the Etuah is brought—it means the Temple of their Great God. At present it is at the entrance of Oparre Harbour.) At this place he began a Prayer, and they all joined in invoking different Deities, which terminated <and concluded> with violent shouts calling on their Great God. At this instant the large bundle wrapt in Red Cloth like an Egyptian Mummy as I have already described, was brought in on a Mans Shoulders, «and» the Cannoe with the Sacrifice was hauled in on <upon> the beach a few Yards from the Morai, Otoo sitting the whole time on a Man's Shoulders. The Priest now quitted the Morai and seated himself at the Sacrifice, «and» Otoo sat opposite to him,—two Drums beat an odd kind of time, and during this the Priest pronounced another prayer or supplication to the Erreerahigh. In this interval they brought three Red Feathers of the breast of a Bird twisted in Cocoa Nutt fibres and presented them to Otoo, and the Rods called Mannooteah, that I have just explained <to Otoo>. This Ceremony lasted a quarter of an hour, when the Sacrifice was brought out on a Pole and laid on the Ground before Otoo with the Head towards him, Drums beating the whole time. The outer Basket <in which> the Body was packed up «in» was now taken off, and the Head exposed. Hammenneemannee the Priest began a supplication in favor «of» Ohodoo and his People, but no reply was at any time made by the King. This Supplicatory Prayer being over, a Grey headed Old fellow, (who I supposed had officiated in this Office to many an unfortunate Wretch,) took up a large splinter of wood, and forcing it into the Socket of each Eye, took out a Mass of corruption which he <divided and> put on two leaves. The Priest began another Prayer, in the course of which one of the leaves was put down on the Stones of the Morai, and the Operator standing before Otoo with the other in his hand, the Priest ordered him to present it to the King,—he received it within four Inches of his Mouth, and at the sentence, Hammamammy, gaped. The Leaf with what they called the Eye was then put by the other and no care taken of them. All this time their Etuah wrapt up on [in?] a piece of Scarlet Cloth was kept on a Man's Shoulders as well as the King, but they now retired to a small pavement or Morai which is called Teppah; here the Etuah and King was put to the Ground, and the Marro being spread out, the King was invested with it, and had it put round him in the manner the common Marro's are worn round the Hips. During this ceremony there was a pretty chant from the Priests. I had agreed to fire three vollies upon the occasion, «and» Tynah told me that I was to fire upon Shouts given by <on> his whole People <shouting>, Maivah Erree, accordingly; as soon as the boy was invested they shouted Maivah Erree (or long live the King—this is our acknowledged King) in a most peircing manner «to the Ear» three & four times, I then ordered a Volley

231

to be fired from the Boat, and with their Shouts it was repeated three times. The Boy was now taken on a Man's Shoulders as before, and with the Etuah were <was> carried back to the great Temple Tebbatabooaitaiah where another Prayer and Chorus was performed. He was then dismantled, and the Marro with the Etuah was taken away by the Priests. [Note: the previous sentence has been crossed out in ML.] In this interval the Body was left unprotected, and we saw the Dogs devouring the remains of the putrid Carcass which <the neglect of it> I found was owing to the offering being an atonement to the Erree and not a particular Sacrifice to the Etuah. The Hogs likewise were neglected in the peace offering, for <but> they were all made a better use of in giving them to us. I don't think there is any immorality in my Idea. Here the whole busyness ended, and noise and feasting ensued, <upon> which I left to themselves <them> and returned on board.

 The Marro since I last saw it was ornamented with some of the Peoples Hair belonging to the Bounty—an ostentatious mark of their connection with the English, and not of respect to the Person it belonged to. It was of a pretty auburn colour, and they told me it was the hair of Skinner who was Barber to the Ship's Company.

 All Men sacrificed to the Etuah are put into the Earth adjoining to the Great Temple or place of Worship; but those who are sacrificed as an atonement to the King are buried under Coral Rocks where the Water has access to them, or left to be devoured by the Dogs. The Water burying Ground <place> lies adjoining to the Morai Woowrooah at the entrance of the Harbour.

Deciphering some of Bligh's Tahitian spellings is speculative; translating them sometimes sheer guesswork. My guess is that 'Mannooteeah' is *manute'a*, whose meaning I guess to be: 'many cross-shaped sticks of wood,' from *manu*, one thousand, or many; *te'a* 'any piece of wood fastened crossways'. (Davies 1851: 263)—However, I shall leave this intriguing and probably insoluble puzzle to more venturesome lexicographers.

Originally—a word more cautious historians shun—Taputapuatea was the name of the *marae*, at Opoa, where 'Oro worship is said to have developed, but as the cult spread the name—as Bligh correctly states—was applied to any *marae* where 'Oro images were kept or 'Oro rites performed, whether it was a permanent land-based temple structure or, as we have seen, a canoe converted to that purpose. As to the literal translation of the word— which of course may not have been its popular meaning—Henry gives it as 'Sacrifices from abroad'. (Henry 1928: 893)

When read in the light of previous entries and editorial comments (e.g., those of April 28th) Bligh's description of the ceremony requires no additional comment. Noteworthy, however, is his remark about the 'better use' having been made of the hogs provided as offerings (i.e., by giving them to him and his people rather than to the deity), and, more interesting to students of Bligh's personality, is the fact that he even *considered* that the action might have smacked of 'immorality'!

A final comment on this day's entry: Bligh recorded that Tina's wives went along in the boat that was headed for the *marae* and its ceremony. The question is, did these two females actually enter the *marae* precincts and witness the ceremony, thereby violating what has been stated to be a strict prohibition? Had they done so—which I doubt—their behavior would have constituted another example of the privilege accorded, or seized by, this imperious pair.

Friday, July 13th

Land and Sea Breezes, Calms with smart Showers of Rain in the Morning. Thermometer from 79 to 81 Degrees.

Employed completing for Sea. Got every thing up from below, roused the Cables up and Washed the Ship with boiling Water to kill Cockroaches. This was our last arduous day work to prepare the Ship for the Plants. Reeved new Yard Tackle Falls and Fore Stay Tackle Fall. Completed our Whale Boat. Hands <employed> making Hay. Dryed Sails.

An apparent <Any appearance of> regret at out <intended> departure is only Visible in the Otoo Family, particularly my Friend Tynah and his Wife Iddeeah—with them it is very evidently sincere. Some others express sorrow; «it is» however «very remarkable to me» the indifference with which the general run of People treat us <is very remarkable>, notwithstanding they all say there will be great sorrow <grief> at our departure. The great proof of indifference is the <that> very few People «who» come about us, and the few attachments that the Natives have formed <that the Natives have formed few attachments> with any of my People. Hitherto I have been accustomed to see them show great concern at parting, and load their Friends with presents of every thing they thought would be desireable to them, but now there is <they offer> nothing remarkable. I can only compare them to some of our English Folks, who ask their Friends to remain in their House, when they wish them out of it; there are many however who seem interested in our well doing. [The last phrase appears also in ML but has been crossed out.]

Tobin's view of the natives' sentiments differs markedly from Bligh's, as will be seen in the following day's entry: was it based on his own cheerier outlook, or on the nature of his own relationships with them?

Saturday, July 14th

Light Westerly Airs and Calms with some smart Showers of Rain. Thermometer from 76 to 82 Degrees.

I began to day to take on board my Plants, received 689 Pots, [marginal note: 'Large Pots 459, Small Ditto 230'] most of which have two Plants in them. Scraped and Greased the Top Masts and brought most of our Articles from the Shore.

>*Abundant Supplies.*
>
>*Our Visitors were numerous to day, and the Seamens Tyo's brought them articles of provisions for their Sea Store. My Friend Tynah and his Wives brought me an abundance of Breadfruit, Plantains, Mahie, Cocoa Nutts and three very fine Hogs. The distress of Tynah and Ideeah at my leaving them is very great but Wyerreddee cares little about us. Poor Tynah is disconsolate at not going with me, altho I have engaged to take his Man, and promised to ask permition of King George for him to be brought home by the first Ship that is sent out. I wish sincerely this kind Friend to us could have his wishes gratified, he deserves a great deal from us.*
>
>*Many of the Natives are desirous of going with us, and have asked their Friends to shut them up in their Chests, and in Casks.*
>
>*Some of the Matilda's People have absented themselves with an intention of staying behind. It <This> gives me no concern but <except> for the injury <I am apprehensive> they may do our Friends by Joining adverse Chiefs.*
>
>*My fatigue to day has been considerable.*

Turning now to Tobin's record for the day:

More than half of the plants were this day embarked, and in the most healthy state, the natives assisting to convey them to the boats, yet not without heavy hearts at the thought of our departure . . . until night the two vessels were attended by canoes laden with various supplies. Hogs were so numerous that many could not be received for want of room to accommodate them. Fowls, the only kind of poultry on the Island, save a solitary gander left by Captain Vancouver a few months before, and which had become a 'pet' at Oparrey, were difficult to procure. Was more attention paid to rearing them, they would soon be abundant.

Among other articles, a quantity of Mahee, which is breadfruit made, after fermentation, into a paste, was taken on board for the stock; this kept a considerable time and was very nutritious. Besides live hogs, a quantity of pork had been salted in the manner described by Captain Cook, which was found to answer equal to any cured in the european way.

Every hour served to convince me of the unfeigned sorrow of these gentle people at our approaching separation. For my Tayo [i.e., 'Itia] I made a selection of every article likely to add to her comforts, but she unfortunately fixed her affections on a fowling piece. Fully convinced that weapons of a destructive kind should, if possible, be witheld from these naturally peaceful beings, I resisted her solicitations for a considerable time; but her heart clung to it, and she became so urgent that, I could not deny my consent any longer, provided it met with our commanders approval. This, by peseverance, she effected, and the gun was recieved with the most greedy satisfaction.

Among other trifles she was left a small portrait of her Tayo [i.e., Tobin himself] with the dates of the arrival and departure of the Providence and Assistant at its back. And here James I cannot refrain from remarking with what friendly care and reverence, a picture of Captain Cook by Webber (painted while at O'tahytey in his last voyage) was preserved by

Plate 27   The watering place, Matavai Bay
Watercolor by George Tobin

Plate 28   Aitutaki canoe
Watercolor by George Tobin

Pomaurey. Nothing I suppose could tempt this amiable chief to part with it. Much did I covet the polygraphic secret, to steal the portrait of the immortal navigator, which was said by those who knew him, to be a most striking resemblance. It has been customary for the different commanders of vessels visiting the Island to note on the back of this picture the time of their arrival and departure. Some other tablet must now be found, as visits have been so frequent, no more space is left. We were not a little hurt at only seeing the bare mention of the arrival and sailing of the Pandora, as our anxiety was great to know what steps had been taken to secure the wretched mutineers of the Bounty. In some degree we were relieved from this doubt by the communication of the Chiefs.

The mind boggles at the thought of Bligh's reaction, had he learned of Tobin's merest wish to steal the famous portrait. (It boggles, also, at the price that the portrait would now bring in an auction at Sotheby's!)

For the delectation of the reader who is also a gourmet here is Captain Cook's recipe for salting pork:

I have now some Pork on board that was salted at Ulietea [Ra'iatea], it is as well tasted and as well cured as any I ever eat, the manner we did it is thus, in the cool of the evening the Hogs were killed and dressed, then cut up the bones taken out and the Meat salted while it was yet hot, the next Morning we gave it a second Salting, packed it in a Cask and put to it a sufficient quantity of Strong Pickle, great care is to be taken that the meat be well covered with pickle other wise it will soon spoile. (Beaglehole 1961: 296)

The Great Navigator waxed even more eloquent in appreciation of native, oven-baked, fresh pork (ibid.: 422–3), but, like most European visitors found 'Mahee' (i.e., *mahi*, fermented breadfruit paste) to be 'sour and disagreable' (Beaglehole 1955: 122), which explains why, on the *Providence*, it was relegated to feeding the accompanying pigs.

Sunday, July 15th

Very Squally Weather and heavy Rain at times with the Wind at West WSW and WNW. Thermometer from 78 to 81 Degrees. Very much Surf in the Bay and Swell.
The Weather to day prevented me from getting all my Plants on board; for it was rather boisterous and very much so at Sea. We however got off two Pots of Avees and 246 Pots of Breadfruit. This with loosing sails to dry <and drying sails> and cleaning Ship, employed us very busily. Mahie [mahi] for Sea Store, Cocoa Nutts and Bread Fruit with a few Hogs, were our Supplies from the Natives. In the Morning I struck my Observatory and finished my Astronimical Observations.
A large Double Cannoe arrived from Oriaitaih (or Ulieteah as it is commonly called)—about 15 Men came in her, Erreeoys. They had a Shed or Hutt in the Middle of it which sheltered 6 or 8 persons. I am sure from the Sea they must have had, these Vessels make better Weather of it than we suppose it possible for them to do.

235

To a great many of the middling Rank of People I made my last presents, and to numerous of the lower Class I gave others, that they might see I remembered with kind attention their friendly behavior to us.

Tynah and the Otoo family continue to Show the greatest regret at our leaving them. No Strangers about us.

The newly arrived Arioi were evidently engaged in one of their regular activities, namely, going on tour. Even for Arioi, however, this journey was a very long one, and may have had something to do with the ceremonies concerning Tu's 'victory' over Matavai, as had been the case with the delegation from Huahine.

Monday, July 16th

Calms and Light Variable Winds with some heavy Rain. Much Swell in the Bay. Thermometer from 76 to 80 Degrees.

Employed bringing the remainder of the Plants on board and various duties in completing for Sea, which kept us at Work the whole day without intermition.

No Strangers about us but the Ulieteah Cannoe People. <To> the principal Man I made a handsome present «to». To Old Otow likewise I paid my last Gift, and made it so truly Valuable, that the poor Old Man could not refrain from shedding tears of gratitude. To the People in general who belonged to Oparre I also gave what was valuable to them, and in doing this with my attendance to give directions and see the Plants properly stowed, I suffered a vast deal of fatigue. By Night the ship was «truly» well fitted and Stowed. Besides the Cabbin I appropriated the Quarter Deck abaft the Mizen Mast and other places to the use of the Plants, which enabled me to take 756 Plants more than could be expected—a vast advantage.

Before Sun Down I embarked my Party amidst a concourse of People who <all> regretted our leaving them, particularly Otoo, the Poor Boy cryed a great deal, and would not quit hold of my hand untill I promised to see them in the Morning, which I intended to do to make him my last present. We saluted him with three Cheers, and they returned us the Compliment with great ardor. Tynah and his Wives with Oreepyah returned to the Ship for the Night. Brought on board the Whale Boat in good order.

And from Tobin:

Accompanied by a vast concourse of natives, our Commandant of the Post, with Pearce and his marines, in the afternoon marched to Point Venus, where boats were in readiness to embark them. When they put off from the shore, three cheers were given by the crews, and returned by the more numerous Islanders, who shed many a tear on the occasion.

Before the day closed Captain Bligh sent me to fill a few casks of water. Not a native

236

was to be seen; grief had drawn them to the other side of the Matavai. It was the first evening for more than three months that Point Venus had not been the scene of festivity and good humour. Our encampment was deserted; a flagless staff bespoke its evacuation, and great was my relief from such a cheerless spot, when I returned to my associates on board.

The ship was unmoored and launch hoisted in, the next morning. Many improvements, as well as to the other boats had been made during our stay to render them more safe in case of accident to the ship in the subsequent part of the voyage, which was by far the most perilous; and as the crew was increased one of the Matildas boats was taken on board. [Marginal note: 'The boats were able to contain all the Crew in case of Shipwreck.']

Both vessels were tumultuously crowded with natives of both sexes, heavily laden with various farewell presents for their English Tayos, who not ungrateful to the kindness of these good people, were equally liberal in return. Young Otoo was about us the whole day nearly, in his Canoe, but as usual could not be perswaded to come on board; the only instance where an unlimited confidence was not placed in us, and we were willing to attribute it to the custom of not entering [any] house but his own.

There was no Heeva or merriment in the evening. Many at sunset took their leave with a tearful eye, while others continued on board the whole night unwilling to lose the last attentions of such of our shipmates as they were attached to.

On this day Captain Bligh sent the following official communication to Portlock:

Sir

Being now ready for Sea and thus far the object of our Voyage fully completed; you are to proceed with me (as in all former cases) in our intended Route home.

Having furnished you with a Copy of my orders, and shewn you how uncertain my route will be between this and Timor, you will readily perceive what an attention is requisite to keep company, and to observe Signals as I may make to you.

Should accident separate us before I reach the Friendly Islands, I shall cruize 24 Hours for you in sight of the Islands Caow [Kao, also called Oghao] and Tofoa. I shall then pass to the North of Bligh's Islands [i.e., Fijian Islands] (of which you have a Map) and proceed round those I discovered off the New Hebrides, where, in Lat of 14 degrees 30 minutes I shall also cruize in sight of the Land 24 Hours. This is the last place of Rendezvous I can fix with any certainty, and you must observe to cruize 24 Hours at each place lest you may get there before me.

Coupang in Timor is the place I propose to complete my Water at. It is situated in 10 degrees 12 minutes S. 124 degrees 41 minutes East of Greenwich.

As the time of the Westerly Monsoon is advancing fast upon us, I with much concern give up the power of examining strange lands, but what will not detain us. I shall therefore make the Coast of Louisiade and take the most direct and effectual means to pass on to Timor with the utmost dispatch, where you may *wait for me such time as you may think advisable and do the best for his Majestys Service. I shall wait for you 8 days, and leave such directions as I may think will satisfy you how to proceed.*

Given under my Hand on board His Majestys
Ship Providence in Matavai Bay 15 July 1792
Wm. Bligh

Herewith you are furnished with
a Complete Sett of Signals both
for Ships and Boats.

Tuesday, July 17th

Light Airs from the Sea and Calms with dark heavy Clouds in the Offin. Thermometer from 75 to 79 Degrees.

By day light we had a number of Cannoes round us, and by Noon a hundred of them, which with necessary duties kept us in confusion in Unmooring Ship. The light Winds we had, and those from the Sea prevented me from getting out, I therefore steadied the Ship with a Stream Anchor after Warping further out into the Bay. Point Venus N 35 [degrees] E, West Head of Tarra S 26 [degrees] W. The River S 80 [degrees] E. Ship in 13 fathoms. Moreah from S 64 [degrees] W to S 87 [degrees] W.

I thought I had nearly done with making presents; but I had a greater throng to day than Yesterday. Most of the lower order of People, begging for something to remember me, and I rewarded them all for their good behavior. All the Otoo Family except the King were with me, but I kept back most of what I intended for them, politically.

I regretted much not being able to get to Sea, our time however was well employed in many essential things respecting the Plants. I wrote letters of my proceedings to my Lords Commissioners of the Admiralty to be taken home by the first Ships, and I wrote to Weatherheads People [i.e., of the Matilda] threatening punishment to them as Deserters, if they did not join in the interest of the Otoo family. At Night as usual Tynah with his Wives Slept on board.

Again, Bligh intercedes in Tahiti's politics. Although he knew full well the narrow limits of the Pomares' secular authority, he was also mindful of their past and present hospitality to visiting English ships—and evidently hopeful of its continuance. Tobin adds a few particulars:

Several men, late of the Matilda, now embarked for a passage home, but four or five remained by choice on the Island, one of whom was a jew convict that had come in her from Port Jackson. [See Bligh entry for July 18th] To those who remained Captain Bligh, with great consideration, addressed a letter exhorting them to peace and good conduct, but if unfortunately, after the departure of the Providence, hostilities should take place to give their Assistance to the Royal party. Old Hamminaminhay, the high priest, was charged with this letter, who, notwithstanding his confidence in our Commander, brought it to several of us to know if it was miti [maita'i] (good) which on being assured, gave him great relief.

Wednesday, July 18th

The Weather came clear to day, but we had such West and North Winds, until 3 OClock in the Afternoon we could not sail. In this interval I had the West end of the Dolphin Bank buoyed and the East part of the next bank, for the deep Water Channel as I was determined to tow out. At 4 we got under way and towed out into a fresh Sea Breeze which was blowing about 2 Miles without the Land. Assistant in Company. We carried 13 14 16 10 16 17 21 21 25 fathoms untill on a parallel with the North part of the Coast and then had no Ground at 35 fathoms. Mustered the Ship's Company.

In the Morning I went to see Old Oberreeroah as she was infirm, and to take my leave of her and Otoo. The latter was absent for a few hours, but <to> the Old Woman I made my last present «to». She showed the most affectionate regard at my taking leave, and I left her with Otow in great distress.

About 9 O'Clock Otoo came off to the Ship in a Double Cannoe, and remained along side untill Noon. He would not come on board, I therefore gave my present to him from my Boat. It consisted of Shirts, Printed Linnen, Large Axes, Knives, Hatchets, Toys, Scissors, Nails, Saws, Beads and several other articles. They were all enumerated amidst a number of People, and very gratefully received. We Parted with shaking hands, and a promise exacted from me to come again to Otaheite.

The Sea Breeze appearing without, brought off every Soul of our acquaintance. I had still numerous presents to make, and I gave them with my warmest regard and good Wishes. Tynah, Ideeah, Oreepyah, and their Servants, requested to be the last out of the ship, by which means, as it blew very strong when I got out in the Breeze, I was under the necessity to keep <of keeping> them all Night, or risk <risking> the loss of my Boat. This delighted the poor People, altho they must have suffered great inconvenience from it.

We had marks both of regret & indifference in leaving this hospitable place. This is the second time I have experienced their friendship and regard, and I have done every thing in my power to reward them. I can venture to say they are sensible of it.

During the Night it blew a hard Gale of Wind at E by S—our passengers however cared little about it. At day dawn I made up my presents for Tynah & Iddeeah and having stored them with an assortment of every article I had and Iron Work in great abundance, the whole was embarked and I ordered them to be landed at Oparre.

*From the most earnest sollicitations of our Friend Tynah, I gave
him a Musquet and 500 rounds of Powder and Shot. It was the least I could do for
him who had served us so well, particularly as his Ennemies would soon be about
him with a superior force.*

*During the absence of the Boat, we kept plying off & on. About
11 OClock she returned and was hoisted in—it continueing to blow away hard we
made Sail under Double Reefs, and at Noon [marginal note: '19 July & here Log
Account begins the 20th 12 Hours earlier than Civil Account'] Point Venus bore S
85 [degrees] E distance 6 or 7 Miles, West Head of Tarrah S 44 [degrees] E 4
Miles and the North part of Moreah N 86 degrees W. Wind at East and
Thermometer 77 Degrees. Served full allowance of Grog.*

*To my astonishment I found a Man (who had always been with
the Botanists in collecting and taking care of the Plants) secreted between Decks.
The Gale was too strong for me to beat back and land him, without much loss of
time, when every moment is of the greatest consequence to me, and I had not a
heart to make him jump over board. While I was debating in my mind what was
best to be done, the Botanists <Gardeners> told me he had been a valuable Man to
them, & would be of great use if I kept him. As this was an act of the Man's own,
I conceived he might be usefull to our Friends in Jamaica in attending the Plants,
about which he knew a great deal; and as he was an active fellow & a Towtow, I
knew the People on Shore would be satisfied with the loss of him expecting to
benefit by it in the end. I thought it not worth delaying <losing> a moments time
to land him, which might have delayed me another day, & therefore directed that he
should be under the care of the Botanists <Gardeners> to look after the Plants.*

*The Chiefs parted very affectionately with Mididdee [marginal
note: 'sometimes called Mydee or Mydeeai']—he left them & his Country without
shedding a Tear, altho a great deal attached to them all <all of them>. Tynah
desired he would see King George, & hoped that a Ship would be sent out for
him—his conversation in my Cabbin on the whole for the last quarter of an hour
«when the Boat was waiting» was like an affectionate creature who was loosing a
valuable Friend; both him however and Iddeeah, parted from us at last with only a
respectfull regard, and answered our three Cheers which were given from both Ships.
I have taken no notice of Wyerreddee as she absented herself on having disobliged Tynah.*

*There is a most worthy & disinterested Couple who live at
Oparre. They are relations to Tynah. The Man is called Morotarrah & the Woman
Toeedooah. She is remarkable for her attention to us & real grief at parting; but my
particular reason for mentioning her is, she received the Matildas People with «the»
warmest hospitality when they arrived after the loss of their Ship. She is a well
grown active Woman—her Husband is strongly infected with a scrofulous disease
about the extremities.*

The Matildas People who <whom> I have taken with me are:

John Marshall—Chief Mate	Thomas Baillie—Ditto	John Thompson—AB
Jas. Norris—Surgeon	John Smith, second—AB	Samuel Dennise—AB
Robert Atkinson—Boatswain	David Monet—AB	John Hopkins—AB
John Potts—Carpenter	Josuah Harper—AB	Stephen Regrove—AB
John Smith, first,—Boy		

Two others John Witstaff and James Gilbert are entered on board the Assistant by my order to Lieut Portlock dated 9th April 1792.

This day every person received their allowance of liquor, & <which is> to be continued as customary.

I delivered my Captain Cook's Picture before I sailed, with a memorandum on the back of the time of my arrival and Sailing, & the number of Plants I had got on board— it was however by mistake dated the 16th for my time of Sailing.

The People of the Matilda who have deserted from me after having made application to be taken home are—

James Conner	William Yaty	Andrew Cornelius Lind
James Butcher	John Williams	

A Person who I am informed was transported for life to Port Jackson & escaped in the Matilda, remains also on the Island, but I could get no further information about him, than he was a Jew [marginal note: 'called Samuel Tollend'].

I have not enterd & run the above Men on my Supernumery List as they did not appear on board, but have left letters to the Commanders of ships who may touch here stating their situation.

This day includes 36 Hours, ending at Noon, on the 19th Civil Account, when the 20th by Log account begins in my next Log.

Ships draught of Water after the Plants were on board and hove short to the last anchord—

Aft 16 feet 9 inches
forward 15 feet 9 inches
By the Stern 1 foot 0 inches

Before the Plants were taken on board the Ship was only 3 Inches by the Stern, so that the weight of them brought her down 9 Inches.

Recapitulation of Plants
Bread Fruit ———— 777 Large Pots
313 Small
35 Tubs
26 Boxes

241

Aahighyyahs or Ayyahs	4 Large Pots
['ahi'a, Eugenia malaccensis, Malay apple]	31 Small Ditto
	2 Tubs
Rattahs	18 Large Pots
[rata, also mape, Inocarpus edulis, Tahitian 'chestnut']	7 Small Ditto
Vees or Avees	8 Large Pots
[vi, Spondias dulcis, native 'mango']	17 Small Ditto
Ettow	2 Large Pots
[tou, Cordia subcordata]	2 Large Pots
Tahitian 'chestnut']	4 Small Ditto
Mattee	5 Large Pots
[mati, Ficus tinctoria]	1 Small Ditto
Oriahs	10 Large Pots
[ore'a, Musa, the 'maiden plantain']	
Peeah	7 Ditto Ditto
[pia, Tacca pinnatifida, arrowroot]	
Vayeehs	2 Ditto Ditto
[fe'i, Musa fehi, 'mountain' plantain]	
Curiosity Plants	2 Large Pots
	8 Small Ditto
	2 Tubs
Total on board of every kind	835 Large Pots
	381 Small ones
	39 Tubs
	26 Boxes
Total Packages	1281
Upon a moderate calculation we suppose the 1151 Vessels of Bread Fruit to contain	2126 Plants
Vessels containing other Fruits	472 Ditto
Ditto Ditto Curiosity Plants	36 Ditto
Total of Plants on Board	2634

Before returning to Bligh's remarks for this day, an excerpt from Tobin's will provide some picture of the nature of what some observers named, 'Bligh's Floating Garden':

If you [i.e., his brother James] refer to the 'Plan and Section' of the Garden on board the Bounty (which is among your fathers books) it will give you a more perfect knowledge of our method of stowing the plants than any thing I can say. It may however be observed that, as well as the great Cabin of the Providence both sides of the after part of her Quarter deck were fitted at

O'tahytey for the same purpose, leaving narrow gangways next to the skylight for the movements of the crew.

Tobin also provides a more colorful description of the Tahitians' reactions to the departure:

As we encreased our distance from the shore the natives reluctantly quitted us, many vainly strove to follow in their canoes, expressing their sorrow by loud and reiterated lamentations, while some who had particularly attached themselves to the vessels or the Post, were seen tearing their hair, and heedless of the pain, wounding their heads with a sharks tooth as on the death of a relation.

And now back to Bligh's entry: '. . . as his [Tina's] Ennemies would soon be about him with a superior force.' Bligh's prophesy, based as it was on his sound knowledge of Tahitian politics, proved correct—although not, perhaps, in the ways he expected.

Daedalus, the laggard storeship for Vancouver's *Discovery* and *Chatham,* anchored briefly in Matavai Bay in February 1793 but her logs recorded no information about current Tahitian politics, so that five years were to pass between the departure of Bligh and the arrival of the next Europeans to provide any record of the local political scene. These were the eighteen Englishmen, and the English wives of five of them, who were landed at Matavai on March 4th, 1797, from the Ship *Duff,* Captain James Wilson, for the purpose of establishing a Protestant mission. By the time of their arrival Tina's brother, Ari'ipaia, had died, and the connubial arrangements of both Tina and of Tu had changed. The fickle Vaiariti had forsaken Tina for one of her lower-class paramours, and Tina was living with a new 'wife', Pepiri, the daughter of a Papeuriri sub-chief. Tu, now sixteen or seventeen, was married to his first cousin, the daughter of his father's sister—while also 'given up to unnatural affections' [i.e., with young men]. (From *Transactions* of the London Missionary Society, quoted in Oliver 1974: 1291)

In comparison, the Tahitians' political life seemed unchanged and, on the surface, serene. Tina continued in active authority over Pare-Arue, and Vaetua over part of Ha'apaino'o; while in Taiarapu, Tina's youngest son, Teri'inavahoroa, continued to exert some influence, and perhaps some authority as well. Meanwhile, in Papara, Temari'i stilled reigned and ruled; and although he remained on polite terms with Tina, his close friendship with Tu, who was his nephew, led him to encourage the latter in his increasing impatience to supercede his father's secular authority over Pare-Arue—an encouragement that was powerfully assisted by the aged but still robust Ha'amanemane. With the passage of time, however, tensions mounted and the following line-up solidified: on the one side, Tina, the still-loyal 'Itia, Vaetua, and Teri'inavahoroa (now called Vehiatua); on the other, Tu, Temari'i, and Ha'amanemane. In August 1798 Temari'i was removed from the line-up through his fatal experiment with gunpowder. This however served only to increase the tension: when some aides of Tina's sent word to Temari'i's supporters that his corpse ought to be thrown into the sea rather than displayed and buried in state, Tu and Ha'amanemane rallied their forces and with the decisively threatening support of some of the musket-armed ex-*Matilda* seamen, intimidated Tina's supporters into surrender. Tina himself, who characteristically was taking the cure at Tetiaroa at the time, thereupon sent a message ceding his secular authority to Tu, so that for a while the latter was political ruler over all of Tahiti—and of Mo'orea as well, Tu having succeeded to his father's influence and authority there.

——But only for a short while. After a series of 'rebellions' Tu and his whole establishment (along with the few English missionaries still on the island) had to flee to Mo'orea, and it was not until 1815 that he gained a more substantial political authority over all of Tahiti and Mo'orea—this time in the guise of a Christian monarch, rather than as principal Vicar of 'Oro—and again with the decisive help of Europeans. (See Newbury 1961 and Oliver 1974, vol. 3)

TAHITI to ENGLAND

The journey homewards lasted twelve-and-a-half months and was in three legs: Tahiti to Timor, Timor to the West Indies (where both vessels were commandeered for five months to assist in the newly declared war against France), and the West Indies to Deptford, where both of them were de-commissioned.

The passage from Tahiti to Timor took ten weeks, two-and-one-half of them spent threading through the dangerous Torres Strait. Bligh himself doubtless measured the success of that leg of the journey in terms of the number of breadfruit plants that survived it, namely, 927 of the 1281 pots, tubs, and boxes loaded aboard at Tahiti. Others will also judge—and acclaim—it for the geographic discoveries made and charted *en route*.

The vessels kept together throughout this leg of the voyage, with the smaller and more maneuverable *Assistant* usually assigned to lead the way through waters thought to be narrow or shoaly. Remarkably, except for some damage to anchors and ground tackling, the seamanship displayed was of such excellence that none was incurred by either ship. And such had been the foresight in victualling the crowded vessels that the only serious shortage experienced was of potable water, and that because of the need to irrigate the precious cargo of plants.

It is beyond the intended scope of this book to reproduce and annotate Bligh's full Journal account of this leg of the journey. That task must await an editor better qualified than the present one in the science of marine geography and in the art of navigation. Instead, there will be presented a cursory account, with a few Journal excerpts, of the passage from Aitutaki onwards, in order to indicate the kinds of physical hazards encountered and the native islanders glimpsed. At Aitutaki, the first stop after Tahiti, the vessels remained long enough to permit a closer view of its inhabitants. Because of that, and because of the thitherto unknown nature of the Aitutakians, the observations recorded during the visit will be reproduced

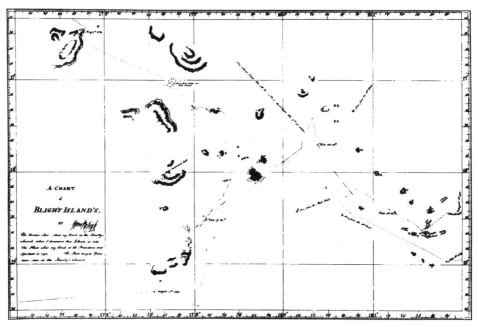

Figure 12a   Bligh's chart of the route of *Providence* through the Fiji Archipelago

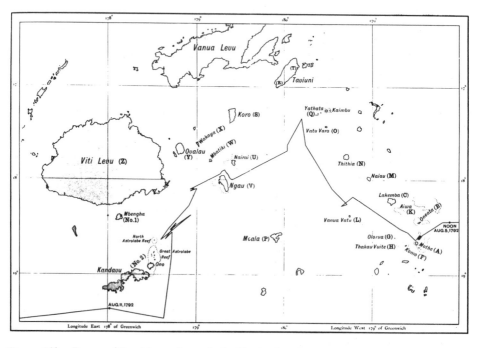

Figure 12b   Route of *Providence* through the Fiji Archipelago

more fully—but placed in an appendix, so as not to interrupt the account of the expedition's main mission, which of course was to deliver its cargo of breadfruit to the West Indies.

After leaving Aitutaki, on July 25th, the ships sailed almost directly west for eleven days, passing within sight of Savage Island (Niue) and some northern islands of the Tonga Archipelago, but too far offshore from them to see any of their inhabitants. Then, on August 5th they reached the eastern islands of the Fiji Archipelago. Some of these had been seen, in fact discovered, by Bligh during his voyage in the *Bounty* launch; others he now saw for the first time—which warrants a fuller reproduction of some of his Journal entries, in which he adopted the procedure of identifying the islands by alphabetic letters. (Figures 12a, 12b)

At 5 O'Clock [August 5th, civil time] I found a dangerous range of Breakers between the Islands A [i.e. Mothe Island] and B [Oneata] where I intended to pass, I therefore hauled in for A and found its North Shore bold too ['too' crossed out in ML] without any Anchorage, and its West side apparently shut up by a Reef which extended to other Islands F, G. and H [Komo, Olorua, and Thakau Viute] where shoals were so numerous standing on in the Night became highly dangerous; for that reason I prefered my present situation, altho not the pleasantest I could have wished for ['for' crossed out in ML]. I hailed Lieut Portlock and told him to keep in with the Island all Night with the West end of the Island bearing from South to SSE, and we preserved our station very fortunately without trouble.

A Cannoe came off to us with two Men in her, who bartered without reserve a few Coco Nutts for Toeys [hatchets] and Nails. I paid them well, and as expected, were <they came> off in the Morning with other two <two other> Men, and sold as many more Nutts, some Spears and Clubs. Two of the Men came on board and looked about them with some surprise. One of them <the Men> had his hair plaited about 4 inches long in his Neck into a number of Tails loaded with black grease, the others wore it short and lime burnt [i.e., deliberately bleached by application of powdered coral-lime]. Some of them had lost [i.e., by deliberate removal] both the little fingers as far as the second joint, and the others only of one hand [partially underlined words crossed out in ML]. They had very few marks of tattowing, one of their Ears [i.e., earlobes] was remarkably long, and had a hole in it that would have taken a large Knife for an ornament. Two others were bored in the common way. Their Beards were rough and no way trimmed, and their persons dirty. We could not understand them except in a few Words which were of the Friendly Island [i.e., Tongan] Language. I happened to mention Tongataboo [Tonga's largest Island], when they got hold of it <of which they took notice>, and I saw they were perfectly acquainted with that Land. The Cannoe has the common Outrigger, but it was on the Starboard side. It differed also in its form to any I had seen, it was open, about 2 feet wide in the middle, sharp at both ends <each end>

247

with a prow that curved a little. Their Paddles were like <those of> the Friendly Island. As I could not delay any time, I made Sail and they quitted us well satisfied with what they had got. The Spears were common for striking fish, and the Clubs were identically the same as <those of> the Friendly Island. One of the Men wore a pretty Pearl Oyster Shell at his breast.

I have no very favorable opinion of the Country, around the shore however were a great many Coco Nutt trees. On the Hills the Trees marked very Strong Winds from the East and SE. There can be no doubt of the Natives being <as> disirous as the Friendly Islanders of intercourse with us, it was remarkable their coming off in th-e Night <their coming off in the Night was remarkable>.

The Sea appeared clear to the WNW but we soon began to discover more Islands, and at Noon we had them on each side of us. A Sailing Cannoe followed us for some time, but at last seeing I would not wait for them <it> returned. The Sail was like the Friendly Island Sails, and there was a small Shed on the Cannoe and about 20 Men.

Mothe, the home of most of the natives seen by Bligh on this occasion, lies about 230 nautical miles east of the nearest island of the Tonga Archipelago. Its native residents were—still are—Fijian in language and social organization, but shared many other cultural traits with the Polynesian-speaking Tongans—partly because of an ancient common heritage and partly as the result of subsequent voyaging between the two archipelagoes.

In his previous passage through the Fiji Archipelago, in the *Bounty* launch, Bligh had entered the area a few miles south of Mothe and thereafter had kept to a fairly straight northwest course, which carried him about midway between the large islands of Viti Levu and Vanua Levu. This time, in the *Providence*, he determined to pass around the southern extreme of the archipelago, which he found to be the island of Kandavu. (Figures 12a, 12b) During this passage the vessels passed within sight of many natives, in canoes and on land, but had no close contact with any of them. Here is Bligh's description of Ngau, the Island identified by him as 'V':

Untill we advanced towards the Islands and opened the Channel fairly, it appeared full of breakers—besides what were round the Shores, there were some broken patches off the West part of U [Nairai]—every way else the passage was fair about 5 Miles wide. The Reefs were steep too <also steep>, for we could not find any bottom, and from the extreme parts of the Island they extend a long way <off>—about 2 Miles.

We ranged along the Shore of V Island [Ngau] and on its West side open to a Valley, formed by the highest lands of the Island, appeared an excellent Harbour or Bay for Ships. Another likely place was seen on the South side. It was at this time nearly dark, I was therefore obliged to give up the Idea of examing those places, and to get a little Sea room for the Night, the land extending from the WSW round by the North to the Island U—the most Southerly Land was very high and extensive to what the others were, it was called Z [Viti Levu].

At day light I made Sail to the Southward. A very high Mountain was seen on the Island Z, and from its likeness was called the Cockscomb, the whole of this Island is very Mountainous, and its SW part terminated as a very high Cape sloping towards the South. An Island lies to the Southward of it called No.1 [Mbengha].

The Island Z either joins or forms a part of the largest Islands of this Archipellego, which I passed between <between which I passed> in 1789.

As land continued to present itself in the south, I determined to sail round its Southern extremity, altho it might cost me a day to accomplish it.

The nearer we came to the Shore «of Island V» [Ngau] the more we became delighted with the Country. We sailed within a Mile of the Reef which surrounds the Shore. Inside the Reef the Water is perfectly smooth and Shoal, and some fine Sandy Beaches. There are some openings in the Reef fit for Boats. About the Reef we saw many Natives striking of [crossed out in ML] fish and tracking their Cannoes about with Poles. On the Shore the Natives were numerous. As we sailed along they followed us waving peices of White Cloth. In general they had a peice round their heads, and a Lance or Spear in their hands. Nothing could exceed the beauty of the Country at this time, it was cultivated far up into the Mountains in a regular and pretty manner. Fine Plantain Walks and Shades of Cocoa Nutt and other Trees were rendered more picturesque by the dwellings that were among them.

It was an uncommon sight in this Sea to see a well built Village on an emminence—here, was a considerable one delightfully situated on the Brow of a Hill amidst a charming Grove of Trees. Some Houses and Plantations were a considerable way up the Mountains. The Houses were all thatched round the Sides and Top with one opening or Door way. Some of them resembled those of the Friendly Islands with the Roof exceeding or overhanging the Base, and the sides <had> a great inclination outwards, so that the Floor is considerably less than the bounds of the roof. Others were something like the Sandwich Island Houses. Everything seemed to show they were <an> industrious and social People, they are notwithstanding much accustomed to War, for their signals were numerous to collect their whole force. On an elevated Hill [marginal note: 'on the North part of the Island'] where we saw a number of the Natives, two Signals were made by Flags hoisted to two detatched Cocoa Nutt Trees, no doubt to alarm the whole Island. On this Hill we could observe a well beaten Road and a Single Hutt which I thought was for the purpose of a Watch House.

They appeared very desirous to have an intercourse with us, and I regretted very much that with the Night I was obliged to relinquish it. Three

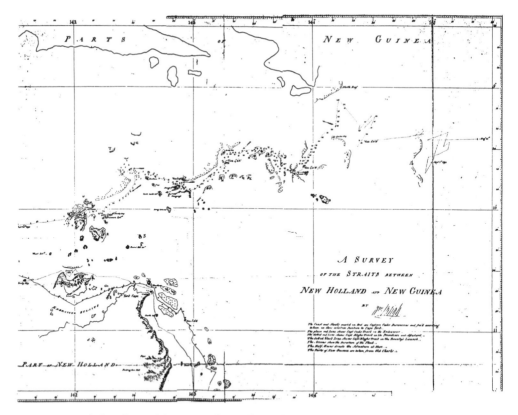

Figure 13a   Bligh's chart of the route of Providence through the Torres Strait

Cannoes came after us, but as they were too late in leaving the Shore, so they failed of coming up with the Ship. In the first Cannoe were seven Men, they were of a very dark Colour, almost a Black—their Heads bound round with White Cloth — had Pearl Oyster Shells pendant from the Neck. One Man stood in the Bow of the Cannoe holding up a Club such as I got at the last Island, and made signs for us to stop and Trade with them. Their Clothing was the common Marro, a strip of Cloth round their Hips. The colour of these Men must certainly have been artificial, for in the other Cannoes the People were rather lighter coloured than the Otaheitians. Their Hair was bushy <without any thing to confine their bushy hair>. These men also showed much desire to trade with us, and held up Cloth to induce us to stop for them. In one of the Cannoes they used a Large Paddle to scull with as the Friendly Islanders do, and without any material error I believe we may consider them to be the same kind of People.

It appeared indifferent to them on which the Outriggers were on, as I observed at the last Island. The form of the Cannoe was the same and the double Cannoe secured by Cross pieces in the common way.

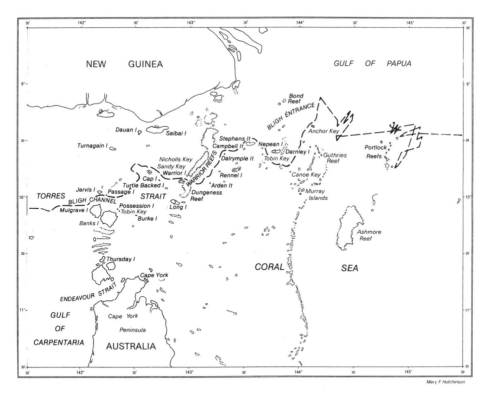

Mary F Hutchinson

Figure 13b   Route of *Providence* through the Torres Strait

At Whytootackee I observed the Natives blacked their Skin with Grease and Smut—here they certainly do the same. It is an undoubted mark of ferocity.

Etc. Etc.

After the detour around Kandavu the ships, always keeping together, headed for New Guinea and the Torres Strait. On the way they followed the *Bounty*-launch track and passed through the Banks and Torres groups of islands, without contact with any natives save for a distant view of a hundred or so on Bligh Island (Ureparepara), 'drawn up in some order as if with a design to prevent our landing.' (Entry of August 19th)

The next sighting of natives took place in the Murray Islands, at the eastern side of Torres Strait, where the vessels were cautiously feeling their way through waters strewn with small islands and shoals, and along a track, it is believed, never before travelled by a European vessel. (Figures 13a, 13b) The procedure followed was to anchor during the night-time in as safe a holding as possible, and at first light send out boats to search for west-trending channels deep enough to accommodate the ships. Here is a sample entry exemplifying the physical hazards encountered and the measures taken:

At dawn of day [September 18th] having fully informed Lieut. Portlock how to proceed, I sent two Boats on board of him with orders to Weigh and lead out between the Islands V and U. Unfortunately in weighing our Anchor, it came up with only one Arm—it appeared to have had an old flaw in it. This was a serious loss to me. I ordered the Cable to be bent to the spare Anchor, and a Buoy lashed on the broken Arm of the other.

To render the Boats of use to us we were obliged to Sail under close Reef Top Sails, for it blew so fresh they could not keep a head of us otherwise. As we advanced to the Westward passing between Black Rock and Passage Island, we saw several lofty Islands to the Southward of the opening between [islands] V and R. Soon after we discovered reefs one overlapping another—arranged of Rocky Keys to the Westward, and about the Northside of Island V, with Shoal Water from the Northermost key round to island U and Passage Island. To the North of Island U I have before remarked the probability of <their being> no Passage, I had therefore no great prospect but to creep through the way I was going. The Assistant being advanced farther on, was obliged to come to an Anchor, and the Flood Tide was running so strong that I could not beat out of the labrynth I was in, to wait untill I could explore farther with my Boats which were now making the Signals of danger in every direction. Lieut. Portlock was so situated that he feared to make the Signal for me to follow him; but as my anchoring ground was bad, and he made the Signal for good bottom where he was, and I thought the place more sheltered; I bore up, conning the Ship from the Mast Head between the Reefs. When I came near the Assistant, I found the Tide running at a fearfull rate, I therefore furled all Sails before we came to and anchored. The rapidity with which the Cable run out can only be conceived by those who have seen Ships brought up in a strong Tide; but to my horror, when the half Cable came out, it had the Dog Stopper on, which altho I cut it immediately, the Ship brought up so violently, that the Anchor came home; and by letting go a second Anchor I had it but just in my power to save the Ship from the Rocks. The Men (who were Quarter Masters) that <who> had done this Act, were no more faulty than their Officer who was in the Tier to command them. I therefore did not punish them as I could not with propriety flog him. The Master declared he had never given the order for the Stopper to be put on; and it appeared it was done to prevent too much Cable going out, that they might not have the trouble to get it in again. [All of the partially underlined words crossed out in ML]

Untill slack tide nothing could be done but to prepare <except preparing> to get the Anchors up. We were now Anchored on the North part of Island V. It has a barrier of Rocky Keys and Reefs around it, forming narrow guts of passages with Shoals all the way to Island U. The pass I thought the most elligible for us, bore W by S between some Rocky Keys not a ⅙ of a Mile across, and about 1 Mile distant from us; to examine which I ordered away two Boats with Lieutenants Guthrie and Tobin. I directed them to land on one of the Isles from whence ['from' crossed out in ML] they might be able to see the Shoals; and after examining the Anchorage to report to me by Signal, if it was good and the Passage practicable.

The Island V appeared a miserable burnt up country—it had nevertheless Wood in some places. The Rocky Keys that were about it resembled those off the Coast of Norway. Between the Northermost of those Keys and Island U is «a» space of about 3 Miles that promised a safe passage; but from our own Mast Heads it appeared so shut up with Shoals <that> I did not attempt to explore it minutely.

We saw four Cannoes lurking along shore towards the Assistant.

The Strength of Wind and Tide, with our Anchors among Rocks, made me anxiously look for Slack Water and the reports from the Boats. About 3 O'Clock the Boats made the Signal for good Anchorage. At 4 O'Clock the Tide began to slack, and by 5.20 I had both my Anchors, with the loss of one of the arms of the Best Bower, and both Cables much rubbed. The Assistant weighed without accident, and I made her Signal to lead. Lieut Portlock had his orders from me to Anchor in the first good ground he should meet with.

Lieut. Guthrie met me as I was passing the 1st narrows, about 1 Mile from our last Anchorage; and I now found we had neither good anchorage or <I found they had neither met with good anchorage nor> a convenient Channel for the Ships to pass through; on the contrary, we were in a worse situation than before. Rocks with bad bottom all round us, and a dreadfull Tide running. In the midst of all these dangers Night obliged me to Anchor with little certainty of keeping from the Rocks untill Morning. <On the return of Lieuts. Guthrie and Tobin they alledged as an excuse for their making Signal that they did not think I would have weighed, but their inexperience at sea pleaded with me as the only excuse for them, for they had express signals with them, which they should and could have made for the Ships to lie fast like they were.>

After a miserable Night day light threatened us with a Storm; but Sun rising brought more favourable Weather, and having given Lieut. Portlock his orders to lead through such pass as might appear best with the Wind we had, and sent the Boats to lead a head of him, I made the Signal to Weigh at Slack Tide. We were under Sails with a Weather Tide, and ranging along the Keys off the NW part of Island V, and Reefs on the North, in a Channel about ¾ Cable length wide, and that winding; I passed (into an open Sea) between two Keys, on the Starboard hand, and one on the larboard. No land to be seen from the South round by the West to North. There appeared foul ground on the West side of V, for we saw two large detached Rocks, one of which was about 3 Miles from the Shore.

At 9 O'Clock an hour after we were clear of the Rocks, we again fell into Shoal Water ———— [etc., etc.]

Some of the natives encountered in the Torres Strait proved to be as treacherous as the rocks and shoals. On the morning of September 5th, when he was out in a boat exploring for a safe passage, Tobin was overtaken by a large canoe:

Mr Tobin informed me he was overtaken by a Cannoe about 50 feet long with 15 Men in her—that when about 15 yards from him, they offered him a Cocoa Nutt which he refused, making signs to them to proceed to the Ship. Upon this they immediately got their Bows ready, and he saw their intention was to send some Arrows at him; in self defence therefore, he says he was obliged to fire at them, and the whole Boats Crew, 7 Men, fired into the Cannoe and no doubt did some mischief, for the poor Wretches immediately quitted them. This was the most meloncholy account I could receive, all my hopes to have a friendly intercourse with the Natives were now lost.

Bligh's pessimism was not entirely warranted, inasmuch as some peaceful bartering did take place nearby and only two days later:

At One O'Clock a Cannoe came alongside with 10 Men in her, but as the Assistant made the Signal to follow her, they had not time to <was under Sail I had not time to let them> come on board. They expressed much surprise, and seemed mortified at our getting under way, for they had been to the Assistant and traded with great fairness. Mr Tobin's battle seems to have been of no consequence. [This sentence has been crossed out in ML—perhaps after a later attack, on September 11th.]
  We found difficulty in weighing our Anchor, the ground was so good. At ½ past 3 Anchored for the Night under the lee of an Island called F [Stephen's Island], and here the Cannoe which <who> had left us came to the ship again, and traded their Bows and Arrows—Clubs and Spears, with great fairness; for large Nails and Toeyes [hatchets] which they called Toorick. They showed great surprise. Three of them came on board but could not be enticed below. They are about the Middle size, quite black and wooley headed with Beards—Stark naked—Some of them had lost several of their Teeth. Some had their foreheads daubed red—Some had a few feathers stuck in their Wool — Some had the Skin on the point of the Shoulder raised in circular Rims, that together formed a kind of Badge about the size of a Water-mans. The Septum of the Nose was pierced, in which they wore a Ring of Shell or Bone, to distend it, of ¾ Inch Diameter. The Ear was pierced in common <of all of them was pierced> . . . [etc., etc.]

Another peaceful meeting occurred two days later, but on September 11th there took place the most hostile encounter experienced during the entire expedition. The location was near the center of the strait, in the vicinity of Dungeness and Warrior islands:

We were not long under Sail before we saw the Cannoes that were about Dunganess and Island P [Warrior Island] nine in number <containing> from 8 to 20 Men in each, paddling towards the Ships. Some went towards the Assistant but the strongest party came to us, and made signs that Water and Food was to be had at Island P—a word they generally made use of was Wabbah Wabbah, pointing to their belly and holding up a Bamboo which I considered was for the use of holding Water. They expressed great astonishment at the Ship and at the Men at the Mast heads, and altho we offered them ropes they would not come alongside, but showed a distrust and design. I was just considering the amount of all these symptoms <intention of this conduct> when I saw the Assistant fire at some Cannoes, (as did our Cutter,) and alarmed me <was alarmed> by the Signal she made for assistance. It was now known the Cannoes had made an Attack, and those about us were intending to do the same. I knew mischief was done by these Wretches to our poor little Companion [i.e., the Assistant!] and some Arrows were fired at us. It was now not a time to trifle—my ships might be on Shore in a few minutes without active and careful conduct to prevent it, and it remained a serious point who were to be masters of this Neighborhood. I settled <who were to be Masters of this Neighborhood was a very important matter. I determined> it immediately by discharging two of the Quarter Deck Guns with round and Grape. The Contents of one carried destruction with it, and horrible consternation. They fled <The Natives jumped> from their Cannoes into the Sea and Swam to Windward like Porpoises. <If my situation had not been among rocks and shoals I would not have quitted them untill I had shown them we were their friends. The Assault was unprovoked.>

Three of *Assistant's* crew were wounded by the arrows—not seriously, it was thought at the time, but one of them died of his wounds a fortnight later.

Thereafter, the only perils to the ships were in the form of rocks, shoals, high winds and swift tides, until September 21st, when they emerged into the open sea—to celebrate which their companies spent the following Sunday 'without work and happy to a degree that they had passed the Reefs of New Guinea'. A week later Timor was sighted, and on October 2nd, civil time, the ships anchored in Coupang Roads to a friendly shoreside salute of fifteen guns.

The ships remained at Coupang eight days. Some of the officials who had befriended Bligh during the *Bounty*-launch visit were still there, and warmly hospitable. However, the stay was marred by the death of the seaman who had been struck by an arrow in the Torres Strait, and by the climate and the malarial setting of the place. Several crew members contracted fever and dysentry while there, and Bligh himself was ill most of the time:

During my stay here I had not a moments intermition from a violent head ach, and times slight touches of the Fever. About Mid-day my Brains felt like being in a state of boiling. From 8 in the Morning to 5 in the Afternoon I dared not expose myself to the Sun, and in that interval I suffered a great deal from the extreme heat of the land, which caused the Winds to be heated and to parch everything it blew upon. The houses too, from the Red tyling that forms the Roof, were heated like Ovens, so that Morning and Evening were the only parts of the Day at all bearable. For 7 months not a drop of Rain had fallen and perhaps not until the middle of November will the [wet] Season set in.

In contrast, his Tahitian passengers seemed pleased with the place:

Our Otaheite Friends who had hitherto seen nothing to make up to them for leaving their own Country were exceedingly delighted with the Houses and sight of Europeans, as it conveyed to them some Idea of what they were to see in England.

On the other hand, they received further practice in ethnic prejudice:

They dislike the Malay People because they had dirty mouths and black teeth [i.e., from chewing betel nut]. Seeing a few of them in Chains created some surprise, but as soon as they knew the cause [doubtless from breaking Colonial rules] they were satisfied it was just and proper.

While at Coupang the ships' botanists-gardeners collected 92 pots of plants (including mangoes, Mava plums, areca nuts, and a seed-bearing breadfruit) and the ships' supplies of water were replenished. There also Bligh learned about the shipwreck of the *Pandora*, whose 99 survivors (out of 133 crew and captive mutineers) had arrived there in September 1791. (*Pandora's* Tahiti-built shallop had parted company before the shipwreck and had sailed directly to Batavia.)

From Coupang the ships sailed without stop to St. Helena, where they arrived December 17th, 272 more containers of breadfruit having died *en route*. Another casualty was Thomas Lickman, one of the Marines and according to Bligh, 'a poor, worn-out creature' who had died 'through catching cold and from an improper use of arrack [at Coupang].'

Acting on Admiralty instructions Bligh presented several plants, including twelve breadfruit, to St. Helena's Governor and saw them safely planted. In the message to Bligh conveying their appreciation the officials expressed their 'warmest gratitude towards His Majesty [!] for his goodness and attention for the welfare of his subjects', and added, that the sight of the ships 'had raised in them an inexpressible degree of wonder and delight to contemplate a floating garden transported in luxuriance from one extremity of the world to the other.' In his Journal Bligh expressed pleasure in finding the place so English and healthful, and the women so 'fair and pretty'.

After taking on 'all needful refreshment' the ships sailed for the

West Indies and reached St. Vincent after a passage of twenty-seven days, during which another seaman, Thomas Galloway, died, reportedly from dysentery contracted at Coupang.

This visit marked Bligh's first to the West Indies since 1787, when he had been there in the merchant service in the employ of his wife's uncle, Duncan Campbell. What a change the intervening years had wrought for him! Then, one of a number of men engaged in prosaic merchant trade; now, a celebrity at the conclusion of a hazardous mission, which his West Indian hosts believed would bring considerable financial benefits to themselves. The latter expressed their appreciation in writing, in warm hospitality, and in gifts—to Bligh a piece of plate valued at one-hundred guineas, to the ships' companies fresh beef in the form of two bullocks. The visit was marred only by the loss of two more seaman: Henry Smith, who fell overboard and drowned, and John Thompson (one of the *Matilda*'s men), who deserted.

After depositing a consignment of plants (and taking on some local ones destined for Kew Gardens), the ships sailed for Jamaica. On arrival, February 4th, the rest of the plants were unloaded there and at other West Indies ports, and some local, Kew-bound ones taken on board. One of the gardeners, James Wiles, along with his Tahitian assistant, 'Jacket', were left there to transplant and tend the breadfruit.

(The ultimate destinations of the breadfruit and other plants collected at Tahiti are listed in Powell 1973.)

Departure for England was delayed by news of France's declaration of war. Both ships were assigned to the Commander of the West Indies Station, who made much use of them in convoying other British ships and in capturing those of the enemy, until June 10th, when they received orders to proceed to England. On June 17th they sailed together in convoy, and on August 7th anchored at Deptford—where on September 9th Bligh wrote the final entry in his Journal—in what must be one of the record understatements in maritime history:

This voyage has terminated with success, without accident [to the ships' hulls] or a moment's separation of the two ships. It gives the first and only satisfactory account of the pass between New Guinea and New Holland, if I except some vague accounts of Torres in 1606; other interesting discoveries will be found in it.

In Jamaica Bligh had received a letter from local officials and other beneficiaries of his expedition; it read, in part:

March 20th, 1793

Sir,

I am authorized in the name of the Committee appointed to act in the reception of the Bread Fruit and other valuable plants lately received, to assure you in their name of the *high sense they entertain of your exertions and great merit in bringing to so happy a conclusion the beneficient object of our most gracious Sovereign in this most arduous task committed to your charge.*

> I am, etc.
> Henry Shirley

Equally satisfying to Bligh must have been the scene at the termination of the ships' commission, as reported in the *Kentish Register* for September 6th, 1793:

His Majesty's ship *Providence* . . . was paid off at Woolwich. It was a scene highly gratifying to observe the cordial unanimity which prevailed amongst the officers; the decency of conduct and the healthy and respectable appearance of the seamen, after so long and perilous a voyage, not one of whom but evinced that good order and discipline had been invariably observed. The high estimation in which Captain Bligh was deservedly held by the whole crew, was conspicuous to all present. He was cheered on quitting the ship to attend the Commissioner; and at the dock-gates the men drew up and repeated the parting acclamation. (Quoted in Mackaness 1951: II 28)

Although the crew—the 'People'—in general may indeed have held their Captain in 'high estimation'—he got all but four of them home alive and in good health; the lashings he ordered had been relatively few and those well deserved; etc.—that attitude most certainly did not prevail, with 'cordial unanimity', among the officers of his ship. While those among them who recorded their opinions on this point did appear to respect Bligh's seamanship, one of them, Lieutenant Bond, became embittered, and another, Flinders, antipathetic, because of Bligh's sometimes overweening and insensible manner towards themselves. Tobin also acknowledged Bligh's shortcomings in this respect but, characteristically, was more tolerant of them (for example, in his letter to Francis Bond of December 1817, reproduced in Mackaness 1949: 32–3).

Nor was the crew's 'acclimation' echoed throughout the nation (as had been the case after Bligh's return from the *Bounty* voyage). Shortly after his arrival home the Royal Society awarded him its Gold Medal, and in due course elected him a Fellow (for 'distinguished services' in navigation, botany, etc.), but elsewhere he was coolly treated or ignored. For one thing, the general public of a nation at war with an adversary only twenty-five miles away had no interest in the charting of a passage through a strait on the other side of the world. And as such things often go, the transplanting of the breadfruit was credited by the general public more to the famous Sir Joseph Banks, who had promoted the expedition, than to the man who had carried it out. More crucial for Bligh, however, was the coolness he experienced at the Admirality. For example, the then First Lord granted an audience to Lt. Portlock long before one was permitted the waiting Bligh, and it was not until April 1795 that Bligh received his next—and not very important—command. That coolness, near to hostility in some naval circles, had been incited mainly by influential relatives of two of the *Bounty* mutineers—of Fletcher Christian and of the convicted but then pardoned Peter Heywood. And it was for a while chilling enough to delay promotions also to the young officers who had accompanied Bligh on the *Providence*. (As Tobin wrote in his private Journal: 'It is hard of belief that this [hostility towards Bligh's alleged behavior during the *Bounty* voyage] could have extended to the officers of the *succeeding* voyage. Yet we certainly thought ourselves rather in the 'back ground'.') In the case of Bond, his next promotion did not take place until 1800—eighteen years after becoming a lieutenant. (He eventually lived down the association, however, and rose to the rank of rear-admiral.) Tobin's rise was also slow; despite the 'interest' of Lord Nelson, and a very active period of hard-fought naval actions, he did not 'make' post-captain until 1802.

During the years immediately following the *Providence* voyage Flinders fared somewhat better than Tobin and Bond. And then, in 1795 he sailed to Australia and embarked on a career of maritime exploration and mapping that was to win him immortal fame—though few earthly rewards.

Portlock also fared better than Bond and Tobin in the years immediately after the Tahiti voyage (perhaps because of having been on the *Assistant*, and not the *Providence*?). He was promoted to the rank of commander shortly after his return to England and saw much action in the war, but his later naval career was plagued, and retarded, by ill health.

As for *Providence*'s Second Lieutenant, James Guthrie, he disappeared into the anonymity from which he had in 1790 emerged, there being no official records of any promotions after service on the *Providence*, nor of the date of his death. (Personal communication of February 17th, 1987, from C. J. Ware, National Maritime Museum, Greenwich)

More happens to be known about the fates of the Tahitians, who had left their homeland for an enticing new life. Alas, neither of them was to survive very long. 'Jacket', the one who had remained in Jamaica to assist Gardener Wiles, died after only a short stay. And of his compatriot Maititi, Tobin recorded: 'a british grave recieved him . . . a few short weeks after setting his foot on a british shore [i.e., in England].'

Returning to Bligh himself, while the stigma implied in his widely employed nickname, 'Bounty Bastard Bligh', remained with him to the end, he doggedly—and often valiantly—pursued a career in Government service, including several naval battles and the governorship of New South Wales, until, as a retired vice-admiral, he died in London in 1817.

As for the plants of breadfruit delivered to the West Indies, after so much time and effort and privation (some of it fatal) by so many men, they adapted exceedingly well to their new localities. And, according to a study carried out in the 1960s:

Though at first the inhabitants of [the British West Indies] were slow in acquiring a taste for the fruit, it has long since become an integral part of their diet. It is absolutely relied upon in rural areas, where breadfruit, in its season, is eaten three times a day. (Powell 1973: 7)

Appendix
Aitutaki

At 4:30 p.m. on July 24th (civil time) 1792, six days after leaving Tahiti, *Assistant* signalled the sighting of Aitutaki (Bligh's 'Whytootackee') bearing SW by ½ W, distant 4 or 5 leagues. During the following 24 ½ hours the two ships remained in the vicinity of the island and the voyagers experienced a close and friendly contact with some of its natives—the last of its kind they were to enjoy before reaching Timor. This was Bligh's second glimpse of the island; the first occurred on April 11th 1789, six and a half days out of Tahiti and seventeen before the *Bounty* Mutiny. In fact, Bligh is credited with its 'discovery,' *Bounty* having been the first known European vessel to sight the island. Bligh's remarks regarding that first visit will provide a background to those written in 1792:

I had little reason to expect any New Discovery, as my Track, altho not traversed by any one before, yet was bordering so near on others, that I scarce thought it probable to meet any land. At daylight however we discovered an Island of a Moderate height with a round Conical Hill towards its northern extreme. The N.W. part made in a perpendicular head, but the S.E. slopes off to a point. As I advanced towards it, a Number of Small Keys were seen from the Mast head lying to the S.E., and at Noon could Count nine of them. They were all covered with Trees, and the large island had a most fruitful Appearance. The Shore was bordered with Flat land, with innumerable Cocoa Nutt and other Trees, and the higher Grounds were beautifully interspersed with Lawns. I could not get near the Shore on account of the Wind, nevertheless there appeared broken Water between all the Keys, and I am inclined to think they are all joined by a Reef. I saw no Smoke or any sign of Inhabitants, it is scarcely to be imagined however that so charming a little spot is without them.

I became more anxious this Afternoon to determine the limits of this Land then I had before considered it worthy of my attention, for I found it highly dangerous to any Ships that might come this Way both from the Low Keys lying to the S.S.E. of the Main Island and a Reef which I saw extending considerably to the Westward with a Small Key on it, which was conspicuous to us from a few Cocoa Nut Trees, whose tops only appeared above the horizon. I therefore determined keeping the Land on the N.W. during the Night and to wait the event of another day, which without any predetermination the Wind and Weather would have made me do the same thing. It was noon before I drew in with the Islands again, when I had all but the Wester[mos]t Key nearly under the extent of the large Island, so that the extremes were Westermost Key and Eastermost part of the Great Island, which, as the bearings express, only extended 19 degrees. A prodigious Surf broke on every part within our view.

By my protracted bearings I find my course and distance since Yesterday Noon to be S.S.W. 5 ½ Miles which gives 2 Miles in Long[itu]de. The Time Keeper gives One Mile, and the D.R. 8 Miles; this trifling difference is therefore more likely to be the error in calculation than in any Current.

As I drew nearer to the Southermost Key I discovered from aloft that there were a number of Natives within the Reefs, but as the Sea broke dreadfully round them I imagined none were capable of getting through it to come out to us, let their inclination have been ever so Strong. I was however agreeably surprized by a Visit from four Men in a Single Cannoe. They paddled Straight for the Ship without making a Single Stop untill they were alongside, when without any kind of fear or astonishment, after receiving a few Beads from me, they came into the Ship. One Man seemed to have some ascendency over the Others, and him only had the Curiosity to look a little about the Ship, but none of them would go below. My People had just been to dinner and had left some of their fresh Pork in a Bowl, which was given to them on being asked for, and they eat it Voraciously with some boiled Plantains. Two of the Men had each a large Mother of Pearl Shell hung at their breasts, pendant from the Neck by plaited human Hair. On being told I was the Erree, the principal person immediately came and joined Noses with me, and presented me his Shell and tyed it round my Neck, and now being perfectly reconciled to their situation, they Seated themselves, and I had time to endeavor to make enquiries, which as their language was in some degree like Otaheite I got this information.

They called the Island Whytootackee and the Eree, Lomack Kaiah. They said they had no Hogs, Dogs or Goats upon the Island neither had they Yams or Tarro, but Plantains, Vees, Fowls and Breadfruit they said were in great abundance, and also Cocoa Nutts. As All that I have mentioned was in their View there could be no mistake between us, I had also a Pompion [pumpkin] hanging up, and they immediately called it Oomarra ['umara], which is the Ulietea [Ra'iatean] name for it, but the Otaheitans called it Enoah [noha]. [Note: 'umara, or its cognate forms, is the word for 'sweet potato' throughout this part of Polynesia; Bligh evidently was mistaken in thinking that the Ra'iateans applied the name to the local 'pumpkin'. D.O.]

Notwithstanding they said there were no Hogs, Yams or Tarro, they called them by Name, and I am rather Inclined to beleive they were imposing upon me. I nevertheless thought it my duty, As I could do it conveniently, to supply them with those Articles, and I therefore Ordered a fine Young Boar and Sow into their Cannoe, with some Yams and Tarro. I also gave each of them a knife and a fine Toey [hatchet], some Nails, Beads and also a Looking Glass; the latter they handled and examined as a Monkey would do, but Nails and Toeys they were acquainted with and call them Aouree [Tahitian: auri], which is the common [Tahitian] Name for Iron.

When I have given my present to the different Men, they were preparing to leave us, and the Cheif of the Cannoe took possession of everything I had given to the others; one of them only, showed any signs of disatisfaction, they however joined Noses, and were reconciled. As the evening was coming on I became desirous for them to leave the Ship, but to my astonishment two out of the four were [wished] to remain on board for the Night, and the others were to come for them in the Morning. I would have treated their confidence with the utmost gratitude and regard, but it was impossible to say how far it might be in my power to land them in the Morning without subjecting myself to accidents and delay, and as to the punctuality of their friends coming for them, it was by no means absolutely certain; I therefore desired them to go into the Cannoe; which they did reluctantly and left us. They were also solicitous for some of us to go on shore with them.

These People are just the same as those of Hervey Isles, in their appearance at first sight, but they are certainly more docile and inoffensive. They were fishermen who had been upon the Reefs, their complexion therefore being very dark, and their persons very Meagre, made them perhaps not a true sample of their Countrymen. They had naturally strong black Hair which they wore loose about the Neck, but from the extreme heat of the Sun and the Salt Water, (like all fishermen) great part of it was turned of a brown or reddish Colour. The Cheif of the Cannoe was tatowed on the Thighs and the Legs, with four small Strakes across the Upper Arms, something like a Spear, the others had the same Strakes across the hollow of the Knee, but neither were marked on the posteriors as the Otaheiteans. They wore a Marro like most other Islanders and had besides some Cloth [bark-cloth] and Matt like those of the Friendly Islands [Tonga] which was wrapt round their middle. They had one Spear in the Cannoe, which they gave me; it was a common Pole pointed with the hard Toa Wood. Not a Single Article besides had they in their Cannoe, not even a Cocoa Nutt or a Gourd of Water. The Cannoe was made of One Peice of Timber with the common outrigger. The Stern had a small elevation, and round the Gunwale long poles were lashed to Strengthen the Upper part of the Cannoe. The head was no way remarkable or was their Paddles materialy different from most others.

I could not discover if they had any knowledge of Hervey Islands [Manuae and Te Auotu], but I think there is little doubt of it, as from them only could they have got a knowledge of Iron. The distance between those Islands is 54 Miles in the direction S. 67 E. and N. 67 W. Should this Island be without such essential articles as I have already mentioned, it would be of little avail for any ship to stop at it, but I am doubtfull of the information I received, and as the Natives are disposed to trade and will be more so, a Ship coming this way may make it worth her while to stop a day or two with them under the West side of the Island. Could Anchorage be found it would be one of the most desireable little Spots in the South Sea, but within the Keys it is all Shoal Water & without not fathomable.

This Island which the Natives call Whytootackee is about 10 Miles in Circuit; its North part lies in Lat. 18 [degrees] 50 minutes S, and its South end in 18 [degrees] 54 minutes S. Eight Sm[al]l Islands or Keys lie off to the S.S.E. of it and one to the W.S.W. The Southermost lies from a Round Hill on the N. part of the Island S. 30 E. by Compass 7 Miles, and is in Lat. 18 [degrees] 58 minutes S. The Isld itself is not above 2½ Miles from E. to W., but the Reef and Keys to the Southd of it extends 8 Miles. Every Key was covered with Trees among which, as well as on the large Island, were many that from their peculiar branches I supposed to be the Toa. The Beaches were Brilliantly White. The Long[itude] of the Hill on the North part of the Isld is by the Time Keeper 200 [degrees] 19 minutes E. and by my Account 199 [degrees] 48 minutes E. and the Variation of the Compass may be considered to be 8 [degrees] 14 minutes E.

The Language of these Islanders, altho at first in conversation [it] did not appear to be like the Society Islands, Yet many of their Words may be said to be identically the Same, and in any respect [does] not differ more from the Otaheiteans than the Uleitea [Ra'itea] or Huheine [Huahine] People do. (Bligh 1937: II 94–6)

Bligh overestimated somewhat the overall dimensions of the island but his fix for its location was remarkably close. And, as he wrote, the natives of Aitutaki were virtually identical in physical type with those of the nearby Hervey Islands, whom he had seen during the visit of *Discovery* and *Resolution* in 1777. Moreover, he was correct in his judgment about the close similarity of the Aitutakians' language to that of the Tahitians.—But let us proceed with his observations and opinions of 1792:

I determined to take a look at Whytootackee not only to endeavour to gain some information <not only> respecting the proceedings of the Pandora, but <also> of the Bounty—to ascertain its exact situation, and to examine the West side of it for Anchorage. I went round the East and SW part of it when I first discovered the Island in the Bounty.

The land is remarkable by a round Hill which lies near the northermost extremity, and it is of a very conspicuous height [i.e., 450 feet].

After a boisterous Night I bore away, and having passed the NE side of the Island we hauled round the North end, and kept working under the lee of the land trying for Anchorage which we did not find, having sounded with 140 fathoms of line without striking the bottom. From the North point the land inclines first SW by S (by Compass) then S ¾ W, and from the Westermost point SE by S to the South point of the Island.

What I have to remark new on the Geography of this land is, that for an extent of 3 Miles on the West side is <there> perfect <perfectly> good shelter for a Ship under Sail. The border round the Shore is a steep reef at a small distance from the Beach, where I believe in moderate weather our ['our' deleted in ML] Boats may land with safety. The Assistant sounded with 180 fathoms of line about ½ Cables length from the Breakers but could get no bottom.

My Sketch of the Island [Figure 14] will give a just Idea of it. It is remarkable that I made the Longitude of the round Hill in my last Voyage to be 200 [degrees] 19 minutes E by my T[ime] Keeper and this time from a mean of my three Time Keepers 200 [degrees] 17 minutes E, from whence I conclude that

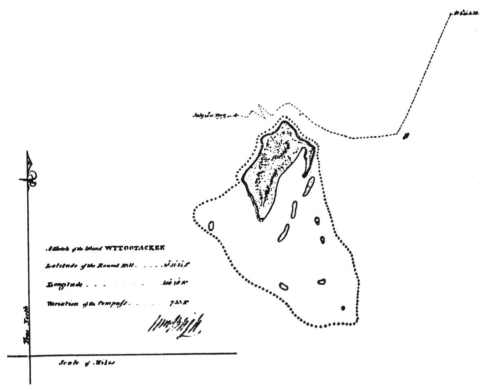

Figure 14   Bligh's map of Aitutaki

200 [degrees] 18 minutes E is very near the truth after so short a run from Otaheite. My situation with respect to latitude is the same, and [in?] every nautical remark, I shall therefore conclude my discription as I did then.

This Island which the Natives call Whytootackee is 10 Miles in Circuit its north part lies in 18 [degrees] 50 minutes S and its South end 18 [degrees] 54 minutes S. Eight small Keys (or Quays) lie off to the SSE of it and one to the WSW. The Southermost lies from round Hill S 30 [degrees] E by Compass 7 Miles and is in latitude 18 [degrees] 58 minutes S. The Island itself is not above 2½ Miles from East to West but the limits of the Reef that surrounds it are nine Miles from North to South, and about 7 from East to West.

It is beautifully clothed with Wood, and exceeds any place, I ever saw, in Cocoa Nut Trees. A great number of them on the East side are without their branches, and even to leeward many of them were in the same state, I therefore apprehend the Island is subject to severe Storms of Wind.

We had no sooner got round the north end of the island than we observed several Hutts on the Shore, and the Natives about their Cannoes. As soon as we were well under the lee of the Shore they launched through the Surf and came

265

off to us. As the Assistant was able to keep nearest the Shore, the [in ML 'the' is crossed out] most of the Cannoes went to her: three came alongside of us, and I made presents to them <the People> of Beads and Iron Work, for which they gave a few worthless Spears and Breastplates. They had not a Cocoa Nut or any article of food with them, some Cocoa Nutts however were carried on board the Assistant. They were confident of our good intentions towards them, and instead of any look of surprise and astonishment, it was <expressed> rather complacency and admiration. They asked for Togee Nooee [to'e nui?], which is the New Zeland name for a large Hatchet or Toeey—a great part of their language was Otaheitean, yet the two Men [i.e., Tahitians] I have with me did not understand them so readily as I did myself. On the whole I was satisfied in my enquiries. They said no White person had been or was on the Island. That they had seen three Ships or Vessels—They named Brittanee and Otaheite very distinctly, and spoke of a Person who <whom> they called Oheedidee [HitiHiti]. They called the Island Whytootackee, and named particularly Comackkaiah, and Tongawarre, as Erees of the Island. They knew all our plants, and called the Breadfruit Cooroo [kuru; Tahitian 'uru] and Pork Boackah [Tahitian pua'a], the latter is a Friendly Island [Tongan] name—taking their expression literally it was to be <I> understood they had no Hogs on shore, but I suspect they meant to say they were scarce. Fowls were in abundance. The Scraps of Cloth [barkcloth] they brought off with them was <were> of the Friendly Island kind. The Men were above the middle size—had very good regular features—were fleshey, and <showed> no mark of a want of food. Their Heads covered with strong black Hair were very lousy, and I observed that some of them had had their faces smutted, the remains of it being evident about the Eye brows and under the Throat. Their dress was only a marro [loin cloth], and the Pearl Shell pendant from the neck by plaited human Hair. Their Colour is darker than an Otaheitean. They spoke of their Women [marginal note: 'called Evahini [vahine] same as at Taheiti'] lasciviously, some of them were in the Cannoes that went alongside the Assistant. The Men were tattowed on the Legs, Thighs and Arms. The Legs & Thighs of two Men were <so> fully tinctured as to loose their natural colour of th Skin. In all I observed about 15 Cannoes, some of them might have had 20 Men, I distinctly counted 15 & 9, & 11 in others. Some of the Cannoes had high black feathered ornaments at the Sterns. Within the Reef they were managed by setting Poles [i.e., by poleing]—those that were alongside of us were hallowed out of the trunk of the Breadfruit tree without any acarf or piece, except in the length, to increase which, they injudiciously join the ends of one piece of hallowed Trunk to the end of the other, by sewing as it may be called, without forming a Scarf to strengthen it, perhaps to make up for this, is <to make up for this is perhaps> the reason for their supporting the Gunwales by long Poles being ['being' crossed out in ML] lashed along the edge. The Outriggers are common, and, like all I have seen, on the larboard side. I saw not any with Sails.

The dwellings or Hutts on the Beach were only shelter for Fishermen, they were made like the common Sheds at Otaheite, but I saw some lofty Houses under and among the Cocoa Nutt Trees that had the exact form of those among the Sandwich Islands—they looked like Hay Stacks.

I do not think we saw above four hundred persons including every person we could discover with our Glasses.

It blew so violently that the Natives showed some apprehension of being drifted off the land, but notwithstanding this, two Men wished to stay with us, and others gave our Otaheite Men an invitation to go on Shore, for which with much incivility they laughed at them. On my looking at the scrap of Cloth that one of them had in his hand he conceived I wanted it, and with an apology gave it in a manner which delighted me—'Terah airaddee no te tye'—Take it - you are wellcome, but it is wet with the Sea.

Here was no sign of any Wreck about the Coast. It is clear that the Pandora was here, as I am confident of their description of Oheediddee the Otaheitean who sailed with Capt. Edwards [partially underlined words crossed out through in ML]. His Shallop probably made <was> the 2nd Vessel, the Natives spoke of, and as to the 3rd I fear they allude to my touching there in the Bounty—but for this I should flatter myself Capt. Edwards had taken her.

One of the Natives who came on board had a very ulcerous Throat and Neck, evidently the same disease as the people of Otaheite are subject to.

At 5 O'Clock in the Evening I bore away in a hard Gale of Wind, regretting very much I could have no further intercourse.

Besides the Breast Plates and Spears, I got some Fish Hooks like the Taheite Mattow, made of Turtle Shell, the line was made of Cocoa Nutt husk, also a Stone Adz or Ettoey, the Edge of which was circular like a Gouge.

In contrast to Tahiti, almost nothing was recorded by the earliest European visitors about the indigenous culture of the Aitutakians. Between Bligh's two visits H.M.S. *Pandora* spent one day there *en route* home with the *Bounty* people captured at Tahiti, but her officers recorded even less about the island than did those of *Providence* and *Assistant* After that, other European vessels doubtless called there briefly from time to time but the island's lack of accessible anchorages discouraged longer visits. In fact, close and continuous contact commenced only in 1821 when the English missionary, John Williams, stationed two Tahitian mission teachers there. Those and subsequent agents of the London Missionary Society succeeded quickly in transforming many aspects of the indigenous culture, but evidently had little or no interest in recording for posterity the nature of the 'heathen' institutions they helped to replace. Because of the similarity of the Aitutakians' language to those of nearby islands, such as Rarotonga, and even Tahiti, it is plausible to *infer* that they resembled them closely in many other cultural respects as well, including social organization and religion. But the only information recorded about the indigenous culture of Aitutaki itself comprises a few of their oral traditions (Low 1934–35), a description of some of their tattoo patterns (Gudgeon 1905), and a catalogue of their modern-day, but to some extent 'indigenous' arts and crafts (Buck 1927). Thus, Bligh's few and brief ethnographic remarks will be annotated below as the unconnected and non-contextualized fragments that they are, and in the order that he wrote them, beginning with: 'a few worthless Spears and Breastplates'.

Even the normally curious and voluble Tobin disposed of the Aitutakians' bartered artifacts in a few off-hand words:

Nails and toeys [hatchets] were received with great satisfaction by them, for which they exchanged their only ornament, a pearl shell hung to a collar of human hair plaited and worn about the neck. Besides this article they disposed of some spears, the end part jagged and formed of a hard, dark-coloured wood. Their spears, I am inclined to think, are only used as an implement for fishing. There was besides in one of the canoes a club not unlike (though shorter) some we had procured at Otaheite which had been brought from Toubouai, an island to the southward.

George Hamilton, surgeon of the *Pandora* (which had called at Aitutaki on May 19th, 1791) had a better opinion of these artifacts:

Here we purchased from the natives a spear of most exquisite workmanship. It was nine feet long, and cut in the form of a Gothic spire, all its ornaments being executed in a kind of alto relievo; which, from the slow progress they made with stone tools, must have been the labour of a man's whole life . . .

. . . the men [wear] a gorget of the exact shape and size as at present wore by officers in our service. [*gorget*, 'A piece of armour for the throat. A gilt crescent-shaped badge suspended from the neck, and hanging on the breast, formerly worn by officers on duty.' O.E.D.] It is made of the pearl oyster-shell. The centre is black, and the transparent part of the shell is left as an edge or border to it, which gives it a very fine effect. It is slung round the neck with a band of human hair, or the fibres of cocoa nut-shell, of admirable texture, and a rose worked at each corner of the gorget, the same as the military jemmy of the present day. (Thomson 1915: 123) [*jemmy*, 'spruce, neat, smart; neatly made (also foppish)' O.E.D.]

It would appear that Bligh's interest in 'natives', including their artifacts and customs, had become almost exhausted upon leaving Tahiti, when that interest had been encouraged by the bearing such matters had upon his mission. Or perhaps he was simply weary, or bent on discovering news of the *Bounty*, or intent on getting his precious breadfruit to their destination. In any case, the worthy Portlock showed much more interest—albeit unpunctuated!—in trading with the Aitutakians (and of course was in contact with more of them than were Bligh and Tobin, who were anchored farther offshore):

The Natives thick along the Beaches and several canoes [paddling] along shore within the Reef

*and soon after came out three of their canoes along side the Assistant without any [solicitance?]
and one went along side the Providence, in one of the Canoes that came along side the Assistant
there appeared to be three men of some note, and one of them I take to be a priest, as he had
in each hand a piece of white cloth and a Branch of the Cocoanutt tree made up something like
the Otaheitian Bonnets which he handed into me. I received and considered them as a token
of Peace and friendship and the man that I suppose to be the Priest before and after I had recd
the present repeated a number of words which I suppose to be a prayer. I made him a suitable
return and several of them came immediately into the ship and made use of the Common South
sea mode of saluting us (that is by joining noses) a very [friendly?] trade now commenced and
for our Nails Towes [hatchets] Beads Rings etc (which they seemed exceedingly fond of) they
parted with every thing they had in their canoes and indeed some of them almost stript themselves of all their cloth and threw it into the ship without any return being expected, but I made
a point of rewarding their liberallity by giving them some large towes and spike nails which
delighted them exceedingly. The articles of Provisions which they brought of were Plantains and
Cocoanutts and I saw a piece of dressed Bread Fruit in one canoe. The other things that I procured from them were some small Pieces of Cloath small mats 4 Paddles and 5 spears and three
Gorgets. Their cloth is much like that of the Friendly Islands, being stout and some of it very
prettily glazed and printed in a very regular manner red black and white in [nearly?] small
squares, their matts are small and coarsely made but wrote [wrought?] with more taste than
the Otaheitian mats as they are wrote with different colour rushes which had a very pretty
effect. Their Paddles are about the common size which is about 5' 7ins long and 9 inches broad
very neatly made and pains taken to ornament them, on one side the Blade nearly at the Grasp
is some very neat work cut out like Cornish work and on the other side just above the Point of
the Paddle is a ridge off about ½ an inch above the Surface of the Blade and besides those ornaments they take much pains in staining them with a kind of Black dye, not in general but in
variety as their fancy may direct, their Spears are about 12 feet long thick in proportion some
of them made of the hard Towa wood [toa, Casuarina equisetifolia, iron wood] and very
much barbed [over?] the Point others made of the Burou tree [purao, Hibiscus tiliaceus]
and headed with the Towa wood and one I got was Pointed with two pieces of the Stingarays
tail and must be a very dangerous weapon. I also got one weapon of about 8 feet [long?] made
of the Towa tree and shaped like an officers spontoon ['spontoon, a species of half-pike or hal-
berd carried by infantry officers in the 18th century', O.E.D.] their gorgets which are suspended from the neck with a wreath of human hair hangs just below the chin (and wether for
ornament or service I cannot justly say, but am rather inclined to think for both, as it no doubt
looks very well and may [in case time?] of Battle fend of a Blow from a Spear) is made of a
single large Pearl shell of about 6 inches diameter worked by some means very smooth and
beautifull. I also procured another ornament which they wear about the Neck or head, this consists of what I call the Palm nutt strung upon a beautiful Pink coloured rush. I am inclind to
think the rush is staind others think not.*

Returning to the less admiring (but more grammatical) remarks of
Bligh: 'a great part of their language was Otaheitean, yet the two Men [i.e.,
Tahitians] I have with me did not understand them so readily as I did myself.'
The language was indeed very close to Tahitian (about as close as, say, Danish

to Swedish) and the circumstance that the Tahitians did not 'understand' it may be attributed to their native parochialism, or to their deliberate wish to distance themselves from these unsophisticates (for example, Bligh's statement, '[some Aitutakians] gave our Otaheite Men an invitation to go on Shore, for which with much incivility they laughed at them'). In Portlock's opinion: 'Their language is I rather think more like the New Zeland than the Otaheitian and the manner of speaking, quicker than the Otaheitian and by no means so soft and pleasant. They ask for a hatchet by the same name that the Newzelanders do, that is Togey however any person that understand well the one language may likewise understand most of the others.' —An accurate statement, on all counts.

——'[The Aitutakians] spoke of a person whom they called Oheedidee.' This statement of Bligh's is a puzzle. HitiHiti had left the *Pandora* before the vessel visited Aitutaki, and although he had been aboard the *Resolution* when Cook sighted the nearby Hervey Islands, in 1773, there had been no direct contact with any Hervey Islanders on the occasion. In 1777 both *Resolution* and *Discovery* called there, and this time their ships' companies made contact with the inhabitants, who perhaps then learned of the existence of HitiHiti from the accompanying Omai, and passed that information to the Aitutakians.

——'no Hogs on shore': Bligh was correct in his conclusion; the Aitutakians did possess pigs and they may indeed have been scarce.

——'Their Colour is darker than an Otaheitean' etc: Portlock gives a fuller description of them:

The People we saw are in general above the Common height and remarkably well and strong made and have something of the wild look of the New Zelander about them . . . The men of this Island appear to have good manly countenances are rather above than below the Common height and are in general very stout strong made men. Their hair some have short and others very long and in general black some few we observe with light or redish coloured hair this I suppose proceeds from their hair being staind by a kind of clay [or perhaps lime?] pasted on it a practice common amongst the Friendly and Sandwich Islands. Some of the oldest men I observd had long beards but in general the men appeard to have been close shaved by shells or other means and several had their faces painted intirely black. I think it appeard as if daubd over with sut . . . [They] are tatowd about the legs arms and bodys but none of them that we saw had their posteriors tatowd as is the Custom at Otaheite, Mr Franklin observd to me that he saw a man cut upon the arm as is the manner of the Natives of Africa [i.e., artificially scarified] but I did not see it myself and am rather inclined to think as it does not appear general to think that those marks he saw must have been the Effect of accident, in one of the Canoes that came along side were three women each I should [judge?] upwards of thirty years of age very stout poorly clad and by no means desirable one of them had lost an eye and had scarcely cloth enough on to cover her waist, however they were very cheerfull and seemed highly delighted with a sight of the ships. One of my officers says that [he] observed the women were as tatowd as much about the legs as the men were. I did not notice this myself.

——'Cannoes': Bligh's description of the ones he saw tallies well with the types still in use in 1926, including the 'injudicious' manner of joining the hull segments. (Plate 28) Although he saw none, sails were doubtless in use, probably rectangular ones of pandanus matting. Bligh evidently judged the Aitutakian canoes to be so inferior to those of Tahiti as to warrant few words about them; Portlock, who saw more of them close-to, was more favorably impressed:

The Canoes of this little spot are of the double and single kind more numerous than might be supposed from the size of the Island. I think we saw upwards of a Dozen none carrying less than 5 Men the long single ones carrying some eight some ten and the Double ones of which kind we saw I think four carrying at least 16 men all the Canoes that came near us were armed with Spears and those weapons like the spontoon but I saw no other kind of weapon. Their Canoes are made from the single tree hollowed out and kept exceedingly white and clean ornamented all round with a little red kind of pea with a black eye stuck on the outside of the canoe and strengthend by a piece of wood about 1½ inch thick that is securely lashed within and just below the Gunwale of the canoe. The largest that we saw was about 40 feet long and between the gunwales about 1 ft 4 inches wide increasing to about 2 feet in the middle or broadest part of the [beam?] and round at the bottom. They are very handsomely made and finished tapering away gradually from the middle towards each end and [then?] terminates in a Blunt Point. Some of the large ones were ornamented also by having a kind of gallows erected on the stern post of the Canoe of about 6 or 8 feet high decorated with many man of war birds feathers.

——'lofty Houses . . . that had the exact form of those among the Sandwich Islands': the Hawaiian-like, pointed-roofed ('Haystack like') houses described by Bligh did in fact exist on Aitutaki, but were eventually replaced by rectangular ones, at the behest of the missionaries. (Buck 1927: 38)

——'I do not think we saw above four hundred persons': when the pioneer missionary, John Williams, visited the island in 1821 he estimated the population to be about 2000 (Williams 1937: 20); there is no known reason for it having been much larger, or smaller, than that of 1792.

Upon quitting the island at 5:00 p.m. Bligh 'regretted' that he could have 'no further intercourse' with its inhabitants, but after Tahiti, Aitutaki was undoubtedly anti-climactic, and he clearly had a much larger objective on his mind.

Bibliography

Adams, Henry, *Memoirs of Arii Taimai*, Paris, 1891.

Beaglehole, J. C. (ed.), *The Journals of Captain Cook on his Voyage of Discovery*, 3 volumes, Cambridge: Cambridge University Press, 1955, 1961, 1967.

_____ *The Endeavour Journal of Joseph Banks: 1768–1771*, 2 volumes. Sydney: Angus & Robertson Ltd, 1962.

Bligh, William, *The Log of the Bounty, Being Lieutenant William Bligh's Log of the proceedings of his Majesty's Armed Vessel Bounty in a Voyage to the South seas, to Take the Breadfruit from the Society Islands to the West Indies*, 2 volumes. London: Golden Cockerel Press, 1937.

_____ *The Log of H.M.S. Providence*. London, 1976 (facsimile of Admiralty Copy, limited edition).

Bougainville, L. A. de, *Voyage autour du monde sur la Frégate du Roi La Boudeuese et la flûte L'Étoil en 1766, 1767, 1768, 1769*, Paris, 1771. (Second edition in 2 volumes, 1772; English translation by J. R. Forster) London, 1772.

Buck, P. H. (Te Rangi Hiroa), 'The material culture of the Cook Islands (Aitutaki)', *Board of Maori Ethnological Research Memoir*, volume 1, New Plymouth, 1927.

Callander, John, *Terra Australis Cognita: or, Voyages to the Terra Australis, or Southern Hemisphere*, 3 volumes. Edinburgh, 1766–68.

Carrington, Hugh (ed.), *The Discovery of Tahiti: A Journal of the Second Voyage of H.M.S. Dolphin round the World, under the command of Captain Wallis, R.N., in the Years 1766, 1767 and 1768, written by her Master, George Robertson*. London: Hakluyt Society, 1948.

Commerson, Philibert, 'Sur la Découverté de la Nouvelle Isle de Cythere ou Tahiti, *Mercure de France*, November 1769. (Reprinted in Corney 1914: 461–6.)

Cook, James, *A Voyage towards the South Pole and round the World . . . in the years 1772, 1773, 1774, and 1775*, 2 volumes. London, 1777.

_____ A Voyage to the Pacific Ocean in the years 1776, 1777, 1778, 1779, and 1780, 3 volumes. London, 1784. (Volume 3 compiled by J. King.)

Corney, B. G. (ed.), *The Quest and Occupation of Tahiti by Emissaries of Spain during the Years 1772–1776*, 3 volumes. London: Cambridge University Press, 1913, 1915, 1919.

Dalrymple, Alexander, *An Historical Collection of the Several Voyages and Discoveries in the South Pacific Ocean*, 2 volumes. London, 1770–71.

Davies, John, *A Tahitian and English Dictionary*. Tahiti: London Missionary Press, 1851.

Dixon, George, *A Voyage round the World: but more particularly to the North-West Coast of America*. London, 1789.

Ellis, William, *Polynesian Researches*, 2 volumes. London: Fisher, Son and Jackson, 1829.

Fairchild, H. N., *The Noble Savage: A Study in Romantic Naturalism*. New York: Columbia University Press, 1928.

Forster, Georg, *A Voyage round the World in his Brittanic Majesty's Sloop, Resolution, Commanded by Captain James Cook, during the Years 1772, 3, 4 and 5*, 2 volumes. London: B. White, J. Robson, P. Elmsley, and G. Robinson, 1777.

————— 'O-Tahiti', *Göttingisches Magazin der Wissenschaft und Litteratur*, volume 1, no. 1, Göttingen, 1780.

Forster, J. R., *Observations Made During A Voyage round the World in Physical Geography, Natural History and Ethic Philosophy*, Part 6. London: G. Robinson, 1778.

Gough, B. M. (ed.), *To the Pacific and Arctic with Beachey: The Journal of Lieutenant George Peard of H.M.S. 'Blossom'—1825–1828*. Cambridge: Cambridge University Press, 1973.

Green, R. C. and Kay, 'Religious Structures of the Society Islands', *New Zealand Journal of History*, volume 2, 1968.

Gudgeon, W. E., 'The origin of the *ta-tatau* or heraldic marks at Aitutaki Island', *Polynesian Society Journal*, volume 14, 1905.

Hammond, L. D. H. (ed.), 'Rélation de la décourverté que vient de faire Mr. de Bouguainville d'une Isle qu'il a nommée La Nouvelle Cythere'. Paris, November 1769. (English translation by L. D. H. Hammond, *News from New Cythera: A Report of Bougainville's Voyage 1766–1769*. Minneapolis: University of Minnesota Press, 1970.)

Hawkesworth, John, *An Account of the Voyages undertaken . . . for making Discoveries in the Southern Hemisphere*, 3 volumes. London, 1773.

Henderson, G. C., *The Discoverers of the Fiji Islands: Tasman, Cook, Bligh, Wilson, Bellinghausen*. London: J. Murray, 1933.

Henry, Teuira, *Ancient Tahiti*. Bernice P. Bishop Museum Bulletin no. 48. Honolulu, 1928.

Hoare, M. E. (ed.), *The Resolution Journal of Johann Reinhold Forster: 1772–1775*, 4 volumes. London: Hakluyt Society, 1982.

Jacquier, Henri, 'Le mirage et l'éxotisme tahitiens dans la littérature', *Bulletin de la Société d'études Océaniennes*, volume 7, 1944.

Keevil, J. J., *Medicine and the Navy*, 3 volumes. Edinburgh: E. & S. Livingstone, 1957. (Volume 3 by C. Lloyd and J. L. S. Coulter.)

Kennedy, Gavin, *Bligh*. London: G. Duckworth & Co. Ltd, 1978.

Lagayette, Pierre, *Henry Adams et les mers du sud: The Memoirs of Arii Taimai*. Pau: Université de Pau et des Pays de l'Adour. 1973.

Lamb, W. K. (ed.), *A Voyage of Discovery to the North Pacific Ocean and Round the World, 1791–1795*. 4 volumes. London: The Hakluyt Society, 1984.

Lee, Ida (Mrs C. B. Marriott), *Captain Bligh's Second Voyage to the South Sea*. London: Longman's Green & Co., 1920.

Levy, Robert, *Tahitians: Mind and Experience in the Society Islands*. Chicago and London: University of Chicago Press, 1973.

Lewis, Michael, *A Social History of the Navy, 1793–1815*. London: George Allen & Unwin Ltd, 1960.

Lloyd, Christopher, *The British Seaman, 1200-1860: A Social Survey*. London: Collins, 1968.

Low, D., 'Traditions of Aitutaki', *Polynesian Society Journal*, volumes 43 and 44, 1934–35.

McCormick, E. H., *Omai: Pacific Envoy*. Auckland: Auckland University Press, 1977.

Mackaness, George, *The Life of Vice-Admiral William Bligh, R.N., F.R.S.*, 2 volumes. New York and Toronto: Farrar & Rinehart, Inc., 1931.

————— (ed.), *Some Correspondence of Captain William Bligh, R.N., with John and Francis Godolphin Bond 1776–1811*. Australian Historical Monographs, no. 19, Sydney, 1949.

————— (ed.), *Fresh Light on Bligh: Being some Unpublished Correspondence of Captain William Bligh, R.N., and Lieutenant Francis Godolphin Bond, R.N., with Lieutenant Bond's Manuscript Notes Made on the Voyage of H.M.S. 'Providence'. 1791–1795*, Australian Historical Monographs, no. 29, Sydney, 1953.

Marra, John, *Journal of the Resolution's Voyage in 1772, 1773, 1774, and 1775*. London, 1775.

Mortimer, George, *Observations and Remarks made during a Voyage . . . in the Brig Mercury . . .* London: T. Cadell, J. Robson, and J. Sewell, 1791.

Newbury, Colin, *The History of the Tahitian Mission, 1799–1830. Written by John Davies, Missionary to the South Seas Islands, with Supplementry Papers from the Correspondence of the Missionaries*. London: Cambridge University Press, 1961.

Oliver, Douglas, *Ancient Tahitian Society*, 3 volumes. Honolulu: University Press of Hawaii, 1974.

————— *Two Tahitian Villages*. Hawaii: Institute of Polynesian Studies, 1931.

Orsmond, John, Notes. Unpublished manuscripts in the Mitchell Library, Sydney, n.d.

Pacific Islands Pilot, volume 3, 8th edition. London: Hydrographic Office of the Admiralty, 1957.

Powell, Dulcie, 'The voyage of the plant nursery, H.M.S. Providence 1791-1793'. *Bulletin of the Institute of Jamaica, Science Series*, no. 15, 1973.

Revue Maritime et Coloniale, tome 70, Paris, 1881.

Rutter, Owen (ed.), *The Journal of James Morrison, Boatswain's Mate of the Bounty* . . . London: The Golden Cockerell Press, 1935.

Spate, O. H. K., 'Splicing the Log at Kealakekua Bay: James King's Sleight-of-Hand', *Journal of Pacific History*, volume 19, no. 2, 1984.

Thomson, Basil (ed.), *Voyage of H.M.S. Pandora*. London: Francis Edwards, 1915.

Wales, William, *Remarks on Mr Forster's Account of Captain Cook's last Voyage round the World in the Years 1772, 1773, 1774, and 1775*. London, 1778.

Williams, Glyndwr, 'Seamen and Philosophers in the South Seas in the Days of Captain Cook', *Mariner's Mirror*, volume 65, no. 5, 1979.

Williams, John, *A Narrative of Missionary Enterprises in the South Sea Islands*. London: J. Snow, 1837.

Wilson, James, *A Missionary Voyage in the Southern Pacific Ocean, Performed in the Years 1796, 1797, 1798, in the Ship Duff, Commanded by Captain James Wilson*. London: T. Chapman, 1799.

Index

compiled by Elmar Zalums

276

Text set in 11½ point Goudy Old Style
Bligh's journal set in 12 point Chancery light italics
Other journal extracts set in 10½ point Novarese book italics
Of this edition 2000 copies have been printed